EU Law for Irish Students

EU Law for Irish Students

BRUCE CAROLAN

GILL & MACMILLAN

Gill & Macmillan
Hume Avenue, Park West
Dublin 12
with associated companies throughout the world
www.gillmacmillan.ie

© Bruce Carolan 2004
ISBN-13: 978 07171 3107 5
ISBN-10: 0 7171 3107 6
Print origination in Ireland by Carole Lynch

**A catalogue record is available for this book
from the British Library.**

**For Don and Diane,
in memory of our mother and father**

CONTENTS

PREFACE

Trying to write a textbook on European Union law for Irish students is as difficult as trying to paint a moving train.

While I was writing this book, the member states of the European Union signed the Treaty of Nice. This Treaty proposed significant changes to the institutional structure of the European Union, to allow the accession of ten new member states from central and eastern Europe in May 2004. In June 2002, Ireland's voters rejected the Treaty in a referendum, stalling the implementation of the Treaty (and the completion of this textbook).

A second referendum was held, and Ireland's voters approved ratification of the Treaty of Nice, which came into effect in February 2003. However, shortly thereafter, Valéry Giscard d'Estaing presented a Draft Treaty establishing a Constitution for Europe to the Italian Presidency of the European Union, along with a timetable that proposed agreement on the new Constitution by December 2003. The Draft Constitution, among other things, proposed further changes to the EU institutional structure. The manuscript for this textbook was revised to comment upon some of the most important recommended changes.

The EU member states failed to agree a new Constitution by December 2003, largely as the result of the refusal of Poland and Spain to accept a reduction in their voting strength in the Council of Ministers, as proposed in the Draft Constitution. As of this writing, the task of seeking agreement to the new Constitution falls to the Irish Presidency of the European Union, and, failing agreement there, to the Dutch presidency in the latter half of 2004.

This textbook includes the revisions effected by the Nice Treaty, and discussion of some of the major proposals contained in the Draft Constitution. The reference to the Draft Constitution Articles is to the version of the Draft Treaty presented to the Italian Presidency on 18 July 2003. I have retained discussion of the Draft Treaty because it is likely that a Constitution ultimately will be adopted and because discussion of the changes proposed in the Draft Constitution will help with a deeper understanding of current EU law.

Having addressed the long path to publication, I will turn to the book itself.

This book should prove useful to a wide range of people interested in the law of the European Union. It will serve as an accessible introduction to a complex subject for students of commerce, law or political science.

Practitioners who may not have studied the law of the European Union in law school, or who may have fallen behind in this rapidly changing area of law, will find this book provides a good overview and a quick update of recent (and forthcoming) developments in the most important areas of EU law.

The book has been written with one eye on the syllabus for the EU Law, Final Examination – First Part, of the Law Society of Ireland. The book should prove an invaluable revision aid for those intending to sit the FE-1 exam in EU law. The chapters cover virtually all of the main areas of the EU FE-1 examination for the Law Society of Ireland: sources of community law; European Union institutions; general principles of law; supremacy and direct effect; application and enforcement of EU law; challenges to acts of Community institutions; free movement of persons, services and establishment; and competition law of the European Union.

Many courses for the study of the law of the European Union are divided into three parts. The first part consists of institutional and constitutional issues. The second part consists of the substantive law of the European Union. The third part comprises competition law.

This book roughly follows the three-part division common to 'omnibus' classes in the law of the European Union. The first part of the book describes the institutions of the European Union, their powers, and their relationship to each other. The most significant political institutions include the European Council, the Council of Ministers, the Commission and the European Parliament. The Court of Justice of the European Communities and its associated court, the Court of First Instance, are also considered. The first part of the book also considers the relationship between the law of the European Union and domestic Irish law. This involves consideration of the judicially-created doctrines of direct effect and supremacy.

The second part of the book considers the substantive law of the European Union. This consists primarily of the so-called 'four freedoms': free movement of goods; free movement of workers; free movement of services/establishment; and free movement of capital. Most introductory courses skip over the final freedom, free movement of capital, and this book is no exception.

The third part of this book briefly addresses the competition law of the European Union. This is sometimes added on to the end of a survey course in the law of the European Union (perhaps being lectured after the Spring Break), and is sometimes offered as a separate course. It is important, in part, because domestic Irish competition law is patterned after European Union law. Also, intending solicitors are expected to have an academic knowledge of competition law before proceeding on to the vocational training necessary to become qualified.

The Treaty of Amsterdam, which became effective in 1999, attempts to simplify the law of the European Union by renumbering the Treaty Articles. This worthwhile attempt creates confusion in the short to medium term, because so many of the important cases discussing Treaty Articles refer to the previous numbering system. For some time, it will be necessary to refer to both the old and new numbering system, and this book will follow that convention. By and large, the new numbering scheme will be referred to first, followed by the old numbering scheme.

In this book, we will be concerned chiefly with two treaties: the Treaty on European Union; and the European Community Treaty. Most of the references to Treaty Articles will be to Articles contained in the European Community Treaty, although there will occasionally be references to the Treaty on European Union. Some authors distinguish between the Treaties by always including a reference such as EC Article 234 or TEU Article 6. By and large, we will not follow this convention where references are to the EC Treaty. Because we will deal primarily with the European Community Treaty, students can assume that the Articles cited are from the EC Treaty unless the Article is clearly designated TEU, to indicate that we are referring to the Treaty on European Union.

I would like to thank Una Butler, BL, part-time lecturer in EU law at the Dublin Institute of Technology, for her extremely helpful contributions to the final four chapters of the book, which freed me to revise earlier chapters in light of the proposed Constitution for Europe. I also wish to thank Dr. Fergus Ryan, whose encouragement and thoughtful comments improved the chapters he reviewed. Similar thanks are due to Ciaran Walker of London, England, and to Anna-Louise Hinds of the National University of Ireland (Galway). (Of course, any errors are my own.) Thanks also to the Dublin Institute of Technology, which attempted to provide me with space and time to write, when space and time were in short supply at the Institute. Thanks are also due to the University of Florida, Warrington College of Business, where I was a visiting professor in Spring 2001. Finally, I wish to thank the Stetson University College of Law, where I was visiting professor in the academic year 2003-2004, for their hospitality and support in the final stages of this book. I particularly wish to thank Connie Evans and Sharon Gisclair, and the entire Faculty Support Staff, for their diligence and hard work.

I have attempted to provide an accurate statement of the law of the European Union as of the date of publication. I would appreciate any errors being brought to my attention, through my publisher, Gill & Macmillan.

Bruce Carolan
Gulfport, Florida, USA

TABLE OF CASES

TABLE OF STATUTES

EC LEGISLATION

Treaties

EUROPEAN CONVENTIONS

CONSTITUTION OF IRELAND

UNITED KINGDOM LEGISLATION

NORTHERN IRELAND LEGISLATION

Chapter 1

A BRIEF HISTORY OF THE EUROPEAN UNION

POST-WORLD WAR II EFFORTS TO INTEGRATE EUROPE

A very brief overview of the history of European integration, and of the European Union, is helpful in understanding the substance of Community law.

The modern history of European integration – and of the European Union – commences in the period following World War II. Military, political and economic considerations all played a role in the plan for European integration, and in the development of the European Union. The hope was that European integration in some form or fashion would prevent a recurrence of war in Europe. This remains a major motivating factor in continuing efforts for European integration.

Another major post-World War II influence on desires for European integration was a fear of the spread of communism, and, to a lesser extent, a concomitant fear of domination of European affairs by the United States (which was engaged in a Cold War with the former Soviet Union). A strong Europe (including a stronger Germany which, in its weakened state, was at risk of Soviet domination), could hold back the 'communist threat', and simultaneously reduce US influence in Western Europe (which might otherwise be required under the threat of Soviet expansion).

Before addressing the history of the European Union specifically, it is necessary to consider several developments that occurred in the immediate post-World War II period, but which are unrelated to the EU.

THE COUNCIL OF EUROPE

Perhaps the most significant post-war international development prior to the birth of the modern European Union was the meeting of the 'Congress of Europe' in The Hague, Netherlands, in 1948. This resulted in a Treaty establishing the Council of Europe in 1949. The Treaty established a Parliamentary Assembly and a Committee of Ministers. The Council of Europe was intended to propose international treaties or conventions for its (initially) twenty-four member states.

EUROPEAN CONVENTION ON HUMAN RIGHTS

Perhaps the most important accomplishment of the Council of Europe was the adoption in 1950 of a treaty popularly known as the European Convention on Human Rights (which is formally known as the European Convention for the Protection of Human Rights and Fundamental Freedoms). The overriding purpose of the ECHR was to prevent another holocaust, such as had occurred in Germany during World War II.

The Convention provided, contrary to the typical international convention, that individuals could invoke its protection by bringing an action in a special court in Strasbourg, France (after attempting to resolve their complaint initially in their domestic courts). However, in recognition of the sovereignty of the signatory states, a member state expressly had to agree to allow itself to be sued in Strasbourg. Also, if the court ruled that a member state was in violation of the Convention, the ultimate sanction was expulsion from the Council of Europe. The judgments of the Court of Human Rights could not be enforced in the same manner as a judgment of a domestic court.

OTHER POST-WAR EFFORTS AT INTEGRATION

Several other international agreements (the North Atlantic Treaty Organisation, the Treaty of Dunkirk, the Organisation for European Economic Cooperation, later expanded and re-named the Organisation for Economic Cooperation and Development) were adopted in the years immediately following the end of World War II. While these may have influenced general thinking on the ultimate shape of European integration, they are separate from the project that led to the European Union.

As we will see, other international organisations tend to be more traditional 'intergovernmental' arrangements, whereby member states retain the full measure of their national sovereignty and proceed primarily by way of 'consensus' or unanimity. The European Union is radically different. To paraphrase the Court of Justice of the European Communities in a case that we will study, the European Union represents a new legal order, for the sake of which member states have sacrificed some measure of their national sovereignty, albeit in limited (but ever-increasing) areas.

TREATIES UNDERPINNING THE HISTORY OF THE EUROPEAN UNION

The history of the European Union is in one sense a history of Treaties. That is, one can trace the development of the Union by following the adoption of a series of Treaties. Another important aspect of the development of the European Union is the expansion of membership through the addition of new member states, from six to a membership of fifteen, to twenty-five member states, and beyond. (Each expansion has occasioned necessary change in the Treaties underpinning the European Union, and have led to the creation of a Draft 'Constitution' for the European Union.)

The most important Treaties in the development of the modern European Union are:

1. the European Coal and Steel Community Treaty, 1951;
2. the European Economic Community Treaty, 1957;
3. the Single European Act, 1986;
4. the Treaty on European Union, 1992 (the 'Maastricht Treaty');
5. the Treaty of Amsterdam, 1997; and
6. the Treaty of Nice, 2002.

Other Treaties include the Merger Treaty, 1965, and the Euratom Treaty, 1957, but these Treaties do not figure as prominently in the development of the European Union as a unique international system of governance.

The European Union is unique in the history of international relations, for reasons pertaining to relationships between member states, and for reasons pertaining to the relations between individual citizens and the European Union. Certain aspects of this uniqueness were present from the outset, and other aspects developed as the European Union developed. We will focus first on relationships between member states under the Treaties that came to form the basis of the European Union.

INTERGOVERNMENTALISM VERSUS SUPRANATIONALISM

One way to think of relationships between sovereign states is to place these relationships on a continuum. The ends of this continuum are represented by concepts known as intergovernmentalism and supranationalism.

Traditionally, the relationships between sovereign nations have stayed closer to the end of the continuum known as intergovernmentalism. That means, essentially, that when several nations entered into agreements, usually called Treaties, they did so by unanimous agreement, and any further developments under these Treaties that might affect the national interest required unanimous agreement.

Under such an international arrangement, all signatory nations are equal, and, more importantly, any one nation, however small, can block proposals that would affect its interests. (In theory, this is how the World Trade Organisation operates.) Often, there is no body to which a sovereign state can appeal if it believes another country is violating the agreement. Its only option is to retaliate by suspending its own obligations toward the offending member state.

At the other end of the continuum is the concept of supranationalism. An international agreement with supranational characteristics might have traits similar to a federal system, such as the United States. (Some authors use the words 'supranational' and 'federal' interchangeably.) That is, there might be institutions or bodies that had powers to compel the signatories to the agreement to take certain actions, even if they did not wish to do so. Further action under a supranational agreement might not require unanimous agreement, meaning a single member could not block a proposal. One way to think about supranationalism is to appreciate that, with supranationalism, the supranational entity becomes greater than the sum of its parts.

TRADITIONAL INTERNATIONAL RELATIONSHIPS: INTERGOVERNMENTAL

Until the Treaties giving rise to the European Union, most international agreements stayed close to the intergovernmental end of the continuum. The Treaty establishing the Council of Europe moved away from a strictly intergovernmental approach, by establishing a Consultative Assembly consisting of representatives from the Parliaments of the signatory nations. However, this Assembly was only a talking shop that merely made recommendations to the Committee of Ministers, which, for the most part, could only decide things unanimously. Decisions of the Committee of Ministers amounted to little more than recommendations to the signatory nations, in any event. The member states were free to ignore these recommendations.

INTRODUCTION OF SUPRANATIONALISM

But the proposals for the European Coal and Steel Community Treaty, 1951, were different. In a famous declaration by French Foreign Minister Robert Schuman on 9 May 1950, France proposed the European Coal and Steel Community Treaty. The proposal entailed putting all of coal and steel production for Germany and France under the control of a supranational body called the High Authority. The High Authority would establish rules guaranteeing free trade in coal and steel between the two countries, and prohibiting anti-competitive practices.

Why coal and steel? One answer is this: these were the industries of war. Coal fueled factories in which steel was converted into bombs and bullets.

The Treaty also proposed the creation of other institutions, including, perhaps most importantly from a supranational perspective, the creation of a court that would resolve disputes. The existence of a court to adjudicate disputes between institutions, or between member states and the institutions, concerning, among other things, the interpretation of an agreement, is an essential characteristic of most federal systems.

EUROPEAN COAL AND STEEL COMMUNITY (ECSC) TREATY, 1951

The ECSC was unique in a number of different ways. Because its framework is relevant to later developments in the European Union, it is worth dwelling on briefly.

First, it represented a new approach to dealing with the loser in war, in this case Germany, following the end of World War II. The usual approach to the vanquished had been to extract reparations and impose onerous conditions designed to prevent war-making capabilities. The ECSC Treaty, by contrast, proposed treating Germany as an equal, and placing the coal and steel industries – the industries of war – under the control of a supranational body with power to compel the participants to abide by certain agreed rules.

Second, it introduced strong federal elements into the relations of the participating nations, and represented a partial surrender of sovereign power in very important areas. That is, the nations who agreed to join the ECSC Treaty would give up the right unilaterally to decide how to operate their coal and steel industries, and, for example, forfeit the right to decide what duties to impose on coal and steel imported from another member state.

Eventually, six countries joined the European Coal and Steel Community. These were France, Germany, Italy, and the three Benelux countries, the Netherlands, Belgium and Luxembourg. The United Kingdom was invited to join, but declined the invitation.

POLITICAL AND DEFENCE COOPERATION – A FAILED EFFORT

After the success of the ECSC Treaty, there was a strong push for further European integration. Specifically, the French government, in response to a proposed North Atlantic Treaty Organisation (NATO), promoted the idea of a European Defence Community (EDC) Treaty. (France feared American military influence in Europe under the proposed North Atlantic Treaty Organisation.) In response to a perceived need for the political coordination of a common European defence, a draft Treaty for a European Political Community (EPC) was proposed. However, ultimately both floundered, and failed. Specifically, although the EDC Treaty was signed, it was never ratified; it died in the French Parliament. The notion of a common defence still poses problems for the French, among others. The dispute over a common European position on the US-led war in Iraq is an example of these divisions.

ECONOMIC INTEGRATION – THE EUROPEAN ECONOMIC COMMUNITY TREATY, 1957

The next step in the creation of Treaties underpinning European integration was the adoption of the European Economic Community (EEC) Treaty and the Euratom Treaty in Rome, in 1957. (These Treaties are sometimes referred to collectively as the Treaties of Rome, 1957. We will consider only the European Economic Community Treaty here, because, as Ireland is not an atomic power, the Euratom Treaty is of less consequence.)

Membership of the European Economic Community initially consisted of the same countries that had joined the ECSC – France, Germany, Italy, and the three Benelux countries, the Netherlands, Belgium and Luxembourg, which, in 1948, had formed their own fledgling customs union.

The EEC Treaty developed from a report prepared by the Belgian Prime Minister Paul-Henri Spaak in April 1956. The goals of the Spaak Report, as it was known, were in some respects less ambitious than those contained in the EPC and EDC Treaties. The Spaak Report limited itself to economic rather than expressly political or military concerns. In other ways, however, the Spaak Report was more ambitious, because it envisaged a multi-stage process leading to the fusion of economic markets across the member states.

Five Stages of Economic Integration

In order to appreciate the significance of the Spaak Report, we can consider various stages of integration between the separate economic systems of two countries. These can be divided into five stages.

The first stage is the creation of a free trade area. Under this arrangement, one country agrees to abolish custom duties on goods imported from a second country. The second country, naturally, agrees to abolish customs duties on goods imported from the first country.

The second stage in economic integration is the creation of a customs union. In a customs union, the two countries agree a set of common customs duties for goods coming from third countries. (A customs union avoids the distortion in trade patterns that would result if goods from a third country were subject to a lower import duty in one country in the free trade area than in the other.)

The third stage of integration is the creation of a common market, in which all the factors of production (which might be designated goods, services, labour, capital) are allowed to flow freely between the two countries. The fourth stage of integration is the adoption of a common economic and monetary policy for the two countries. The fifth stage of integration is complete political (including military defence) integration.

The European Economic Community Treaty and the Stages of Integration

What did the EEC Treaty envision? Among other things, the Treaty sought to promote economic integration of separate national markets. Part One of the Treaty stated that the European Economic Community had as its goals the establishment of a Common Market and the approximation or harmonisation of the economic policies of the member states. This means the creation of similar economic standards or conditions throughout the European Union. It sought to accelerate an increase in the standard of living and bring about closer relations between the states belonging to the EEC.

In order to achieve the goals of the EEC, the Treaty set forth a number of basic principles. The Treaty provided that the Community would establish a timetable for the elimination of customs duties and quantitative restrictions (that is, quotas or measures equivalent to quotas) between member states. The Community would adopt a common commercial policy towards countries outside the EEC (that is, establish a customs union), abolish obstacles to the free movement of persons, services and capital, and adopt a common agricultural policy.

In terms of the five stages of integration outlined above, the EEC Treaty, 1957, clearly would reach the third stage of integration, i.e., the creation of a common market. However, the adoption of common policies in agriculture and transport would bring the proposals into the realm of the fourth stage of integration, the integration of economic policies.

(Of course, after the Treaty on European Union, 1992, the EU is irrevocably committed to monetary integration (e.g., the adoption of a common currency), that is, the fourth stage of economic integration. Proposals for the creation of an EU military rapid response force constitute a form of political/defence integration. Thus, the integration project has advanced along the register of economic integration.)

It is useful to keep the goals set forth in 1957 in mind, however, as they remain at the core of European integration today.

INSTITUTIONS ESTABLISHED BY THE EEC TREATY

The EEC Treaty did more than propose integration of separate national markets. It also created political and judicial institutions to oversee and implement the integration process. The institutions created under the EEC Treaty resembled those that had been created under the ECSC Treaty, with certain differences.

The most important institutions created by the EEC Treaty included a Parliamentary Assembly, a Commission, the Council of Ministers, and a Court of Justice. (The EEC Treaty also established a Court of Auditors, a body to oversee the fiscal affairs of the EEC. It is not a court in the sense that we understand the term in Ireland.)

The Parliamentary Assembly, now called the European Parliament, as envisaged by the original 1957 EEC Treaty, would consist of members of national Parliaments, appointed by the member states. (This would later change to a system of direct elections, after adoption of an Act providing for direct universal suffrage in 1976.)

In general, the EEC Treaty provided that the Commission would be responsible for recommending legislation to the Council of Ministers, and for ensuring that adopted legislation was followed. The Council of Ministers would vote on legislative proposals from the Commission. Initially, unanimity would be required to adopt legislation. However, the EEC Treaty provided that at a later stage a system of weighted voting for the approval of legislation would be adopted.

The EEC Treaty also created a Court of Justice. The court would resolve disputes between Community institutions, between the Community and member states, and between individuals and either the Community or a member state.

(Some years after the ratification of the EEC Treaty, the European Council – consisting of heads of states or government came into existence. In fact, with the exception of France, all are heads of government (e.g., Prime Ministers) as most heads of state (e.g., President) are figureheads or monarchs) of member states. Initially, the European Council was a political body, without formal legal status in the Treaties comprising the Community. However, its existence formally was recognised in the Single European Act, 1986, and its duties were detailed in the Treaty of European Union. The Constitution further elaborates on the function of the European Council.)

Initially, some of the institutions were separate, depending upon the Community that they served – e.g., the European Coal and Steel Community or the European Economic Community. However, the Merger Treaty, in effect since 1 July 1967, created a single European Commission, and single European Council for all the Communities.

SLOWING OF INTEGRATION – FRANCE'S 'EMPTY CHAIR POLICY' AND THE LUXEMBOURG ACCORDS

One of the distinctive characteristics of the European Economic Community was that, over time, the Community would move along the continuum from an intergovernmental type of international body, to a more supranational one. The EEC Treaty provided for different stages, during which the supranational aspects of the Community would increase.

An important aspect of supranationalism was the introduction of a system of weighted voting in the Council of Ministers. This system of weighted voting is known as Qualified Majority Voting (QMV). (Under QMV, each state gets a number of votes that, when considered against the total number of votes, are roughly proportionate to its relative size.) QMV means, among other things, that less than unanimous agreement is required in order to adopt certain legislation. In effect, it means that a member state might be bound by legislation that it opposed.

Another important aspect of supranationalism is self-financing, and in 1965 the Community was poised to increase its autonomy by establishing financing that did not depend solely upon contributions from member states.

In 1965-1966, in order to prevent these moves towards increased supranationalism, France boycotted meetings of the Council of Ministers. This boycott was known as the 'empty chair policy'. It effectively paralysed the Community for a period of seven months.

In order to end the empty chair policy, the member states adopted a compromise known as the 'Luxembourg Accords'. The legal significance of this compromise is uncertain. It is in the nature of a political compromise, which has been followed by member states since its adoption.

The Luxembourg Accords provide, essentially, that if a member state indicates that a legislative proposal before the Council of Ministers involves a very important interest of that member state, then the Council will attempt to reach a unanimous agreement. In essence, each member state retains a veto in the Council of Ministers, if it indicates that the matter under consideration involves a very important interest.

The member states themselves failed to reach agreement in the Luxembourg Accords as to what should happen if it were impossible to reach a unanimous agreement. (France insisted that they would continue trying until unanimity was reached, while the other member states believed a decision could be taken.) However, as a practical matter, the Luxembourg Accords meant that few proposals reached the Council of Ministers unless a consensus was deemed likely. This, inevitably, slowed the integration process, at least on the political front. (Some commentators maintained that the Court of Justice stepped into the breach by giving decisions that furthered integration. We will see that the court gave some significant judgments during this period.)

LORD COCKFIELD, THE WHITE PAPER AND
THE SINGLE EUROPEAN ACT, 1986

In 1985, Lord Cockfield, one of Britain's Commissioners on the European Commission, prepared a 'White Paper' for the Commission: see White Paper from the Commission to the European Council (Milan, 28-29 June 1985), COM(85) 310 final. This report identified approximately 300 non-tariff barriers to a unified market. (Tariff barriers, e.g., customs duties, had been completely eliminated by this stage.) These non-tariff barriers included such things as technical barriers, differing health and safety standards, and financial barriers. (An example of a non-tariff barrier would be a requirement in a particular member state that certain information must be contained on the label of a can of food.) The report recommended a strict timetable for the elimination of these remaining barriers.

Lord Cockfield's report ultimately led to the adoption of the Single European Act (SEA), 1986. It brought about institutional change (e.g., formal recognition of the European Council, creation of a Court of First Instance). However, its primary goal was to revive a stagnant integration process.

The SEA sought to revive a stagnant integration process by setting a deadline for the elimination of remaining barriers, and by extending QMV (Qualified Majority Voting).

Perhaps most importantly, the SEA amended the existing EEC Treaty by adding Article 7a (later renumbered by the Treaty of European Union as Article 8a, and amended and renumbered again by the Treaty of Amsterdam as Article 18). Article 7a stated that 'an internal market shall comprise an area without internal frontiers in which the free movement of goods, persons, services and capital is ensured'. Article 7a further provided that the 'Community shall adopt measures with the aim of progressively establishing the internal market over a period expiring on 31 December 1992'.

The SEA also added Article 100a (Article 95 after the Treaty of Amsterdam). This Article provided that when pursuing the objectives set out in (then) Article 7a, i.e., the completion of the internal market, the Council could act by QMV. Practically speaking, this would make it easier for the Council to adopt proposals set forth by the Commission, as a single member state could no longer block the proposal.

The SEA is one of the most important milestones in the process of European integration. As of the deadline of 1992, approximately eighty per cent of the barriers identified in the 'White Paper' had been eliminated, with some glaring exceptions (the most obvious of which was the need for Irish citizens to show a passport when entering another EU member state).

For his troubles, British Prime Minister Margaret Thatcher removed Lord Cockfield from the Commission.

TREATY ON EUROPEAN UNION

The Treaty on European (TEU), 1992, is perhaps best known because it made provision for a single European currency. It also changed the name of the European Economic Community to the European Community (reflecting that the Community extended to more than simply economic considerations), and introduced the concept of the 'European Union' (leading to confusion over the difference between the European Community and the European Union).

The ratification process associated with the ultimate adoption of the TEU exposed deep political divisions over the process of European integration. The Danish initially rejected the Treaty in a public referendum, and it narrowly passed a public vote in France (where it had been expected to pass easily). Commentators remarked that the public feeling was that the European integration project had become remote from the 'average' European citizen. However, in a second referendum (after minor changes to the proposed Treaty), the Danish population approved the Treaty. (History repeated itself when the Irish electorate initially rejected the Treaty of Nice, but approved it in a second referendum.)

One of the most significant aspects of the TEU, apart from monetary union, was the introduction of a so-called 'Three Pillar Structure'. The first 'pillar' consisted of the European Communities. The Communities were comprised of the Communities created by the European Community Treaty (previously the European Economic Community Treaty), the European Coal and Steel Community Treaty, and the Euratom Treaty. In terms of relative legal significance, in some sense the first pillar would undoubtedly be the largest in a pictorial representation of the 'Three Pillar Structure'. This is because the supranational law-making power of the European Union resides largely within this pillar.

The second and third pillars are separate and distinct from the first, or 'Communities', pillar. These pillars, by and large, are not 'supranational' in character. Decisions by member states under the second and third pillars – on matters such as common foreign and security policy or justice and home affairs – are taken in a more traditionally intergovernmental fashion. That is, decisions often require a unanimous decision rather than a decision taken by, for example, qualified majority vote. Also, the Commission and the Court of Justice of the European Communities – EU institutions with a more federal or supranational character – have less of a role to play in decisions that are made under the second and third pillars. However, in changes brought about by the Treaty of Amsterdam, some of the matters under the third pillar have been transferred to the first, or 'Communities' pillar, and decisions in these areas now possess more of a supranational character. The following paragraphs set out the subject matter of the second and third pillars in more detail. The second pillar is concerned with the Common Foreign and Security Policy. The third pillar is concerned with Police and Judicial Co-operation in criminal matters (originally termed Justice and Home Affairs), including matters such as asylum and integration.

The three pillars share a common institutional base, meaning that the Commission, the Council of Ministers, the European Council, the European Parliament, and the Court of Justice are the same regardless of which pillar we are considering. However, as mentioned, for the second and third pillars, those institutions that are more intergovernmental in nature (e.g., the Council of Ministers and the European Council), play the most active role. The other, more supranational institutions (e.g., the Court of Justice, the Commission), do not have as significant role in the second and third pillars.

The three pillars, on their common institutional base, comprise the entity known as 'The European Union'. The European Union – which, prior to the Treaty of Nice, lacked a formal legal existence – is the overarching structure of which the institutions and pillars are the constituent elements.

TREATY OF AMSTERDAM

The TEU provided for a review of its provisions within five years of its adoption. A Reflection Group was formed to submit a report to the European Council. This report was to outline the issues for an Intergovernmental Conference (IGC). The IGC would propose amendments to the Treaties underpinning the European Union.

The report outlined various issues that should be tackled in any forthcoming revisions to the Treaties. These issues included:
1. expanding parliamentary powers;
2. streamlining decision-making;
3. reviewing the second and third pillars; and
4. strengthening the Union in the eyes of its citizens.
One of the most important issues facing the European Union concerned expansion to the east. It would become impossible for the institutions of the Union to function effectively under current structures and procedures if, as expected, the membership of the European Union expands to twenty-five or thirty countries in the near future.

The resulting Treaty of Amsterdam was widely regarded as a failure. Although it did simplify and strengthen Parliament's role in law-making, and made revisions to the second and third pillars, it failed utterly when dealing with issues of expansion. There were no substantive changes to existing structures or procedures in light of imminent expansion of the European Union.

One of the most significant changes brought about by the Treaty of Amsterdam was the adoption of a system whereby certain 'core' member states could agree to accelerate integration. Other member states would not need to participate, and, importantly, member states who did not participate could not prevent the 'core' member states from agreeing to go faster.

TREATY OF NICE

The European Union postponed consideration of institutional and procedural reform until the Intergovernmental Conference held in Nice in November 2000. At this conference, the European Council adopted a Charter of Fundamental Rights for the European Union. The Nice Treaty, ratified by the member states (after two referenda in Ireland) and in force since February 2003, will be considered in detail in the following chapters. The Nice Treaty largely undertakes the work postponed in the Treaty of Amsterdam. That is, the Treaty of Nice undertakes the institutional reform necessary to accommodate a European Union that will have twenty-five member states by May 2004. In some cases, these institutional changes are quite radical, and subject to some ongoing controversy.

CONSTITUTION FOR EUROPE

Commentators have remarked that, with the ink barely dry on the Treaty of Nice, the European Union began changing the new institutional structures. These changes are contained in the Draft Constitution for Europe. Once again, some quite radical changes are proposed, some of which will be highlighted in the material that follows.

CONCLUSION

Unlike some other areas of law, such as property, the law of the European Union is constantly developing. It changes as quickly as Europe changes, and Europe is changing all the time.

Chapter 2
POLITICAL INSTITUTIONS OF
THE EUROPEAN UNION

INTRODUCTION

Before studying the substantive law of the European Union, it is necessary to learn about the political and judicial institutions of the Union. It is also necessary to study the types of law that can be adopted by the European Union institutions, and the law-making procedures. This chapter discusses the political institutions of the Union, and a following chapter discusses the judicial institutions of the Union. A separate chapter discusses the different types of legislative instruments (laws) that can be adopted by the Union, and the various methods for their adoption.

The major political institutions of the European Union are (in the order in which we will be discussing them) the European Council, the Council of the European Union (commonly referred to as the Council of Ministers), the European Commission, and the European Parliament. (Students should be sure to distinguish between the European Council and the entirely separate and distinct Council of Europe. The Council of Europe is an international body based in Strasbourg that promulgates Conventions, the most famous of which is the European Convention on Human Rights. Students should also be sure to distinguish between the European Council and the Council of the European Union. Although these two latter bodies are both EU institutions, commentators often confuse or conflate them.) We will also discuss, briefly, the Economic and Social Committee, and the Committee of the Regions. These could be regarded as 'political' institutions of the EU, but with much less influence than the major institutions (although the major institutions sometimes are required to consult with these minor institutions before taking action).

Finally, we will consider Common Foreign and Security Policy, and Justice and Home Affairs. These represent the 'second' and 'third' pillars respectively, introduced by the Treaty on European Union.

DYNAMIC NATURE OF INSTITUTIONAL STRUCTURES
OF THE EUROPEAN UNION

The institutions with which we primarily will be concerned are those established by the European Economic Community Treaty of 1957. (In fact, the earlier European Coal and Steel Community Treaty and the Euratom Community Treaty of 1957 also established political institutions similar to those established by the EEC Treaty. That meant that there were three sets of almost identical institutions, each serving a separate European 'community'. However, the Merger Treaty of 1965 largely combined these institutions to provide basically for a single institutional structure for the three separate European Communities.)

The EEC Treaty has been amended over the years to produce the two Treaties with which we are most familiar today, the European Community Treaty and the separate Treaty on European Union. The EEC Treaty has been amended by such measures as the Single European Act, 1986, the Treaty on European Union, 1992, and the Treaty of Amsterdam, 1997. (The dates refer to the signing of these Treaties, and not the later, effective date of the Treaties after the necessary ratifications had taken place.)

Each of the amendments brought about by successive Treaties made changes to the institutional structure of what is now known as the European Union. In addition, various Accession Treaties have been adopted over the years, to provide for expansion of the European Union through the addition of new member states. These Accession Agreements sometimes have brought about minor changes to Treaty Articles relating to the institutions in order to accommodate new member states.

The European Union recently has expanded eastward to include many new member states from Central and Eastern Europe. In May 2004, the European Union accepted the following countries as new members: Cyprus; Malta; Hungary; Poland; Estonia; Lithuania; the Czech Republic; Slovakia; Latvia; and Slovenia. The admission of Bulgaria and Romania has been delayed. Turkey has been given a date when it will be told when negotiations on its membership application will begin.

At the end of 2000, the Nice European Council solemnly reaffirmed the political priority accorded to enlargement (we will see that the Community often 'solemnly reaffirms' measures when it wishes to state a political aspiration, rather than a legally binding commitment). The Nice European Council approved a strategy paper on this topic produced by the Commission.

In order to join the European Union, the ten new member states had to satisfy the economic and political criteria set forth in the 'Copenhagen Criteria'. These criteria included:
1. stable democracy, with respect for human rights, the rule of law and the protection of democracy;

2. a functioning market economy; and
3. agreement to accept the body of EU law.

In October 2002, the Commission recommended closing negotiations with the ten applicant countries listed above. A date has not yet been set to begin negotiations with Turkey (which has the longest-pending application for membership), although the Union has set a date on which it will set a date to begin such discussions.

This expansion of the European Union places a great deal of pressure on the institutional structures. The Treaties underpinning the Union will have to be amended to accommodate these changes. The Nice Treaty includes amendments designed to accommodate enlargement. These amendments effect institutional change that will be phased in over time. However, with the ink barely dry on the Nice Treaty, and after a bruising ratification battle in Ireland, the Union produced a Draft Constitution for Europe, which is designed to effect further change, and, in some ways, to offset or nullify changes in the Nice Treaty.

PROTOCOL ON THE INSTITUTIONS WITH THE PROSPECT OF ENLARGEMENT OF THE EU

Commentators had hoped that the Treaty of Amsterdam would propose institutional changes to accommodate the imminent expansion of the European Union. They were disappointed. The hoped-for changes did not occur in the Treaty of Amsterdam. Instead, the member states adopted a Protocol on the Institutions with the Prospect of Enlargement of the European Union, which was attached to the Treaty of Amsterdam. (The European Union increasingly has come to rely on Protocols in place of formal amendments to the Treaties. The legal status of these Protocols is open to question. Protocols constitute a more intergovernmental form of relationship between the member states.)

The Protocol, now of only historical interest as it has been overtaken by subsequent events, dealt with some of the changes that might be necessitated by the expansion of the European Union. It concerned itself primarily with changes to the Commission and the Council of Ministers.

The Protocol provided that, notwithstanding Article 213 (ex Article 157, which, we shall see, is concerned with the number of members of the Commission) at the date of the first enlargement of the Union, the Commission would comprise one national of each member state. However, this change was subject to a proviso. The proviso was that the weighting of the votes in the Council of the European Union (discussed below) would have to be modified in a manner acceptable to member states who have given up the right to nominate a second member.

The sentiment behind the Protocol is difficult to square with the concept, discussed below, that:

> Members of the Commission shall ... be completely independent in the performance of their duties ... [and] ... shall neither seek nor take instructions from any government. (Article 213, ex Article 157.)

Furthermore:

> [E]ach member state undertakes to respect this principle and not to seek to influence the members of the Commission in the performance of their tasks. (Article 213, ex Article 157.)

If the loss of a Commissioner is tied to voting strength in the Council of Ministers, this suggests that member states regard a Commissioner as an 'agent' of that member state, subject to their instruction. This undermines the notion of independence.

The Protocol also provided that at least one year before the membership of the EU exceeded twenty, a conference of member states would be convened to review the composition and functioning of the institutions.

In essence, the European Union decided to put off a decision until a future date. That date arrived with the Treaty of Nice, which was signed in February 2001.

EXPANSION AND THE TREATY OF NICE

The Treaty of Nice represents a major step forward in making the necessary changes to the institutions of the EU to accommodate expansion. Having said that, as will become clear below, the Treaty of Nice also represents something of a disappointment. While the Treaty confronted the necessary issue of institutional change, its proposed solutions made the governance of the European Union more complicated, and less accessible, to intelligent, interested European citizens. Furthermore, while mechanically providing for expansion, it did not assure that decision-making in an expanded EU would be more efficient. To the contrary, it may be more difficult to take decisions after expansion.

The details of the Treaty will be laid out in more detail below. This introduction will provide a general overview of the way in which, among other things, the size of the European Commission will be addressed in an expanded EU.

The Treaty of Nice changes the composition of the Commission. The change will take place in two stages. From 2005, there will be one Commissioner per member state (that is, the larger member states will give up their second Commissioner). Thereafter, when membership in the EU reaches twenty-seven member states, there will no longer be one Commissioner per member state. Instead, a system of rotation will be put into place, whereby the member states, on an equal basis, will take turns appointing a Commissioner. It is not clear how many Commissioners there will be after the second stage.

This change in representation on the Commission has been accompanied by changes to the voting procedures in the Council, which, in part, serve to 'compensate' the larger states for the loss of a Commissioner.

Finally, the Treaty of Nice repeals the Protocol on the Institutions with the Prospect of Enlargement of the EU.

The Draft Constitution of the European Union takes a different approach altogether. It proposes in Article 25(3), that the Commission staff, in essence, comprise of two groups or tiers. First, there will be a College, which shall consist of a President, the Union Minister for Foreign Affairs/Vice President, and thirteen European Commissioners. Secondly, the President will appoint non-voting Commissioners coming from all of the member states who do not have a member in the College. This proposal proved controversial. The Commission President, Romano Prodi, proposed one Commissioner per member state in response to this proposal. As of this writing, the issue has not been resolved.

These observations illustrate that the Treaties (and Draft Constitution) underpinning the Union may continually change to bring about institutional changes. Thus, this chapter can provide only a snapshot of the institutional structure early in the 21st century, and some sense of the changes wrought by the Treaty on European Union, 1992, the Treaty of Amsterdam, 1997, the Treaty of Nice, 2001 and the Draft Constitution of Europe. However, students should keep attuned to various ongoing changes in the institutional structure of the EU. Indeed, as mentioned in the introduction, this advice applies to all areas of the law of the European Union.

RELEVANT TREATY PROVISIONS

Part One of the Treaty Establishing the European Community sets forth Principles. Articles 2 and 3 state the tasks and activities of the Community. Article 7 (ex Article 4) states that the tasks entrusted to the Community shall be carried out by the following institutions: a European Parliament, a Council, a Commission, a Court of Justice, and a Court of Auditors. Article 7 also refers to the separation of powers between the various institutions of the EU, stating that: '[e]ach institution shall act within the limits of the powers conferred upon it by this Treaty'.

The Council of Ministers, the European Commissioners, and the European Parliament comprise the political institutions of the European Union mentioned in Article 7. (The European Council, consisting of 'heads of state or government', although also a 'political' institution, is not mentioned in Article 7. Instead, it is described in Article 4 of the separate Treaty on European Union.)

The Court of Justice, also mentioned in Article 7, constitutes the judicial institution of the EU (along with the Court of First Instance, brought into creation by amendments contained in the Single European Act, and 'attached' to the Court of Justice). We will discuss briefly the final institution mentioned in Article 7, the Court of Auditors, which provides fiscal oversight of the Union.

Part Five of the Treaty Establishing the European Community provides more detail about the 'institutions of the Community'. Title I of Part Five deals with provisions governing the institutions, and sections 1, 2 and 3 of Chapter 1 deal with the Parliament, the Council and the Commission, respectively. Chapter 3 deals with the Economic and Social Committee and Chapter 4 deals with the Committee of the Regions.

As mentioned, the Common Foreign and Security Policy and the European Union's provisions regarding Justice and Home Affairs exist largely outside the European Community. They are popularly known as the second and third pillars, respectively, that constitute the European Union. We will discuss the second and third pillars and the involvement of the Community institutions in these pillars in this chapter.

UNIQUE SYSTEM OF GOVERNANCE

The governance of the European Union is unique. The European Union may have similarities to forms of government with which we are familiar, but in many ways it stands alone.

For example, in Ireland the Oireachtas, or Parliament, is responsible for proposing, adopting and, in many cases, implementing law. The European Union is different. The European Parliament by and large lacks the power to introduce proposals for new legislation. That role largely falls to the European Commission. Adoption of new legislation is largely the primary responsibility of the Council, although in an ever-increasing number of areas, adoption is accomplished through the joint efforts of the Council and Parliament.

Students may be familiar with a US-style three-part system of government, consisting of executive, legislative and judicial functions divided between three branches of government. Often, this division is accompanied by a system of checks and balances to prevent any one branch of government from dominating the other branches or usurping their functions.

However, it is not possible to divide neatly the functions of the institutions of the European Union into executive, legislative and judicial functions. Executive powers are in some measure shared between the Commission and the Council. Legislative powers often are a joint function of the Parliament and the Council, although the Commission is empowered in limited instances to act legislatively. In some instances, the Commission exercises functions we might regard as judicial.

With these thoughts in mind, we can turn to the first institution we will consider, the European Council.

THE EUROPEAN COUNCIL (TREATY ON EUROPEAN UNION, ARTICLE 4)

The European Council consists of 'heads of state or government', assisted by their Ministers for Foreign Affairs, along with the President and one other member of the Commission (TEU, Article 4, ex Article D). According to Article 4:

> The European Council shall provide the Union with the necessary impetus for its development and shall define the general political guidelines thereof.

The role of the European Council is very broad. It acts as the 'political engine' of the Union. It does not have legislative powers.

The European Council meets at least twice a year (more often, it meets three or four times a year), in a meeting hosted by the country that holds the Presidency of the Council. It submits a written report of its meeting to the Parliament.

The European Council came into existence in the 1960s, during a time of stagnation among the political institutions of the then European (Economic) Community. Its existence was not formally recognised until the ratification of the Single European Act, 1986, although it had held regular meetings for a number of years. The formal responsibilities of the European Council are set forth in the Articles from the Treaty on European Union outlined above. These Articles also introduce an element of democratic accountability into this inter-governmental body by requiring that a report be made to the European Parliament.

The Draft Constitution for Europe makes some changes to the European Council. First, it formally establishes the European Council as an institution (Draft Constitution, Article 20). It expressly states what had been implicit: 'it does not exercise legislative functions'. It provides for quarterly meetings to be chaired by the President of the European Council, which is a newly-created position (Draft Constitution, Article 21). The President, according to the Draft Constitution, shall be elected by a qualified majority for a term of two-and-one-half years, renewable once. The President shall not hold a national mandate.

THE COUNCIL OF THE EUROPEAN UNION (EC TREATY, ARTICLES 202-210)

The Council has been described as the place where the member states can assert their national interests. That is, the Council is perceived as representing the voice of the member states. It is easy to see why. Article 203 (ex Article 146) provides that the membership of the Council shall consist of a representative of each member state at ministerial level, authorised to commit the government of that member state. That is, at present, there are fifteen members, one from each member state.

Several things should be noted at the outset. First, the membership of the Council is not static. As the matters under consideration before the Council change, so does the membership. That is, if the Council is considering a proposal from the Commission regarding an agricultural matter, the Council will consist of agricultural Ministers, including Ireland's Minister for Agriculture. If the matter under consideration concerns the external relations of the European Union, the members most likely will consist of Ministers for Foreign Affairs.

The General Council of the Council of Ministers consists of Ministers for Foreign Affairs, including the Irish Minister. This may reflect the attitude of member states that the European Union really is a 'foreign' body, rather than one that is a part of the domestic legal order.

(Junior Ministers, as well as officials from devolved regions, are able to attend meetings of the Council, so long as they have the power to bind the member state.)

Second, we should note that, unlike with members of the Commission (or of the Court of Justice) the Treaty does not set forth the qualifications required for appointment to the Council. That is because it is a matter for member states to make ministerial appointments, and the Council consists of these representatives.

Based on its membership, we might conclude that the Council is more of an intergovernmental institution, because it is the direct expression of the member states' various national interests. This is true, in part; the Council does represent the 'voice of the member states'. However, we must consider how the Council takes its decisions before we decide whether it is more intergovernmental or supranational in character; as we will see, in certain instances, decisions of the Council (acting with Parliament) may compel member states to act contrary to what they perceive as their own national interests. To the extent that decisions can be taken by less than unanimous agreement (as is the case), the Council has supranational characteristics.

COREPER

Because the Council meets irregularly (and with a changing membership!) it requires the assistance of a full-time body to keep it operating efficiently and effectively. This body is known as the Committee of Permanent Representatives according to Article 207(1) (ex Article 151(1)). It is popularly known as 'COREPER', based on the acronym of its name in the French language. COREPER consists of individuals at ambassadorial level who work full-time on the affairs of the Council.

How does this body assist the Council? The members of COREPER work in advance of the meetings of the Council, determining those issues on which consensus exists, and those that will require further discussion at the meetings of the Council. When the Council meets, they know in advance, thanks to the work of COREPER, which items on their agenda can go through 'on the nod' (because of the advance work in achieving a consensus), and which items will pose more difficulties (and more negotiations).

Presidency of the Council

Article 203 (ex Article 146) provides that the office of the President of the Council shall be held in turn by each member state in the Council for a term of six months in the order decided unanimously by the Council. In the year 2000, the Presidency was held by Portugal for six months, and by France for six months. The year 2001 was divided between Sweden and Belgium. The year 2002 was divided between Spain and Denmark. The first half of 2003 was held by Greece, the second half by Italy. Ireland last held the Presidency of the Council in the second half of 1996, and held the Presidency again in 2004.

The foregoing makes it clear that the usual practice with respect to the Presidency is to divide the year between a larger member state and a smaller one. In practice, there are three member states actively involved in the Presidency held by any one member state. Because the term of six months is relatively short, the member state that holds the Presidency is likely to consult closely with the member state that held the most recent Presidency, as well as with the member state that will hold the next Presidency.

The Presidency is responsible for initiating meetings, establishing the agenda for the meetings, and chairing the meetings. The Presidency is expected to be objective and act for the good of the Community as a whole. It takes an active role in moving Commission proposals through the Council.

A small permanent civil service known as a Secretariat assists the Presidency.

Each member state that holds the Presidency tries to leave its mark. The last time Ireland held the Presidency, in 1996, it did much of the groundwork leading to the eventual Treaty of Amsterdam, such as preparing initial drafts of the Treaty and following up when the Netherlands assumed the presidency in the first half of 1997. (Ireland managed to re-insert certain Treaty provisions that were dropped in drafts prepared by the Dutch Presidency.)

Duties of the Council

According to Article 202 (ex Article 145) the Council shall ensure coordination of the general economic policies of the member states, shall have power to take decisions, and shall confer power on the Commission for implementation of Council rules.

By and large, the vast majority of the work of the Council consists of acting upon legislative proposals from the Commission, either alone, or jointly with the Parliament (which has given rise to the phrase: 'The Commission proposes, the Council disposes').

Decision-making in the Council

How does the Council decide whether to adopt a piece of legislation for the Community? It is useful to refer back at this point to the discussion of intergovernmental versus supranational forms of international organisations. In the typical intergovernmental body, decisions affecting any member usually must be taken unanimously. On the other hand, in a supranational body, decisions can be taken without unanimous agreement. As the membership of the Council appears similar to a typical international body, we might conclude that its decisions must always be unanimous. However, this would be incorrect.

There are at least three ways by which a decision could be reached in the Council. One possible rule of decision would require unanimity. A second possibility would be that a simple majority of members would prevail. A third possibility is that some type of weighted majority vote would be required.

The relevant Treaty Article is somewhat disingenuous. Article 205(1) (ex Article 148(1)) states that: 'Save as otherwise provided in this Treaty, the Council shall act by a majority of its members'. This rule of a simple majority of the fifteen members of the Council would make it appear that the Council is very close to the purely supranational end of intergovernmental-supranational spectrum. However, the fact is that the Treaty rarely provides for decisions by a simple majority.

The vast majority of decisions reached in the Council – either by the Council acting alone or, after TEU, jointly with the European Parliament – require either a unanimous vote, or, increasingly, a Qualified Majority Vote (QMV).

Originally, all decisions were made by a unanimous vote. However, the Treaty of Rome in 1957 provided for qualified majority voting after a transitional period, in areas such as the common agricultural policy and transport policy. (Recall that it was the introduction of qualified majority voting, in part, that caused France to adopt its 'empty chair policy' and that resulted in the Luxembourg Accords.)

The number of issues that can be decided by a qualified majority vote has increased over the history of the EU. After the Treaty of Amsterdam, there were about seventy Articles in the Treaty that required unanimity. After the Treaty of Nice, fewer areas remain in which unanimity is required. In theory, at least, qualified majority voting has become the norm.

The Draft Constitution drops the subterfuge of Article 205(1) of the EC Treaty, and provides that decisions of the Council of Ministers shall be taken by qualified majority except in those increasingly rare situations where the Draft Constitution provides otherwise.

It is clear that it is easier and quicker to reach decisions if less than a unanimous decision is required. Thus, in theory, the spread of QMV will enhance the efficiency of decision-making in the EU.

However, in practice it is not always possible to perceive this to be true. The fact remains that, due to the Luxembourg Accords discussed in a previous chapter – pursuant to which the Council endeavours to reach unanimous agreement if a member state indicates that its 'vital national interest' is at stake – the member states effectively believe that they retain the power unilaterally to veto proposals brought before the Council, regardless of the technical voting procedure involved. As a result, the Council often does not take formal votes at all. Rather, thanks to preparatory work done by COREPER, the member states know in advance of the Council meeting how a vote would turn out if it were taken. If the matter under consideration is one to which QMV applies, and it is clear that there are sufficient votes to prevail under a QMV, then a member state may realise it would be futile to oppose the matter at the Council meeting. The matter before the Council may be approved without a formal vote being taken.

Breakdown of Voting Methods

It is not possible to state a general rule concerning which matters before the Council must be decided by unanimous votes, and which require qualified majority voting procedures or a simple majority. It is always necessary to look at the Treaty Article on which the proposal is based to determine which voting procedure applies. However, it is possible to make some general observations.

Those issues that can be decided by a simple majority tend to be in less controversial areas. For example, the Council may decide its own Rules of Procedure by a simple majority vote (Article 207(3), ex Article 151(3)).

Issues that can be decided by a qualified majority include measures to complete the internal market (Article 95, ex Article 100(a)). (Recall that the adoption of Article 100(a), now Article 95, as the result of ratification of the

Single European Act, 1986, was one of the ways that completion of the internal market was accelerated after a period of slow progress.)

Issues that require unanimous consent include, under Article 308 (ex Article 235), measures necessary to attain one of the objectives of the Community that are not provided for expressly in the Treaty. (Article 205(3), ex Article 148(3), provides that abstentions cannot prevent a decision being regarded as unanimous, where unanimity is required.)

Another example of an area that requires a unanimous vote is harmonisation of indirect taxation, such as VAT and excise duties, under Article 93 (ex Article 99). The French Presidency, with the support of the Commission, sought to introduce QMV in this area through amendments brought about by the Treaty of Nice. The goal was to avoid 'double taxation', and situations where separate tax barriers operate as a barrier to the free movement guarantees of the Treaty. Ireland (and Britain) vigorously opposed the revision of Article 93, and the requirement of a unanimous vote in this area did not change.

At the Nice Summit, Ireland also successfully opposed the introduction of QMV under Article 137(3), which pertains to social security protection for workers. As a result, any country can unilaterally prevent adoption of measures in Council that they believe will damage their national interests.

We began this section by considering whether the Council had intergovernmental or supranational attributes. As we have seen, there is no easy answer. The nature of the Council has changed over time. Technically, more and more decisions are taken by QMV, which enhances the supranational character of the institution. However, political considerations exert other influences. The desire to achieve consensus on important issues means that many decisions appear intergovernmental in nature.

Qualified Majority Voting – the Formalities (before Nice)

Article 205(2) (ex Article 148(2)) stated that when the Council is required to act by a qualified majority, the votes of its members shall carry a certain weight. The weight ranged from two for Luxembourg to eight for Spain to ten for Germany, France, Italy, and the UK. (Ireland's vote was weighted at three.)

The weighting of votes was as follows:

Germany, France, Italy, UK	10
Spain	8
Belgium, Greece, Netherlands, Portugal	5
Austria, Sweden	4
Denmark, Ireland, Finland	3
Luxembourg	2
Total	87

The Article further provided that when the Council was acting on a proposal from the Commission that required a qualified majority vote for its approval, there had to be sixty-two votes in favour. In other cases requiring qualified majority voting (that is, on proposals other than those from the Commission), there had to be sixty-two votes cast by at least ten member states.

The rationale behind the qualified majority voting was to prevent domination of the Council by either a few large states or smaller states acting in concert. For example, even if the five largest member states vote for a proposal, there will be only forty-eight votes in favour. The larger states must attract the support of smaller states to succeed. Similarly, if all the smaller states vote in favour of a measure, they will still lack a qualified majority. They must gain the support of a large member state.

Another way to look at the qualified majority voting procedure is by calculating how many votes were required to block a proposal. Before Nice, with a qualified majority vote of sixty-two votes required, it was necessary to have twenty-six votes to block a proposal. This effectively prevented the Franco-German axis from blocking proposals supported the other member states.

Ioannnina Compromise of 1994

The expansion of the European Union to include three new member states provoked a crisis over the number of votes needed to block a proposal that required a qualified majority. This resulted in a compromise similar to the Luxembourg Accords of 1966, which, as you will recall, ended France's 'empty-chair' policy at the time of the initial move to qualified majority voting. The Luxembourg Accords provided that if a member state announced that its vital national interests were at stake, then the Council would endeavour to reach a unanimous decision.

Prior to the addition of Austria, Finland and Sweden to the European Union, a qualified majority required fifty-four votes out of a total of seventy-six votes. Twenty-three votes were required to block a qualified majority. After the addition of these three new member states, a qualified majority required sixty-two votes. The issue which arose was how many votes should be required to block a qualified majority vote?

The majority of member states took the view that an 'arithmetic adjustment' would be required to the number of votes required to block a qualified majority vote. They believed that the number of votes required to block a qualified majority should increase to twenty-six votes. However, the UK disagreed. It (correctly) perceived that its power to block measures would be diminished, because it would be more difficult to organise enough member states to vote against a proposal. The UK sought to leave the number of votes required to block a qualified majority unchanged at twenty-three votes.

A political compromise was reached. According to this compromise, if enough member states opposed a proposal such that there are at least twenty-three votes but less than twenty-six votes against the proposal, then the President of the Council would endeavour to reach an agreement that had at least sixty-five votes, rather than sixty-two votes. If they failed to reach sixty-five votes, the Council could proceed with sixty-two votes. However, the upshot of this compromise, which was acknowledged in a declaration added to the Treaty of Amsterdam, was that it was easier to oppose a proposal before the Council on which a qualified majority was required.

Nice Summit

At Nice, the member states confronted the issue of an expanded Commission and the weighting of votes in the Council. Various proposals were put forward to deal with both issues. It was generally understood that some type of trade-off was required, whereby a re-weighting of their votes in the Council would compensate larger member states who might lose the right to nominate a second member of the Commission. (This undermines the notion that Commissioners are 'independent' and do not represent a member state's interests on the Commission.) Also on the agenda was discussion of a dual majority, whereby the number of votes required to adopt a proposal under qualified majority voting would have to come from member states representing at least half of the total population of the European Union.

The changes to the Commission are discussed below. Suffice it to say that the larger member states succeeded in obtaining increased voting strength in the Council in exchange for giving up a second Commissioner.

Qualified Majority Voting after Nice

The outcome at Nice was mixed.

On the one hand, QMV voting was extended to approximately thirty new areas. Thus, the trend away from requiring unanimous decisions continued. This should streamline decision-making in the European Union. Some of the areas into which QMV has been extended by the Treaty of Nice include Article 13(2) on anti-discrimination measures, Article 123(4) on the Euro, and, as discussed below, Article 214 on the nomination and appointment of the President of the Commission and its members.

On the other hand, the QMV procedure became more complex. Furthermore, after all the changes are implemented, it will be more difficult to reach a qualified majority than before, and easier to block a proposal that requires QMV.

Many people felt there were three goals at Nice with regard to QMV:
1. extend QMV to more areas;

2.   make QMV simpler and easier to understand;
3.   make QMV easier to achieve.

Seen in this light, the Nice Treaty failed in two out of three areas.

QMV can be broken down into three stages:

1.   Pre-Nice;
2.   changes implemented by the Nice Treaty from 1 January 2005; and
3.   changes implemented by the Nice Treaty when the EU reaches twenty-seven member states. These changes will be implemented by amendments to Article 205 (ex Article 148).

We must also consider the implications of the Draft Constitution for Europe.

Pre-Nice: QMV required sixty-two out of eighty-seven votes to be cast in favour of a measure. The blocking minority was twenty-six.

From 1 January 2005: Annex I of the Treaty of Nice includes a Protocol on the Enlargement of the European Union. It effects changes to QMV. The weights attributed to each member state are changed. The changes are as follows.

Belgium	12
Denmark	7
Germany	29
Greece	12
Spain	27
France	29
Ireland	7
Italy	29
Luxembourg	4
Netherlands	13
Austria	10
Portugal	12
Finland	7
Sweden	10
UK	29
Total	237

According to Article 3 of this Protocol, entitled 'Provisions concerning the weighting of votes in the Council', QMV will require 170 out of 237 votes. The blocking minority will be sixty-seven votes. In addition, after 1 January 2005, if the vote is on a proposal from the Commission, at least a majority of the member states must vote in favour of the proposal. If the vote is on any other matter, at least two-thirds of the member states must vote in favour.

Article 205 (ex Article 148) of the EC Treaty is further amended by the addition of a new paragraph, Article 205(4). That paragraph provides that, where a member state so requests, it must be demonstrated that the member states voting in favour of a proposal constitute at least sixty-two per cent of the population of the European Union. This constitutes a second, demographic 'filter' for the adoption of a measure under QMV.

From EU reaching twenty-seven member states: Annex II of the Nice Treaty consists of a Declaration on the Enlargement of the EU. The weights attributed to each member state are changed again. The new weighted voting system is as follows:

Germany, UK, France, Italy	29
Spain, Poland	27
Romania	14
Netherlands	13
Greece, Czech Republic, Belgium, Hungary, Portugal	12
Sweden, Bulgaria, Austria	10
Slovakia, Denmark, Finland, Ireland, Lithuania	7
Latvia, Slovenia, Estonia, Cyprus, Luxembourg	4
Malta	3
Total	345

QMV will require 258 votes out of 345 votes. The blocking minority will be eighty-seven votes. If the proposal comes from the Commission, the majority of member states must vote in favour of the proposal. On any other measure, two-thirds of the member states must vote in favour of the proposal. It continues the requirement that, upon request, it must be shown that the member states voting in favour of a proposal constitute sixty-two per cent of the total population of the Union.

Note that it will become progressively easier to achieve a blocking minority and prevent adoption of measures in the Council. Presently, it requires approximately twenty-nine per cent of the available votes to block a measure in the Council. After 1 January 2005, it will take approximately twenty-eight per cent of the available votes to block a measure. And after expansion to include twenty-seven member states, it will take only approximately twenty-five per cent of the available votes to block a measure.

Note also that the voting strength of Ireland, and other small and medium-sized member states, will be diminished by the proposed changes. The following table shows the dilution in voting strength. Correspondingly, the voting strength of the larger member states has been increased. Thus, these larger states have been compensated for the loss of a second Commissioner.

The Draft Constitution for Europe appears to simplify QMV significantly. At Article 24, it simply provides for, essentially, two types of QMV: QMV for a measured proposed by the Commission; and QMV for other types of measures. For the first type of QMV (a Commission proposal), such a (qualified) majority shall consist of the majority of member states, representing at least three-fifths of the population of the Union. For other types of proposals, QMV requires two-thirds of member states, representing at least three-fifths of the population of the union. Also, the Draft Constitution empowers the European Council, acting on the basis of unanimity, to change the voting procedures laid down for the Council of Ministers in a particular case. That is, if the Treaty requires a unanimous decision by the Council of Ministers, the European Council can adopt 'on its own initiative and by unanimity' a decision allowing the Council of Ministers to act by qualified majority in that area (Draft Constitution, Article 24(4)). The proposed change to QMV in the Draft Constitution proved to be the 'deal breaker' that prevented its adoption by December 2003. Poland and Spain objected to the reduction in their voting strength, which would have been the result of the new voting method. As of this writing, the issue has not been resolved.

We will turn now to the European Commission.

THE EUROPEAN COMMISSION (EC TREATY, ARTICLES 212-219)

It is necessary to distinguish between:
1. the College of Commissioners, that is, the relatively few members of the Commission who are nominated by the member states and approved by the Parliament; and
2. the Commission bureaucracy, which can be compared to a sort of 'civil service of Europe'.

The Treaty provisions we will discuss deal primarily with the broad responsibilities of the Commission as a whole, and the composition, qualifications and appointment of the College of Commissioners. We will focus on these aspects first, and then briefly set out the structure of the Commission bureaucracy.

Duties of the Commission

Article 211 (ex Article 155) sets out the functions of the Commission. According to this Article, the Commission shall:

1. ensure that the Treaty is applied (that is, act as a sort of 'guardian of the Treaty');
2. formulate recommendations and opinions on matters dealt with in the Treaty;
3. participate in the shaping of measures taken by the Council; and
4. exercise powers conferred on it by the Council.

Of these responsibilities, perhaps the most important is the Commission's role as guardian of the Treaty. As we will see in subsequent chapters, the Commission has the power to bring enforcement actions in the Court of Justice against a member state if it believes the member state has violated Community law. Under powers delegated by the Council of the European Union, the Commission also may investigate violations of Community competition law and levy fines against offenders.

The Draft Constitution does not substantially revise the functions of the Commission. However it adds as a function that the Commission: 'shall ensure the union's external representation'. It also makes explicit what had been implicit: 'Union legislative acts can be adopted only on the basis of a Commission proposal', unless the Draft Constitution provides otherwise.

Composition of the Commission

Article 213 (ex Article 157) provides that the Commission shall consist of twenty members. Only nationals of member states may be members of the Commission. The Commission must include at least one national of each of the member states, and not more than two members of the same member state.

Presently, the larger member states (that is, France, Germany, Italy, Spain and the UK) each provide two members to the Commission. The remaining member states each provide one member.

Expansion of the European Union and Composition of the Commission

One important issue facing the European Union is the composition of the Commission when membership in the EU expands. Smaller member states, such as Ireland, would like to continue to appoint a member of the Commission, according to the procedure outlined below.

Larger member states, such as the UK, would like to retain their two 'slots' on the Commission. In a European Union of twenty or twenty-five or thirty member states, including larger member states such as Poland, it is possible to imagine a Commission of forty or fifty members. This is probably too large for a collegial body such as the Commission.

Commentators had hoped that the European Union would deal with this issue in the Treaty of Amsterdam, that is, that Treaty amendments would be proposed to, e.g., Article 213, to deal with the composition of the Commission in light of expanded membership of the European Union. However, the Amsterdam Treaty was a disappointment in this regard.

Treaty of Nice

The Treaty of Nice, on the other hand, deals with the issue of expansion. As discussed in the section on the Council, the changes in the Treaty are not completely satisfactory, especially in the way it allowed a trade-off of increased voting strength in the Council for a reduced number of Commissioners per member state.

As mentioned at the beginning of this chapter, the Treaty of Nice proposes a change to the composition of the Commission. The changes will take place in two stages. From 2005, there will be one Commissioner from each member state (that is, the larger states will give up their second Commissioner). Thereafter, when the number of member states belonging to the EU reaches twenty-seven, there will no longer be one Commissioner per member state.

Instead of each member state being entitled to appoint a Commissioner, there will be a system of rotation. Member states will, on an equal basis, take turns in appointing a Commissioner. The Treaty of Nice does not clearly specify how many Commissioners there will be, but it is likely there will be twenty Commissioners.

The Draft Constitution seeks to change the composition of the Commission yet again. It provides that, the Commission shall be divided, essentially, into two 'tiers'. The first tier will be a College, and will comprise fifteen members: the President; the Union Minister of Foreign Affairs/Vice President; and thirteen European Commissioners, 'selected on the basis of equal rotation between the member states' (Article 25(3)). The second tier will consist of non-voting Commissioners from member states that do not have a member in the first tier.

The President of the Commission opposed the creation of a 'two-tiered' Commission. He proposed that there continue to be one Commissioner from each member state. However, he suggested that the Commission adopt a 'committee structure' and allow most decisions to be taken by committees with a smaller number of Commissioners. As of writing, the issue has not been resolved.

Appointment of President and Members of the Commission

Before Nice, Article 214 (ex Article 158) provided that the member states nominated the President of the Commission by common accord. Having nominated the President, the member states, by common accord with the nominee for President, nominated the other persons they intended to appoint as members of the Commission. The President and the members were nominated for a term of five years. Thus, unanimity was required under Article 214 prior to the Treaty of Nice.

The Treaty of Nice changes the manner in which the President and the members of the Commission are appointed. Most importantly, it drops the requirement of unanimity in appointing the President and the Commission. Instead, it requires a qualified majority for these appointments.

Specifically, amendments to Article 214 (ex Article 158) provide that the Council, 'acting in the composition of Heads of State or Government and acting by a qualified majority', shall nominate the President. This will prevent a single member state from opposing a nominee for President of the Commission, as the UK did when Belgian Prime Minister Jean-Luc Dehaenne was considered for the Presidency in 1994. (The UK thought Dehaenne was too much of a 'federalist'.)

Similarly, with respect to the Commission, the amendments provide that the Council, acting by a qualified majority, shall draw up the list of Commissioners. After approval by the Parliament, the President and other members shall be appointed by the Council acting by a qualified majority.

The Draft Constitution changes the way in which the President and the other members are selected (Draft Constitution, Article 26). The changes enhance, superficially at least, the role of the European Parliament and increase the powers of the President. The European Council, deciding by a qualified majority, will submit a proposed candidate for President to the Parliament. Member states that are eligible to appoint one of the thirteen (voting) members of the College will each submit a list of three names, on which each gender is represented. The President-elect selects thirteen Commissioners from these lists (there is no requirement of gender representation in the final selection). Finally the President, the thirteen European Commissioners, the non-voting Commissioners, and the proposed Union Minister for Foreign Affairs must be approved by Parliament.

Qualifications of Members of the Commission

The Treaty places much emphasis on the independence of the members of the Commission. That is, members of the Commission must agree to serve the interest of the Community, rather than that of their member state. Article 213 provides that: 'In the performance of these duties, they shall neither seek nor take instructions from any government or from any other body'. Furthermore, '[e]ach member state undertakes to respect this principle and not to seek to influence the members of the Commission in the performance of these tasks'.

Thus, in principle, each member of the Commission is free of the influence of the member state that appointed him or her. It is the Council of the European Union that represents the voice of the member state.

It is reasonable to be sceptical of the claim that Commissioners are not influenced by the member state that appointed them. However, individual Commissioners have demonstrated their independence of their member state. One example of this was Commissioner David Byrne, the former Attorney General of Ireland, who was the Commissioner responsible for Health and Consumer Protection during the outbreak of Foot and Mouth Disease (FMD) in Europe in 2001. He stated that in the event of an outbreak of FMD in Ireland, he would ban exports from Ireland to the rest of the EU. He took this stance in the interest of the EU as a whole, even though it would have devastating consequences for Ireland.

Approval of Nominees

After being nominated, the President and the members of the Commission must be 'subject as a body to a vote of approval by the European Parliament' (Article 214, ex Article 158). In other words, the Parliament can only approve or disapprove of all of the nominees at once. Parliament cannot single out one or more nominees and refuse to approve them. This remains true after the Treaty of Nice, although nomination of the President and the members of the Commission does not require a unanimous decision by the Council, as was the case before the Nice Treaty came into effect in February 2003.

The Commission acts by a majority of its members. Each Commissioner holds one or more 'portfolios', and the member states often haggle over who will receive these portfolios. Examples of these portfolios include:
1. Competition;
2. the Internal Market;
3. External Relations;
4. Health and Consumer Protection;
5. the Environment; and
6. the Budget.

These portfolios roughly correlate to sections of the Commission bureaucracy known as Directorates General, but sometimes a single portfolio overlaps two or more Directorates General.

Each Commissioner is assisted by a cabinet, including a Chef de Cabinet. The members of the cabinet are often senior civil servants from the member state of the Commissioner.

Dismissal of Individual Commissioners or of the Entire Commission

If a member of the Commission can no longer fulfil the conditions for the performance of his duties or if he or she has been guilty of serious misconduct, the Court of Justice may, on application by the Council or Commission, compulsorily retire him or her (Article 216, ex Article 160).

Article 201 (ex Article 144) provides that if the Parliament passes a motion of censure by a two-thirds majority of the votes cast, representing a majority of the members of the European Parliament, then the Commissioner must resign.

The Treaty of Nice strengthens the power of the President to discipline or dismiss a Commissioner. Amendments to Article 217 (ex Article 161) will allow the President to demand the resignation of a Commissioner, after obtaining the collective approval of the Commission.

The Draft Constitution drops the requirement that the President obtain the collective approval of the Commission (Draft Constitution, Article 26). Instead, it simply states: 'A European Commissioner or Commissioners shall resign if the President so requests'.

Resignation of Entire Commission

In March 1999, all of the members of the European Commission resigned. The resignation followed the First Report of the Committee of Independent Experts established by the European Parliament to investigate allegations of fraud, mismanagement and nepotism in the European Commission. The Report likely would have been followed by a vote of censure by the Parliament, and the Commissioners' resignation was a preemptive move to avoid a forced resignation.

As the then President of the Commission, Jacques Santer, said in a statement the day following the resignation, there was no suggestion that any member of the Commission was involved in fraud or corruption. However, the Report did conclude that the Commissioners failed to grasp a sense of responsibilities for the Commission bureaucracy, and, in at least one case, made inappropriate appointments to high-paying jobs. The Report concluded that:

> It is becoming difficult to find anyone who has even the slightest sense of responsibility ... The temptation to deprive the concept of responsibility of all substance is a dangerous one. That concept is the ultimate manifestation of democracy.

After their resignation, the Commissioners continued in their posts pending their replacement. This is provided by Article 201 (ex Article 144). The Commission has undertaken a policy of reform in light of the criticisms contained in the Report.

UNION MINISTER FOR FOREIGN AFFAIRS

The Draft Constitution creates the position of Union Minister for Foreign Affairs (Draft Constitution, Article 27). He or she is appointed by the European Council, acting by qualified majority. He or she shall conduct the union's common foreign and security policy.

STRUCTURE OF THE COMMISSION BUREAUCRACY AND RECOMMENDATIONS FROM COMMISSION

The Commission as a whole can be thought of as the civil service of Europe. However, it is a relatively small civil service, having fewer employees, for instance, than the Republic of Ireland. While there are less than four million people in the Republic of Ireland, there are more than 300 million residents of the European Union.

The Commission bureaucracy is organised into Directorates General (DGs), each of which is concerned with an area of policy for the European Union. There are approximately twenty-four Directorates General. Each DG had a number, and certain DGs, such as DG–IV, which was concerned with competition law, were immediately recognisable by their number. However, in an effort to make the Commission more accessible, the recent practice has been to refer to the Directorates General by their name, such as the Directorate General External Relations (formerly known as DG–1A or 1B), and the Directorate General Transport (formerly known as DG–VII).

Each Directorate General is headed internally by a permanent employee known as a Director General.

The Directorates General are divided further into Divisions. Each Division is headed by a permanent employee known as a Division Head.

In addition to Directorates General, there are Special Services that provide support and assistance to all the DGs. These include the Legal Service and, not surprisingly, the Translation Service. Almost twenty per cent of the Commission bureaucracy is involved with translation services. Eurostat is a special service that collects statistical information about the EU.

Members of a Division report to a Division Head, who in turns reports to a Director General, who in turns reports to one (or more) members of the College of Commissioners. This chain of command more or less describes the route that a proposal for a piece of legislation (for instance, a new regulation or a directive, which we will discuss below) would take on its way to the members of the Commission.

When a proposal for a piece of legislation works its way through the Brussels bureaucracy and reaches the members of the Commission, they must take a decision whether or not formally to propose it to the Council (or to Parliament and the Council). They must take that decision by a simple majority of its members (Article 219, ex Article 163.)

OTHER DECISION-MAKING PROCEDURES OF THE COMMISSION: 'COMITOLOGY'

In most instances, the Commission proposes legislation, which is adopted by the Council or by the Council acting with the Parliament. A catch phrase that is used to describe this usual state of affairs is: 'the Commission proposes, the Council disposes'.

However, in certain instances, the Commission has authority from the Council to adopt legislative instruments, such as regulations and directives (which are discussed in more detail below), of its own accord. Article 202 (ex Article 145) provides that the Council may confer on the Commission powers for the implementation of the rules that the Council lays down. However, when the Commission is empowered to adopt legislation, it does so pursuant to procedures specified by the Council. This is because Article 203 (ex Article 146) provides that the Council may impose certain requirements in respect of the exercise of the powers conferred on the Commission.

Some of these requirements involve the Commission reporting to a Committee, which expresses an opinion on the proposed decision. These Committees generally consist of representatives of different member states. They review the operation of the Commission. These Committee procedures can be very complex and we will discuss them only generally. However, the entire process by which the Commission adopts legislation under this Committee procedure has attracted scholarly attention; the academics studying the process have adopted the term 'Comitology' to describe the process and its implications.

Comitology – Consultative Committee, Management Committee, Regulatory Committee

There are three different procedures we will discuss briefly. In the increasing order of oversight or control of the Council over the Commission decision, these procedures involve either a Consultative Committee, a Management Committee or a Regulatory Committee. That is, the Consultative Committee involves the least power over the shape of the final decision of the Commission, while the Regulatory Committee involves the most power.

In each instance, the Commission informs the relevant Committee of its proposed decision. In the case of the Consultative Committee, the members of the Committee form an opinion, but this opinion is not binding on the Commission. The Commission can take a decision despite a negative opinion. In the case of either the Management Committee or the Regulatory Committee, if the Committee gives a negative opinion, the Commission cannot proceed to a final decision. The Council must become more involved in order for the Commission decision to become final. In the case of the Management Committee, it is the case that if the Council fails to take affirmative steps to block the decision, it can become final. In the case of the Regulatory Committee, however, it may not be enough for the Council to do nothing for the Commission decision to become final. It may be necessary for the Council affirmatively to approve the decision.

This is merely the broadest overview of the procedures that can apply when the Commission is empowered to take its own decisions, e.g., in adopting regulations or directives.

EUROPEAN PARLIAMENT (EC TREATY, ARTICLES 189-201)

The European Parliament consists of directly-elected representatives of the people of the member states. After the accession of Sweden, Finland and Austria, the membership of the European Parliament expanded to 626 members. Prior to Nice, the EC Treaty stated that the number of members of the European Parliament should not exceed 700. However, the Treaty of Nice provides, in Annex I, entitled, 'Protocol on the Enlargement of the EU', that due to expansion of the EU, the total number of members may increase to 732.

Members of the European Parliament

Originally, member states appointed members of the Assembly (as it was then known) from their own national parliaments. The Treaty provided that the Assembly 'shall exercise the advisory and supervisory powers' which were conferred upon it by the then European (Economic) Community Treaty.

Thus, the Parliament was little more than a talking shop, whose members were not directly elected.

By virtue of a Council Decision and Act of 1976, members of the European Parliament (as it is now known) are directly elected. The first direct elections were held in 1979. The Treaty now provides, at Article 189 (ex Article 137) that the European Parliament 'shall exercise the powers conferred upon it by the Treaty'. As stated above, prior to Nice the Treaty provided an upper limit to the number of members of Parliament. 'The number of members of the European Parliament shall not exceed 700' (Article 189, ex Article 137). However, the Treaty of Nice raises this upper limit to 732.

The increase in the total number of members is accompanied by changes in the number of members per member state. Ireland, for instance, had its number of members reduced from fifteen to twelve. Of course, in an expanded Parliament, this will work a double diminution of Ireland's voting strength.

The following table shows the number of members of the European Parliament for member states.

Belgium	22
Denmark	13
Germany	99
Greece	22
Spain	50
France	72
Ireland	12
Italy	72
Luxembourg	6
Netherlands	25
Austria	17
Portugal	22
Finland	13
Sweden	18
UK	72

Increasing Powers of Parliament

The history of the European Parliament is one of increasing powers and responsibility. It has transformed from a body that merely advised and supervised, to a body that is jointly responsible (with the Council) for adopting much of the legislation of the European Union. We will discuss these increasing powers in a subsequent chapter dealing with laws and law-making in the European Union.

For the moment, it is sufficient to note that Article 189 provides simply that: '[t]he European Parliament ... shall exercise the powers conferred on it by this Treaty'. The Draft Constitution, Article 19(1), expands on this, to reflect the correct reality of Parliament's role in the European Union:

> The European Parliament shall, jointly with the Council of Ministers, enact legislation, and exercise the budgetary function, as well as functions of political control and consultation as laid down in the Treaty.

Members of Parliament serve for a five-year term (Article 190). They elect their own President (Article 197, ex Article 140).

Organisation of the Parliament

The members of the European Parliament are affiliated with political parties, which are formed at the European, rather than the national level. Article 191 (ex Article 138a) provides 'Political parties at the European level are important as a factor for integration within the Union'. The two largest political parties are the European People's Party and the Party of European Socialists.

Article 198 (ex Article 141) provides that, except as otherwise provided in the Treaty, 'the European Parliament shall act by an absolute majority of the votes cast'. However, the Treaty provides with respect to important areas of responsibility (such as the joint adoption of legislation with the Council) that the European Parliament must act by other than a simple majority.

Generally speaking, the European Parliament acts through a Committee structure, and it is very important to which Committee a member is assigned.

Ombudsman and Right of Petition

Since the Treaty on European Union, an Ombudsman has been appointed by Parliament and empowered to receive complaints from any citizen of the Union (or anyone residing in the Union) concerning maladministration in the activities of Community institutions (Article 195, ex Article 138e).

Also, the Treaty on European Union bestowed upon citizens of the Union (or persons residing within the Union) the formal right to petition the European Parliament (Article 194, ex Article 138d). (Prior to 1993, citizens had an informal right to petition Parliament.)

Powers of Parliament

As discussed above, the Parliament must approve the appointment of the Commission. It also may pass a motion of censure on the activities of the Commission, and, if the motion carries by a two-thirds majority of the votes cast, representing a majority of the members, the Commission must resign as a body (Article 201, ex Article 144). It was these powers which led to the entire Commission resigning in March 1999.

The Draft Constitution, at Article 19(1), provides that the Parliament shall elect the President of the European Commission. However, this represents largely a cosmetic change. The European Council only submits one candidate for the presidency of the European Commission. Parliament must approve this choice by a majority of its members, or else another 'candidate' must be submitted.

The Council must consult the Parliament before it adopts certain legislation, for example, before the Council adopts directives concerning the Common Agricultural Policy (Article 37(2), ex Article 43). Under the consultation procedure, the Council is free to disregard the opinion of the Parliament. However, the Council is not free to refuse to consult with Parliament: see Case 138/79, *Roquette Fréres v. Council* [1980] ECR 3333.

Parliament must give its assent to certain matters, for example, international agreements that have important budgetary implications (Article 300(3), ex Article 228(3)). This amounts to a power of veto in these areas. Perhaps the most important area in which Parliament has such a veto power is in relation to the accession of new member states to the European Union (TEU, Article 49). However, in certain important areas of international interest, such as the Common Commercial Policy, Parliament effectively has no powers at all.

Parliament also has the power to put questions to the Commission and the Council (Article 197, ex Article 140).

Powers of Parliament with Respect to Legislation

A subsequent chapter deals with the types of law that can be adopted by the European Union, and the ways in which laws are adopted. We will see that Parliament has an important role to play in the adoption of legislation, and that Parliament's powers in this regard have been expanding. The Treaty of Nice expands the number of areas in which the so-called co-decision procedure applies; the co-decision procedure affords Parliament essentially a co-equal role in the adoption of Community legislation.

ECONOMIC AND SOCIAL COMMITTEE AND THE COMMITTEE OF THE REGIONS

Article 7(2) (ex Article 4(2)) of the European Community Treaty provides that:

> The Council and the Commission shall be assisted by an Economic and Social Committee and a Committee of the Regions acting in an advisory capacity.

The Economic and Social Committee was established by the European (Economic) Community Treaty. It is purely an advisory body (Article 257, ex Article 193).

There are 222 members of the Economic and Social Committee. Its membership consists of representatives of the various categories of economic and social activity, including farmers, carriers, workers, professional occupations and representatives of the general public. Normally, one-third represents employers and business, one-third represents workers/unions, and one-third represents miscellaneous categories, including the voluntary and governmental sectors. Each member state is allotted a certain number of members of the Economic and Social Committee; Ireland has nine members

(Article 258, ex Article 194). The number of representatives for Ireland will not change with expansion of the EU. The members are appointed by the Council for four years, and their appointments are renewable. The Treaty of Nice eliminated the need for unanimity in the Council concerning appointments; the Treaty of Nice provides for qualified majority voting to approve appointments to ECOSOC.

The Committee must be consulted by the Council or the Commission where the Treaty so provides. The Committee may be consulted by the Parliament.

The Committee of the Regions was established by the Treaty on European Union. It arose at a time of increasing concern over centralisation in the European Community. It is meant to represent regional interests in Europe. Article 263 (ex Article 198a) provides that a Committee consisting of representatives of regional and local bodies shall be established. It is an advisory body.

Each member state is allotted a certain number of members; Ireland has nine members. This did not change under the Treaty of Nice.

The Committee of the Regions must be consulted by the Council or the Commission where the Treaty so provides (Article 265, ex Article 198c).

COMMON FOREIGN AND SECURITY POLICY AND COOPERATION ON JUSTICE AND HOME AFFAIRS

The Common Foreign and Security Policy, and Cooperation on Justice and Home Affairs are not institutions of the European Union. However, they are part of the EU and share a 'common institutional framework'. That is, various institutions of the European Union (as well as the member states acting in a sovereign capacity) help to implement these policies, and therefore they are included in this chapter.

The Treaty on European Union introduced the Common Foreign and Security Policy, as well as Cooperation on Justice and Home Affairs. These are the 'second and third pillars' that initially existed outside of the Community framework. (Since then, some areas of these pillars have been brought inside the Community.) As the names imply, these policies are concerned with developing a common foreign and security policy, and introducing a method of cooperation in matters of justice and home affairs, such as immigration policy.

Implementation – Common Foreign and Security Policy

Common foreign and security policy typically is not implemented like Community policies, such as the common agricultural policy. The primary actors in the common foreign and security policy are the member states and the institutions of the European Union in which the member states have the most influence, that is, those institutions that are more intergovernmental in nature. These would include the European Council and the Council of the European Union. Those Community institutions that are more supranational in nature, for instance the Commission, the Court of Justice and the European Parliament, do not play a major role in the common foreign and security policy.

The Treaty on European Union provides that the Commission is to be fully associated with the work carried out regarding the common foreign and security policy. However, the Commission does not have the sole power to initiate proposals in this area, as is the case with Community legislation. It shares this power with the member states, effectively diluting its law-making powers in this field.

The common foreign and security policy is implemented by means of 'common positions' and 'joint actions'. These types of legal instruments differ greatly from the types of laws that will be discussed in a subsequent chapter. Common positions and joint actions more closely resemble the types of instruments resulting from traditional intergovernmental international bodies.

Implementation – Justice and Home Affairs

Cooperation in the field of Justice and Home Affairs (since re-named Provisions on Police and Judicial Cooperation in Criminal Affairs) brings together the Ministries of Justice of the fifteen member states. It is meant to provide an opportunity for dialogue and cooperation between the police, customs and justice departments of the member states. A major area of concern is the immigration policies of the member states with respect to nationals of countries outside the European Union. Another major and related area of concern is the asylum policies of the member states.

The major players in this area, again, initially, were the member states and those institutions of an inter-governmental nature, such as the Council and the European Council. Initially, the more supranational institutions, such as the Commission, the Court of Justice and the European Parliament, had less influence in the area of Justice and Home Affairs than in other areas within the Community framework.

However, due to amendments contained in the Treaty of Amsterdam, certain areas within Justice and Home Affairs have been moved within the Community framework. Specifically, Title IV (formerly Title IIIa) has been adopted, and is entitled 'Visas, Asylum, Immigration and Other Policies Related to Free Movement of Persons'.

CONCLUSION

This chapter provides an overview of the major (and minor) political institutions (and policies) of the European Union. Another major institution, the Court of Auditors, could have been included in this chapter, as it is not a court at all, but rather an institution concerned with fiscal oversight of the EU. However, for reasons of space consideration, we have included it in a separate chapter, one that deals with the judicial institutions of the EU.

What should be apparent from reading this chapter is the extremely dynamic nature of the structure of European Union institutions and policies. Particularly since the Treaty on European Union, there seems to be an acceleration in the rate at which institutions are changed, re-named, their powers re-defined, etc. Some of these changes (e.g., Parliament's increasing role in law-making) are driven by a desire to make the Union appear to be more democratic and responsive to citizens' concerns about transparency and democratic accountability. Other changes (e.g., changes to the membership of the European Commission and to voting procedures in the Council of the European Union), are driven by the expansion of the Union to twenty-five member states. Some changes (e.g., Common Foreign and Security Policy) could be perceived as a shift away from internal market considerations towards Union concerns about representation on the world stage. A student should ask himself or herself questions, such as whether the Union has succeeded in becoming more democratic and transparent and whether the changes to the Commission membership and QMV voting procedures are effective in absorbing the new member states while allowing the legislative agenda to move forward. By visiting the European Union website and following the news, many other questions will suggest themselves. Forming your own answers will deepen your knowledge of these important issues.

Chapter 3
JUDICIAL INSTITUTIONS OF
THE EUROPEAN UNION

COURTS OF THE EUROPEAN UNION

There are three 'courts' of the European Union. (As will become clear in a later chapter, every national court in a member state of the European Union is, in a real sense, also a court of the European Union, capable of applying European Community law. However, at this point, we will limit our attention to those courts formally operated by the European Union.) The word 'courts' appears in quotation marks because, in fact, one of the courts is not a court at all. Rather, as noted previously, it is concerned with fiscal oversight of the European Union.

The three courts are:
1. the Court of Justice of the European Communities;
2. the Court of First Instance; and
3. the Court of Auditors.

Only the first two courts perform judicial functions. The Court of Auditors provides fiscal oversight of the institutions of the European Union. We primarily will be discussing the first two courts, the judicial institutions of the European Union. However, we will include a brief discussion of the Court of Auditors at the conclusion of the chapter, even though, technically, it does not belong in a chapter devoted to 'judicial' institutions.

The Draft Constitution provides, at Article 28, that: '[t]he Court of Justice shall include the European Court of Justice, the High Court, and specialised courts'. Initially, this appears to affect minimal change to prior structures.

TREATY AND OTHER PROVISIONS

Part Five of the European Community Treaty deals with the institutions of the Community. Chapter 1 establishes the institutions, and Section 4 of this chapter concerns the Court of Justice (of which the Court of First Instance is a part). Treaty Articles 220 to 245 (ex Articles 164 to 188) deal with the Court of Justice.

In addition to the Treaty Articles, there is a Protocol on the Statute of the Court of Justice, a Council Decision on the Court of First Instance, and Rules of Procedure of the Court of Justice. These supplementary provisions must be considered, in order to come to a full understanding of the composition and procedures of the courts. Also, the Nice Treaty includes a Protocol on the Enlargement of the European Union that contains important changes to the courts. Finally, Article 28 of the Draft Constitution concerns the Court of Justice. It can be difficult keeping these sources of authority separate, and we will try to indicate to which source we are referring when it is relevant.

The Treaty of Nice, as will become clear, is concerned largely with making the changes necessary to accommodate new member states, as the Union expands to include central and eastern European countries. It should not be surprising that this expansion has implications for the courts of the European Union, and the Treaty of Nice attempts to deal with changes necessary to allow the courts to continue functioning in an effective manner.

The Treaty of Nice makes four basic changes to the Court of Justice and the Court of First Instance. Two of these changes concern personnel of the courts and two concern the jurisdiction of the courts. The personnel changes concern the number of judges and the role of the Advocate General. The jurisdictional changes concern expanding the jurisdiction of the Court of First Instance and the creation of specialised judicial panels.

We will first consider the Court of Justice of the European Communities, its personnel, its procedures and its jurisdiction, before considering the role of the Advocate General (who, technically, is part of the personnel of the Court of Justice) and the Court of First Instance. We will then briefly consider the court that is not a court, the Court of Auditors.

COURT OF JUSTICE OF THE EUROPEAN COMMUNITIES (EC TREATY, ARTICLES 220-245)

Article 7 (ex Article 4) of the EC Treaty states that the tasks entrusted to the Community shall be carried out by, among others, a Court of Justice. Article 221 (ex Article 165) provides that the Court of Justice shall consist of fifteen judges.

Prior to the accession of Sweden, Finland and Austria in 1995, there were thirteen judges on the Court of Justice. Each of the twelve member states appointed one judge each and the four largest member states – Italy, UK, France and Germany – took turns appointing the thirteenth judge. An odd number of judges was required by reason of Article 15 of the Protocol on the Statute of the Court of Justice, which provided that decisions of the court are valid only when an uneven number of its members sit in deliberations, and because certain cases had to be decided by the whole court (known as a 'plenary' session).

The Treaty of Nice amends Article 221, to provide that the Court of Justice shall consist of one judge from each member state. (Note that prior to Nice, the EC Treaty specified the number of judges, but not their nationalities. Thus, in theory, there could have been two judges from one member state. For instance, if Ireland had appointed someone from Northern Ireland, there would have been two judges from the UK.) Article 28 of the Draft Constitution also provides that the Court of Justice shall consist of one judge from each member state.

Thus, as new member states join the European Union, they will be allowed to appoint a judge to the Court of Justice. (Some member states opposed continued expansion of the Court of Justice. They proposed a smaller court, perhaps consisting of nine judges. Clearly, this would not have included an appointee from each member state. However, this proposal failed. Each member state believed it important to have its own national legal traditions represented on the Court of Justice.)

Thus, as the European Union expands, the membership of the Court of Justice will expand also. As the court functions as a collegial body, this expanded membership may make it more difficult for the court to operate.

As mentioned above, the operations of the court are governed by the Statute on the Court of Justice and by Rules of Procedure. A Protocol to the Treaty of Nice amends these instruments. (The Treaty of Nice also provides that future changes to the Rules of Procedure can be made by a qualified majority vote of the Council. Previously, a unanimous vote of the Council was required to amend this instrument. The court probably would prefer to have power to amend its own Rules of Procedure, but this was not forthcoming.)

Prior to the Treaty of Nice, the Treaty provided that the court would sit in plenary session, but was also permitted to sit in chambers of three and five. Article 221 allows the court to sit in chambers on any type of matter, but they must sit in plenary session if a member state or a Community institution that is a party to a proceeding asks it to do so.

The expansion of the court by the addition of new judges for each new member state might make it unwieldy to sit in plenary sessions. If there were twenty-seven judges, one for each member state, it might not be possible to deliberate in an orderly fashion. How does the Treaty of Nice deal with this?

The Treaty of Nice provides for a Grand Chamber (Protocol to the Nice Treaty on the Enlargement of the European Union (Nice Protocol), Article 16). It will comprise eleven judges, with a quorum of nine. The Grand Chamber will sit when a member state or Community institution that is party to the proceedings requests. Thus, due to the Treaty of Nice, although the number of judges on the Court of Justice will increase with each new member state, the Court of Justice will decide most important cases in a Grand Chamber, rather than in a plenary session of the full court.

Who will be a member of the Grand Chamber? The membership will include the President of the Court, and the Presidents of the five-judge chambers established under Article 221, and other judges to be appointed according to the Rules of the Court.

The creation of a Grand Chamber may create a two-tiered court. That is, a certain number of judges (those appointed to the Grand Chamber) will hear the most important cases. Other judges will sit on five-judge panels and hear cases of lesser importance.

Appointment of Judges

According to Article 223 (ex Article 167) judges must possess the qualifications required for appointment to the highest judicial offices in their respective countries, 'or [be] jurisconsults of recognised competence'. The latter provisions allow 'academic lawyers', e.g. professors at law schools, to be appointed to the Court of Justice.

The judges must be chosen from persons 'whose independence is beyond doubt' (Article 223).

The judges are appointed by common accord among the member states, and, in practice, each member state appoints one judge to the Court of Justice. The Protocol on the Statute of the Court of Justice (Court Protocol) provides at Article 4 that the judges may not hold any political or administrative office, or engage in any other occupation (unless granted an exemption to do so).

Judges are appointed for (renewable) six year terms, according to Article 223 (ex Article 167). This length of term is left unchanged by Article 28(2) of the Draft Constitution.

The appointments are staggered so that there is a partial replacement of judges every three years. That is, first eight judges are replaced, and then, when those eight have been sitting for three years, the remaining seven are replaced. The judges elect the President of the Court of Justice, for a term of three years. The President fixes the dates and times of sittings of the court (Article 25 of the Rules of Procedure of the Court of Justice).

Removal of Judges

Article 6 of the Court Protocol provides that a judge may be removed from office by a unanimous judgment of the judges and Advocates General (discussed below) of the court that the judge in question can no longer fulfil the obligations of office. (Naturally, the judge being removed is not counted in determining the unanimous vote.) If removed from office, the replacement judge serves the remainder of the term of the judge who has been removed (Court Protocol, Article 7).

Sittings of the Court

At the outset, it should be noted that the court sits in Luxembourg, rather than in Brussels, where many of the other institutions of the European Union are located. It is also important to distinguish between the Court of Justice of the European Communities, (which is re-named the European Court of Justice by the Draft Constitution), and the quite separate and distinct European Court of Human Rights, which sits in Strasbourg, France (one of the locations in which the European Parliament sits, to confuse matters further). Commentators sometimes mistakenly place the Court of Justice in Belgium, rather than Luxembourg, and/or refer to judgments of the European Court of Human Rights as if they were decided by the Court of Justice of the European Communities.

Prior to the Treaty of Nice, the Treaty provided, at Article 221 (ex Article 165) that the Court of Justice sat in plenary session. (Plenary session means that all the judges sit at once to hear a case.) However, it was rare that all fifteen judges sat at once to hear a case.

This was because Article 221 (ex Article 165) also provided that the court could form chambers, each consisting of three, five or seven judges, in order to hear particular categories of cases. There was no limitation in the Treaty on the types of cases that could be assigned to a chamber.

A plenary session of the court was required when a member state or a Community institution that was a party to the proceedings before the court so requested (Article 221, ex Article 165). Prior to the Treaty on European Union, the court was required to sit in plenary session in any case brought by a member state or a Community institution; now it need only do so in such cases if requested.

Even if the court sat in plenary session, this did not necessarily require that all fifteen judges hear the case. Only seven judges were required to constitute a quorum under Article 15 of the Protocol.

As noted above, the Treaty of Nice substantially revises the sittings of the Court of Justice. Article 221 of the EC Treaty is amended to provide that the Court of Justice shall sit in chambers or in a Grand Chamber. The Protocol on the Statute of the Court of Justice is amended. It provides that:

> [T]he court shall form chambers consisting of three and five judges. The judges shall elect the Presidents of the chambers from among their number. The Presidents of the chambers of five judges shall be elected for three years. They may be re-elected once. The Grand Chamber shall consist of eleven judges. It shall be presided over by the President of the court. The Presidents of the chambers of five judges and other judges appointed in accordance with the conditions laid down in the Rules of Procedure shall also form part of the Grand Chamber.

The Grand Chamber will sit when a member state or a Community institution that is party to the proceedings so requests.

Article 16 of the Protocol, after the Treaty of Nice, provides that the Court of Justice shall sit in plenary session (that is, all of the judges sitting) in certain limited instances (e.g., dismissal of ombudsman, Commissioner or member of the Court of Auditors). It also provides that where the court considers that a case before it is of exceptional importance, it may decide, after hearing the Advocate General, to refer the case to the plenary session.

Jurisdiction of the Court of Justice

We will be exploring some particular aspects of the Court of Justice in greater detail in other chapters. However, it is useful to consider the principal heads of the jurisdiction of the European Court of Justice.

Article 220 (ex Article 164) states that: 'The Court of Justice shall ensure that in the interpretation and application of this Treaty the law is observed'. Article 28 of the Draft Constitution provides that it shall ensure respect for the law in the interpretation and application of the Constitution.

The Court of Justice renders judgments on cases before it, or gives opinions on questions put to it concerning, for example, whether the European Community Treaty allows the European Union to become a signatory to the European Convention on Human Rights.

The judgments of the Court of Justice can be divided into two categories. One category consists of judgments resulting from preliminary rulings given in cases referred to the Court of Justice from courts or tribunals of member states under Article 234 (ex Article 177). We will discuss this system of preliminary rulings, an important aspect of the court's jurisdiction, in a later chapter.

The other category of the court's judgments consists of actions brought directly in the Court of Justice. This branch, in turn, can be further divided into two principal types of direct actions.

One principal type of action brought directly in the Court of Justice is an enforcement action brought by the European Commission against a member state under Article 226 (ex Article 169). In this type of case, the Commission brings an action in the Court of Justice alleging that the member state has failed to fulfil its obligations under the Treaty. The court has jurisdiction to give a judgment that the member state has failed to fulfil its obligations, and, since amendments introduced by the Treaty on European Union, the court can impose a monetary penalty on the member state (Article 228, ex Article 171). We will discuss these types of enforcement actions in greater detail in another chapter.

The other principal type of action brought directly in the Court of Justice is an action against one of the institutions of the European Union. These actions may be brought by another institution, by a member state, or, in rare instances, by an individual (Article 230, ex Article 173). This type of action will be discussed in greater detail in a following chapter.

Under Treaty Article 227 (ex Article 170) another type of action brought directly in the Court of Justice is an action by one member state against another member state claiming that the member state has failed to fulfil its obligations under Community law. However, this has been used rarely by member states and is essentially a dead letter. For an example of a case brought by one member state against another, see Case 141/78, *France v. UK* [1979] ECR 2923. One reason there may be few cases brought by one member state against another is because it might impair diplomatic relationships between two member states. Far better to lobby the European Commission to bring an action against a member state, and let the Commission incur the other member state's wrath (as well as the expense!)

Finally, the Court of Justice has appellate jurisdiction over actions commenced in the Court of First Instance. That is, a party dissatisfied with a ruling of the Court of First Instance can, in appropriate circumstances, appeal to the Court of Justice.

The Draft Constitution continues to provide that the Court of Justice shall have jurisdiction over 'original' actions (i.e., 'action brought by a member state, an institution or a natural or legal person'), and over preliminary rulings (Draft Constitution, Article 28(3)). Article 28 also provides that the Court of Justice shall 'rule on the other cases provided for in the Constitution'.

Procedures of the Court of Justice

In the Court of Justice, there is much more emphasis on written documents than in oral presentations. The Rules of Court are far more detailed with respect to written procedures (Articles 37-44 of the Rules of Procedure), than they are with respect to oral procedures (Articles 55-62 of the Rules of Procedure). The written submissions essentially contain the entire case of the party, including evidence as well as legal arguments. However, Article 47 of the Rules of Procedure does permit the court to require that certain facts must be proved by witnesses. The court can summon witnesses before it to provide testimony.

One judge is usually assigned as Judge Rapporteur of a case. He or she prepares a summary of the points made by the parties in their written submissions and outlines generally the case before the court. He or she is meant to read this report in court. (Article 18 of Protocol). On the date of the hearing, the parties are given a limited time to make their oral argument to the court. The court typically asks few questions. The Advocate General subsequently makes his or her recommendation in open court. The matter invariably is taken under advisement by the court, and a judgment is rendered some time later.

Judgment of the Court

Article 63 of the Rules of Procedure provides that the judgment of the court shall contain, among other things, the date of its delivery, the names of the President and the judges taking part in it, the name of the Advocate General, the description of the parties, a statement of the forms of order sought by the parties, a statement that the Advocate General has been heard, a summary of the facts, the grounds of the decision, and the operative part of the judgment, including any decision as to costs.

Certain aspects of the court's judgment should be noted. Only one judgment, that of the court, is delivered. There are no dissenting opinions. This is not to say that the judges entirely agree with the judgment (remember that decisions of the court shall be valid only when an uneven number of its members is sitting in deliberations: (Court Protocol, Article 15). However, it is not possible when reading the judgment or opinion of the court to discern the position of any particular judge.

There are various reasons why a single judgment is to be preferred. It prevents individual judges from being accused of bias in favour of their member state. Equally important, it protects judges from being penalised by their member state for a decision (such as by a refusal, by a member state, to re-appoint a judge). It also may help to prevent confusion, although the resulting decisions can themselves be difficult to fathom.

The official reports of the Court of Justice are the Reports of Cases of the European Court of Justice and the Court of First Instance. These are known as the European Court Reports. In addition to the judgment of the court, the Reports also set out the report of the Judge Rapporteur and the recommendation of the Advocate General.

The judgments of the court can be quite sparse and vague. This may be because most of the judges are from a civil law background, where courts produce sparse judgments. Sometimes, one paragraph of the judgment seems to contradict another paragraph. This may result from the need to build a majority in favour of a judgment; the judges in deliberations may 'horse trade' on various paragraphs to be included in the judgment. A judgment may represent a compromise among various opinions of the court.

Recall also that the judgment of the court appears in all the official languages of the European Union. (The working language of the court is French.) Statements that appear quite clear in one official language may become ambiguous in another language.

Advocates General

Judges are not the only personnel on the Court of Justice. Article 222 (ex Article 166) provides that the court 'shall be assisted by eight Advocates

General'. (There was a ninth Advocate General appointed from 1 January 1995 until 6 October 2000, because of difficulties arising from Norway's failure to ratify accession to the European Community. Certain changes had been made in anticipation of Norway joining the European Union at the same time as Sweden, Finland and Austria. However, for the second time, Norway voted against membership in the EU in a public referendum. The expansion of the Court of Justice and the addition of an Advocate General had been anticipated, but proved unnecessary. We will only speak of the eight Advocates General provided for at present.)

The Advocate General does not have a counterpart in the Irish judicial system. His (or her) function is similar to that of the commissaire du gouvernement in the French Conseil d'Etat. According to Article 222 (ex Article 166) the function of the Advocate General is:

> to make, in open court, reasoned submissions on cases brought before the Court of Justice, in order to assist the court in the performance of the task assigned to it.

In other words, the Advocate General gives a non-binding, independent opinion to the court, based on the submission of the parties to the case.

The Treaty of Nice preserves the role of the Advocate General. The number of Advocates General will remain at eight. After the Treaty of Nice, the number of Advocates General may be increased upon request of the court, upon a unanimous vote of the Council (Article 222). The Treaty of Nice also contemplates that the Advocate General may assist the Court of First Instance (as we will see, until now, the Court of First Instance did not have an Advocate General; instead, a judge of the Court of First Instance could undertake that role if it was felt necessary). However, amendments to Article 224 proposed by the Treaty of Nice provide that the Statute of the Court: 'may provide for the Court of First Instance to be assisted by Advocates General'.

Why have an Advocate General?

The Advocate General prepares a preliminary opinion for the court, in which he recommends a particular decision. This opinion is not binding on the court, but is highly influential. (Occasionally, the popular media treat the recommendation of the Advocate General as if it were a final judgment of the court, and fail to distinguish between it and the court's later subsequent judgment.) The Advocate General's recommendation is usually more detailed and covers the issue in greater depth than the subsequent judgment of the court, and is a good place to get an overview of the law in a particular area.

There are several reasons why an Advocate General is useful. Many cases reach the Court of Justice without the benefit of a full trial in a lower court and an opinion from an inferior court. In a typical appeal, the appellate court has the record of the proceedings in the lower court and, sometimes, the lower court's reasoning as to why it ruled as it did. The record from the lower court helps to focus the issue on appeal. For reasons that will be discussed later, this is often lacking in the Court of Justice. The recommendation of the Advocate General can help focus the issues in the same way that a record from a lower court might do so.

Also, parties such as member states and Community institutions sometimes intervene in a case. The Advocate General can summarise and critique these submissions.

The Treaty of Nice makes one minor change to the Advocate General's participation. Until now, the Advocate General has participated in all cases coming before the Court of Justice, regardless of how trivial. The Treaty of Nice amends Article 223 to provide that the Advocate General shall make a reasoned submission: 'on cases which, in accordance with the Statute of the Court of Justice, require his involvement'. This should speed up decision-making in relatively simple and straightforward cases, where a recommendation of the Advocate General might not be necessary to make a decision.

Qualifications and Appointment of the Advocates General

The Advocate General must possess the same qualifications as are necessary for appointment as a judge of the court. That is, he (or she) must 'possess the qualifications required for appointment to the highest judicial offices in their respective countries or who are juriconsults of recognised competence' (Article 223, ex Article 167).

The Advocate General's independence must be beyond doubt, and he or she is not allowed to hold any other employment during the term of appointment.

Advocates General are appointed for six years, and every three years there is a partial replacement, with four being replaced. The Advocates General are appointed by common accord of the member states, although the practice is that the larger member states appoint at least four Advocates General, while the remaining four positions rotate among smaller member states. Ireland has had one Advocate General, Nial Fennelly. He is now a member of the Irish Supreme Court. (Fidelma Maher, an Irish barrister, now sits on the Court of First Instance.)

COURT OF FIRST INSTANCE

The Court of First Instance was created by the Single European Act, 1986. It is attached to the Court of Justice and has jurisdiction to hear certain types of cases determined by the Council of Ministers (Article 225, ex Article 168a). The court was created to help with the heavy caseload that was building up in the Court of Justice.

Limits on Types of Cases before the Court of First Instance

The jurisdiction of the Court of First Instance, originally created by the Single European Act, has gradually expanded. However, certain limitations on the court's jurisdiction remain.

Originally, the Court of First Instance was created to hear only competition cases and staff cases (that is, cases brought by employees of Community institutions complaining about employment matters). This was expanded to include cases brought by non-privileged parties (that is, parties other than Community institutions).

Prior to the Treaty on European Union, the relevant Article (then Article 168a, now Article 225) provided that:

> The Court of First Instance shall not be competent to hear and determine actions brought by member states or by Community institutions or questions referred for a preliminary ruling under Article 177 [now Article 234].

The Treaty on European Union removed the limitation regarding cases brought by member states or by Community institutions, thereby expanding the court's jurisdiction. It remained the case, however, that: 'The Court of First Instance shall not be competent to hear and determine questions under Article 234 [ex Article 177]' (Article 225, ex Article 168a).

The Treaty of Nice expands the jurisdiction of the Court of First Instance to allow for that court to hear preliminary references brought under Article 234. Amendments to Article 225 by the Nice Treaty provide that:

> The Court of First Instance shall have jurisdiction to hear and determine questions referred for a preliminary ruling under Article 234, in specific areas laid down by the Statute.

Article 225, as amended by the Treaty of Nice, provides that, even if empowered to hear a particular preliminary reference, the Court of First Instance need not do so, and may refer the matter instead to the Court of Justice if, in the opinion of the Court of First Instance: 'the case requires a decision of principle likely to affect the unity or consistency of Community law'.

The expansion of the jurisdiction of the Court of First Instance to hear cases under Article 234 (ex Article 177) will reduce the heavy workload of the Court of Justice.

Appointment to and Qualifications of Judges of the Court of First Instance

The qualifications required for appointment to the Court of First Instance are not quite as demanding as those required for the Court of Justice. Article 225 (ex Article 168a) provides that:

> The members of the Court of First Instance shall be chosen from persons whose independence is beyond doubt and who possess the ability required for appointment to judicial office.

(Note that appointment to the Court of Justice required abilities sufficient for appointment to 'the *highest* judicial offices'.)

The members of the Court of First Instance are chosen by common accord among the member states. Members are appointed for terms of six years and retiring members are eligible for appointment. The membership is partially renewed every six years.

Appeals from Decisions of the Court of First Instance

A party may appeal a decision of the Court of First Instance to the Court of Justice (Protocol, Article 49). The appeal must be brought within two months of the decision (Protocol, Article 49). The appeal is limited to points of law (Protocol, Article 51).

Member states and Community institutions that were not party to the original proceedings before the Court of First Instance may intervene for the purpose of bringing an appeal (Protocol, Article 49).

If the appeal succeeds before the Court of Justice, the court will quash the decision of the Court of First Instance and either enter judgment itself, or send the case back to the Court of First Instance (Protocol, Article 54).

Specialised Judicial Panels

The Treaty of Nice provides in amendments to Article 220 that:

> judicial panels may be attached to the Court of First Instance under the conditions laid down in Article 225a in order to exercise, in certain specific areas, the judicial competence laid down in this Treaty.

After the Treaty of Nice, Article 225a will provide that the Council, acting unanimously, may create judicial panels to hear and determine at first instance certain classes of action or proceeding brought in specific areas.

What this means is that 'specialised' courts may be created to hear matters such as competition law or intellectual property cases.

The Draft Constitution, in Article 28, continues to provide for 'specialised courts'.

COURT OF AUDITORS (EC ARTICLES 246-248)

The Court of Auditors does not perform a judicial function. Instead, the court is charged with providing fiscal oversight of the Community. Article 248 (ex Article 188c) provides that: 'The Court of Auditors shall examine the accounts of all revenues and expenditures of the Community'. It is responsible for determining 'whether all revenue has been received and all expenditure incurred in a lawful and regular manner and whether the financial management has been sound' (Article 248(2), ex Article 188c(2)).

The Court of Auditors draws up an annual report after the close of each financial year. This report is forwarded to the other institutions and published, along with replies from other institutions, in the *Official Journal of the European Communities*.

At present, the Court of Auditors consists of fifteen individuals, appointed by the Council, acting unanimously after consulting with Parliament (Article 247, ex Article 188b). They are appointed for a term of six years.

The Treaty of Nice amends Article 247 to provide that the Court of Auditors shall consist of one national from each member state, and that they shall be appointed by the Council acting by a qualified majority after consulting with the European Parliament.

CONCLUSION

A strong court is a distinctive characteristic of a 'federal' or supranational system. We will see that the Court of Justice and the Court of First Instance are very strong institutions. Some of the most important developments in EU law have resulted from decisions of the Court of Justice. It should not be surprising, then, that the court system has expanded since the creation of the European Economic Community in 1957. First, there was the creation of the Court of First Instance by the Single European Act, and the subsequent expansion of that court's jurisdiction. Recently, there has been the creation of special courts, further expanding the power and influence of the courts. The most recent and controversial development has been the Nice Treaty's creation of a two-tiered court. Students may wish to consider the implication of this development on EU governance.

Chapter 4
SOURCES OF COMMUNITY LAW AND LAW-MAKING

FROM INSTITUTIONS TO LAW AND LAW-MAKING

In previous chapters we have discussed the political and judicial institutions of the European Union, their general characteristics and their responsibilities. We are now going to take a closer look at one of the important functions of the institutions of the European Union. That function is the creation of European Union law. We will review the sources of law in the European Union, the characteristics of that law, and the role of various institutions in the creation of that law.

Generally speaking, this chapter is divided into two parts. The first part deals with the types of Community legislation, and the procedural and substantive requirements for its valid adoption. The second part deals with the way in which this legislation is adopted.

In other words, Part One deals with the results of the law-making process. Part Two deals with the law-making processes themselves.

In dealing with the way in which legislation is adopted, our focus will be on some of the political institutions of the Union. The institutions with which we will be primarily concerned are the Commission, the Council and the European Parliament.

The judicial institutions do not play a prominent role in the creation of legislative instruments. (This is not to say that the judicial institutions do not 'make' law; some of the most important legal doctrines in EU law are judge-made.) However, the political institutions sometimes fight between themselves as to whether the proper procedures have been followed in adopting new law, and the Court of Justice of the European Communities may be called upon to resolve these disputes. The Court of Justice also is involved in deciding whether member states have followed the proper steps in implementing European Union law.

This chapter will deal with European Union law largely from the perspective of express requirements for the creation of legislative instruments laid down in the European Community Treaty. In a later chapter, we will consider European Union law from another perspective. We will look at the relationship between European Union law and the national legal orders of the member states. This will involve national constitutional considerations, as well as European Union law that is largely judicially created.

PART ONE: SOURCES OF COMMUNITY LAW

In considering sources of European Union law, we should not forget Treaty Articles. The Articles of the European Community Treaty are often overlooked when listing sources of law in the European Union. Due in part to the doctrine of Direct Effect, which is discussed in a subsequent chapter, the Treaty Articles themselves are an important source of Community law in the national legal order.

Community law can be divided into two parts:
1. Primary law: the European Community Treaty and the Treaty on European Union (as well as provisions of the other Treaty, Euratom) constitute the primary source of law.
2. Secondary law: secondary sources of law consist of the types of legislation that can be enacted by the Community institutions.

Our primary emphasis in this chapter will be on the types of legislation that can be created by the Community institutions pursuant to express terms of the European Community Treaty.

EC Treaty, Article 249 and Types of Legislation

The first paragraph of Article 249 (ex Article 189) provides:

> In order to carry out their task in accordance with the provisions of this Treaty, the European Parliament acting jointly with the Council, the Council and the Commission shall make regulations and issue directives, take decisions, make recommendations or deliver opinions.

There are two points to note. The first is that, prior to Treaty amendments brought about by the Treaty on European Union, 1992, the Article provided that: 'In order to carry out their task in accordance with the provisions of this Treaty, *the Council and Commission shall ... '*. That is, there was no express reference in the Article to the role of Parliament in the adoption of legislation. The Treaty on European Union changed this to make Parliament's role in the adoption of legislation more visible in the text of the Treaty. The Treaty of Amsterdam continued this process, by further enhancing Parliament's role in the adoption of legislation.

Second, note that the Article specifies four distinct types of legal instruments. (There actually are five, but the last two usually are grouped together and treated as if they were one type of legal instrument.) These are:

1. Regulations;
2. Directives;
3. Decisions;
4. Recommendations and Opinions.

Article 32 of the Draft Constitution changes the names of the instruments that can be adopted in the European Union. It also creates some new types of instruments. According to Article 32, 'in exercising the competences conferred on it by the Constitution, the Union shall use as legal instruments ... European laws, European framework laws, European regulations, European decisions, recommendations, and opinions'. Some of these legal instruments are the same as pre-existing legal instruments; some are new. We will highlight some of the proposed changes where necessary.

Types and Characteristics of Legal Instruments

Article 249 (ex Article 189) specifies the characteristics of the foregoing types of legal instruments. The second, third, fourth and fifth paragraphs of Article 249 provide:

> A regulation shall have general application. It shall be binding in its entirety and directly applicable in all member states.

> A directive shall be binding, as to the results to be achieved, upon each member state to which it is addressed, but shall leave to the national authorities the choice of form and methods.

> A decision shall be binding in its entirety upon those to whom it is addressed.

> Recommendations and opinions shall have no binding force.

One might argue that these legal instruments appear in Article 249 in descending order of importance. The argument might be as follows. Regulations are effective immediately, while directives typically envisage some further, time-consuming, efforts to become effective, so, in this sense, one might claim that regulations are more 'important'. Regulations and directives potentially affect many persons, sometimes tens of millions of persons, while decisions in theory bind only those to whom they are addressed. So one might argue that decisions are less important than regulations and directives. Finally, recommendations and opinions are non-binding. Member states need not, and often do not, implement recommendations and opinions into national law. Hence, they often appear at the bottom of a list of importance.

If we review Article 32 of the Draft Constitution, we will see which of the new types of legal instruments simply are re-named versions of the preexisting legal instruments, and which are new. Article 32 provides:

A European law shall be a legislative act of general application. It shall be binding in its entirely and directly applicable in all member states.

A European framework law shall be a legislative act binding, as to the result to be achieved ... but leaving the national authorities entirely free to choose the term and means of achieving that result.

A European regulation shall be a non-legislative act of general application for the implementation of legislative acts. ... It may either be binding in its entirety and directly applicable ... or binding as regards to the results to be achieved ... A European decision shall be a non-legislative act, binding in its entirety ... to whom it is addressed. Recommendations and opinions ... shall have no binding force.

We will examine each of these provisions in turn. Before we do that, however, we will look at the Treaty Articles that impose obligations regarding the adoption of all of the foregoing forms of Community legal instruments.

Substantive and Procedural Requirements for the Valid Adoption of Community Law – Introduction

Certain European Community Treaty Articles impose obligations for the valid adoption of legal instruments. Some of these obligations are substantive, and some are procedural. Substantive obligations, generally, mean that the substance of the legal instrument must meet certain requirements. Procedural obligations, generally, mean that certain steps have to be followed. Failure to fulfil these obligations can result in the court ruling that the legal instruments are invalid.

The Draft Constitution also requires that certain substantive and procedural requirements be met for the valid adoption of EU law.

There are two primary obligations under the European Community Treaty. The first is that every legal instrument must be based on a Treaty Article. This is a substantive obligation (it concerns the substance of the legal instrument). The second obligation is that a legal instrument must state the reasons for its adoption and must be published or notified in order to take effect. These constitute procedural obligations (i.e., steps that must be followed).

The first obligation arises from the fact that the European Community – from which legal instruments generally issue – is a Community of limited competence. In other words, the Community only has the competence attributed to it by the Treaties that underpin the European Union. Therefore, there must be a clear basis in this Treaty (or in other Community law that is itself based on the Treaty) for any legal instrument adopted by the Community.

The second obligation arises by reason of policy and natural justice. It is not fair to bind people to a law of which they do not have notice, even if this notice is technical in nature and unlikely to come to most people's attention.

Furthermore, there should be reasons behind the adoption of laws affecting European citizens.

The explanations for the adoption of Community legislation can prove useful to the Court of Justice if there is a legal challenge to the validity of the legislation.

Treaty Articles and Substantive and Procedural Requirements

Article 253 (ex Article 190) provides that:

> [R]egulations, directives and decisions adopted jointly by the European Parliament and the Council, and such acts adopted by the Council and Commission, shall state the reasons on which they are based and shall refer to any proposals or opinions which were required to be obtained pursuant to this Treaty.

Article 37 of the Draft Constitution continues this requirement:

> European laws, European framework laws, European regulations and European decisions, shall state the reasons on which they are based and shall refer to any proposals or opinions required by the Constitution.

Article 254 (ex Article 191) sets forth requirements that must be met for the valid adoption of Community law. These requirements vary according to the type of legal instrument involved, and the method of its adoption.

Regulations, directives and decisions adopted pursuant to the co-decision procedure (explained below) set out in Article 251 (ex Article 189b) must be signed by the President of the European Parliament and published in the Official Journal of the European Communities. They enter into force on the date specified in them or, in the absence of a specified date, on the twentieth day following their publication.

Regulations and directives addressed to all the member states must be published in the Official Journal and enter into force on the same terms as in the previous paragraph.

Finally, other directives and decisions must be notified to those to whom they are addressed and take effect upon such notification.

Similar requirements concerning signature and publication are set forth in Article 38 of the Draft Constitution.

Basis of Legal Instruments

Community institutions sometimes dispute whether the legal instrument is based on the proper Treaty Article. This can be a significant issue, because different Treaty Articles specify different voting methods for the adoption of legal instruments, as well as different procedures for adoption. One Treaty Article might require a unanimous vote in the Council, while another Treaty Article might require only a qualified majority. One Treaty Article might require that Parliament play an essentially equal role (to the Council) in the adoption of the legislation, while another Treaty Article might require only that Parliament be consulted. If a member state (or the Commission) opposed, for example, a certain directive, it might argue that the legal instrument was based on the wrong Treaty Article, and should have been based on another Article.

In Case C-84/94, *United Kingdom v. Council* [1996] ECR I-5755, the UK argued that a directive pertaining to working hours had been based on the wrong Treaty Article. The Council had adopted the directive pursuant to then Treaty Article 118a (now a substantially-revised Treaty Article 138), which stated that the Council could adopt directives concerned with worker health and safety by a qualified majority vote. The UK argued that issues pertaining to working time were not sufficiently related to health and safety to justify using Article 118a. The UK argued that another Treaty Article, which required a unanimous vote, should have been used to adopt the directive. The court rejected this argument and ruled in favour of the Council, but this case illustrates how one can use the substantive requirement to challenge Community legal instruments.

Similarly, if reasons are not given for the adoption of a legal instrument, or if a party believes the reasons are inadequate, a challenge can be based on a failure to fulfil the obligations imposed under Article 253 (ex Article 190).

Choice of Appropriate Legal Instrument

The Council, either acting jointly with Parliament or upon a recommendation from the Commission, sometimes has the choice as to which type of legal instrument to adopt. In other instances, the Treaty sets forth what type of legal instrument must be adopted.

For example, Article 42 (ex Article 51) concerns the free movement of workers. It provides that the Council shall (acting pursuant to a procedure described below): 'adopt such *measures* in the field of social security as are necessary to provide freedom of movement for workers' (italics added). Clearly, under this Article, the Council would be free to make regulations, issue directives, take decisions or issue recommendations or opinions.

In other areas, the options are more limited. For example, Article 40 (ex Article 49) is also concerned with the free movement of workers. It provides that the Council shall 'issue directives or make regulations'.

Article 39(3)(d) (ex Article 48(3)(d)) is even more restrictive. It provides that the right of workers to remain in the territory of a member state after having been employed there 'shall be embodied in implementing *regulations* to be drawn up by the Commission' (italics added). (This is an example of an area in which, contrary to the usual procedure, the Commission is empowered to adopt legal instruments. The resulting legal instrument is Commission

Regulation 1251/70 on the right to remain in a member state after having been employed in that state.)

The Draft Constitution appears a bit more flexible regarding the choice of legislative instrument. Article 37 of the Draft Constitution provides that:

> unless the Constitution contains a specific stipulation, the institutions shall decide, in compliance with the procedures applicable the type of act to be adopted in each case, in accordance with the principle of proportionality set out in Article 9.

Characteristics of Particular Legal Instruments – Regulations

So what are the characteristics of a regulation? The language of Article 249 (ex Article 189) helps to identify some of the relevant issues.

According to Article 249:

> A regulation shall have general application. It shall be binding in its entirety and directly applicable in all member states.

Thus, by its terms, Article 249 suggests that a regulation applies to a wide number of categories of people (general application), and not to a small subset of people (as we will see is the case with decisions). It is binding in its entirety, and not simply binding as to the results to be achieved (as we will see is the case with directives).

Regulations and Meaning of 'Directly Applicable'

A regulation is 'directly applicable' in all member states. The term 'directly applicable' can be given at least two meanings. One meaning concerns the relationship between international and national law, and the other, related, meaning concerns the ability of individuals to invoke international law in the national courts. (This latter concept has come to be known as 'direct effect'.)

As we will see in a subsequent chapter, some member states, such as Ireland, require that domestic law must be changed in order to make international law applicable inside the country (see Article 29.6 of the Irish Constitution). That is, ordinarily the Oireachtas must adopt a piece of legislation that transposes international law into the Irish national law. Also, international law typically concerns relations between sovereign states, and individuals rarely can rely on international law directly in their domestic courts.

One meaning of 'directly applicable' is that a regulation becomes part of the domestic law of the member state without the need for implementing national legislation. This is most likely the meaning intended by the drafters of Article 249 (ex Article 189). It would be extremely time-consuming if every regulation adopted by the Community had to be transposed into national law by a national legislature. The direct applicability of regulations means that this form of Community legal instrument takes a short cut into domestic law.

Another possible meaning of 'directly applicable' is that individuals can rely upon or invoke the regulation in the Irish national courts. This is similar to but slightly distinct from the previous notion that regulations are transposed automatically into the national law.

Technically, regulations are a species of international law. Typically, individuals cannot rely upon or invoke international law in the domestic courts of a country with a dualist legal system, such as Ireland. This was true with respect to the European Convention on Human Rights which, prior to 'incorporation' into Irish law, could not be invoked in the Irish national courts, even though Ireland had signed the Convention.

It is not clear whether the original signers of the EC Treaty intended that regulations could be invoked by individuals in the national courts. However, as we shall see in a subsequent chapter, the Court of Justice has concluded that regulations can be invoked or relied upon by individuals in the national courts. This is an important characteristic of regulations.

Characteristics of Directives

Article 249 provides that:

> A directive shall be binding, as to the results to be achieved, upon each member state to which it is addressed, but shall leave to the national authorities the choice of forms and methods.

This Treaty Article very cleverly accommodates the differing legal systems of the various member states. Typically, a directive dictates an outcome or result and a deadline by which the member states must achieve that result. The member state ordinarily adopts a domestic law (or statutory instrument) in advance of the deadline. That is, the state implements the directive into national law. The member state informs the European Commission – the policing agency of the European Union – of the steps it has taken to implement the directive. The European Commission may bring an enforcement action against the member state if it believes the state has not properly implemented the directive into national law.

Note that a directive is binding 'upon each member state to which it is addressed', while a regulation has 'general application' and is 'directly applicable'. In other words, regulations have universal application, that is, they are applicable in all member states. Directives, on the other hand, can be selectively applied, that is, addressed only to some of the member states.

We have indicated above, in the section on regulations, that individuals can rely upon them in front of national courts, that is, that regulations have 'direct effect'. In a subsequent chapter, we will consider whether directives also are capable of having direct effect. We will see that this is a very complex issue that has not been resolved to the satisfaction of all.

Characteristics of Decisions

'A decision shall be binding in its entirety upon those to whom it is addressed'. The European Commission often employs decisions in the area of competition law. In other words, if the Commission suspects a violation of competition law has occurred it may conduct an investigation and issue a decision finding a company or individual to have violated competition law. The decision will be binding upon the individual or company to whom it is addressed.

A decision is more 'targeted'. It should be possible to 'name' the individuals and/or firms that are affected by a decision.

Characteristics of Recommendations and Opinions

Recommendations and opinions often are referred to as 'soft law'. They are not binding, but they may set out important policy positions of the European Community.

Article 211 (ex Article 155) provides that the Commission shall have the power to formulate recommendations or deliver opinions on matters dealt with in the Treaty. Recommendations usually are said to issue on the initiative of the Commission, while opinions usually are a response to a question posed by a member state.

Also, if recommendations or opinions are not observed by a member state, these non-binding measures may be followed by binding measures such as directives or regulations.

If we refer to back to the earlier listing of legislative instruments set forth in Article 33 of the Draft Constitution, we see that many of the same terms are employed. At first glance, it appears that regulations under the European Community Treaty are renamed 'European laws', while directives are renamed 'European framework laws'. Apart from this change, the new instruments share the relevant characteristics of a regulation and directive described above and in Article 249. The Draft Constitution, however, creates new types of instruments: 'European regulations' defined as a 'non-legislative act'. Furthermore, a 'European decision' is created by the Draft Constitution, which resembles the European Community Treaty 'decisions', but with potentially broader application. Recommendations and opinions appear unchanged.

PART TWO: THE LEGISLATIVE PROCESS

The manner in which the European Community adopts legislation (e.g., regulations, directives, decisions, recommendations and opinions) is complex. For years, a standard catchphrase was: 'the Commission proposes and the Council disposes'. This phrase implied that the Commission was the primary source of legislative proposals, while the Council of Ministers, voting according to one of the voting procedures described earlier, makes the final decision whether to adopt the proposed legislation. While not exactly untrue, this view was a crude simplification of a legislative procedure that could take a number of different forms.

However, with the increasing role of Parliament in the adoption of legislation, it is no longer even roughly accurate to say: 'the Commission proposes, and the Council disposes'. Now it is more accurate to say: 'the Commission proposes, and, most times, the Parliament and Council dispose'.

There is a series of basic points to keep in mind in considering the legislative procedures of the European Union. First, it is unlikely that a student would be required to describe in detail the various procedures by which laws are adopted in the EU. If called upon to do so, it most likely would be in the context of describing the changing nature over time of the roles played by the Commission, the Council and the European Parliament in the adoption of Community legislation. The changes in procedures over time reflect the recasting of institutional balance, mainly in favour of the European Parliament. As we will see, the role of the European Parliament in the adoption of Community legislation has progressively increased in succeeding amendments to the Treaties underpinning the Union.

Second, there is no single legislation-making body in the European Community, as there is in Ireland and other parliamentary democracies. In national law, we are used to laws being enacted by the Oireachtas. Indeed, the Irish Constitution, at Article 15.2, provides that only the Oireachtas may do so. However, in the European Union, the Commission, the Council and the European Parliament all have varying roles to play in the adoption of legislation. Sometimes other Community institutions, such as the Committee of the Regions or the Economic and Social Committee also participate in the adoption of legislation.

Third, there is no single procedure by which legislation is adopted. Instead, there are various procedures specified in the Treaty for the adoption of legislation. Furthermore, there is no single guiding principle for establishing which procedure applies in the context of a piece of legislation. The applicable procedure depends upon the Treaty Article under which the legislation is adopted. The Treaty Article will specify which procedure must be followed.

The authors Paul Craig and Gráinne DeBúrca specify six different methods by which legislation can be adopted in the European Union, and provide a detailed overview of each of these methods (see Craig and DeBúrca, *EU Law: Text Cases and Materials*, 3rd ed., Oxford University Press, 2003). We will follow the lead of those authors, and divide these six methods into two groupings. We will concentrate principally on the second of these two groupings. In the first group, we can place the following four legislation-making procedures:

1. the Commission acting alone;
2. the Council and Commission acting alone;
3. the Council and Commission in consultation with Parliament; and
4. the Council and Commission acting with the Parliament's assent.

These are relatively simple procedures; in three of them, the power of the European Parliament is relatively minor; in the fourth and final procedure, the power of the European Parliament is, in a limited sense, maximised, but in a very blunt way that limits its effectiveness.

In the second grouping we can place the so-called 'co-operation' procedure specified by Treaty Article 252 (ex Article 189c) and the 'co-decision' procedure specified by Treaty Article 251 (ex Article 189b). These are complex procedures, in which the European Parliament plays a significant role in the adoption of the final legislation, particularly in the co-decision procedure. The co-operation procedure was added by the Single European Act, and the Treaty on European Union added the co-decision procedure. The Treaty of Amsterdam simplified the co-decision procedure and extended its applications. Each of the amendments in the successive Treaties has had the effect of strengthening the European Parliament's role in the adoption of legislation. This demonstrates that the power of the European Parliament in legislation-making in the EU has increased over time.

The Treaty of Nice extends the co-decision procedure and limits the co-operation procedure in such a way as to render the co-operation procedure practically obsolete. In the future, in an extended number of areas, Parliament will act as an almost equal partner with the Council under the co-operation procedure.

The First Group of Legislation-Making Procedures

In the first group of legislation-making procedures, we included the Commission acting alone, the Commission and Council acting alone, the Commission and Council acting after obtaining the opinion of Parliament, and the Commission and Council acting after obtaining the Parliament's assent.

Little needs to be said about these procedures, as the descriptions given set forth what each procedure is all about. In certain rare instances, the Commission is empowered by the Treaty to adopt legislation on its own. Similarly, there are certain instances in which the maxim 'the Commission proposes and the Council disposes' is accurate. The Treaty allows some laws to be adopted by the Commission and Council without any input from the European Parliament.

In some instances, the Commission proposes, and the Council can dispose of the proposal, e.g., adopt a directive or a regulation, only after having obtained the opinion of Parliament (and/or the Economic and Social Committee and the Committee of the Regions). The Council can ignore the opinion of the European Parliament (or the other Committees). However, the Council cannot act without obtaining the opinion of Parliament. If the Council adopts a piece of legislation without obtaining the opinion of Parliament (or, in appropriate circumstances, the other Committees), the Court of Justice will strike down the resulting legislation.

In certain areas, usually involving very important decisions such as the admission of new member states to the European Union, the Commission and the Council can act only upon the assent of the European Parliament. The Single European Act added this provision, and the Treaty of Amsterdam expanded the areas subject to it. This means that the Parliament has an absolute veto power over these decisions.

(Note that while the assent procedure gives the European Parliament a veto power, it is a very crude and blunt instrument. Parliament might like many aspects of a proposal over which it has such veto power, but have reservations about certain portions of the measure. It would prefer to be able to limit its objections to those aspects of the measure to which it objects. However, under the assent procedure it does not have this option. This limits the effectiveness of its powers.)

We can turn to the EC Treaty for examples of these procedures. Under Article 39(d)(3) (ex Article 48(d)(3)) a worker is entitled to remain in the territory of another member state after having been employed in that state, 'subject to conditions which shall be embodied in implementing regulations to be drawn up by the Commission'. Thus, this Treaty Article provides for the Commission to act alone in adopting Community legislation, in this instance a regulation.

Article 49 (ex Article 59) provides that the Council may, acting by a qualified majority on a proposal from the Commission, extend the provisions of the chapter on free movement of services to nationals of a third country who are established within the Community. This is an example of 'the Commission proposes, and the Council disposes', i.e., of the Council and Commission acting alone.

Article 93 (ex Article 99) provides that the Council shall, acting unanimously on a proposal from the Commission and after consulting the European Parliament (and the Economic and Social Committee) adopt provisions for the harmonisation of legislation concerning various types of taxes. This provides an example of the Council and the Commission acting after obtaining an opinion from Parliament.

The Second Group of Legislation-Making Procedures

The second group of legislation-making procedures are considerably more complex than the first group, and apply to more areas of legislation. This group consists of the co-operation procedure under Article 252 (ex Article 189c) and the co-decision procedure under Article 251 (ex Article 189b).

The Co-operation Procedure

The co-operation procedure envisions a multi-stage procedure for the adoption of legislation, in which each stage depends upon what has occurred in the previous stage. When a Treaty Article requires that the co-operation procedure outlined in Article 252 must be followed (which, after Nice, is increasingly rare), the procedure is as follows.

The Council, acting by a qualified majority on a proposal from the Commission, after considering the opinion of Parliament, adopts a common position. The Council communicates its common position to the European Parliament; the Commission and Council also communicate to Parliament the reasoning that led to the common position and the Commission's position.

The Parliament has three months within which to act on the common position. If it fails to act, then the Council can adopt the common position. On the other hand, if the Parliament approves the Common Position, then the Council can adopt it.

However, the Parliament may, within three months, either reject the common position, or propose amendments to the common position. The Parliament must act by an absolute majority of its members (rather than simply a majority of those voting) in order to reject a common position or propose amendments. What happens next depends upon whether Parliament decides to reject the common position or offer amendments.

If the Parliament has rejected the common position, then the Council may adopt the common position only by unanimity. (Recall that the common position originally was adopted by a qualified majority vote.) Thus, in this situation, Parliament, combined with one member state, can block the proposal.

If the Parliament has proposed amendments to the common position, the proposal goes from Parliament to the Commission. The Commission has one month to examine the proposals. The Commission then sends the re-examined proposal to the Council, which consists, essentially, of the original common position and those amendments as proposed by the Parliament which it has accepted. It also sends the Council those proposed amendments that it has rejected, along with reasons for rejecting them.

The Council can adopt the re-examined proposal, that is, the original common position along with the proposed amendments by Parliament that have been accepted by the Commission, by a qualified majority vote.

If the Council wishes to adopt any of the amendments proposed by the European Parliament that have not been accepted by the Commission, the Council can do so only by a unanimous vote. If the Council wishes to amend the re-examined proposal, that is, the common position and amendments accepted by the Commission, it may do so only by unanimity.

In other words, the Council can act without the Commission's consent only by unanimity. See also Article 250 (ex Article 189a) which provides that 'where, in pursuance of this Treaty, the Council acts on a proposal from the Commission, unanimity shall be required for an ... amendment to that proposal ...'.

Several things should be noted about the co-operation procedure. First, note that the Parliament does not have an absolute veto over legislation pursuant to this procedure. If the Parliament rejects the common position, the Council can still adopt it, albeit only by a unanimous vote.

If the Parliament proposes amendments to the common position, these must be 'vetted' by the Commission. Only those amendments that have passed scrutiny by the Commission can be adopted by a qualified majority vote. If the Council wants to adopt some of Parliament's proposed amendments that have not been included in the Commission's re-examined proposal, it can do so only by a unanimous vote.

Although this co-operation procedure is a far cry from Irish national procedures that place virtually all legislative powers in the Irish Parliament, note that the co-operation procedure, introduced by the Single European Act, constitutes a considerable advance on the consultation procedure which preceded its introduction.

First, under the co-operation procedure, the Parliament gets two 'readings' of the proposal. It is consulted before the adoption of a common position, and it is allowed to review, and propose amendments to, the common position adopted by the Council.

Note also that the Council and Commission must respond to amendments proposed by the Parliament. The Commission must review the amendments under a deadline, and must send a report to the Council that includes the re-examined proposal (including amendments it has adopted) and reasons for rejecting other proposed amendments. Although the Commission retains the upper hand in dealing with the proposed amendments (as the Council can only adopt amendments with which the Commission disagrees by a unanimous vote), this is a strengthening of Parliament's role when compared to the consultation procedure. In the consultation procedure, the Commission and the Council can completely ignore Parliament's opinion and adopt the Commission's proposed legislation without further input from Parliament.

However, after amendments wrought by the Treaty of Nice, the co-operation procedure will be primarily of historical interest. Furthermore, the

Draft Constitution proposes a procedure that renders both the co-operation procedure and the co-decision procedure obsolete. An understanding of both the co-operation and co-decision procedures will help us understand the changing role of the institutions of the European Union in the making of EU law. For the moment, however, the most significant procedure is the co-decision procedure.

The Co-decision Procedure

The co-decision procedure specified in Article 251 (ex Article 189b) was added by the Treaty on European Union and simplified by the Treaty of Amsterdam. It was extended to new areas by the Treaty of Nice. Apart from the assent procedure to be followed in certain limited areas, it provides for the greatest input by the European Parliament in the legislative process. The addition of the co-decision procedure to the Treaties underpinning the European Union, and its extension to new areas in the recent Treaties of Amsterdam and Nice represent an increase in the role of the democratically-elected European Parliament in making laws for the EU. The extension of the co-decision procedure to more areas of law-making within the EU is a process that is likely to continue in the future, in an effort to enhance the democratic legitimacy of the Union by reducing the so-called 'democratic deficit'.

The co-decision procedure is similar to the co-operation procedure, in that what takes place at any stage depends upon what has occurred at an earlier stage.

Under the co-decision procedure, the Commission submits a legislative proposal simultaneously to both the European Parliament and the Council. The Parliament gives its opinion on the proposal to the Council. The Parliament may endorse the proposal in the form in which the Commission has proposed it, or it may offer amendments. If the Parliament approves the proposal, the Council may adopt the proposal by a qualified majority vote. If the Parliament proposes amendments to the proposal, and the Council accepts the amendments, then the Council may adopt the amended proposal by a qualified majority vote.

Of course, the Parliament may not approve of the proposal, or may offer amendments that the Council is not willing to accept. If this occurs, then the Council adopts a common position and communicates it to the Parliament, along with its reasons for adopting the common position. The common position refers to the common position of the Council alone; it may not represent the 'common position' of both the Council and the Parliament. (The Commission also communicates its reasons to the Parliament.)

Upon receipt of the common position by the Parliament, three things may occur. First, the Parliament may approve the common position, or not take a decision within the three months allowed for it to do so. If either of these things occurs, then the proposal is deemed to have been adopted, and becomes law.

The Parliament may reject the common position, by a majority of its members (not simply a majority of those voting). If this occurs, than the proposal is deemed not to have been adopted, and it does not become law.

Note that, unlike the co-operation procedure, the Parliament has the power at this stage in the co-decision procedure to defeat the proposal by a majority vote of its members. The Parliament does not have such an ultimate 'veto' power under the co-operation procedure, and this reflects the added power of the Parliament under the co-decision procedure.

The third possible outcome after Parliament receives the common position is that the Parliament may propose amendments to the common position (by an absolute majority of its component members). Parliament forwards the amended text of the common position (containing the proposed amendments) to the Council (and to the Commission). The Commission delivers an opinion to the Council; the Commission either approves or disapproves of the proposed amendments.

If this third outcome occurs, this, in turn opens up various possibilities. If the Commission approves all of the amendments, then the Council can adopt the amended common position by a qualified majority vote. If the Commission has not approved of some of the amendments, however, the Council can adopt these amendments only by a unanimous vote.

If the Council does not approve of the amendments, the President of the Council and the President of the Parliament must convene a meeting of the 'Conciliation Committee'. The Commission assists the Conciliation Committee. The membership of the Conciliation Committee consists of an equal number of members of the Council and of the European Parliament.

The Conciliation Committee attempts to agree the language of a joint text. If they succeed, then the joint text is put before the Council and the Parliament for adoption. If the Council approves the joint text by a qualified majority vote and if the Parliament approves the joint text by an absolute majority of its members, then the joint text is adopted. If either of the institutions fails to adopt the joint text, then the proposal is not adopted.

This represents a second point in the co-decision process where the Parliament has the power to 'veto' a proposal.

If the Conciliation Committee is unable to agree a joint text, then the proposal is deemed not to have been adopted.

THE DRAFT CONSTITUTION AND THE LAW-MAKING PROCEDURE

The Draft Constitution contains provisions for law-making at Article III-302. The procedure is very similar to the co-decision procedure outlined above. With respect to the adoption of European laws or framework laws (roughly equivalent to 'regulations' and 'directives' in pre-Draft Constitution terms), the procedure is as follows.

The Commission submits its proposal to both the European Parliament and the Council of Ministers simultaneously. In the Draft Constitution, the subsequent procedures are divided into sections with various headings, which makes following the procedure somewhat easier. The headings are 'First Reading', 'Second Reading', 'Conciliation', 'Third Reading', and 'Special Provisions'. (The 'Special Provisions' are not especially relevant to our consideration of legislative procedures and will not be discussed here.)

First Reading

After the Commission has submitted a proposal to both the Parliament and the Council of Ministers, the European Parliament adopts its position and communicates it to the Council. If the Council adopts the Parliament's position (unlike in previous versions of the 'co-decision' procedure, the voting method is not expressly stated), the proposed act is adopted.

If the Council of Ministers does not approve the Parliament's position, the Council adopts its own position, and communicates it to Parliament, along with the reasons which led the Council to adopt its position. (The Commission also informs Parliament of its position.)

Second Reading

Parliament then faces a deadline of three months. If it fails to act on the Council's position, the proposed act is adopted. Of course, the Parliament may approve the Council's position, which also means the act is adopted.

Parliament may, on the other hand, reject the Council's position (a majority of the component members are required to reject the position). If this happens, the act is not adopted. That is, this ends the procedure.

A third possibility in the second reading is that Parliament, by a majority of its component members, amends the position of the Council of Ministers. If this happens, the Parliament forwards the amended text to the Council of Ministers and to the Commission. The Commission delivers an opinion on these amendments.

If the Commission approves Parliament's amendments, then the Council of Ministers can adopt the amended text by a qualified majority, and the act will be adopted. If the Commission does not approve all the amendments, then the

Council can only approve those amendments by a unanimous vote. If it does so, the act is adopted.

If the Council does not approve all the amendments, then the President of the Council, in agreement with the President of the European Parliament, shall convene a meeting of the Conciliation Committee.

Conciliation

The Conciliation Committee shall consist of an equal number of members of the Council of Ministers (or their representatives), and members representing the European Parliament. They have the task of reaching agreement on a joint text, by a qualified majority of the members of the Council of Ministers (or their representatives) who are present, and by a majority of the members of Parliament who are present. If they are unable to agree a joint text within six weeks of the matter having been referred to conciliation, the act is not adopted. That is, the procedure comes to an end.

Third Reading

If the Conciliation Committee approves a joint text, the European Parliament, acting by a majority of the votes cast (this is potentially a much smaller number required than a majority of its component members: it is easier to pass this joint text in Parliament), and the Council of Minister, acting by a qualified majority (not unanimity), can adopt the act in question in accordance with the joint text, in which case, the act is adopted. If they do not do this in six weeks, the act is not adopted, and the procedure ends.

(Short extensions to the time allowed are permitted – the period of three months can be extended by one month, and the period of six weeks can be extended by two weeks.)

These procedures appear slightly less complicated than the co-decision procedure under the Amsterdam and Nice Treaties (which itself represented a minor simplification of the procedure outlined originally in the Treaty on European Union).

CONCLUSION

The legislation-making procedures of the Union are complex. The pursuit of democratic accountability is hindered where the procedures by which laws affecting citizens of the EU are adopted are difficult, if not impossible, for an educated citizen to understand. The Community should attempt to further streamline its legislation-making procedures to enhance the goals of openness and democratic accountability. The Draft Constitution appears to do this, and students can evaluate, over time, whether these efforts have been successful.

In addition to the complex legislative procedure described in this chapter, a student must become familiar with the different types of legislative instruments that can be adopted, and their various characteristics. This can be difficult. Students have probably thought of 'law' as being undifferentiated. They may be aware of Acts of the Oireachtas and statutory instruments. But EU law has far more variations than domestic law. However, to understand the relationship between Irish domestic law and EU law, it is necessary to have a basic understanding of the different types of 'law' that can be adopted in the European Union, e.g., regulations, directives and decisions. The next chapter discusses the relationship between EU and Irish law, and a student should ensure he or she knows the different types of legislative instruments that can be adopted before proceeding to the next chapter.

Chapter 5

THE RELATION OF EUROPEAN UNION LAW TO NATIONAL LAW – DIRECT EFFECT AND SUPREMACY

SOURCES OF EUROPEAN UNION LAW

From a previous chapter, we are familiar with various sources of European Union law. These sources include: Treaty Articles; regulations; directives; decisions; and recommendations (see Article 249, ex Article 189). Other potential sources of European Union law include international agreements, and what have come to be known as 'General Principles of European Union law'. The latter includes the judicially-created Fundamental Principles of Human Rights.

The Draft Constitution for Europe re-names some of the foregoing legislative acts, and creates some new, non-legislative acts. These changes should not affect the analysis of the relationship between European Union law and Irish national law.

This chapter investigates the nature of European Union law, and, more particularly, the relationship between European Union law and national law. (For our purposes, we will concentrate on Treaty Articles and the types of law set forth in Article 249.)

CAN EUROPEAN UNION LAW BE RELIED ON IN NATIONAL COURTS? THE QUESTION OF DIRECT EFFECT

One of the issues that arises when considering the relationship between European Union and national law is whether European Union law can be invoked in national courts by individuals, in the same manner that an individual can invoke Irish law in domestic courts. That is, can a person invoke European Union law as a source of individual rights before the Irish courts?

This concept is known as 'direct effect'. The issue is, does European Union law have direct effect? Or is it the case that individuals must assert claims under European Union law before a special court (such as was the case under the European Convention on Human Rights)?

Can only member states invoke European Union law? Is European Union law available to individual citizens? If European Union law does have 'direct effect', does this apply to all the sources of European Union law, or only to some? Can European Union law be invoked against private individuals, or only against member states?

It should be clear immediately that the enforcement and effectiveness of European Union law is greatly increased if an individual can invoke it in the national courts. It is much easier to bring an action in a local court. Far more parties are available to detect violations of European Union law if individuals, and not only member states, can invoke it.

We will see that the 'effectiveness' of European Union law enforcement plays an important part in the Court of Justice's consideration of whether European Union law has direct effect.

Two Preliminary Issues: Recognition of Law, Substance of Law

There are at least two preliminary issues when considering whether European Union law can be invoked in the national courts, that is, whether it has direct effect.

The first issue is whether the national legal order recognises European Union law as a source of authority.

For example, prior to the creation of the Irish Free State, the island of Ireland was governed by a British legal system. After the Parliamentary elections resulting in the formation of the First Dáil, a revolutionary Irish government passed laws. However, the dominant British legal order refused to recognise the First Dáil as a source of authority. As a result, an individual could not invoke this law in the British-controlled Irish courts. In other words, this law lacked direct effect.

Related to this issue is whether the relation between European Union and national law should be decided by reference to European Union law, or by reference to the domestic constitutional legal order. This issue implicates national constitutional law.

The second issue is whether the substance of the European Union law is such as to provide an enforceable right. That is, are the terms of the European Union law relied upon sufficient to provide a claim in a court of law?

For example, some national institutions, e.g., universities, provide a Charter of Student Rights, but expressly state that the provisions of the Charter do not give rise to legally-enforceable rights. Thus, the provisions of the Charter lack direct effect because of the character of the Charter itself.

We will consider these issues in turn. We will see that the Court of Justice has considered both issues.

Supremacy of European Union Law

If European Union law can be invoked and relied upon by an individual in the national courts, the issue arises as to which law is supreme. That is, if European Union law and national law conflict on a point, which should prevail?

Dualist versus Monist Legal Systems

To better understand the issues involved in considering whether European Union law has direct effect, we first look at the differing nature of national legal systems. Some national legal systems are regarded as 'monist' and others as 'dualist'.

In a monist legal system, all forms of law, domestic and international, are regarded as belonging to the same general sphere of 'law'. There is little or no qualitative difference between national and international law, and the effect given to either typically depends upon interpretation given to each by a national court interpreting the national constitutional order. In a monist system an individual can, in appropriate circumstances, invoke and rely upon international law as a source of individual rights in the national courts.

In a dualist system, there is a strict division between national and international law. International law and national law are regarded as occupying two entirely different spheres. International law cannot be invoked by an individual in the domestic courts of a country with a dualist legal system. International law only becomes part of the domestic legal order if the legislature takes steps to incorporate the international law into the national law.

Ireland possesses a dualist legal system. The Irish Constitution provides that international law becomes part of Irish law only if the Oireachtas takes the necessary steps (e.g., adopting legislation) in order to make the international law part of domestic law.

EUROPEAN UNION LAW AND DIRECT EFFECT – *VAN GEND EN LOOS*

The issue of whether European Union law – specifically Treaty Articles – has direct effect arose in Case 26/62, *Van Gend en Loos* [1963] ECR 1.

In that case, a lawsuit was filed in Dutch courts. The claim was that the Netherlands had increased the import duty on a good from another member state, in violation of then Article 12 (now Article 25) of the then European Economic Union Treaty. (Import duties had not yet been completely eliminated under the multi-stage process set out in the Treaty, but member states were forbidden from increasing existing duties.)

The Dutch officials defended that the import duty had not been raised. The imported good in question merely had been reclassified under another tariff heading with a higher import duty. The Dutch argued that European Union law did not prohibit the reclassification of goods.

Issue: Can an Individual Rely on a European Union Treaty Article in a National Court?

Before the Dutch court could consider whether then Article 12 (now Article 25) had been violated, it had to consider a preliminary issue. That issue was whether an individual could invoke Article 12 (now Article 25) in the national courts. Because the Dutch court was not sure of the answer, and because a decision on this issue was necessary to give judgment, the Dutch court made an Article 234 (ex Article 177) reference to the European Court of Justice.

The matter was referred to the European Court of Justice, which considered the issue of direct effect of Treaty Articles.

The Jurisdictional Issue

The government of the Netherlands, joined by Belgium, argued that the Court of Justice lacked jurisdiction to consider this issue. They argued that the question of the relation between national and European Union law was a national constitutional issue for the national courts to decide. However, the Court of Justice concluded that it was only interpreting the provisions of the relevant Treaty Article. This provided it with jurisdiction under Article 177 (now Article 234).

Having decided it had jurisdiction to consider the issue, it considered whether Article 12 (now Article 25) had 'direct effect'. In order to reach this decision, it considered the 'spirit, the general scheme and the wording' of the Treaty Articles.

A 'Purposive' or 'Teleological' Approach to Interpretation of the Treaty

Take particular note of the court's approach to interpreting the Treaty in *Van Gend en Loos*. This can prove helpful in analysing the court's approach to other issues that might arise under the law of the European Union.

The court could have taken a narrow or strict view of whether Article 12 had direct effect. That is, the court could have asked: 'Does Article 12 expressly provide that individuals may invoke its provisions in a national court?' If the issue had been framed that way, the court would have concluded that Article 12 did not have direct effect, because the Treaty Article did not expressly state that it did.

Most students routinely accept the direct effect of European Union law in the national legal order. However, the Court of Justice could have ruled differently, and it is worth considering the effect of an alternate ruling. This will provide insight generally into the manner in which the Court of Justice approaches issues before it.

If the Court of Justice had concluded that individuals could not invoke Treaty Articles in national courts, this would *not* mean that European Union law could not be enforced. For example, the European Commission could have brought an enforcement action against the Netherlands under then Article 169 (now Article 226). That Article provides that the Commission may bring an action in the Court of Justice against a member state if the Commission believes the member state is not fulfilling its obligations under European Union law. Therefore, if the Commission believed that the tariffs imposed by the Netherlands violated Article 12 (now Article 25) it could have brought an enforcement action against the Netherlands.

Also, then Article 170 (now Article 227) provides that a member state may bring an action in the Court of Justice against another member state if it believes that state has violated the Treaty. This provided another avenue for enforcing Article 12.

Also, if the Court of Justice had concluded that Article 12 lacked direct effect, that would not necessarily have been the last word on the matter. In the face of such a ruling from the Court of Justice, the member states would have been free to amend the Treaties to provide for direct effect. It is open to debate whether the founding member states intended Treaty Articles (not to mention directives) to have direct effect. We should also recall that Advocate General Roemer recommended that the court not find that Article 12 (now Article 25) had direct effect. He sided with the Netherlands and Belgium that the issue was one for the national legal orders.

However, in *Van Gend en Loos*, the court did not confine itself to the express words of the Treaty Article or the likely intent of the founding member states. Instead, the court took an approach that has come to be termed 'purposive' or 'teleological', because it is concerned with promoting the purpose of the European Union. As noted, the court turned to 'the spirit, the general scheme and the wording' of the Treaty. Note that the 'wording' of the Treaty, which some might regard as most important in interpreting its provisions, appears last in the list of considerations.

The Spirit, the General Scheme and the Wording

The court noted that the objective ('spirit') of the Treaty was to establish a Common Market. Because the functioning of a Common Market was of concern to individuals, this implied that the Treaty was more than an agreement that created mutual obligations between member states (the situation in a typical international agreement). The court buttressed this point by noting that the Treaty established institutions that were endowed with powers to affect individuals as well as member states.

The court also cited Article 177 (now Article 234). This Treaty Article provided a system whereby national courts could refer to the Court of Justice issues pertaining to the interpretation of the Treaty. Article 177 (now Article

234) thus supported a conclusion that the Treaty envisaged that individuals would raise Treaty Articles in the national courts, which might lead to Article 177 (now Article 234) references.

Three governments made submissions to the court, in which they argued that enforcement of Article 12 (now Article 25) should be left to the European Commission (or to member states). The court rejected this argument with the observation that just because the Commission or a member state could invoke Article 12, this did not imply that an individual could *not* invoke the same Article.

In considering whether Article 12 (now Article 25) should have direct effect, the court observed, significantly, that:

> The vigilance of individuals concerned to protect their rights amounts to an effective supervision in addition to the supervision entrusted by Articles 169 and 170 [now Articles 226 and 227] to the diligence of the Commission and of the member states.

We will see that the effectiveness of European Union law is of great importance to the Court of Justice in interpreting the relationship between national law and the law of the European Union.

In a famous phrase, the court stated:

> The conclusion to be drawn from this is that the European Union constitutes a new legal order of international law for the benefit of which states have limited their sovereign rights, albeit within limited fields, and the subjects of which comprise not only member states but also their nationals. Independently of the legislation of member states, European Union law therefore not only imposes obligations on individuals but is also intended to confer upon them rights which become part of their legal heritage.

In other words, regardless of whether a member state had enacted national legislation to give effect to the provisions of a Treaty Article, individuals enjoyed rights under European Union law which could be invoked in national courts.

CONDITIONS FOR DIRECT EFFECT

The court also indirectly laid down conditions that a Treaty Article would have to satisfy in order to have direct effect. With one exception, these conditions still must be satisfied whenever asking if a provision of European Union law, such as a Treaty Article, has direct effect.

Article 12 provided, among other things, that: 'member states shall refrain from ... increasing [customs duties on imports]'.

The court stated that the substance of Article 12 was suited for direct effect because:

1. the Article laid down a prohibition, that is, a negative rather than a positive obligation;
2. it was clear and unconditional;
3. it was not subject to any conditions; and
4. its implementation did not depend upon further legislation being introduced under national law.

The Court of Justice soon dropped the requirement of a negative rather than a positive obligation. The other three conditions, variously stated, remain. In order for a Treaty Article to have direct effect, it must be clear and unambiguous, it must be unconditional, and it must not depend upon further implementing measures under national law (or under European Union law, for that matter).

SUMMARY

Van Gend en Loos and the doctrine of direct effect occupy such an important position in European Union law that it is worth summarising the state of European Union law after this early ruling. In *Van Gend en Loos*, the court faced the issue whether it had jurisdiction to consider whether a Treaty Article had direct effect, or whether this question had to be resolved by national courts considering national constitutional law. It concluded that it had jurisdiction to resolve the issue (contrary to the recommendation of the Advocate General). It further considered whether, under European Union law, a Treaty Article was capable, generally, of having direct effect. It concluded that a Treaty Article was capable of producing direct effect, based on the 'the spirit, the general scheme and the wording of the Treaty'. The foregoing issues were constitutional in nature, that is, these issues considered whether European Union law would be recognised in a separate legal order.

Finally, the court considered what characteristics a Treaty Article must possess before it could have direct effect. This issue concerns the substance of the law, and whether it is capable of being relied upon by an individual. The court essentially laid down four requirements (one of which was later dropped).

REMAINING ISSUES – DIRECT EFFECT OF OTHER FORMS OF EUROPEAN UNION LAW

As with many judicially-created doctrines, the doctrine of direct effect, while solving the issue before the court in one particular case, raised a host of issues when considered in other contexts in which the doctrine might apply.

For example, *Van Gend en Loos* involved a Treaty Article. What about other types of European Union law? Did regulations have direct effect? What about directives? In *Van Gend en Loos*, the parties accused the member state of violating European Union law. What if one accuses a private party of violating European Union law? Does the doctrine of direct effect mean that European Union law can be invoked in national courts against a private party?

We will consider these issues in turn.

Regulations and Direct Effect

In Case 39/72, *Commission v. Italy* [1973] ECR 101, the Court of Justice of the European Union ruled that regulations have direct effect.

The case for the direct effect of regulations is fairly straightforward. Recall that Article 249 (ex Article 189) sets out the types of legislation that can be adopted by the European Union. One type of legislation is a regulation.

With respect to a regulation, Article 249 (ex Article 189) provides that:

> A regulation shall have general application. It shall be binding in its entirety and directly applicable in all member states.

The express language of the Treaty Article itself seems to indicate that a regulation should have direct effect, if we understand 'directly applicable' to mean essentially the same thing as direct effect.

It is probable that the founding member states intended regulations to have 'direct effect'. They most likely intended that regulations would become part of the national legal orders of the member states without the need for implementing legislation. Many of the six founding member states shared a monist perspective on international law. Thus, the fact that an individual could invoke a regulation in national court would not necessarily have offended their domestic legal orders.

Directives and Direct Effect

The issue whether directives have direct effect is not so straightforward. This issue has remained one of the most contentious issues in European Union law.

The issue of direct effect of directives was considered by the Court of Justice in Case 41/74, *Van Duyn v. Home Office* [1974] ECR 1337. The British Government considered the activities of the Church of Scientology to be contrary to public policy. The Secretary of State, exercising powers granted him under British law, adopted a ruling that any foreign national seeking to enter the UK in order to work for the Church of Scientology would be refused leave to enter.

Ms Van Duyn was a Dutch national, and a member of the Church of Scientology. She had worked for the Church of Scientology in the Netherlands, and sought to enter the UK to take up work with the Church at its college in Sussex. She was refused leave to enter pursuant to the Secretary of State's instruction.

Ms Van Duyn brought an action in the British High Court. She claimed that the refusal of leave to enter violated European Union law. She sought to rely on Article 39 (ex Article 48), which guaranteed the free movement of workers. She also sought to rely on Directive 64/221, which concerned the right of member states to exclude foreign nationals based on public policy. In particular, Ms Van Duyn sought to rely on Article 3 of Directive 64/221, which provided that: 'Measures taken on the ground of public policy ... shall be based exclusively on the personal conduct of the individual concerned'.

Ms Van Duyn argued that her membership in the Church of Scientology did not constitute 'personal conduct', and so the decision to refuse leave to enter violated, among other things, Article 3 of Directive 64/221.

Before the British High Court could consider the substance of Ms Van Duyn's arguments, however, it had to consider whether Treaty Article 39 (ex Article 48) and Directive 64/221 could have direct effect. That is, was Ms Van Duyn able to invoke and rely upon this European Union law in the national courts?

The UK eventually dropped its argument that Treaty Article 39 (ex Article 48) lacked direct effect. The issue remaining was whether Directive 64/221 (and, more particularly, Article 3 of Directive 64/221) could have direct effect. The court concluded that it could have direct effect.

The UK argued that directives generally, and Directive 64/221 in particular, could not have direct effect. It pointed out that Article 249 (ex Article 189) distinguished between regulations and directives. With respect to regulations, the Treaty Article expressly stated that regulations were directly applicable. The UK argued that, from this, one could conclude that directives lacked direct effect, because the Treaty contained no reference to direct applicability and directives.

The court rejected the UK's argument, and found that directives could have direct effect. It essentially gave three reasons in support of its conclusion.

First, the court stated that simply because regulations had direct effect, this did not mean that other forms of European Union law lacked direct effect. Such a conclusion would be contrary to the wording of Article 249 (ex Article 189) which says that a directive shall be binding on a member state.

Secondly, the court held that:

> [T]he useful effect of such an act [i.e., a directive] would be weakened if individuals were prevented from relying on it before their national courts and if the latter were prevented from taking it into consideration as an element of European Union law.

This reasoning harks back to the court's concern about the effectiveness of the Community law, as expressed in the earlier case of *Van Gend en Loos*.

Thirdly, the court stated that:

[Article 234 (ex Article 177)] empowers national courts to refer to the court questions concerning the validity and interpretation of all acts of the European Union institutions [including directives] ... [and] implies ... that these acts may be invoked by individuals in the national courts.

Note that this reason invokes and relies upon the express wording of a Treaty Article.

Conditions for Direct Effect of Directives

Having concluded that directives were capable, generally, of producing direct effect, the court then considered whether the conditions for direct effect had been met in the case before it. This is the second step in determining whether a law can be relied upon, i.e., whether the law itself possess characteristics capable of being relied upon. The court essentially restated the conditions laid down in *Van Gend en Loos* (that is, three of the conditions, as the requirement of a negative prohibition had been dropped). This is, the directive had to be:
1. clear and unambiguous;
2. unconditional; and
3. not dependent on further implementing measures.

The court concluded that Article 3 of Directive 64/221:

confers on individuals rights which are enforceable by them in the courts of a member state and which the national courts must protect.

In other words, that Article 3 of Directive 64/221 had direct effect.

REMAINING ISSUES – DEADLINES AND VERTICAL VERSUS HORIZONTAL DIRECT EFFECT

The court ruling in *Van Duyn* immediately spawned issues pertaining to the application of the doctrine of direct effect of directives in other contexts. Some of these issues continue to engage the court. An early issue concerned whether directives could have direct effect before the deadline for implementing the directive into national law had expired. A more troublesome issue concerned whether a directive could be invoked against a private individual (horizontal direct effect), or if directives were only directly effective when invoked against a member state (vertical direct effect).

We will consider these issues in turn.

Direct Effect of Directives and Deadlines for Implementation

From a previous chapter, we know that directives bind member states to achieve a certain result, but leave the choice of forms and methods of achieving that result to the member states. In practical terms, that means that the directive includes a deadline by which the member states are meant to have implemented the directive into national law.

What if an individual seeks to rely on the direct effect of a directive before the deadline for its implementation has passed? In other words, can an individual invoke a directive in the national courts before the deadline has passed? (This issue did not arise in *Van Duyn*, because the deadline for implementing Directive 64/221 had passed.) The answer is no. It is not possible to rely on a directive before the deadline for its implementation has passed.

The issue was addressed in Case 148/78, *Pubblico Ministero v. Tullio Ratti* [1979] ECR 1629. In *Ratti,* an Italian company began labelling its products according to the requirements of a pair of European Union directives. The Italian Government had failed to implement these directives. However, the deadline for implementation had not expired with respect to one of the directives. Italian law contained its own requirements for the labelling of the products, and provided for criminal penalties for non-compliance. Ratti was prosecuted for violating the Italian law. In his defence, he invoked the European Union directives. In other words, he sought to rely on the direct effect of the directives.

The Italian court made a reference to the Court of Justice on the issue of whether Ratti could invoke the non-implemented directives in national court.

Directives and Conditions for Direct Effect

The Italian government sought to argue that an individual could never invoke a non-implemented directive in national court, because the conditions for direct effect were not fulfilled. Specifically, directives by their nature require that member states implement the directive into national law by legislation or otherwise. A 'positive legislative measure under national law', in the words of the *Van Gend en Loos* judgment, always will be required in the case of a non-implemented directive. On the surface, this would make it appear that one of the conditions for direct effect could never be fulfilled with respect to directives. But, we know from *Van Duyn* that non-implemented directives can have direct effect. How did the court resolve this?

The court rejected Italy's argument, at least with respect to directives as to which the deadline for implementation had passed. The court's rationale was based in estoppel. That is, it might be true, technically, that one of the conditions for direct effect had not been met. However, it would not be right to allow a member state to rely on its own wrongdoing (i.e., the failure to implement the directive on time) in order to prevent an individual from relying on the directive. If the directive had been implemented on time, the individual would not be forced to rely on its direct effect.

According to the court:

> [A] member state which has not adopted the implementing measures required by the directive in the prescribed periods may not rely, as against individuals, on its own failure to perform the obligations which the directive entails.

Direct Effect of Directives Before Expiry of Deadline for Implementation

The court took a different view with respect to directives as to which the deadline for implementation had not expired. The court ruled that an individual could not rely on the direct effect of a directive before the deadline for implementation had passed.

According to the court:

> It is only at the end of the prescribed period and in the event of a member state's default that the directive ... will be able to have [direct effect].

What this means with respect to the direct effect of directives is that we must always ask the following question: 'Has the deadline for implementing the directive into national law expired?' In essence, this adds an additional requirement for the direct effect of directives, one that is often overlooked.

However, the most complex issue with respect to the direct effect of directives concerns whether directives can be invoked against a private party. Notice that in all the cases we have discussed so far, an individual sought to invoke the terms of a directive against a member state (against the UK in *Van Duyn,* against Italy in *Ratti*). This is known as asserting the directive 'vertically'. Asserting a non-implemented directive against an individual is known as 'horizontal' direct effect. The issue is, do non-implemented or improperly implemented directives have 'horizontal' direct effect? The next section considers this complex issue.

Vertical versus Horizontal Direct Effect

The Court of Justice definitively answered the question whether directives have horizontal direct effect in a case where the issue was not really necessary for the decision. That case was Case 152/84, *Marshall v. Southampton and Southwest Hampshire Area Health Authority (Teaching)* [1986] ECR 723. The court said directives did not have horizontal effect. However, after the court announced its decision, it began issuing decisions which minimised the effects of that decision, so much so that commentators and Advocates General were impelled to urge the court, unsuccessfully, to reverse its original decision.

The court has stuck to its original ruling against direct effect, despite pressure from various Advocates General to rule in favour of the horizontal direct effect of directives. However, the court has developed other doctrines, such as giving a broad definition to what constitutes an emanation of the state, indirect effect and damage actions against a member state for failure to implement a directive. These judicially-created doctrines have minimised the impact of a lack of direct effect. We will consider these doctrines in turn.

No Horizontal Direct Effect for Directives

In *Marshall*, Ms Helen Marshall worked for the Health Authority. She lost her job pursuant to a Health Authority policy that set the retirement ages for men and women at the ages established under British law for eligibility to draw a state pension. Women became eligible to draw a state pension at age 60, and men became eligible to draw a pension at age 65. So, according to Health Authority policy, the normal retirement age for women was 60 and for men was 65, even if a woman wanted to continue working for a longer time. (In fact, Ms Marshall worked until age 62; nothing in the national legislation *required* an employer to fix an earlier retirement age for women.)

After her dismissal, Ms Marshall brought an action in a British Industrial Tribunal, claiming that the unequal retirement ages discriminated against her on the basis of her sex. The Tribunal found that the UK Sex Discrimination Act, 1975, did not prohibit different retirement ages for men and women. However, on appeal, the Court of Appeal referred a question to the European Court of Justice, concerning unequal retirement ages and the EC Equal Treatment Directive, 1976. The Equal Treatment Directive, Council Directive 76/207, required equal treatment of men and women in employment. The UK relied upon the earlier-adopted UK Sex Discrimination Act as implementing the later 1976 Directive. However, Ms Marshall's case posed the issue whether the directive had been properly implemented, and, if not, whether the directive itself prohibited unequal retirement ages. In other words, Ms Marshall sought to invoke the directive itself in UK national courts, that is, to rely on the direct effect of Directive 76/207, since the implementing national legislation did not provide her with a remedy.

The Health Authority opposed Ms Marshall by raising a number of arguments. The Authority argued that it was not the member state and that, therefore, the directive could not be invoked against it. In other words, the Authority argued that it was essentially a private party, and that directives lacked horizontal direct effect, that is, that directives could not be relied upon against private parties. Ms Marshall, naturally enough, argued against this position, and argued for the horizontal direct effect of directive.

On this point, Ms Marshall lost. The court ruled unequivocally that directives lacked horizontal direct effect. According to the court:

> A directive may not of itself impose obligations on an individual and ... a provision
> of a directive may not be relied upon as such against such a person.

The court has never veered from this position although, as we shall see,
subsequent court decisions have minimised the impact of this ruling.

What was the court's rationale for ruling against direct effect? The court
pointed out that the express wording of Article 189 (now Article 249) provides
that directives are binding 'upon each member state to which it is addressed'.
Therefore, directives could not be binding upon individuals, because the
Treaty did not say they were.

Recall, however, that the court has not limited itself to the express wording
of the Treaty in deciding other issues of European Union law, such as the
doctrine of direct effect itself. It usually considers the 'spirit, the general
scheme and the wording' of the Treaty, in what is known as a 'purposive' or
'teleological' approach. The court's approach to the horizontal direct effect of
directives represents a departure from this approach.

Note also that the court has ruled that *Treaty Articles* do have direct effect.
In Case 43/75, *Defrenne v. Sabena* [1976] ECR 455, the court considered
whether Article 119 (now 141), had horizontal direct effect. The court wrote:

> [T]he prohibition on discrimination between men and women applies not only to
> the action of public authorities, but also extends to all agreements which are
> intended to regulate paid labour collectively, as well as to contracts between
> individuals.

Minimising the Lack of Horizontal Direct Effect – Part 1: Organ of the State

Ms Marshall won her case in the Court of Justice, despite the court's ruling
that the directive she sought to rely on lacked horizontal direct effect. How
was that possible? The court concluded that the Health Authority could be
regarded as an organ of the state, and that, therefore, Ms Marshall could rely
on the established vertical direct effect of directives. The Health Authority
had argued that it should only be considered an organ of the state when
performing its duties as a Health Authority, e.g., providing health services,
and not when it was acting in a capacity similar to a private enterprise, e.g.,
hiring and firing employees. The court rejected this argument, stating that:

> Where a person involved in legal proceedings is able to rely on a directive as
> against the state he may do so regardless of the capacity in which the latter is
> acting, whether employer or public authority.

What is an Organ of the State? – Foster v. British Gas

The court provided further clarification of which bodies constituted an organ
of the state in Case C-188/89, *Foster v. British Gas* [1990] ECR I-3313. The

claimants in *Foster* wanted to rely on the Equal Treatment Directive to challenge unequal retirement ages for men and women in British Gas. However, British Gas had been privatised, although it was still a monopoly provider of gas in the UK and a nationalised industry.

The court provided greater detail on what constituted an organ of the state. It stated that:

> A body, whatever its legal form, which has been responsible, pursuant to a measure adopted by the state, for providing a public service under the control of the state and has for the purpose special powers beyond those which result from the normal rules applicable in relations between individuals, is included in any event among the bodies against which the provisions of a directive capable of having direct effect may be relied upon.

Thus, in considering whether a body is an organ of the state, we must consider:

1. whether it is charged by law;
2. to provide a public service; and
3. whether it has special powers beyond those applicable in relations between private individuals.

The Court of Justice has ruled that directives can be relied on against tax authorities (Case 8/81 *Becker* [1982] ECR 53), the police (Case 222/84, *Johnston v. Chief Constable of the RUC* [1986] ECR 1651) and local authorities (Case 103/88 *Costanzo* [1989] ECR 1839), as well as public health services (*Marshall*, cited above).

Minimising Lack of Direct Effect – Part 2: Indirect Effect

The definition of an organ of the state can reach only so far. Eventually, a case could arise in which an individual who sought to invoke a directive against a private body would not be able to do so because of the lack of horizontal direct effect. It is easy to see the potential problem. Imagine a woman worked for a private employer in a member state where the Equal Treatment Directive had not been implemented properly, such as the UK. If that woman were forced to retire at an earlier age than a man, she would not be able to bring an action and rely on the Equal Treatment Directive. Meanwhile, a woman working at an organ of the state would be able to rely on the directive, and successfully challenge her dismissal. Two citizens with identical complaints would not have the same rights.

Indeed, precisely this occurred in the British case of *Duke v. GEC Reliance* (House of Lords) [1988] 1 All ER 627. A woman sought to challenge the unequal ages of retirement for men and women imposed by her private employer. The House of Lords held that, despite the ruling in *Marshall* (cited above) that unequal retirement ages violated the Equal Treatment Directive, the plaintiff's case in *Duke* had to be dismissed because she worked for a private employer and the directive could not be invoked against a private party.

The Court of Justice has sought to further minimise the lack of horizontal direct effect through the doctrine of indirect effect. The leading cases are Case 14/83, *Von Colson and Kamann* [1984] ECR 1891 and, particularly, Case C-106/89, *Marleasing v. La Commercial Internacionale* [1990] ECR I-4135.

Von Colson *and National Laws Implementing European Union Law*

In Case 14/83, *Von Colson*, two German women sought employment in a German prison. They were denied the posts on the basis of their sex. They brought a complaint of sex discrimination in the German courts, and won. However, German law provided for a very small award of compensation – basically, the out-of-pocket expenses for attending the job interview. The women would have preferred the German court to order that they be given the job.

The German national court made a reference to the European Court of Justice. The issue was whether European Union law required a specific remedy, for example, that the employer be ordered to hire the women.

The court ruled that European Union law, in this instance, the Equal Treatment Directive, did not impose a requirement that German national law provide a specific remedy, for instance, the offer of a job. However, the court stated that:

> [I]n applying the national law and in particular the provisions of a national law specifically introduced in order to implement Directive 76/207, national courts are required to interpret their national law in the light of the wording and the purpose of the directive in order to achieve the result referred to in the third paragraph of Article 189 [now Article 249].

The previous paragraph contains the seeds of the doctrine of indirect effect. It means, in essence, that when the national court is interpreting national law (particularly national law adopted to implement a European Union directive), the national court must do so in light of the purpose of the directive, in order to give it binding effect in national law. Once again, the 'effectiveness' of Community law has played an important part in the court's decision-making process.

Extension of Indirect Effect – Marleasing

The court developed and extended the doctrine of the indirect effect of directives in Case C-106/89, *Marleasing v. La Commercial Internacionale* [1990] ECR I-4135.

Marleasing brought an action in Spanish national courts against La Commercial Internacionale. Marleasing sought to 'pierce the corporate veil' and have the defendant company's articles of incorporation declared void. The grounds that Marleasing sought to rely on were that the defendant company had been formed for the purpose of defrauding creditors. This was arguably a basis for voiding the articles of association under Spanish law. However, a directive had been adopted, Directive 68/151, that sought to harmonise the grounds for voiding articles of association in the member states. This directive did not include the grounds relied on by Marleasing under Spanish law.

Spain had not implemented the directive into national law. Therefore, it was not like the situation in *Von Colson,* where the national law had been adopted to implement European Union law. The national law in *Marleasing* was adopted before the directive had been adopted. Thus, the court could not indulge in the rationale that it was interpreting national law in light of an earlier-adopted directive.

The defendant company sought to rely on the non-implemented European Union directive. That is, it sought to invoke the direct effect of the directive against Marleasing to prevent Marleasing from using grounds other than those specified in the directive.

However, directives do not have horizontal direct effect. Did this mean that Marleasing was able to rely on Spanish national law, even though European Union law (in the form of the relevant directive) did not provide this as a basis for voiding the articles of association? Or was the defendant company able to invoke European Union law, to prevent Marleasing from using a ground not contained in the directive?

The Spanish court made a reference to the Court of Justice. It asked whether the directive could be invoked against a private party. The Court of Justice ruled that the directive did not have direct effect. That was not the end of the matter, however. The court stated that:

> [I]n applying national law, whether the provisions in question were adopted before or after the directive, the national court called upon to interpret it is required to do so, as far as possible, in the light of the wording and the purpose of the directive in order to achieve the result pursued by the latter and thereby comply with the third paragraph of Article 189 [now Article 249] of the Treaty.

Therefore, in practical terms, this meant that the Spanish court would be required to interpret national law in the light of Directive 68/151 and conclude that Marleasing could not rely on grounds outside of those contained in the directive.

What is the basis for this 'interpretive obligation'? Article 10 of the EC Treaty (ex Article 5) imposes an obligation on member states to take all appropriate measures to ensure fulfillment of the obligations arising out of the Treaty. That obligation extends to the national courts, in interpreting national law intended to implement European Union law.

The doctrine of indirect effect goes a long way towards minimising the effects of the lack of horizontal direct effect of directives. However, it cannot cover all possible situations, such as when there is no national law that can be interpreted in the light of the non-implemented or incorrectly implemented directive. The Court of Justice has sought to further minimise the lack of horizontal direct effect by another judicially-created doctrine – damages against a member state for failure to implement a directive.

Part 3: Damages Against a Member State for Failure to Implement a Directive – Francovich

The court effectively further minimised the lack of horizontal direct effect of directives in Cases C-6/90 and C-9/90, *Francovich and Bonafaci v. Italy* [1991] ECR I-5357, even though the issue of horizontal direct effect was not directly at issue in these consolidated cases.

The European Union had adopted a directive, Directive 80/987. The purpose of the directive was to protect individuals who worked for companies that became insolvent. It did this by requiring member states to set up a fund from which employees who were owed money by employers could make a claim.

Italy did not implement the directive into national law before the expiration of the deadline for doing so. The Commission brought an enforcement action against Italy, and the court ruled that Italy had violated its obligations under European Union law by the failure to implement the directive. However, Italy had not yet implemented the directive by the time the *Francovich* case arose.

In *Francovich,* two individuals worked for companies that became insolvent. When they were unable to obtain compensation from the state (because Italy had not implemented Directive 80/987 and set up a fund for compensation), they brought suit against Italy in the Italian national court.

They sought to invoke the terms of the directive against Italy. Because they sought to invoke the directive against a member state, they could rely on the fact that directives have vertical direct effect.

Recall, however, that directives (or any form of European Union law) may lack direct effect for other reasons. Specifically, recall that we began the chapter by outlining the conditions for direct effect announced in *Van Gend en Loos*. These conditions are first, the European Union law must be clear and unambiguous (or clear and precise), second, it must be unconditional, and, third, it must not depend on further legislative measures. (Of course, the third condition falls away when we are considering directives that have not been properly implemented. As to directives, we ask whether the deadline for implementation has expired.)

In *Francovich*, the court concluded that Directive 80/987 lacked direct effect either because it was not sufficiently precise or because it required further implementing measures in the form of setting up the fund from which individuals were to be compensated. (The court was not altogether clear in its reasoning.)

Therefore, the parties could not rely on the directive as against Italy. (Essentially, then, they were in the same position as individuals who sought to rely on a directive against a private party.)

The court did not stop there, however. It went on to consider 'whether a member state is under an obligation to make good damage done to individuals arising out of the failure' to implement a directive. The court concluded that a member state could be liable in damages for its failure to implement a directive.

Rationale for Damages for Failure to Implement a Directive

The court based its conclusion that a member state could be liable in damages for failure to implement a directive on 'the general scheme and basic principles of the Treaty'. The court emphasised, once again, that:

> [T]he full effectiveness of European Union provisions would be affected and the protection of the rights they recognise undermined if individuals were not able to recover damages when their rights were infringed by a breach of European Union law attributable to a member state.

Furthermore, the court stated that:

> [The] obligation on member states to make good the damage is also based on Article 5 [now Article 10] of the Treaty, under which the member states are bound to take all appropriate measures, whether general or particular, to ensure fulfillment of the obligations arising under European Union law. This includes the obligation to make good the unlawful consequences of a breach of European Union law.

Conditions for Liability

The court laid down three conditions for liability. First, the directive must confer rights on individuals. Second, it must be possible to determine the rights conferred by reference to the directive. Third, there must be a causal relationship between the failure to implement the directive and the damages suffered.

We can see that the claimants in *Francovich* would meet all three of the conditions for liability. The directive conferred rights on people like the claimants, it was possible to determine those rights by looking at the directive, and the damages resulted from failure to implement the directive.

The *Francovich* conditions for liability would appear to extend to situations where the directive lacked direct effect because a party sought to invoke it against a private party. Thus, the principles established by

Francovich can be seen as another means of minimising the lack of horizontal direct effect of directives.

Further Developments of Liability for Member State Violations of European Union Law

As we have seen repeatedly, a major court decision such as *Francovich* immediately spawns questions that are not answered in the original judgment. For example, did the principle of member state liability extend to other violations of European Union law, apart from the failure to implement a directive? Was it necessary to have a previous court ruling that the member state was in violation of European Union law, as had been the case in *Francovich*? Was there strict liability for a violation of European Union law, regardless of how innocent the breach? (*Francovich* did not mention fault as one of the conditions of liability.)

The Court of Justice has developed an entire jurisprudence after *Francovich*, concerning the remedies available in national courts for a violation of European Union law. This jurisprudence is considered in detail in a following chapter. However, at this point, we can summarise a few points that are covered in more detail in a later chapter.

The Court of Justice has ruled that member states can be liable for violations of European Union law other than the failure to implement a directive. It is not necessary for the court to have found the member state in violation of European Union law before liability can arise. However, there is not strict liability for a violation of European Union law.

In Cases C-46/93 and C-46/93, *Brasserie du Pecheur and Factortame* [1996] ECR I-1029, the court clarified the conditions giving rise to member state liability for violation of European Union law. The court stated that:

> European Union law confers a right to reparation where three conditions are met: the rule of law infringed must be intended to confer rights on individuals; the breach must be sufficiently serious; and there must be a direct causal link between the breach of the obligation resting on the state and the damage sustained by the injured parties.

Thus, some element of fault is required for liability. Specifically, the breach of European Union law must be sufficiently serious.

The court clarified what is meant by 'sufficiently serious' in Case C-392/93, *R v. HM Treasury, ex parte British Telecommunications plc* [1996] ECR I-1631 and in Cases C-283, 291 and 292/94, *Denkavit International* [1996] ECR I-5063. Essentially, the court looks at a variety of factors, including the scope of the discretion left to the member state in implementing European Union law, the clarity of the instructions, and previous communications from the European Commission (the policeman of the European Union) regarding a claimed infringement of European Union law.

THE FUTURE OF HORIZONTAL DIRECT EFFECT
OF DIRECTIVES

Much of the foregoing discussion follows from the ruling of the Court of Justice that directives did not have horizontal direct effect. In some ways, it would seem things would be much simpler if directives could be invoked against private individuals. Is there any possibility that the court may someday change its mind and rule that directives are capable of having horizontal direct effect?

It seems unlikely the Court of Justice will conclude that directives are capable of horizontal direct effect. At least two Advocates General have recommended that the court change its ruling in this regard. The court has refused to do so.

In Case C-91/92, *Dori v. Recreb* [1994] ECR I-3325, Advocate General Lenz recommended that the court rule that directives were capable of horizontal direct effect. In Case C-316/93, *Vaneetveld v. Le Foyer SA* [1994] ECR I-763, Advocate General Jacobs invited the court to rule that a directive could be invoked against a private individual. However, in both cases the court adhered to its ruling that directives lack horizontal direct effect. *Dori* was a ruling of the full court, emphasising the importance of the decision.

The recommendations of the Advocates General in *Dori* and *Veneetveld* provide a good overview of the arguments in support of horizontal direct effect for directives. Students interested in pursuing this issue further are referred to the recommendations.

SUPREMACY OF EUROPEAN UNION LAW OVER
NATIONAL LAW

Implicit in the question of the direct effect of European Union law is the question of supremacy. That is, which law is supreme, European Union law or national law?

We will see that although the Court of Justice and the member state of Ireland both conclude that European Union law is supreme to national law, their reasoning is not necessarily identical. This represents a possible source of tension between the domestic and the European Union legal orders.

VIEW OF THE COURT OF JUSTICE ON SUPREMACY

From the cases we have discussed so far it would seem that from the perspective of the Court of Justice, European Union law is supreme. For example, although the issue was not discussed expressly in the judgment in *Van Gend en Loos*, the logical implication of the court's discussion of the direct effect of Article 12 (now Article 25) was that it superceded national law on custom duties.

This was the clear implication of the court's language in *Van Gend en Loos*. The court stated:

> [T]he European Union constitutes a new legal order of international law *for the benefit of which the states have limited their sovereign rights, albeit within limited fields*, and the subjects of which comprise not only member states but also their nationals [italics added].

The court directly addressed the issue of the supremacy of European Union law in Case 6/64, *Costa v. ENEL* [1964] ECR 585. The court concluded that European Union law was supreme to national law, even national law that was enacted after the European Union law in question.

It gave various rationales for this supremacy. Essentially, it concluded that member states had irrevocably surrendered a measure of their national sovereignty when they joined the European Economic Union. The court in *Costa v. Enel* stated that:

> The transfer by the states from their domestic legal systems to the European Union legal system of the rights and obligations arising under the Treaty carries with it a permanent limitation of their sovereign rights, against which a subsequent unilateral act incompatible with the concept of the European Union cannot prevail.

VIEW OF IRELAND ON SUPREMACY

When the Court of Justice gave its opinion regarding the reasons for the supremacy of European Union law, it is not clear that it was taking into account the constitutional legal orders of the member states. Of course, there were only six member states at the time, and the court could not be expected to consider the constitutional legal orders of countries such as Ireland, that might become a member state in the future.

In Ireland, upon joining the European Union, the Constitution was amended by referendum. As a result, a new Article, Article 29.4.3° was adopted. This Article provides that:

> No provision of this Constitution invalidates laws enacted, acts done or measures adopted by the state necessitated by the obligations of membership of the [European] Communities or prevents laws enacted, acts done or measures adopted by the Communities, or institutions thereof, from having the force of law in the state.

Thus, from the Irish perspective, European Union law is supreme because Irish domestic law, and in particular Irish constitutional law, has been amended to provide for the supremacy of European Union law.

This arguably contrasts with the perspective of the Court of Justice of the European Communities. The court view seems to be that by reason of accession to the European Union, Ireland irrevocably surrendered a measure of national sovereignty over certain limited areas.

The tension between European Union and national views of the supremacy of European Union law could arise if Ireland amended its Constitution to provide for the supremacy of national law in one of the areas covered by European Union law. That is, if Ireland took: 'a subsequent unilateral act incompatible with the concept of the European Union'.

From the viewpoint of the Court of Justice, amending the Irish Constitution would not affect the supremacy of European Union law. It is not clear that Ireland would have the same view of the matter. However, until such time as European Union and Irish law seriously clash over a concrete issue, this tension is unlikely to boil over into a real issue.

CONCLUSION

Direct effect and supremacy are perhaps the two most important legal doctrines in all of European Union law, and both are judicially created. *Van Gend en Loos* may be the most important judgment ever given by the Court of Justice, and it was given against the recommendation of the Advocate General. It is difficult to overemphasise the importance of these doctrines. The Law of the European Union is a type of international law, and historically, international law was seen as the concern of sovereign states. In other words, the individual is not typically a subject of international law. In practical terms, this means an individual cannot invoke international law in the domestic legal orders, e.g., in the national courts. However, thanks to the Court of Justice, the law of the European Union is unique. Under the proper circumstances, an individual can invoke EU law in the national courts, and obtain a remedy. The law of the European Union is, truly, 'a new legal order'.

Chapter 6

REMEDIES IN NATIONAL COURT FOR VIOLATION OF COMMUNITY LAW

THE EC TREATY AND REMEDIES FOR VIOLATION OF COMMUNITY LAW

The judicially-created principle of direct effect means that, in proper circumstances, an individual can invoke Community law in Irish national courts. This feature distinguishes Community law from many other species of international law. However, direct effect raises the issue of the remedies that may (or must) be provided in national courts if a violation of Community law is proved.

The issue can be illustrated with a simple example. Article 141 (ex Article 119) of the European Community Treaty provides, among other things, 'Each member state shall ensure that the principle of equal pay for male and female workers for equal work or work of equal value is applied'. We know from Case 43/75, *Defrenne* [1976] ECR 455, that Article 141 (ex Article 119) has direct effect, at least that portion of the Treaty Article which guarantees equal pay for equal work.

Assume that a woman working in a civil service job discovers that she is being paid less per hour than a man who holds the same job. Assume, for the moment, that there is no Irish law that prohibits this. If she wishes, we know that she has the right to sue in Irish courts and rely on Article 141, which prohibits discrimination based on sex for pay of equal work. If she prevails, is that the end of the case?

Clearly not. The woman would be entitled to some remedy for violation of European Union law. But what remedy? We can return to Article 141 to see if it provides an answer. It does not. The Treaty Article only establishes the rule of equal pay for men and women for equal work. It does not state what remedy should be provided. We might think that the remedy is so obvious that it is not necessary to state it expressly – the woman would be entitled to money damages equal to the difference between the pay she and the male co-worker have received.

However, other remedies suggest themselves. What about differences in compensation that will arise in the future? Can the court make an award of money damages to cover continuing differences in rates of pay? This might be too speculative, given that the woman might leave her job at some point.

Does that mean the woman will have to return to court periodically to sue for the continuing difference in compensation? That seems unfair, or an inefficient use of court resources.

It might be preferable for the court to issue an order compelling her government employer to adjust her pay scale to make it equal to the man's pay scale. But does the court have the power to compel the government to make such an adjustment? If the court has that power, must it order that the woman's salary be raised to equal the man's salary? Or could the court order that the man's salary be lowered to equal the woman's salary? In other words, could equality be achieved by making each party equally miserable on a lower rate of pay?

Again, Article 141 does not provide an answer to these questions. The answers could be provided by Community legislation. That is, the Commission could propose that the Council (and Parliament) adopt legislation that harmonises the remedies available in national courts for a proven violation of Community law. However, to date the Commission has not made such a proposal, and it is unlikely to do so, except in certain limited circumstances.

Court of Justice Fills the Lacuna

Thus, it has fallen to the Court of Justice of the European Communities to develop, judicially, the remedies that are available in the national courts for a violation of Community law.

The following sections review the court's jurisprudence in the creation of a set of remedies in the national courts for violation of European Union law. The court has not always been forthright in its pronouncements on these issues, and this can make it difficult to reconcile its case law on the subject.

We will consider an Irish case that posed the issue of remedies available for a proved violation of Community law. Some might argue that the Irish courts avoided confronting the issue of whether they had power under Community law to fashion remedies that were not available under national law, and furthermore, that the courts ignored their obligation to seek clarification of this issue from the European Court of Justice.

On the issue of remedies in national court for violation of Community law, commentators have spoken of 'three generations' of jurisprudence of the Court of Justice of the European Communities. (See the following: Curtin and Mortelmans, 'Application and Enforcement of Community Law by the Member States: Actors in Search of a Third Generation Script', in *Institutional Dynamics of European Integration* (1994), p. 423; O'Keefe, 'Third Generation Remedies and Sex Equality Law' in *Sex Equality Law in the European Union* (1996), p. 294.)

These three generations can be stated in simple terms at the outset.

Three Generations of Court Jurisprudence

The 'first generation' of court jurisprudence consisted of the principle that Community law had direct effect and was supreme to national law. The second generation established the principle that it was for national courts to fashion remedies according to national law, subject to the requirements of non-discrimination and effectiveness of the remedy. The third generation established the potentially contradictory principle that Community law itself provided a source of power for national courts to fashion remedies for violation of Community law. These Community-law-based remedies might be greater than the remedies available for violation of analogous national law.

We can consider these three generations in greater detail using a specific Treaty Article to illustrate our points.

Article 12 (ex Article 6) of the European Community Treaty prohibits discrimination based on nationality. The Treaty, however, does not state expressly whether an individual who believes she has suffered such discrimination may bring an action in the national court to vindicate the principle of non-discrimination contained in Article 12.

First Generation – Direct Effect and Supremacy

Early cases of the Court of Justice considered this lacuna and ruled that, in appropriate circumstances, Treaty Articles (and other forms of Community law), have 'direct effect' and can be invoked in national courts by aggrieved individuals to challenge national legislation which allegedly violates Community law. (See Case 26/62, *Van Gend en Loos v. Nederlandse Administratte der Belastigen* [1963] ECR 1 and Case 106/77, *Amministrazione della Finanze dello Stato v. Simmenthal SpA* [1978] ECR 629.)

These well-known early rulings of the European Court have been labelled the 'first generation' of court decisions regarding the creation of remedies in national courts for violations of Community law.

Second Generation – National Autonomy Subject to Two Constraints

The 'second generation' of decisions by the Court of Justice addressed an issue that arose from the early doctrines of direct effect and supremacy. This issue was whether Community law was a source of remedies for a claimant who prevailed under Community law in the national courts. This issue concerned the relationship between national and Community law. These second-generation cases of the European Court of Justice adopted a minimalist approach to the obligations imposed on national courts under Community law: national courts, applying national law, had an obligation to fashion remedies for violation of European Union law, subject to minimal constraints imposed by Community law.

Community law imposed two constraints, known as non-discrimination and effectiveness. The first constraint required that the remedy provided by the national court must not be less favourable than the remedy provided for a violation of a similar national law (non-discrimination). The second constraint required that national law must not render it virtually impossible or excessively difficult to obtain a remedy (effectiveness). (See Case 158/80, *Rewe-Handelsgessellshaft Nord mnH v. Hauptzollamtkiel* [1981] ECR 1805 and Case 265/78, *Ferwerda v. Produktschap voor Vee en Vlees* [1980] ECR 617.)

The European Court of Justice, in *Rewe-Handelsgesellshaft Nord mbH v. Hauptzollamtkiel*, expressly stated that Community law was *not* a source of remedies in the national court:

> [A]lthough the Treaty has made it possible in a number of instances for private persons to bring a direct action, where appropriate, before the Court of Justice, it was not intended to create new remedies in the national courts to ensure the observance of Community law other than those already laid down by the national law.

Although the court has continued to acknowledge the sentiments expressed in *Rewe-Handelsgesellshaft*, we will see that it is difficult to reconcile the quoted language with the outcomes of other cases before the Court of Justice.

'Political Reasons' for Second Generation Jurisprudence

The second-generation cases avoided a potential political conflict. This conflict might arise if remedies for a violation of Community law exceeded remedies for a violation of a similar national law. These second-generation cases also may have encouraged national courts to apply Community law, because of the national courts' familiarity with the national law on remedies. National courts, in their role as Community courts applying Community law, might be reluctant to apply Community law if novel or unusual remedies were required.

Potential Conflict: Second Generation Jurisprudence and Uniformity of EU Law

These second-generation cases, however, allowed for the possibility that national law might not adequately protect rights arising under European Union law and that the effectiveness of European Union law might be undermined. Furthermore, and perhaps more significantly, if national law determined the remedies for violation of European Union, different remedies might be available in different member states for a violation of the same

Community law. The need for effectiveness and uniformity in European Union law put pressure on the European Court of Justice, in the absence of Community legislation harmonising remedies in national court for violation of Community law, to fashion substantive remedies under Community law.

Two cases marked a turning point in the court's thinking. As a result of these cases the principle of effectiveness became more important than the principle of national autonomy in fashioning remedies in the national courts for a violation of Community law.

A Turning Point in the Court's View of Remedies?

These cases are:

1. Case 14/83, *Von Colson and Kamman v. Land Nordrhein-Westfalen* [1984] ECR 1891; and
2. Case 222/84, *Johnston v. Chief Constable of the RUC* [1986] ECR 1651.

These cases, and others, particularly the later case of Case 271/91, *Marshall v. Southampton AHA (Marshall 2)* [1993] 3 CMLR 293, elevated the principle of the effective judicial protection of rights under Community law to a general principle of Community law. This was certain to create tension with the competing principle that it was for national courts, applying national law, to fashion remedies for violation of Community law.

In *Von Colson*, the plaintiffs prevailed on a claim of sex discrimination under German national law, which ostensibly had implemented a Community directive, Council Directive 76/207, that mandated equal treatment of men and women in employment. German law provided for the payment of a nominal sum (essentially the expenses incurred in the unsuccessful job application) as the remedy.

The plaintiffs did not argue that the remedy provided by German law was less favourable than that available under national law for similar actions; nor did they claim that the German law made it impossible or excessively difficult to obtain a remedy. The German law therefore seemed to comply with the requirements of non-discrimination and effectiveness established by the 'second generation' cases of the European Court of Justice.

The European Court, however, held that the terms of the directive and Article 5 (now Article 10) of the European Community Treaty required that the remedy provided by Germany be effective. Community law required that:

> [C]ompensation must ... be adequate in relation to the damage sustained and must therefore amount to more than purely nominal compensation such as, for example, the reimbursement only of the expenses incurred in connection with the application.

Community law therefore dictated the minimum requirements for the remedies chosen by the member state. This represented a greater incursion into national law than that of the second-generation cases that had preceded *Von Colson*.

In *Johnston v. Chief Constable of the RUC*, the plaintiff challenged national legislation that precluded her claim for sex discrimination in the face of a certificate from the Secretary of State for Northern Ireland stating that the allegedly discriminatory act was necessary for national security: see Article 53(2) of the Sex Discrimination (Northern Ireland) Order 1976 (SI 1976/1042). Such a certificate constituted irrefutable evidence under the national law that grounds existed for derogating from the principle of equal treatment in employment.

The Court of Justice emphasised that an effective judicial remedy in the national courts for violation of a right protected by Community law was a general principle of Community law. This general principle of law, according to the court, was common to the constitutional traditions of the member states and was contained in Articles 6 and 13 of the European Convention for the Protection of Human Rights and Fundamental Freedoms. The court concluded that the remedy provided by the UK failed to satisfy the requirements of Community law. Once again, Community law penetrated national law and imposed substantive conditions on remedies for violation of Community law.

Third Generation of Jurisprudence – EU Law as a Source of Remedies

In the 'third generation' of European cases concerning national judicial protection of Community rights, European Union law has become the source of remedies for violation of European Union law. However, the court has not always spoken forthrightly on the issue.

Spanish Fishermen and the Power to Grant an Injunction against the Crown

Case C-218/89, *Factortame Ltd. v. Secretary of State for Transport (Factortame I)* [1990] ECR I-2433, illustrates the European Court's *sotto voce* or indirect method of assuring effective judicial protection of rights under Community law. In *Factortame I*, Spanish fishermen challenged British regulations under the Merchant Shipping Act, 1988 (i.e. the Merchant Shipping (Registration of British Shipping Vessels) Regulations 1988), which imposed a nationality requirement for the registration of British ships. The national law was intended to thwart 'quota hopping' under the Community's common fisheries policy.

The plaintiffs alleged irreparable harm and sought interim relief to enjoin enforcement of the regulations. The House of Lords concluded it lacked power under national law to grant the requested relief and made an Article

234 (ex Article 177) reference to the European Court of Justice. The House of Lords asked if it had the *power* to grant such relief under European Union law. Under British law, the courts lack power to grant an injunction against the Crown, which, in practical terms, means that the court cannot enjoin an Act of Parliament.

Lord Harwich stated:

> I am clearly of the opinion that, as a matter of English law, the court has no power to make an order which has these consequences.

The request for a preliminary ruling from the House of Lords stated that:

> ... the national court has no power to give interim protection to the rights claimed by suspending the application of the national measure pending the preliminary ruling.

The British court asked whether the national court had either the obligation or the power under Community law to grant the interim protection (*Factortame v. Secretary of State for Transport (No. 1)* [1989] 2 All ER 692, 703).

The European Court of Justice, however, avoided the issue whether Community law provided national courts with the power to fashion remedies for a violation of Community law. The European Court framed the issue as:

> [W]hether a national court which, in a case before it concerning Community law, considers that the sole obstacle which precludes it from granting relief is a rule of national law must disapply that rule.

The court ruled that the national court must 'disapply' the rule of national law and grant the interim relief.

If we consider the European Court's decision in a vacuum, that is, only in light of the decision of the Court of Justice judgment, *Factortame I* is located within the second generation of the court's case law regarding remedies in national court. The judgment adheres to the basic formula that national courts need not create new remedies for violation of Community law; they need only provide such remedies as are available under national law subject to the twin requirements of non-discrimination and effectiveness.

If we consider the ruling in the context of the reference from the House of Lords, however, *Factortame I* appears to be within the third generation of the European Court's cases on remedies in the national courts. The House of Lords concluded it lacked power to grant interim relief; the European Court concluded it had such power under Community law. Commentators have sought to reconcile these positions. See, e.g.: Ross, 'Beyond *Francovich*' (1993) 56 MLR 55; Lewis and Moore, 'Duties, Directives and Damages in European Union Law' [1993] PL 151; Steiner, 'From Direct Effect to *Francovich*' (1993) 18 EL Rev 3; Flynn, 'Taking Remedies Too Seriously? National Procedural Autonomy in the European Court of Justice' (1996) 31 Irish Jurist 110.

However, Advocate General Mischo had no doubt that Community law was a source of remedies in the national courts when he wrote:

> Since Case 213/89 *Factortame*, there can no longer, I think, be any doubt that in certain cases community law may itself directly confer on national judicial authorities the necessary powers in order to ensure judicial protection of those rights, even where similar powers do not exist in national law.

See Cases C-6 and 9/90, *Francovich and Bonifaci v. Italy* [1991] ECR I-5357, Opinion of Advocate General Mischo at paragraph 53.

CONDITIONS FOR LIABILITY FOR VIOLATION OF COMMUNITY LAW

There is no longer any doubt that the European Court of Justice clearly has fashioned substantive remedies from Community law. This is the 'third generation' of European case law on national judicial protection of Community law. In the well-known *Francovich* case, the plaintiffs worked for employers who became bankrupt. A Community directive required member states to establish a fund from which employees such as the plaintiffs could obtain unpaid wages. Italy failed to implement this directive and was found by the European Court of Justice to be in violation of Community law in an enforcement action brought by the European Commission. The plaintiffs subsequently sought to rely upon the terms of the non-implemented directive in the national court. The Court of Justice ruled on an Article 177 reference that the directive lacked direct effect. The European Court ruled, however, that the plaintiffs could obtain an award of damages against Italy for the failure to implement a directive. The court found that the principle of member state liability in damages for a violation of Community law was inherent in the system of the European Union law (particularly the principle of the effectiveness of Community law), and could be found in the obligations imposed by Article 5 of the Treaty.

The conditions for member state liability were threefold:
1. the directive must accord rights to the individual concerned;
2. the rights must be identifiable from the terms of the directive; and
3. there must be a causal link between the breach of Community law and the damages claimed.

Francovich unambiguously represented a new cause of action in the national courts which had its source in Community law.

CLARIFICATION OF PRINCIPLES ESTABLISHING LIABILITY FOR VIOLATION OF COMMUNITY LAW

In subsequent cases, the European Court of Justice clarified the conditions of member state liability for a violation of Community law. Liability could arise for violations of Community law other than an outright failure to implement a directive, liability in the national court did not depend upon a prior ruling of European Court that the member state had violated Community law, and liability could arise where a directive had direct effect. See: Cases C-46/93 and 48/93, *Brasserie du Pecheur SA v. Federal Republic of Germany (Factortame III)* [1996] 2 WLR 506; Case C-392/92, *British Telecommunications (BT)* [1996] QB 615; Case C-5/94, *R v. Maff, ex parte Hedley Lomas (Ireland) Ltd*, not yet reported; Cases C-178 and 179/94 and C-188 and 190/94, *Dillenkofer and Others v. Federal Republic of Germany* [1996] ECR I-4845.

Where damages are claimed for acts other than a failure to implement a directive in a timely manner (such as the allegedly faulty implementation of a directive or an alleged violation of a right established under a Treaty Article), the conditions for liability of the member state are similar to those necessary to establish liability against an institution of the European Community: the rule of law infringe must be intended to confer rights on individuals; the breach must be sufficiently serious; and there must be a direct causal link between the breach of the obligation resting on the state and the damage sustained by the party.

According to the court in *Factortame III* (at paragraph 79), while the law of the member state might be relevant to determining whether, under European Union law, the breach has been sufficiently serious, this cannot be the determinative consideration:

> The obligation to make reparation for loss or damage caused to individuals cannot, however, depend upon a condition based on any concept of fault going beyond that of a sufficiently serious breach of Community law. Imposition of such a supplementary condition would be tantamount to calling in question the right to reparation founded on the Community legal order.

NATIONAL LAW CANNOT IMPOSE ADDITIONAL REQUIREMENTS FOR LIABILITY

The post-*Francovich* cases reiterate that member state liability in damages for breach Community law has its source in Community law, regardless of whether national law provides for such liability. Furthermore, member state rules on such liability cannot require that a claimant show more than a sufficiently serious breach of Community law. For example, in *Bourgoin SA v. Ministry of Agriculture, Fisheries and Food* [1996] QB 716, the British Court of Appeal held that, in order to obtain damages against a public body for breach of a Treaty Article, it was necessary to prove an abuse of power or other tort. This ruling is suspect under current Community law. See Craig, '*Francovich*, Remedies and the Scope of Damages Liability' (1993) 109 LQR 595, 603.

INCREASING COURT WILLINGNESS TO PENETRATE NATIONAL LAW

The case of *Zuckerfabrick* illustrates the European Court of Justice's willingness to penetrate national law to assure a uniform remedy in the national courts for violation of Community law: see Joined Cases C-14/88 and C-92/89, *Zuckerfabrick Sukrdithmarschen AG v. Hauptzollamt Itsehow and Zuckerfabrik Soest GmbH v. Hauptzollamt Paderborn* [1991] ECR I-415. For a discussion of the significance of *Zuckerfabrik*, see Curtin, 'The Decentralised Enforcement of Community Law Rights: Judicial Snakes and Ladders', in *Constitutional Adjudication in European Community and National Law* (1992).

In *Zuckerfabrik*, the issue was whether national courts had jurisdiction to grant interim relief suspending enforcement of national laws that were based on Community law. The European Court ruled that the national courts had the power to suspend enforcement of national measures based on Community law. It addressed the issue of the conditions under which such a remedy could be granted. Although the court acknowledged its 'second generation' formula that national procedural law governed the conditions for the granting of such relief, it observed in paragraph 5 of its judgment that:

> [T]hose conditions differ according to the national law governing them, which may jeopardise the uniform application of Community law.

The European Court concluded that the uniform application of Community law is a fundamental requirement of the Community legal order. Thus, Community law required national courts to apply uniform conditions in deciding whether to suspend enforcement of national law based on Community law.

The effects of *Francovich*, *Factortame* and *Zuckerfabrik* were summarised in O'Keefe, 'Third Generation Remedies and Sex Equality Law', in *Sex Equality Law in the European Union* (Wiley, 1996) as follows:

> All three cases demonstrate the introduction of common remedies to enforce Community law rights by the setting aside of national law, the granting of new

procedural rights for interim relief, and the introduction of new causes of action. It is clear that the effect on the national procedural rules will be enormous.

IRELAND AND REMEDIES IN NATIONAL COURT: THE *BLOOMER* CASE

The issue of the remedies available in national courts for violation of Community law arose in the case of *Bloomer v. Incorporated Law Society of Ireland* [2000] IR 383, in the Irish Supreme Court, affirming in part, reversing in part, *Bloomer v. Incorporated Law Society*, unreported, Irish High Court, 22 September 1995.

In *Bloomer*, graduates of Queen's University, Belfast, sued the Law Society of Ireland in the Irish High Court. They challenged the refusal of the Law Society to grant them exemptions from entrance examinations to the Law School at the Law Society. Regulations adopted by the Law Society pursuant to its statutory powers provided that graduates of certain law schools in the Republic of Ireland enjoyed an exemption from these entrance examinations. Essentially, the Queen's students argued that their legal education was sufficiently similar to that of Irish law graduates that the denial of the exemptions was unfair, and a form of discrimination based on nationality. Discrimination based on nationality, of course, violated then Article 6 of the EC Treaty (now Article 12).

Ms Justice Laffoy of the Irish High Court ultimately ruled that the denial of exemptions to the Queen's law graduates constituted a form of discrimination based on nationality, and therefore violated EC law. The issue arose as to the proper remedy.

The Queen's students sought the benefit of the exemptions enjoyed by the Irish law graduates. However, Justice Laffoy concluded that Irish constitutional law prevented her from making an order directing the Law Society to amend its regulations in order to grant the exemptions to the Queen's students. Instead, she found that her power under the Irish Constitution was limited to striking down the exemptions, and, henceforth, requiring that all applicants to the Law School at the Law Society sit the entrance examinations. In other words, she achieved 'equality' by making everyone equally miserable. She also dismissed the lawsuit brought by the Queen's students, as she could not grant the relief they sought. She assessed hundreds of thousands of pounds in costs against the students who had proved that they had been discriminated against.

Justice Laffoy never considered whether she might have power under Community law to fashion some form of affirmative relief that would have compelled the Law Society to amend its regulations in order to eliminate discrimination. The Supreme Court overturned the award of costs against the Queen's students and allowed them a portion of their own costs as the 'successful' party – they had, after all, proved a violation of Community law. However, the Supreme Court also did not consider whether Community law might have provided a basis for fashioning a remedy for the violation of Community law. Nor did the court make a reference under what was then Article 177 (now Article 234) to the Court of Justice of the European Communities asking whether it had such power.

As we will see in a subsequent chapter, the failure to make an Article 177 (now 234) reference might have violated Ireland's obligations under Article 10 (ex Article 5) to: 'take all appropriate measures ... to ensure the fulfilment of the obligations arising out of this Treaty ... '.

Bloomer also illustrates the importance for a lawyer to keep an eye on all aspects of Community law at all times, from initiating possible causes of action to the concluding remedies in a case.

CONCLUSION

In a subtle way, the issue of remedies available in an Irish court for a violation of European Union law illustrates some of the tension between the Irish courts and the Court of Justice of the European Community. On the one hand, national courts, including the Irish national courts, play a critical role in ensuring the all-important 'effectiveness' of European Union law. Thanks to the doctrine of direct effect, every Irish court is, in effect, also a court of the European Union. This is a tremendous source of power for Irish courts and probably inclines the courts to look favourably on the task of ensuring the effectiveness of European Union law.

On the other hand, the Irish courts have tremendous respect for the Irish Constitution, and might resist fashioning remedies that do not comport with the constitutional constraints on the Irish court's power to grant remedies. At the end of the day, a student must be attuned to these tensions, in addition to being aware of European Union law as a source of remedies.

Chapter 7
GENERAL PRINCIPLES OF EUROPEAN UNION LAW

GENERAL PRINCIPLES AS A SOURCE OF EUROPEAN UNION LAW

In an earlier chapter, we discussed various sources of European Union law. We identified, for example, the Treaty Articles themselves, and various types of 'secondary' legislative instruments such as regulations, directives, decisions, and recommendations and opinions. However, the general principles of European Union law represent another important source of European Union law. These General Principles of European Union law are the subject of this chapter. Many of the court decisions we will consider pre-date the creation of the European Union, and the court's references were to 'European Community'. We will refer to 'Community Law' throughout much of the chapter. Students should appreciate that these principles apply in European Union law and that, for most intents and purposes, we can use 'Community Law' and 'Union Law' interchangeably.

Genesis of General Principles of European Union Law

The Treaty Articles and secondary legislation provide a comprehensive set of rules for resolving a vast number of issues or disputes that conceivably could arise as the project for European integration proceeds. However, it would be impossible for the drafters of the Treaty Articles or of secondary legislation to anticipate every possible issue that might arise. Invariably, issues will arise for which there is no clear answer under the existing set of rules.

In the absence of a clear set of rules pertaining to a particular issue or area, it is natural that a dispute might arise. The parties to the dispute might invoke the assistance of the national or European Union courts to resolve their dispute. The courts will be called upon to interpret and apply existing European Union law to resolve the dispute. In the absence of a clear answer, the national courts may or must make an Article 234 (ex Article 177) reference to the Court of Justice of the European Union.

What if there is no clear principle in the existing body of European Union law to resolve the issue before the European Court of Justice? Can the Court of Justice simply rule that existing European Union law does not cover the dispute before it and not resolve the dispute?

The Court of Justice has responded to this lacuna by formulating what are known as General Principles of European Union law. These principles, which are not expressly set forth in Treaty Articles or secondary legislation, have the force of European Union law. They represent an independent source of European Union law.

Legitimacy of General Principles of European Union Law

Elsewhere, we have described the European Union as having only attributed or limited competence. That is, the Union has only those powers expressly ascribed to it in the Treaty or in secondary legislation which itself must be based explicitly on Treaty articles. The Union does not have general or free-ranging competence. In the absence of attributed competence, for instance, the Union cannot adopt laws binding on member states. For example, it is unlikely the Union could adopt a regulation setting the curriculum in second-level schools – such as requiring that all students study a second language – because there is no express Treaty Article that would empower the Union to adopt such legislation.

How is it then, that the Court of Justice of the European Union can adopt 'General Principles of European Union law' which have the same force as other forms of European Union law? Doesn't this amount to a type of free-ranging competence that we have said is not permitted by our understanding of how the Union operates?

There are various Treaty Articles that could be relied upon to argue the legitimacy of the court's adoption of General Principles of law. For example, Article 220 (ex Article 164) provides that: 'The Court of Justice shall ensure that in the interpretation of this Treaty the law is observed'. Article 230 (ex Article 173) specifies the grounds on which the court can annul the act of a Union institution. One of these grounds is 'infringement of this Treaty or of any rule of law relating to its application'. Both of these Treaty Articles imply that there is some type of 'law' distinct from and independent of the 'law' as it is provided in the Treaty itself. In other words, the Treaty itself empowers the court, in interpreting and applying European Union law, to rely on higher principles of abstract 'law'. It is this separate and distinct 'law' that provides the court with power to announce General Principles of law.

From Where do General Principles Originate?

We will see that the court suggests different origins for General Principles of law, depending upon the general principle that is involved. For example, in Case C-13/94, *P v. S and Cornwall County Council* [1996] ECR I-2143, a person, P, was fired from employment after revealing that she was undergoing a sex change operation, to change sex from a man to a woman. She claimed that her termination violated European Union law.

(Although P was biologically male, her condition, gender dysfunction, meant that she believed she was in some truer sense a woman, despite having the physical characteristics of a man. In her view, and those of her doctors, she sought to align her physical sex characteristics with her true sex as a woman. The Advocate General and the court referred to P throughout their opinions by the feminine pronoun.)

European Union law did not expressly prohibit discrimination against transsexuals or against persons who intended to have a sex-change operation. The relevant European Union law consisted, primarily, of the Equal Treatment Directive, Directive 76/207. This directive, however, merely forbid employment discrimination between men and women – it did not forbid discrimination against someone who wanted to change sex from a man to a woman.

Nevertheless, the court ruled that P's firing violated European Union law. How is this possible? The court ruled that Directive 76/207 was:

> ... simply the expression, in the relevant field, of the principle of equality, which is one of the fundamental principles of European Union law.

In other words, the prohibition of discrimination based on sex was the tip of the iceberg. It was merely the specific manifestation of a much broader principle of equality, which forbid 'irrational' discrimination, such as that based on stereotypes and not related to the ability of the person to perform a job. The court ruled that discrimination against transsexuals violated this broader General Principle of European Union law, and therefore, European Union law itself.

In the *P* case, the court suggested that the General Principle of European Union law originated or was located in European Union law. We will see that, in other instances, European Union law can be inspired by the national laws of the member states.

The General Principles of European Union Law – Some Preliminary Remarks

What are the General Principles of Law? Because these principles are not contained in the Treaties or the secondary law of the Union, there is no one place where we can look for a definitive list of these principles. The General Principles are judicially created, and a listing of them must be derived from the court decisions in which they are established.

Several observations should be made. First, because a list of these General Principles must be derived from court decisions, there may be some minor variations in how these principles are described. For example, some commentators speak of a general principle of non-discrimination and others speak of a general principle of equality. Are these the same principles? Do they have the same elements?

Second, the list of General Principles of European Union law is dynamic. That is, there is always a possibility that the Court of Justice may announce a new General Principle. Thus, it is important to understand how the court behaves when it announces a General Principle of European Union law, because it may be possible in the future to persuade the court to adopt a new principle.

Third, General Principles of European Union law may subsequently be adopted by the law-making institutions of the European Union, after the court has announced them. This has been true particularly in the field of human rights, which are discussed below. After the court developed human rights jurisprudence, reference to human rights protections was included in subsequent Treaty amendments. At a summit in Nice, the Union 'proclaimed' a Charter of Fundamental Rights (although the enforceability of these rights by private citizens remained an open question). The Draft Constitution for Europe expressly incorporates this Charter. This illustrates the transition from judicial pronouncement to express law of the European Union.

General Principles of European Union Law – a Catalogue

So what are the General Principles of European Union law? A catalogue of such principles, although not exhaustive, would include:
1. fundamental human rights;
2. proportionality;
3. legitimate expectations; and
4. non-discrimination.

These are the principles discussed in this chapter. However, other principles catalogued by commentators include retroactivity and vested rights (see Hartley, *The Foundations of European Union Law*, 4th ed., Oxford University Press, 1998), as well as the right to a hearing and equality.

Other possible General Principles include effective judicial protection of union rights, which is discussed in the chapter on Remedies in National Court for Violation of Community Law.

FUNDAMENTAL HUMAN RIGHTS

One General Principle of European Union law is generally described as 'fundamental human rights'. What are fundamental human rights? Again, in the absence of a clearly defined Treaty Article or piece of secondary legislation, there is no definitive written statement of this General Principle. Instead, it must be derived from the judgments of the Court of Justice. The Principle itself is dynamic; its meaning can change with each court pronouncement of what it means. Thus, in order to come to an understanding of what constitutes fundamental human rights in European Union law, we must review the development of this principle.

Because of the increasing importance of human rights in the Union legal order, we also will consider how the Union has incorporated human rights principles into the Treaties underpinning the Union. Finally, we will discuss the Charter of Fundamental Rights adopted by the Union at the Nice Summit in 2000, and incorporated into the Draft Constitution for Europe.

The Draft Constitution provides, at Article 7, that:

> The Union shall seek accession to the European Convention for the Protection of Human Rights and Fundamental Freedoms. Such accession shall not affect the Union's competences as defined in the Constitution.

If the Union accedes to the European Convention on Human Rights, this should eliminate the possibility of conflicting interpretations of virtually identically-phrased human rights guarantees. This conflict in interpreting human rights differently is discussed below.

Overview of Court's Development of Human Rights Jurisprudence

We will summarise briefly the development of human rights jurisprudence by the Court of Justice. We will then look at the important cases in this area and attempt to derive an understanding of what constitutes fundamental human rights in the court's jurisprudence. We also will consider briefly the court's view of suggestions that the European Union sign up to international human rights treaties, such as the European Convention on Human Rights.

Initially, the Court of Justice ruled that it did not have jurisdiction to consider human rights issues. This reflected the primarily economic concerns of the European Economic Community Treaty, and the lack of any explicit human rights protections contained in it. However, the court gradually changed its opinion on this matter, and concluded that European Community law did protect human rights. Why did the court change its mind? Some commentators suggest that a threatened 'revolt' by national courts – which insisted on evaluating European Community law against human rights protections contained in national constitutions – caused the Court of Justice to 'discover' human rights protections in European Community law.

The court gave shape to these human rights protections over a series of decisions. But if these protections are not written down anywhere, how did the court decide what these protections consisted of? We will see that the court drew on a variety of sources – including national constitutional law and international treaties – to give concrete substance to the vague guarantee of human rights protection.

Human Rights in European Union Law – a Brief History

The Court's Initial Reluctance to Invoke Human Rights Protections

The Court of Justice resisted initial attempts by individuals before it to invoke human rights protections. Its reluctance was understandable. These claims initially were based on national constitutional guarantees of human rights. In a precursor to later decisions that formally established the supremacy of European Union law, the court in the early human rights cases ruled that national constitutional law could not be used to challenge Community action.

Recall also that the Treaty of Rome, 1957, created the European *Economic* Community. In other words, there had been a conscious choice to limit the scope of European integration to economic matters. This choice had been made in light of the failure of the earlier attempts to create a European political union. The court undoubtedly was reluctant to expand its jurisprudence outside the scope of the limited Community competence created by the early Treaties.

However, neither the supremacy of European Community law nor the limited competence of the European Economic Community prevented individuals from claiming that their human rights had been infringed by Community action. After initially rebuffing these attempts, the Court of Justice did an abrupt 'about face' and ruled that European Community law protected fundamental human rights. This rapid change in attitude followed a conflict between national courts and the Court of Justice. This conflict threatened to undermine the supremacy of European Community law.

Early German Cases: Stork *and* Geitling – *Court Rejects Human Rights Arguments*

The earliest cases involving human rights claims arose out of Germany. After World War II, Germany adopted a national constitution that contained strong human rights protections. The Germans were sensitive to human rights concerns, and wanted to prevent the human rights abuses that occurred under the Third Reich from being repeated. It was inevitable that someone would invoke these human rights guarantees against Community action.

The earliest cases arose not under the EEC Treaty, but under the earlier European Coal and Steel Union Treaty. However, the principles announced in these decisions applied to the EEC Treaty as well.

One of the first cases was Case 1/58, *Stork v. High Authority* [1959] ECR 17. Recall that the High Authority was a European Commission-type organisation set up by the European Coal and Steel Union Treaty. In *Stork*, a coal wholesaler invoked German human rights guarantees to challenge a decision of the High Authority. The court rejected this argument. The court wrote:

> The High Authority is not empowered to examine a ground of complaint which maintains that, when it adopted its decision, it infringed principles of German constitutional law.

The principle announced in *Stork* is consistent with the court's later judgments concerning the supremacy of European Community law: national law cannot be used to challenge European Community law.

However, in Cases 36, 37, 38 and 40/59, *Geitling v. High Authority* [1960] ECR 423, the court went further. In *Geitling*, another party from Germany sought to rely on fundamental human rights guarantees to challenge Community action. The court rejected this argument. It repeated its ruling that the German national law could not be used to challenge European Community law. It also wrote:

> European Community law, as it arises under the ECSC Treaty, does not contain any general principle, express or otherwise, guaranteeing the maintenance of vested rights.

In other words, while *Stork* refused to consider human rights complaints based on German national law, the *Geitling* case suggested that European Community law itself contained no human rights protections.

About Face: Stauder *and the Court's 'Discovery' of Human Rights*

The Court of Justice did an 'about face' in Case 29/69, *Stauder v. City of Ulm* [1969] ECR 419. The European Community had adopted a plan to reduce the 'butter mountain', i.e., excess butter supply in Europe (created by the trade distorting Common Agricultural Policy), and thereby support butter prices. Under the scheme, national governments were empowered to distribute excess butter to needy individuals. The City of Ulm in Germany adopted a 'voucher' scheme, under which an individual filled out a coupon and gave it to a merchant in return for butter.

Mr Stauder claimed that, because the scheme adopted by the City of Ulm required him to identify himself on the coupon, this violated his rights to human dignity. He did not want to have to reveal his identity to a stranger on a coupon that indicated that he was impoverished. He challenged the Community scheme on the ground that it violated his fundamental human rights.

Under *Stork* and *Geitling*, it would have seemed that his arguments should have been rejected. Under *Stork*, he could not invoke the German Constitution. Under *Geitling*, there were no human rights protections under European Community law.

However, the court did not reject his argument (although it did not rule in his favour, either). The court examined the Commission decision under which the City of Ulm had adopted the scheme to distribute butter to the needy. It concluded that the Commission decision did not require that people identify themselves in order to get the butter.

Therefore, the court wrote:

> [I]nterpreted in this way the provision at issue [i.e., the challenged Commission decision] contains nothing capable of prejudicing the fundamental human rights enshrined in the general principles of European Community law and protected by the court.

Thus, in *Stauder* the court implicitly acknowledged that the general principles of European Community law protected 'fundamental human rights', even though it found that the Commission decision did not violate these rights. (The court often rules in this way, that is, announcing a broad principle of human rights protection, and simultaneously finding that it has not been violated.)

Why did the Court Change its Mind?

Commentators have suggested that the Court of Justice did a u-turn on the issue of human rights protection because of a potential 'constitutional' conflict with the national courts. The conflict arose because of the potential for certain national courts, particularly in countries with strong constitutional protection of human rights, such as Germany, to review European Community law against the human rights protections contained in national law. National courts might rule that a certain European Community law violated fundamental human rights protections in the national Constitutions, and refuse to give effect to that European Community law. Such a development would threaten the supremacy of European Community law, and, ultimately, might undermine the uniformity of European Community law. If this happened, the entire process of European integration might be threatened.

Thus, some have suggested that the Court of Justice developed human rights jurisprudence because of concerns over European integration, and not out of concern for human rights.

The Sources and Substance of Human Rights

Sources: The Handelsgesellschaft *and* Nold *Cases*

The terse statement in *Stauder* represented the court's 'discovery' of human rights protection in European Union law. However, the decision begged various questions. What were the sources and substance of European Union law regarding human rights?

Over a series of cases, the court has developed this area of its jurisprudence. It is now accepted that human rights protections are 'inspired' or derived from various sources. These sources include:

1. constitutional traditions common to the member states;
2. international human rights treaties to which member states are signatories or on which they have collaborated;

3. other miscellaneous international law, such as international conventions regarding working conditions; and
4. other sources, such as national non-constitutional principles concerning the attorney-client privilege.

Constitutional Traditions Common to the Member States

An early case to consider the sources of European Union law regarding human rights was Case 11/70, *Internationale Handelsgesellschaft v. Einfur-und Vorratstelle für Getreide und Futtermittel* [1970] ECR 1125. In this case, a German trader challenged a Council regulation concerning export licenses for maize. Under the regulation, the trader provided a money deposit for a license to export a certain amount of maize within a specified period of time. If the trader did not export all of the maize before the deadline, the trader lost some of the deposit. The trader lost a deposit and brought an action in German national court seeking a refund. The trader claimed that the regulation violated German national law concerning fundamental human rights. The German court made a reference to the Court of Justice

The Court of Justice rejected the argument that German national law could be used to challenge the regulation. However, it said the regulation could be evaluated using analogous human rights principles in European Community law. What were these principles and where did they come from? The court wrote that:

> [R]espect for fundamental rights forms an integral part of the general principles of European Community law protected by the Court of Justice.

Furthermore, these rights are 'inspired by the constitutional traditions common to the member states', even though they are 'ensured within the framework of the structure and objectives of the Community'. In other words, although the rights protected under national and European Community law might be identical, it is European Community law that applies, and not national law.

(In *Handelsgesellshcaft*, the Court of Justice ruled that the regulation did not violate principles of fundamental human rights, and sent the ruling back to the German national court to apply it. However, the German national court found that the regulation did violate German national law. This outcome illustrates the potential constitutional 'crisis' caused by the differing national and Union court attitudes to human rights protection.)

International Treaties Pertaining to Human Rights

The Court of Justice expressly expanded the sources of fundamental human rights protections in Case 4/73, *Nold v. Commission* [1974] ECR 491. In *Nold*, a coal wholesaler claimed, among other things, that a Commission decision violated guarantees of human rights. The decision made it more difficult for Nold to purchase coal from its usual supplier and threatened Nold's business.

The Court of Justice stated that: 'fundamental rights form an integral part of the general principles of [Community] law'. In indicating the source of these rights, the court made the now-familiar observation that: 'the court is bound to draw inspiration from constitutional traditions common to the member states'. However, the court went on to identify an additional source of rights. The court wrote that:

> [I]nternational treaties for the protection of human rights on which the member states have collaborated or of which they are signatories, can supply guidelines which should be followed within the framework of European Community law.

(*Nold* also represented a 'give with one hand, take with the other' decision. That is, although the court decided that Nold could obtain the protection of human rights protections, it found that the Commission decision did not violate these protections.)

Other International Agreements

The Court of Justice has identified other international agreements as providing guidance or inspiration in articulating human rights guarantees under European Community law. For example, in Case 149/77, *Defrenne v. Sabena* [1978] ECR 1365, the court found that the elimination of sex discrimination constituted one of the fundamental rights guaranteed under General Principles of European Community law.

In reaching this conclusion, the court referred to the European Social Charter of 18 November 1961 and Convention No. 111 of the International Labour Organisation of 25 June 1958. This approach illustrates one of the other sources of 'inspiration' for the protection of fundamental human rights under the General Principles of European Union law.

Other Sources of 'Inspiration'

In Case 155/79, *AM&S Europe Ltd v. Commission* [1982] ECR 1575, a company objected to producing documents to the Commission on the ground that these documents were covered by the attorney-client privilege. The issue was whether European Community law included the attorney-client privilege. In deciding this issue, the court wrote that:

> European Community law ... must take into account the principles and concepts common to the laws of those states.

The court concluded that the 'principles and concepts' common to the member states included: 'observance of confidentiality ... as regards certain communications between the lawyer and client'.

Thus, a type of human rights protection can arise from non-constitutional national sources, such as the doctrine of attorney-client privilege.

Substance of Human Rights Guarantees

By identifying the source of human rights guarantees under the General Principles of European Union law, we have also identified much of their substance. If the court draws 'inspiration' from the European Convention on Human Rights in forming European Union law regarding protection of human rights, then it is likely that the protections offered by the ECHR are also contained in European Union law. Also, if common constitutional traditions provide guidance in shaping European Union law, then it is likely that there are similar protections.

In some senses this is true. In Case 130/75, *Prais v. Council* [1976] ECR 3727, a woman alleged that she had been discriminated against because she was Jewish. Specifically, she complained that a competitive examination for Union employment was set on a Jewish holiday; as a result she could not sit the exam. European Community law did not expressly prohibit discrimination based on religion. However, Article 9 of the European Convention on Human Rights did prohibit religious discrimination. The Court of Justice did not dismiss the woman's complaint on the basis that European Community law did not prohibit religious discrimination. Instead, it ruled that European Community law prohibited religious discrimination (as did the Convention on Human Rights). (The court ultimately ruled against the woman, however, because she had not informed the Commission at the time she applied of her inability to sit the exam on certain religious holidays.)

Thus, *Prais* represents a case where European Union law arguably is the same as the law contained in the Convention on Human Rights. By and large, if a right can be identified under the European Convention on Human Rights, one can argue that this same right exists under European Union law as a fundamental human right. (Similarly, if one can identify common constitutional traditions, or provisions of international treaties to which member states have subscribed, then one can argue that these form part of European Union law under the General Principles of Law. In other words, the catalogue of fundamental human rights under the General Principles of Law can be derived from the sources of these rights in the court's human rights jurisprudence.)

Conflicts in Human Rights Protections – Court of Justice v. Court of Human Rights

However, cases of the Court of Justice have demonstrated that the Court of Justice does not always interpret the European Convention on Human Rights in the same way as the European Court of Human Rights. This raises the possibility that two standards of human rights protections might arise from essentially the same source. For example, in Cases 46/87 and 227/88, *Hoechst AG v. Commission* [1989] ECR 2859, the Court of Justice rejected the argument that the European Community law right of privacy applied to a business. It reached this conclusion based on its interpretation of Article 8 of the European Convention on Human Rights. However, Craig and DeBúrca point out that in a subsequent case, *Chappell*, App. No. 10461/83, Series A, No. 152A, the European Court of Human Rights suggested that the right of privacy contained in Article 8 might apply to businesses.

Also, the Court of Justice ruled in Case 374/87, *Orkem v. Commission* [1989] ECR 3283 that the right to a fair trial guaranteed in Article 6 of the European Convention on Human Rights did not guarantee a right of silence. Therefore the Court of Justice concluded there was no similar human right in European Union law. However, the European Court of Human Rights ruled to the contrary in *Funke v. France*, App. No. 10828/84, Series A, No. 256A.

Questions also arise over the manner in which the Court of Justice surveys national law and in its application of human rights principles. In Case C-13/94, *P v. S and Cornwall* [1996] ECR I-2143, the Court of Justice concluded that European Union law forbid discrimination against transsexuals, in part based on what it perceived as changing attitudes in the member states. However, in Case C-249/96, *Grant v. Southwest Trains* [1998] ECR I-621, the Court of Justice ruled that European Union law did not forbid discrimination against homosexuals. Its conclusion, again, was based in part on its perception of national attitudes. These are difficult conclusions to reconcile, and cast doubt on the court's ability to articulate and apply human rights protections.

Why Not Sign the European Convention on Human Rights?

Various EU institutions and commentators have suggested that the European Community or European Union could accede to the European Convention on Human Rights. This could avoid the possibility of inconsistent interpretations of the Articles of the Convention by the Court of Justice and the Court of Human Rights.

However, if the Union agreed to accede to the European Convention on Human Rights, this would place the European Court of Human Rights above the European Court of Justice in being the final interpreter of the Convention on Human Rights.

Not surprisingly, perhaps, the Court of Justice has concluded that it is not possible for the European Community to accede to the Convention. (At the time of its opinion, the European Union did not have legal personality.) In Opinion 2/94 on Accession by the Union to the European Convention for the

Protection of Human Rights and Fundamental Freedoms [1996] ECR I-1759, the court wrote that: 'as Community law now stands the Community has no competence to accede to the Convention'. According to the court, it would be necessary to amend the Treaties underpinning the European Union to allow the Community to accede to the Convention. No amendments to the Treaties were proposed in Amsterdam or Nice. Rather, the Union has responded to the court's pronouncements on human rights by adopting various changes to European Union law, including Treaty amendments. However, in the Draft Constitution, it is proposed that the European Union accede to the European Convention on Human Rights.

Changes to Treaties in the Area of Human Rights

Article 6(1) (ex Article F(1)) of the Treaty on European Union states that:

> The Union is founded on the principles of liberty, democracy, respect for human rights and fundamental freedoms, and the rule of law, principles which are common to the member states.

Article 6(2) (ex Article F(2)) of the Treaty on European Union states that:

> The Union shall respect fundamental rights, as guaranteed by the European Convention for the Protection of Human Rights and Fundamental Freedoms signed in Rome on 4 November 1950 and as they result from the constitutional traditions common to the member states, as general principles of European Union law.

These Treaty Articles did not create new law. Instead, they formally acknowledged the prior rulings of the Court of Justice to the same effect.

Article 7(1) of the Treaty on European Union (ex Article F.1(1)) does create new law. It states that the Council, meeting in a composition of the heads of state or government and acting by unanimity on a proposal by one-third of the member states or by the Commission and after obtaining the assent of the European Parliament, may determine the existence of a serious and persistent breach by a member state of the principles mentioned in Article 6(1). The Council, acting by a qualified majority, may suspend certain rights under the Treaty with respect to the offending member state. For the purposes of this Article, the Council acts without taking into account the vote of the representative of the government of the member state accused of the violation.

EU Charter of Fundamental Rights

The European Council met in Nice in December 2000, to consider changes to the Treaties so as to permit expansion of the European Union.

However, at the Nice summit, the Union 'proclaimed' a Charter of Fundamental Rights. The precise legal effect of this action is subject to debate. The Charter was not included in a Treaty amendment. Instead, it was adopted through a 'joint proclamation' by the Council, the European Parliament and the Commission. It does not have binding effect, in the manner of other forms of European Union law.

The Presidency Conclusions published by France at the conclusion of the summit described the Charter as 'combining in a single text the civil, political, economic and societal rights hitherto laid down in a variety of international, European or national sources'. According to the Conclusions, 'The European Council would like to see the Charter disseminated as widely as possible amongst the Union's citizens'. However, 'the question of the Charter's force will be considered later'.

It is easy to understand why certain member states may have opposed giving binding effect to the rights contained in the Charter of Fundamental Rights. Some of the rights in the Charter are civil or political rights recognised throughout the member states, such as the right to be free from torture, and the right to free expression. However, other rights are social and economic in nature, and include such things as the right to a job placement service. Not all member states would regard these rights as 'fundamental'. Member states also would disagree whether violations of such 'rights' can be properly determined by a court of law. These member states might feel these issues are best left to the political process.

Ireland (and the UK) opposed giving legal force to the rights contained in the Charter of Fundamental Rights. Ultimately, Ireland's position prevailed. Some of these rights may be incorporated formally into European Union law, in a way that they become enforceable in a national court. The Draft Constitution for Europe formally incorporates the Charter of Fundamental Rights, although the enforceability of the rights set forth therein is still open to question.

OTHER GENERAL PRINCIPLES OF EUROPEAN UNION LAW – PROPORTIONALITY, LEGITIMATE EXPECTATIONS, NON-DISCRIMINATION

Fundamental human rights attract considerable attention as a General Principle of European Union law. However, there are other important principles. Some of these have their genesis in the national law of the member states, and some seem related to principles of fundamental human rights. We will discuss briefly three of these principles: proportionality; legitimate expectations; and non-discrimination.

Proportionality

Proportionality is a legal concept that is familiar in the German national legal order. It has been adopted in European Union law as a means to test administrative or other actions of member states or Union institutions, among other things.

Generally speaking, the 'test' of proportionality involves asking the following set of questions. First, are the interests that the administrative action seeks to promote legitimate? In other words, is a proper goal being pursued? Second, do the means chosen advance the (legitimate) goal that is being pursued? Finally, are the means chosen the least restrictive available? Are these means 'proportionate' to the goal?

If the challenged measure fails one of the three tests, then it must be struck down.

In another chapter we will discuss Case 120/78, *Rewe-Zentrale AG v. Bundesmonopolverwaltung für Branntwein (Cassis de Dijon)* [1979] ECR 649. In *Cassis de Dijon*, an importer of fruit liqueur from France to Germany challenged a German law that prohibited importation of certain alcoholic drinks if they did not have a high enough alcohol content. The importer argued that this violated the guarantee of free movement of goods. The Germans sought to defend the German rule on the basis that it was necessary to fight alcoholism. They claimed that low alcoholic content drinks encouraged people to drink more and to become alcoholic.

The court rejected this argument. In terms of our proportionality criteria, the rule violated the second requirement. In other words, discouraging alcoholism is a legitimate goal, so the first requirement of proportionality is met. However, the means chosen did not rationally advance the legitimate goal. Many people dilute stronger liquor before drinking it, so prohibiting the import of low alcoholic content drinks does not fight alcoholism. Instead, the rule was seen as a means of favouring German manufacturers of fruit liqueurs, who made a drink with a stronger alcohol content.

At the opposite extreme, imagine if the death penalty were imposed for illegal parking. Discouraging illegal parking is a legitimate goal. Imposing the death penalty would definitely advance the goal. But the means chosen are not proportionate to the goal, nor are they the least restrictive.

Legitimate Expectations

The General Principle of 'legitimate expectations' covers a number of different activities. For one thing, it largely prohibits the adoption of retroactive measures. For instance, in the field of criminal law, most people intuitively understand that a person cannot be criminally punished for performing an act that was legal at the time it was performed. This would violate principles of natural justice.

A similar principle applies in European Union law, and extends to civil as well as criminal matters. However, we must distinguish between various types of retroactivity.

First, there is the situation of true retroactivity where, for example, a law is passed requiring someone to perform an act (such as paying a fee or completing a form) when that was not required at the time the act was performed.

There is also a system of quasi-retroactivity, whereby a person is granted permission to engage in certain conduct for a period of time, and that permission is withdrawn before the deadline elapses.

Both types of retroactivity may be reached by the European Union law principle of legitimate expectations.

Non-discrimination

European Union law contains a number of express prohibitions on discrimination. For example, since the Treaty of Rome, the European (Economic) Treaty has contained a prohibition against discriminating against women in rates of pay (Article 141, ex Article 119). In recent Treaty amendments, and in secondary legislation, there have been more express references to prohibitions on discrimination. For example, Article 13 (ex Article 6a), introduced by the Treaty of Amsterdam, empowers the Council to take appropriate action to combat discrimination on a wide range of grounds, including sex, racial or ethnic origin, religion or belief, disability, age or sexual orientation.

Council Directive 76/207, the so-called Equal Treatment Directive, mandates member states to implement into national law the principle of equal treatment of men and women in employment.

However, as the Court of Justice made clear in Case C-13/94, *P v. S & Cornwall* [1996] ECR I-2143, the express non-discrimination references in European Union law are the tip of the iceberg. In other words, the express prohibitions on discrimination contained in, for example, the Equal Treatment Directive, are the specific manifestation of a broader principle of non-discrimination.

What is the broader principle of non-discrimination contained in the General Principle of European Union law? Essentially, it is a requirement on member states and Union institutions not to discriminate arbitrarily against individuals on the basis of characteristics that are not relevant to their abilities. Very often, these characteristics are innate, and cannot be changed by the individual, such as race and sex.

CONCLUSION

From earlier chapters, we are aware that some of the most important legal doctrines in European Union law (e.g., direct effect, supremacy) are judicially created. It should not surprise us that the Court of Justice has been willing to announce other important judicially-created doctrines, such as fundamental human rights and proportionality. We also have seen that European Community Treaty Articles lend support to the conclusion that the court has power to announce/create these doctrines.

However, we should not lose sight of how dramatic the development of General Principles of European Union law is. With regard to fundamental human rights, it is as if the court suddenly discovered an entire US Bill of Rights-style document and incorporated it into its jurisprudence. When one considers that the Charter of Fundamental Rights is meant to be merely declaratory of existing, judge-made law, the drama is even more startling. Students may consider whether the court has been too aggressive in its discoveries.

Chapter 8

ENFORCEMENT OF EUROPEAN UNION LAW BY THE COMMISSION

INTRODUCTION – DIFFERING MEANS OF COMMUNITY ENFORCEMENT

There are various ways in which European Union law may be enforced. Thanks to the judicially-created doctrine of direct effect, an individual may enforce European Union law. For example, as a defence of a criminal or civil action, an individual might raise the law of the European Union. For instance, a defendant sued for breach of contract might raise as a defence that the contract violated European Union law. As we will see, this is the way EU competition law often is raised. See, e.g., Case 56/65, *Société Technique Miniére v. Maschinenbau Ulm GmbH* [1966] ECR 235. Or a defendant in a criminal action might claim that the national law under which he or she is being prosecuted violated European Union law. As we will see in the chapter dealing with free movement of goods, European Union law was raised as a defence by the criminal defendants in the famous case of Case 8/74, *Procureur du Roi v. Dassonville* [1974] ECR 837.

Another way that European Union law can be enforced is in an action brought by one member state against another. Article 227 (ex Article 170) provides that where a member state considers that another member state has failed to fulfil an obligation under the Treaty, it shall bring the matter before the Commission. If after three months, the Commission has not taken any action against the allegedly offending member state then the complaining member state may bring the matter before the European Court of Justice. Article 227 has been used very rarely. See Case 141/78, *France v. UK* [1979] ECR 2923.

Enforcement by the Commission

One of the primary methods for the enforcement of European Union law is an enforcement action brought by the Commission. Recall that one of the functions of the Commission is to act as 'guardian of the Treaties'. It is in this capacity that the Commission polices violation of European Union law by member states and takes steps to remedy these violations. In one sense, the Commission is the 'police officer' of the European Union.

Enforcement by the Commission has certain advantages over individual enforcement. The Commission obviously has greater resources than an individual, or even a large company. However, the Commission has discretion whether or not to prosecute violations of European Union law, and in certain instances, the Commission might choose not to pursue a violation. In that instance, an individual might have more incentive to pursue an enforcement action.

Relevant Treaty Articles – an Overview

The relevant Treaty Articles concerning Commission enforcement actions are Article 226 (ex Article 169) and Article 228 (ex Article 171). The former Article concerns the steps the Commission may take administratively to remedy a violation of European Union law. The latter Article outlines an enforcement action in the Court of Justice brought by the Commission against a member state. The Draft Constitution of Europe does not appear to substantially change the procedure as outlined below; essentially identical procedures are outlined in Article III of the Draft Constitution.

EC Treaty, Article 226

Article 226 (ex Article 169) provides that if the Commission considers that a member state has failed to fulfil an obligation under the Treaty, the Commission shall deliver a reasoned opinion on the matter after giving the member state an opportunity to submit its observations. If the state does not comply with the reasoned opinion within the period laid down by the Commission, the Commission may bring the matter before the Court of Justice.

EC Treaty, Article 228

Article 228 concerns an action brought before the Court of Justice on an alleged violation of the European Community Treaty by a member state. Prior to amendments brought about by the Treaty on European Union, Article 228 (at the time Article 171) merely provided that if the Court of Justice found that a member state had failed to fulfil an obligation under the Treaty, it could issue a declaration. The declaration would provide that: 'the state shall be required to take the necessary measures to comply with the judgment of the Court of Justice'.

Enforcement of Court's Judgment – Treaty on European Union Amendments

In other words, prior to the Treaty on European Union, the judgment of the court in an enforcement action amounted to a declaratory judgment that the member state had violated European Union law and needed to mend its ways. There was no formal method of compelling the errant member state to comply with the judgment. As we will see, Article 228 was amended by the Treaty on European Union to give some potential 'bite' to the judgment of the Court of Justice, by empowering the Commission to bring a separate action before the Court of Justice. In this action, the Commission can allege that the member state has not complied with the court's prior judgment. At the conclusion of the latter action, the court is empowered by the amended Article 228 to impose fines on the member state.

Violations of European Union Law and Defences

The enforcement of European Union law prompts the question: what constitutes a violation of European Union law? We will see that a number of acts or omissions can violate European Union law (e.g., failure to implement a directive by the deadline). These specific acts violate a general Treaty provision (Article 10, ex Article 5), which requires that member states take all steps to ensure fulfillment of European Union law and abstain from measures which could jeopardise EU objectives.

  We will also see that there are few defences to a Community enforcement action, and that, in certain instances, the Commission can continue an enforcement action even after the member state takes steps to comply with European Union law.

Enforcement Actions – Formal and Informal/Administrative and Judicial

Before focusing on the specific provisions of the relevant European Community Treaty Articles, it helps to divide the Commission's enforcement action into stages. Enforcement actions by the Commission typically have an informal and a formal stage. Furthermore, we also can consider that Commission enforcement actions are divided between administrative and judicial stages. The informal steps by the Commission to remedy a perceived violation of European Union law take place before the formal administrative steps outlined in Article 226 and the formal judicial steps outlined in Article 228.

Informal and Formal Stages

The technical nature of the relevant European Community Treaty Articles can distract from the fact that the Commission resolves many alleged infringements of the Treaty through informal means.

  The initial contact usually involves the Director General of the relevant Commission Directorate contacting a representative of the member state, usually the member state's permanent representative to the EU. In this initial informal contact, the relevant Directorate General sets out the Commission's position regarding the alleged failure of the member state to fulfil an obligation under the Treaty.

The matter may be resolved at this informal stage. Either the member state agrees to change its practices, or it convinces the Commission that a violation has not occurred.

Letter of Formal Notice

If the matter is not resolved in this early, informal stage, the Commission then sets out its position in a formal letter to the member state. This represents the start of the formal, administrative stage of the enforcement proceedings. The member state ordinarily is given several months to respond to this letter.

It should be noted that the Commission must draft the letter setting out its position with some care. The Commission may be bound by the position it takes in the letter, and not allowed to introduce new factual claims later. See, e.g., Case 51/83, *Commission v. Italy* [1984] ECR 2793. However, if factual claims were clearly laid out at the earlier, informal stage, this may remedy deficiencies in the later formal stages, such as the formal letter from the Commission or the reasoned opinion. See, e.g., Case 23/84, *Commission v. United Kingdom* [1986] ECR 3581.

The matter may be resolved at this stage of the proceedings. The member state may submit observations in which it successfully argues that it is not in violation of the Treaty (although this would seem unlikely), or it may give an undertaking to remedy the alleged violation.

If the matter is not resolved at this stage, it proceeds along the administrative stage. The next stage in the administrative enforcement proceeding is the reasoned opinion by the Commission, setting forth its views regarding the failure to fulfil an obligation under the Treaty.

Reasoned Opinion

In the reasoned opinion, the Commission sets out its theory of the violation of European Union law by the member state. The Commission may be bound by this legal theory at later stages in the enforcement proceedings, just as it may be bound by factual assertions contained in the letter of formal notice. See, e.g., Case 7/69, *Commission v. Italy* [1970] ECR 111.

At least two issues arise with respect to the reasoned opinion. The first issue is the degree of detail that must be contained in the reasoned opinion. That is, how reasoned must the reasoned opinion be? The second issue is the length of time that the member state must be given to respond to the reasoned opinion. In other words, how quickly must the member state give a response to the reasoned opinion?

Reasoning in Reasoned Opinion

If the Commission fails to state adequate reasons in its reasoned opinion, the court may annul the Commission action, or deem the subsequent action before the court inadmissible. However, the Commission's reasoning in the reasoned opinion need only set out a clear statement of the Commission's theories that the member state has violated European Union law. In Case 7/61, *Commission v. Italy* [1961] ECR 317, Italy defended an enforcement action by arguing that the Commission's reasoned opinion failed to set out sufficient reasons. The court stated:

> The opinion referred to in Article 169 [now Article 226] must be considered to contain a sufficient statement of reasons to satisfy the law when it contains – as it does in this case – a coherent statement of the reasons which led the Commission to believe that the state in question has failed to fulfil an obligation under the Treaty.

Time to Respond to a Reasoned Opinion

A member state typically has several months in which to respond to a reasoned opinion. However, the amount of time granted to a member state may be considerably shorter. In Case 74/82, *Commission v. Ireland* [1984] ECR 317, the Commission gave Ireland only five days within which to change laws that had been in effect for many years. Ireland defended on the ground that it had not been given enough time to comply. Ultimately, the court ruled against Ireland – the Commission had granted Ireland additional time to comply with the reasoned opinion and had delayed in bringing an action before the court – however the court criticised the Commission for its initial short deadline.

Of course, if the Commission has engaged in lengthy informal discussions with the member state or has granted the state considerable time to respond to the letter of formal notice, this might justify a shorter deadline to respond to a reasoned opinion.

If the member state fails to comply with the reasoned opinion within the time limits set by the Commission, then Article 226 provides that the Commission 'may bring the matter before the Court of Justice'. This marks the start of the judicial stage of the Commission enforcement action.

Action before the Court of Justice

If the Commission proves to the court's satisfaction that the member state has violated European Union law, the court gives a declaratory judgment that: 'the state shall be required to take the necessary measures to comply with the judgment of the Court of Justice'.

As noted above, before amendments brought about by the Treaty on European Union, there was no formal method of compelling a member state to comply with the judgment of the court. The most that the Commission could do would be to initiate another proceeding under Article 226 (ex Article 169) pointing to the failure to comply with the judgment of the court as being a violation of European Union law. This would require repeating the same steps that had led to the court judgment: informal contacts, formal letter of notice, reasoned opinion, culminating in another action under Article 228 (ex Article 171). Obviously, this would have been unwieldy and time-consuming.

Enforcement of Court Judgment after the Treaty on European Union – Article 228

However, as the result of the Treaty on European Union, Article 228 (ex Article 171) was amended. The amendment provided that if the Commission considered that the member state had not taken measures to comply with the judgment of the court it could take certain steps. Specifically, the Commission could, after giving the state an opportunity to submit its observations, issue a reasoned opinion specifying the points on which the state had not complied with the judgment of the Court of Justice.

If the member state failed to take the necessary steps to comply with the court's judgment within the time limit laid down by the Commission, the Commission could bring the case before the Court of Justice. In the action before the court, the Commission could specify the amount of the lump sum penalty payment it thought should be imposed by the court in the circumstances.

If the Court of Justice found that the member state had not complied with the judgment, it could impose a lump sum penalty payment on the member state.

WHAT CONSTITUTES A VIOLATION OF EUROPEAN UNION LAW?

Various acts or omissions by a member state may constitute a failure to fulfil its obligations under European Union law. However, these failures typically are framed in a particular manner.

Article 10 (ex Article 5) of the European Community Treaty provides that:

> Member states shall take all appropriate measures, whether general or particular, to ensure fulfillment of the obligations arising out of this Treaty or resulting from action taken by the institutions of the Community. They shall facilitate the achievement of the Community's tasks.

It further provides that member states: 'shall abstain from any measures which could jeopardise the attainment of the objectives of this Treaty'.

Thus, although there are a number of categories of activities that could violate European Union law (e.g., failure to implement a directive on time, failure of a court to make an Article 234 (ex Article 177) reference although required to do so), these would probably be framed as a violation of Article 10. That is, the specific violations of European Union law constitute a general failure to take all appropriate measures to ensure fulfillment of European Union law, or represent a measure that could jeopardise the attainment of Treaty objectives.

We can now consider various acts and omissions that constitute a failure to fulfil obligations under the Treaty.

Failure to Implement a Directive

A directive is a form of legislative instrument that, by its nature, requires certain action by the member state in order to implement it into the national law. Article 249 (ex Article 189) provides that a directive shall be binding, as to the result to be achieved, but shall leave to the national authorities the choice of form and method. The directive specifies the result to be achieved, and sets forth the deadline within which it is to be accomplished by the member state.

For example, Council Directive 80/987 concerned the approximation of laws of the member states relating to the protection of employees in the event of the insolvency of their employers. It provided, generally, that member states had to establish institutions that would guarantee the payment of final wages to an employee who worked for a company that went bankrupt. The directive provided that: 'member states shall bring into force laws ... necessary to comply within the directive within thirty-six months' of the notification of the directive.

Italy failed to bring into force laws necessary to comply with the directive. The Commission brought an Article 226 (ex Article 169) enforcement action against Italy. The Court of Justice ruled in Case 22/87, *Commission v. Italy* [1989] ECR 143 that Italy had failed to fulfil its obligations under European Union law, because it had failed to implement the directive on time.

This directive later became the subject of the famous Joined Cases C-6/90 and C-9/90, *Francovich v. Italy* [1991] ECR I-5357. This case helped establish the principle that a member state could be liable in damages for its failure to fulfil its obligations under European Union law. In *Francovich*, employees of a company that had gone bankrupt sought to rely on Directive 80/987 in Italian national courts to obtain payment of wages they had lost upon their employer's bankruptcy. Recall that the Court of Justice ruled that the directive did not have direct effect. However, the individuals were able to sue Italy directly for damages suffered due to their failure to fulfil its obligations under European Union law, which had been established by the earlier judgment in Case 22/87, *Commission v. Italy* [1989] ECR 143.

Failure to Implement a Directive Properly or Completely

Sometimes the failure to fulfil an obligation arises from a member state's failure to implement a directive properly or completely. It may have taken some steps to implement the directive, but these steps may be improper or incomplete.

As an example of a failure to implement a directive properly or completely, we can point to Case 14/83, *Von Colson and Kamann v. Land Nordrhein-Westfalen* [1984] ECR 1891. In that case, two women unsuccessfully applied for jobs in a German prison. They brought a sex discrimination suit in the German courts. Germany previously had adopted national laws to implement the 1976 Equal Treatment Directive, Council Directive 76/207, and the plaintiffs had relied upon this German law in bringing their claim. They succeeded in proving in national court that they had been discriminated against on the basis of their sex. However, the national law that had implemented the directive provided only for a very small amount of maximum compensation in damages, essentially the travel expenses incurred in going to the interview.

The Court of Justice, on an Article 234 (ex Article 177) reference, ruled that these damages were inadequate. It stated that although the directive allowed Germany to devise its own method of compensating people who proved a violation of the directive: 'full implementation of the directive ... does entail that sanctions be such as to guarantee real and effective judicial protection'. Germany had failed to guarantee real and effective judicial protection, and we can conclude from this opinion that Germany failed to implement the directive properly or completely.

Failure to Implement a Directive Adequately in Law of Member State

Another failure to fulfil European Union law arises from what we might describe as a failure to implement a directive adequately. This is a subtle distinction from failure to implement a directive completely. The failure to implement a directive adequately does not concern the substance of the national law adopted to implement a directive (as was the case in *Von Colson*). Instead, it concerns the type of legal steps taken by a member state to implement an EC directive into the national law.

We are familiar with the requirement that the results to be achieved in the national law must be completed within a deadline. But what steps are adequate? Is it adequate that administrative measures are adopted to implement the directive into national law? Or must some stronger measure be adopted?

The court considered this issue in Case 102/79, *Commission v. Belgium* [1980] ECR 1473. The Council issued directives with a view towards eliminating barriers to the free movement of motor vehicles. The directives did this by requiring the harmonisation of vehicle inspection requirements throughout the European Union (then known as the European Economic Community). The directives envisioned that there would be uniform inspection requirements throughout the member states. An identical certificate would be issued to a vehicle owner who passed this inspection. Member states would be required to register a vehicle if the owner produced an inspection certificate from any member state. In other words, the owner could not be required to produce a certificate from the member state in which he wanted to register the vehicle, if he could produce an inspection certificate from another member state. Clearly, this would encourage people to buy vehicles in other member states – that is, encourage the free movement of vehicles – since they would not face dual inspection requirements.

The member states faced a deadline for implementing the directive into national law. Belgium did not change its domestic laws to implement the directive. The Commission brought an enforcement action. Belgium defended on the grounds that, while it had not amended its laws, it had changed its administrative practices to implement the directive. That is, anyone who presented an inspection certificate from another member state would be allowed to register his vehicle without having to obtain a Belgium inspection certificate (even though Belgium law said a Belgium inspection certificate was required in order to register a vehicle in Belgium). Thus, the issue arose: is a change in administrative practice sufficient to implement a directive?

The Court of Justice ruled against Belgium, and concluded that Belgium had failed to fulfil an obligation under the Treaty. Belgium had not implemented the directive properly. It gave three reasons for its decision. First, administrative practices can be easily changed. Second, people might not be aware of the administrative practice. Third, producers of vehicles in other member states might not be aware of the practice, and could not promote the sale of vehicles to residents of Belgium with the argument that they need not have the vehicle inspected in Belgium. This last consideration would undermine the goal of the directives to promote free movement of vehicles.

TYPE OF 'LAW' REQUIRED TO IMPLEMENT DIRECTIVE

From *Commission v. Belgium*, we have some idea of what is not sufficient to implement a directive into national law. However, the case does not tell us affirmatively what is required to implement a directive into national law.

In Case 97/81, *Commission v. Netherlands* [1982] ECR 1791, the court provided guidance on what was required to implement a directive into the national law. In that case, the Commission brought an enforcement action against the Netherlands for failure to implement a directive that set forth certain minimum standards for surface table water. The Netherlands defended on the ground that the setting of these standards was a matter for the local authorities (we will see that this has been invoked as a defence in other enforcement actions), and that these local authorities implemented the directive through local administrative measures.

The Court of Justice rejected the Netherlands' defence, and found that it had failed to fulfil an obligation under European Union law. The court ruled that implementation of a Community directive required that the member state adopt national provisions of a binding nature. Thus, it is not enough to point to administrative measures, or to actions taken by local authorities as being adequate for implementing directives.

DEFENCES TO AN ENFORCEMENT ACTION

Member states have raised various defences against enforcement actions brought by the Commission under Article 226. Although some of these defences seem reasonable, they have not always been successful.

Implementation Depends on Local or Regional Governments

In Case 1/86, *Commission v. Belgium* [1987] ECR 2797, Belgium was in the process of adopting a federal system of government. Under the new federal system, certain powers were transferred to federal regions, and were no longer to be under the control of the central government. Some of these powers included powers necessary to implement Community directives. For example, the power to set groundwater standards was transferred to the federal regions.

The Community adopted a directive on groundwater standards. Belgium failed to implement the directive by the deadline. The Commission brought an enforcement action against Belgium. Belgium defended by arguing that it lacked central power to implement the directive into national law. These powers now rested with the federal regions.

The Court of Justice rejected Belgium's argument and found that it had failed to fulfil an obligation under European Union law. The court ruled that a member state may not point to circumstances in its internal legal system to justify a failure to implement a directive.

Other Member States are in Breach of European Union Law or Deadline too Short

It is no defence to argue that other member states are in violation of European Union law. In Case C-146/89, *Commission v. United Kingdom* [1991] ECR 3533, the Court of Justice wrote that:

> [A] member state cannot justify its failure to fulfil obligations under the Treaty by pointing to the fact that other member states have also failed, and continue to fail, to fulfil their own obligations.

Unlike other forms of international agreements, the European Community constitutes a 'new legal order' rather than a system of mutual reciprocal obligations that can be abandoned if another party fails to abide by the agreement.

A member state may not defend against an enforcement action by arguing that the deadline for implementing the directive is too short: see Case 52/75, *Commission v. Italy* [1976] ECR 277. The member state has an obligation to raise the issue of the short deadline at the earliest opportunity so as to afford the Commission the opportunity to select a longer deadline, or to negotiate an extension of the deadline with the member state.

MAY A MEMBER STATE BE LIABLE FOR THE ACTS OF NATIONAL COURTS?

It would appear that a member state may be liable for the actions of the national courts, even though these courts are independent of the control of the central government. In Case 14/83, *Von Colson and Damann v. Germany*, cited above, the Court of Justice ruled that the German national courts had an obligation under Article 10 (ex Article 5) of the European Community Treaty to interpret national law in order to provide effective judicial protection for rights created under European Union law. The European Union law at issue in that case was the Equal Treatment Directive. In theory, if the national court failed to fulfil its obligation under Article 10 to give effective judicial protection to the rights created by European Union law, this could amount to a violation of European Union law. In an enforcement action against a member state for the acts of the national courts, the member state could not defend on the ground that the national courts were independent bodies over which the central government had no authority. Recall that in *Commission v. Belgium,* cited above, the Court of Justice ruled that a member state could not rely on circumstances in its internal legal system to defend against an enforcement action.

Advocate General Warner reached this conclusion in Case 30/77, *R. v. Bouchereau* [1977] ECR 1999, in which he wrote that an enforcement action could be brought against a member state if the national court deliberately ignored or disregarded European Union law. The Commission initiated Article 226 (ex Article 169) actions against France when it claimed that the Cour de Cassation manifestly disregarded European Union law.

The Commission would be very hesitant to bring an action against a member state for the action or inaction of a national court. Practically speaking, in most instances, the national Constitution would leave the government of the member state powerless to compel the national court to change its ways. Perhaps more importantly, under the system of references from the national courts to the Court of Justice, the national courts are important institutions in ensuring the effectiveness and uniformity of European Union law. The Commission would be unlikely to undertake action that might upset the important role of the national courts.

ENFORCEMENT ACTIONS AGAINST A MEMBER STATE THAT HAS COMPLIED WITH EUROPEAN UNION LAW

What if the member state has remedied the violation of European Union law, but has not done so until after the deadline set by the Commission in the reasoned opinion? Can the Commission proceed with its enforcement action under Article 226, or will the court rule that the issue is 'moot'?

The Court of Justice has ruled that a Commission enforcement action is admissible even if the member state has remedied the violation of European Union law after the deadline set forth in the reasoned opinion.

In Case 240/86, *Commission v. Greece*, [1988] ECR 1835, the court explained its reasoning behind considering an enforcement action even if the member state has remedied the violation after the deadline in the reasoned opinion has expired. The court wrote:

> [E]ven where the default has been remedied ... an interest still subsists in pursuing the action. The interest may consist in establishing the basis for a liability which a member state may incur [in the future], by its failure to fulfil its obligations, towards those to whom rights accrue as a result of that failure.

CONCLUSION

Unlike many international agreements, the law of the European Union provides a strong mechanism for the enforcement of European Union law, including the imposition of penalties on a member state for a violation. Many other international agreements only provide for a 'name and shame' procedure, that is, the naming of members who violate the international agreement.

The European Commission acts as the 'police officer' of the European Union. It is empowered to enforce EU law, which it attempts to do informally. If informal attempts fail, however, the Commission is able to take formal steps, up to and including bringing a lawsuit against a member state in the Court of Justice. Since adoption of the Treaty on European Union, the Commission can seek, and the court can impose, fines on a member state.

The ability of the Commission to obtain sanctions against a member state is a strong indication of a system that is 'federal' or 'supranational' in character.

Chapter 9

REFERENCES FROM NATIONAL COURTS TO THE EUROPEAN COURT OF JUSTICE

DUAL ROLE OF NATIONAL COURTS

Pursuant to the doctrine of direct effect, individuals may invoke European Union law in the national courts. The national courts must fashion an effective judicial remedy for a proven violation of European Union law.

In some sense, then, national courts play a dual role. They are courts of the member states in which they are located, but they also function as courts of the European Union.

RISK OF NON-UNIFORM APPLICATION OF EUROPEAN UNION LAW

There is at least one major issue to consider when reviewing the role of national courts in the implementation of European Union law. That issue is uniformity. In other words, how does the Community ensure that national courts in the member states do not apply European Union law differently in the same factual situation?

As of the time of writing, judges from fifteen different member states are involved in the implementation of European Union law through the national courts. This will increase to up to twenty-five judges with the expansion of the Union to include new member states from central and eastern Europe. Each of these member states has its own legal system and tradition. Some member states have a common law tradition, while others operate under a civil law system. Court structures vary from member state to member state.

With such variations between the judicial systems and legal traditions of the member states, the risk of a non-uniform application of European Union law is very high. If left to their own devices, courts in different member states might reach contrary conclusions in virtually identical situations. For example, the national courts in one member state might decide that a different retirement age for women and men does not violate the Equal Treatment Directive, Council Directive 76/207. The national courts of another member state might conclude that a different retirement age for men and women does violate the Equal Treatment Directive.

If national courts of different member states applied European Union law differently, there could be a number of adverse consequences. First, as a practical matter, parties with a dispute under European Union law might seek out a national court likely to provide a favourable ruling. That practice is known as 'forum shopping'. More importantly however, a lack of uniformity in the application of European Union law would undercut the entire project of creating 'an area without internal frontiers in which the free movement of goods, persons, services and capital is ensured ...' (Article 14, ex Article 7a). Courts in some member states might interpret certain national measures (e.g., health and safety measures) as not violating EU law regarding the free movement of goods, while courts in other member states might reach an opposite conclusion. The integration project would be back to square one.

Article 234, Preliminary References and Ensuring Uniformity

Article 234 (ex Article 177) helps ensure uniformity in the application of European Union law by the national courts. Consideration of Article 234 is relatively straightforward; the language of the Article itself sets out the primary issues to be considered. This is different from other areas of European Union law (e.g., direct effect, supremacy, fundamental human rights), where the Treaty itself does not provide express guidance concerning the issues to be considered. Despite the relatively direct approach to Article 234, some observations are warranted.

In short, Article 234 provides a mechanism by which member state courts may or must refer a question on the interpretation of European Union law to the Court of Justice of the European Communities. The Court of Justice provides an answer to the question and the national court applies the law, as interpreted by the Court of Justice, to the dispute before it.

A preliminary reference is not an appeal from the national court to the Court of Justice. Typically, proceedings in the national court are held in abeyance while the Court of Justice considers the Article 234 reference from the national court. Also, the right to make a preliminary reference, in appropriate circumstances, rests with the national court, and not with the parties. The parties cannot insist upon or stipulate to a reference. The national court alone decides whether to make a reference. In Ireland, parties cannot appeal a decision by the national court to make a reference.

The Court of Justice does not render judgment in the case in which the question has been referred. Instead, the Court of Justice provides an interpretation of European Union law, and the national court applies it to render a judgment. Sometimes, the Court of Justice ruling is so specific, and makes such detailed reference to the facts of the case giving rise to the reference, that, in practical terms, it appears to be deciding the case. But it is the national court that enters judgment after applying European Union law. That is why the procedure is known as a *preliminary* ruling or a *preliminary* reference.

A large proportion of the Court of Justice's caseload is devoted to considering Article 234 references from the national courts. (This may explain why the Nice Treaty has amended the European Community Treaty to allow the Court of First Instance to accept preliminary references under Article 234.) Some of the most prominent cases in the jurisprudence of the Court of Justice arose through a reference under Article 234. For instance, Case 26/62, *Van Gend en Loos* [1963] ECR 1, which announced the doctrine of direct effect, was decided after an Article 234 reference from the Dutch national courts.

Van Gend en Loos also illustrates the importance of uniformity in application of European Union law. Imagine the effect on the internal market if some national courts ruled that Treaty Articles had direct effect and could be invoked in national courts, while other national courts decided the same Treaty Articles did not have direct effect. Article 234 is largely the reason why the Community does not face the risk of such non-uniformity.

Article 234 and Issues Posed

Article 234 provides:

> The Court of Justice shall have jurisdiction to give preliminary rulings concerning:
> (a) the interpretation of this Treaty;
> (b) the validity and interpretation of acts of the institutions of the Community and of the ECB;
> (c) the interpretation of the statutes of bodies established by an act of the Council, where those statutes so provide.
> Where such a question is raised before any court of tribunal of a member state, that court or tribunal may, if it considers that a decision on the question is necessary to enable it to give judgment, request the Court of Justice to give a ruling thereon.
> Where any such question is raised in a case pending before a court or tribunal of a member state against whose decisions there is no judicial remedy under national law, that court or tribunal shall bring the matter before the Court of Justice.

The Draft Constitution for Europe, at Article III-279, contains approximately the same language as Article 234 of the European Community Treaty, although it refers to 'the interpretation of the Constitution' and drops the reference to 'the validity and interpretation of the statutes of bodies, etc.' which had become a dead letter. Thus, the concepts of this chapter likely would apply to the corresponding provisions of the Draft Constitution.

The three paragraphs of Article 234 raise three issues that can be considered in turn. First, what issues may be referred to the Court of Justice (or, to phrase it more closely to the text of Article 234, over what issues does the court have jurisdiction)? Second, which national courts or tribunals 'may' make a reference to the Court of Justice? Third, which national courts or tribunals 'must' (or 'shall') make a reference to the Court of Justice?

Certain issues arise by implication from the express language of Article 234. The third paragraph of Article 234 says that certain courts '*shall* bring the matter before the Court of Justice'. That raises the issue of whether this command is literal, or if there might be exceptions to the seemingly mandatory requirement. (For example, would it be necessary to refer a case that was factually identical to the case of *Van Gend en Loos*?) We will consider these three issues in turn.

JURISDICTION OF COURT OF JUSTICE – WHAT MATTERS CAN BE REFERRED?

The first paragraph of Article 234 specifies what matters can be referred from the national courts, by setting out the jurisdiction of the Court of Justice on an Article 234 reference. The first sub-paragraph states that the Court of Justice shall have jurisdiction to give a preliminary ruling concerning 'the interpretation of this Treaty'. This is straightforward enough; *Van Gend en Loos* is an example of an Article 234 (ex Article 177) preliminary reference on the interpretation of the Treaty. In that case the reference concerned whether Treaty Articles were capable of producing direct effect.

The second sub-paragraph provides that the court shall have jurisdiction to give preliminary rulings on the validity and interpretation of 'acts of the institutions of the Community and of the ECB'. ECB stands for the European Central Bank and, in practical terms, does not figure prominently in the preliminary reference scheme. (The reference is dropped in the Draft Constitution.) 'Acts of the institutions of the Community' includes legislative instruments such as regulations, directives, recommendations and opinions. These play a prominent role in the court's jurisdiction under Article 234. The court can give preliminary rulings in matters involving non-binding recommendations and opinions but, in practice, most cases arising under Article 234(1)(b) involve regulations and directives.

The third sub-paragraph gives the Court of Justice jurisdiction to consider 'the interpretation of the statutes of bodies established by an act of Council'. The meaning of this provision is obscure, and not of much practical significance. (It is dropped in the Draft Constitution.)

WHICH COURTS OR TRIBUNALS MAY MAKE A REFERENCE?

Article 234 provides that 'any court or tribunal of a member state' may make a reference under Article 234 if that court or tribunal 'considers that a decision on the question is necessary to enable it to give judgment'. The question is thus posed: what is a 'court or tribunal' for the purposes of Article 234?

Court or Tribunal

The issue of what constitutes a 'court or tribunal' in turn prompts an issue that must be decided before considering the definition of these terms. The preliminary issue that arises is whether the terms 'court or tribunal' should be defined by national or by European Union law.

The Court of Justice has ruled that the definition of 'court or tribunal' is an issue for Community and not national law. It has given a broad interpretation to the phrase. This hardly is surprising given that the purpose of Article 234 is to promote uniformity in European Union law, and that purpose is served both by a Community definition of these terms and a broad definition under European Union law. (Otherwise, member states that wanted to limit the number of references to the Court of Justice might designate only a small number of judicial bodies to be courts or tribunals under national law.)

The Court of Justice of the European Communities considered the issue of what constitutes a court or tribunal in Case 61/65, *Vaasen-Goebbels* [1966] ECR 261. A Dutch social security board of some type attempted to make a reference under then EC Treaty Article 177 (now Article 234). The reference was opposed on the ground that the Dutch body that had made the reference was not a 'court or tribunal' as those terms were understood under Dutch law.

The court ruled that the fact that the body making the reference was not regarded as a court or tribunal under national law did not preclude the Dutch body from being a court or tribunal for the purposes of Article 234. The issue was one of Community, and not of national law.

Functional Definition of Court or Tribunal

The court then turned to the issue of whether, under European Union law, the referring body was a 'court or tribunal'. The court took a functional approach. That is, it based its decisions on the functions or characteristics of the body, rather than deciding the issue based on, inter alia, how the body was defined in national law. The court concluded that the body was a 'court or tribunal' capable of making an Article 234 reference. Certain functions of the Dutch body were important in concluding that it was a court or tribunal. These functions were:

1. it was established under law;
2. it exercised a judicial function; and
3. it had a judicial character.

Court or Tribunal May Include Private Body

A later, similar case is Case 246/80, *Broekmeulen v. Huisarts Registratie Commissie* [1981] ECR 2311. This case arguably extends the ruling of the *Vaasen-Goebbels* case. The *Broekmeulen* case means that, in appropriate circumstances, even private bodies may be a 'court or tribunal' for the purposes of Article 234.

In *Broekmeulen*, a Dutch body called the Appeals Committee for General Medicine sought to make a reference under then Article 177 (now Article 234). The case involved a Dutch doctor who had qualified to practice medicine in Belgium but had been refused the right to practice medicine in the Netherlands. The initial decision to refuse permission had been taken by the Registration Committee of the Royal Netherlands Society for the Promotion of Medicine. The Royal Netherlands Society was a private association. Its procedures provided that an appeal could be taken from a decision of the Registration Committee to the Appeals Committee for General Medicine.

If one did not obtain permission to practice medicine from the Royal Netherlands Society, one could not, as a practical matter, practice medicine in the Netherlands. No one had ever appealed a decision of the Appeals Committee to the ordinary courts.

The Court of Justice ruled that the Appeals Committee was a court or tribunal for the purposes of Article 177 (now Article 234) despite the fact that it was a private body. The court took a functional approach in reaching its decision. The facts that influenced the decision were that:

1. the Royal Netherlands Society existed by Government permission and benefited from government cooperation;
2. it decided matters which implicated important issues of European Union law (in this case the freedom of establishment);
3. its proceedings were adversarial in nature and legal representation was allowed; and
4. in practical terms, the decision of the Society was final, as there was no record of an appeal being taken to the ordinary courts.

Limits to Court's Interpretation of 'Court or Tribunal'

The expansive interpretation of the meaning of 'court or tribunal' is not unlimited. For example, an arbitrator deciding issues between parties pursuant to an arbitration clause in a private agreement ordinarily will not be a 'court or tribunal' capable of making an Article 234 reference to the Court of Justice. See Case 102/81, *Nordsee Deutsche Hochseefischerei GmbH* [1982] ECR 1095. In *Nordsee*, the court found, inter alia, that there were insufficient links between the parties and the Government.

Also, in order to be a 'court or tribunal' the body must be required to reach a decision; ordinarily, a body that has discretion to avoid taking a decision will not be a court or tribunal, even though its proceedings may appear quite judicial in nature. See Case 138/80, *Borker* [1980] ECR 1975. In *Borker*, an attempted reference from the Paris Bar Association was refused because the Association did not have an obligation to render a decision in the case before it.

WHAT COURTS MUST ('SHALL') MAKE A REFERENCE?

Paragraph 3 of Article 234 provides that certain courts must (or 'shall') make a reference to the Court of Justice. A court must make a reference (if a decision on European Union law is necessary to give judgment) if it is 'a court or tribunal of a member state against whose decisions there is no judicial remedy under national law'.

In Ireland, the Irish Supreme Court is a court that must make a reference, if a decision on European Union law is necessary to give judgment. However, is the Supreme Court the only court that must make a reference?

Abstract versus Concrete Interpretation of Article 234(3)

An issue arises regarding the interpretation of the phrase: 'against whose decisions there is no judicial remedy under national law'. Intuitively, we might think this phrase applies only to the highest court of a member state, such as the Irish Supreme Court. In the abstract, one can say that the Irish Supreme Court is a court against whose decisions there is no judicial remedy in Irish law.

However, in particular, concrete cases, there are instances when there are no judicial remedies against decisions of lower courts in national court systems. For example, if the Irish High Court denies leave to appeal, and the Supreme Court does not allow leave to appeal, then, in concrete terms, the High Court is a court 'against whose decisions there is no judicial remedy under national law' at least in this example. Does that mean that the High Court can, in certain circumstances, be under an obligation to make an Article 234 reference?

The answer to this question was not entirely clear. At least one commentator thought that, in such a case, the High Court was a court 'against whose decisions there is no judicial remedy under national law'. However, a recent judgment of the Court of Justice has clarified the issue. The High Court (or courts like it in other member states) is not a court against whose decisions there is no judicial remedy: see Case C-99/00, *Lyckeskog* [2002] ECR I-4839.

The language of Article 234 seems to favour the abstract interpretation of the relevant phrase from paragraph 3. The phrase speaks of *decisions*, in the plural, suggesting that paragraph 3 imposes the obligation to refer only on national courts as to which one can say there is no appeal from their *decisions*, generally.

However, the Court of Justice initially seemed to favour the concrete interpretation of paragraph 3 of Article 234. In Case 6/64, *Costa v. ENEL*, it regarded an Italian magistrate as if it were a tribunal against whose decisions there was no judicial remedy, because there was no judicial remedy in the particular case (although appeals were allowed in other cases).

A leading commentator on European Union law accepted this interpretation. Professor Arnull wrote that the third paragraph of then Article 177 applies in the UK context to:

> [A]ny court, even if not the highest court, against whose decisions there is no appeal in the instant case. Accordingly, the Court of Appeal is obliged to refer if leave to appeal to the House of Lords is not granted.

(See Arnull, 'References to the European Court' (1990) 15 *European Law Review* 375, 388.)

In Case C-99/00, *Lyckeskog* (2002) ECR I-4839, however, the Court of Justice dispelled this notion, framing the issue as:

> [W]hether a national court or tribunal whose decisions will be examined by the national Supreme Court ... only if that Supreme Court declares the appeal to be admissible is to be regarded as a court or tribunal against whose decisions there is no judicial remedy under national law ... .

The court said no, because:

> The fact that examination of the merits of such appeals is subject to a prior declaration of admissibility by the Supreme Court does not have the effect of depriving the parties of a judicial remedy.

Also, on the examination of admissibility, if an issue of EU law arises, the Supreme Court will have an obligation to refer the case to the Court of Justice.

WHAT IS THE SCOPE OF THE OBLIGATION TO REFER?

The third paragraph of Article 234 provides that if a decision on European Union law is necessary to render judgment, a court against whose decisions there is no judicial remedy under national law must ('shall') make a reference to the Court of Justice. Is this literally true? Is the obligation to refer absolute? Are there any exceptions to the obligation to refer?

Generally speaking, we can imagine three situations arising. First, the case before the national court might be exactly the same as a previous case. Secondly, the case might not be factually identical, but the Court of Justice might have ruled on the law pertaining to the case, and it might be a simple matter to apply that law to the case. Thirdly, the Court of Justice might not have addressed the legal issue involved in the case, but the answer might be perfectly clear.

Three Possibilities – Identical Previous Case, Previous Case Law, Obvious Answer

Very generally, the foregoing scenarios outline the three exceptions to the obligation to refer under the third paragraph of Article 234.

In Joined Cases 28-30/62, *Da Costa* [1963] ECR 31, the facts were virtually identical to the earlier case of *Van Gend en Loos*. The Dutch court (which, as a civil law court, was not necessarily familiar or comfortable with the common-law doctrine of precedent) made a reference to the European Court of Justice. The Dutch court asked whether it was obliged to make an Article 177 reference in light of the fact that the Court of Justice previously had decided a virtually identical case. The Court of Justice said it did not have to make a reference. It wrote:

> Although paragraph (3) of Article 177 unreservedly requires courts or tribunals of a member state against whom there is no judicial remedy under national law ... to refer to the court every question of interpretation raised by them, the authority of an interpretation under Article 177 already given by the court may deprive the obligation of its purpose and thus empty it of its substance. Such is the case especially when the question raised is materially identical with a question such has already been the subject of a preliminary ruling in a similar case.

CILFIT *and the Doctrine of* Acte Claire

In Case 238/81, *CILFIT* [1982] ECR 3415, the Court of Justice addressed the remaining two exceptions to the obligation to make a reference under paragraph 3 of then Article 177. These exceptions are:
1. when there is previous case law of the Court of Justice applicable to the dispute; and
2. when there is no previous case law, but the answer to the issue is obvious.
The Court of Justice ruled that it is not necessary to make a reference in either situation. With respect to the first situation, that is, where there is case law on point, the court wrote that the obligation to refer does not apply:

> [W]here previous decisions of the court have already dealt with the point of law in question, irrespective of the nature of the proceedings which led to those decisions, [and] even though the questions at issue are not strictly identical.

The court also ruled that, in appropriate circumstances, the national court might not have an obligation to refer even if there is no previous ruling of the Court of Justice concerning the issue. This is known as the doctrine of *acte claire*, and derives from the French judicial system. According to the court:

> The correct application of European Union law may be so obvious as to leave no scope for any reasonable doubt as to the manner in which the question raised is to be resolved.

However, with respect to the doctrine of *acte claire*, the Court of Justice laid down various conditions. These conditions are so stringent that some people would contend that they have swallowed up the exception; that is, that no national court could in good faith determine that the conditions had been met. If so, then national courts, practically speaking, remain under an obligation to refer whenever there is no previous judgment of the Court of Justice concerning the issue, even if the answer appears obvious.

Conditions Required to Satisfy Acte Claire *Doctrine*

Before a national court bound by paragraph 3 of Article 234 can conclude that it need not make a reference, it must take account of a number of factors. First, the national court must be convinced that the matter is equally obvious to the courts of the other member states and to the Court of Justice. Second, it must reach this conclusion while taking account of the characteristic features of European Union law and difficulties in its interpretation. Third, it must consider that Community legislation is drafted in several languages and conclude that the answer is obvious regardless of the official language considered. Fourth, it must take account that European Union law uses terminology that is unique to it, and that words used in the Community legal order may not have the same meaning as the identical words in national law. Fifth, the issue must be placed in the context of European Union law as a whole.

The national court must take account of all the foregoing factors. If, after doing so, it can confidently say that the correct application of European Union law is so obvious as to leave no scope for any reasonable doubt, then it does not have to make an Article 234 reference.

What would appear so obvious as to leave no scope for any reasonable doubt is that it is virtually impossible for a national court to satisfy the conditions laid down to invoke the doctrine of *acte claire*.

Acte Claire *and Other Exceptions not Applicable when European Union Law at Issue*

In Case 314/85, *Firma Foto-Frost* [1987] ECR 4199, the Court of Justice ruled that national courts do not have the power to declare acts of Community institutions invalid. (The national court may, however, reject a claim on the basis that the Community act is valid.)

In practical terms, this means that if a decision on the validity of an act of a Community institution is necessary to render a decision, the national court must make an Article 234 reference, notwithstanding the exceptions outlined above.

NATIONAL COURT STILL FREE TO MAKE A REFERENCE

If the conditions for an exception exist, this merely eliminates the obligation to make a reference under Article 234. The national court still retains the power to make an Article 234 reference, no matter how obvious the answer to the issue might appear.

The Court of Justice made this clear in *CILFIT*, cited above. The court wrote:

> [I]t must not be forgotten that in all such circumstances national courts and tribunals, including those referred to in paragraph (3) of Article 177 [now Article 234] remain entirely at liberty to bring a matter before the Court of Justice if they consider it appropriate to do so.

However, the Court of Justice does not necessarily have to give a full judgment in every reference. Under Article 104(3) of the court's Rules of Procedure, the Court of Justice can reply to a reference with a citation to an earlier ruling by the Court of Justice, if the court feels that the issue posed is identical to a question on which it previously has ruled.

WHEN WILL THE COURT OF JUSTICE REFUSE A REFERENCE?

The Court of Justice has refused to consider a reference. The court has done so when it considered that the reference posed purely a hypothetical question, and when it thought the parties had sought to contrive a 'test' case.

In Case 138/80, *Borker*, cited above, the Paris Bar sought to refer to the Court of Justice the question whether European Union law was violated by the refusal of a German court to admit a French attorney to appear before it. The Court of Justice refused to consider the reference because the Paris Bar had no power to compel the German court to admit the French attorney regardless of the answer to the question. The Court of Justice therefore regarded the question as hypothetical and refused to answer the question.

In Case 104/79, *Foglia v. Novello* [1980] ECR 745, the court refused to consider a reference in a case where the court concluded that the parties had contrived the dispute between them to contest the validity of national taxes under European Union law.

In Case C-413/99, *Baumbast v. Secretary of State for the Home Department* (2002) ECR I-7091, a US citizen, R, challenged her deportation from the UK on the grounds that it violated EU law. Before the matter was decided by the European Court of Justice, R was granted indefinite leave to remain in the UK. The UK challenged the admissibility of the Article 234 reference on the ground there was no remaining dispute. The court rejected the argument:

> [L]eave was granted under English law and the questions of the rights conferred under Community law ... [have] not been resolved definitively.

Thus, 'mootness' may not lead the court to reject a preliminary reference.

CONCLUSION

The system of preliminary references from the Irish courts (or any member state national court) to the Court of Justice is a very clever method for promoting the uniform interpretation of European Union law. The European Community Treaty is fairly straightforward on the cases in which a national court may or must make a reference, but a number of issues have arisen that have required the Court of Justice to interpret the meaning of Article 234.

We should not be surprised that, when called upon to do so, the Court of Justice has favored an interpretation of Article 234 that maximises the circumstances in which an issue of European Union law will be referred to it for interpretation. Students must keep in mind, however, the rare possibility that the Court of Justice will refuse to entertain an Article 234 reference.

Chapter 10
LEGAL CHALLENGES TO ACTS OF COMMUNITY INSTITUTIONS

INTRODUCTION

Any system of governance that claims to be based on the rule of law must provide some method by which affected parties (or stakeholders) may challenge the acts of the institutions established by the system. This also is a feature of any system that claims to be 'constitutional' in nature. Typically, especially in a constitutional system, this challenge is mounted through the courts of the system. Although certain governmental institutions are less susceptible to direct challenge than others – for instance, the Supreme Court of Ireland – the fact that these less-susceptible institutions are embedded within a system of governance that includes checks and balances between institutions insulates them somewhat from criticisms such as a lack of democratic legitimacy. In part, the lack of a means for challenging acts of certain international organisations – such as the World Trade Organisation, a body whose decisions are largely immune from direct challenge by some affected stakeholders – has fuelled criticism of the WTO and generated support for the international 'anti-globalisation' movement.

Does the European Union provide a means by which the acts of institutions of the European Union may be challenged? The short answer is yes. Article 230 (ex Article 173) and Article 232 (ex Article 175) provide a means by which actions (or inactions) of the institutions of the European Union can be challenged in the Court of Justice of the European Communities. Hence, one can argue that the European Union passes this test of the 'legitimacy' of its claim to be a (constitutional) system based upon the rule of law.

However, we shall see that not all 'stakeholders' are created equal in the scheme by which acts of institutions may be challenged. There are, at present, at least three 'tiers' into which we must assign those who would seek to challenge acts of Community/Union institutions. (The Draft Constitution changes this, but not much else, in this area of EU law.)

Those who wish to challenge such acts can be classified as:
1. privileged;
2. quasi-privileged; and
3. non-privileged.

The privileged class of challengers comprises member states and the institutions of the European Union. They have an automatic right to bring an action in the Court of Justice of the European Communities seeking to challenge an act of an institution. In other words, they have 'standing' or, in more formal terms, they satisfy the 'locus standi' requirements for bringing such an action in the Court of Justice.

The quasi-privileged class previously comprised the European Parliament and the European Central Bank. The Treaties originally did not provide for challenges by these institutions to the acts of other institutions. The Court of Justice ruled that they could make challenges to protect their own interests, however, and the Treaty Article subsequently was amended (in the Treaty on European Union) to allow for this. The Nice Treaty amends the Treaty Article further, to provide the European Parliament with the same 'standing' as the other 'privileged' institutions of the European Union.

The non-privileged class comprises everybody else, and includes 'natural persons', that is, you and me. It also includes private companies which, technically, are 'legal persons'. We will see that individuals (you and me and companies) have very limited 'standing' in the Court of Justice to bring a legal action challenging an act of an institution of the European Union. The relevant Treaty Article has been interpreted in such a way as to make it extremely difficult for an individual to satisfy the requirements of 'locus standi'. By and large, individuals never leave the starting gate, that is, never satisfy the preliminary requirements for bringing an action before the Court of Justice.

Although we will spend considerable time talking about the requirements of 'locus standi', it is important to remember that this is not the only requirement that must be satisfied in order to successfully challenge an act of a Community institution. That is, one may have 'standing' to bring a case, but still lose the case. In order to prevail in a legal action, it is necessary to show:
1. that the act that is being challenged is one that is open to challenge under Community law; and
2. that there is a proper basis for the challenge, that is, that one of the grounds for challenging an act has been satisfied.

We will address the foregoing issues in the order in which they appear in the relevant Treaty Articles. We will focus primarily on Article 230 (ex Article 173). Many of the issues in the context of Article 230 are relevant to Article 232 (ex Article 175), e.g., standing and acts that can be challenged. (Article 232 is the less-frequently used Article, for challenges to failure to act by an institution.)

RELEVANT TREATY ARTICLES

Article 230 (ex Article 173) is the most relevant to our discussion. It consists of five paragraphs, which are quoted below:

Article 230 [judicial review of EC acts]

The Court of Justice shall review the legality of acts adopted jointly by the European Parliament and the Council, of acts of the Council, of the Commission and of the ECB, other than recommendations and opinions, and of acts of the European Parliament intended to produce legal effects vis-à-vis third parties.

It shall for this purpose have jurisdiction in actions brought by a member state, the European Parliament, the Council or the Commission on grounds of lack of competence, infringement of an essential procedural requirement, infringement of this Treaty or of any rule of law relating to its application, or misuse of powers.

The Court of Justice shall have jurisdiction under the same conditions in actions brought by the Court of Auditors and by the ECB for the purposes of protecting their prerogatives.

Any natural or legal person may, under the same conditions, institute proceedings against a decision addressed to that person or against a decision which, although in the form of a regulation or a decision addressed to another person, is of direct and individual concern to the former.

The proceedings provided for in this Article shall be instituted within two months of the publication of the measure, or of its notification to the plaintiff, or, in the absence thereof, of the day on which it came to the knowledge of the latter, as the case may be.

These five paragraphs essentially concern themselves with the following issues (in the following order):
1. the acts that can be challenged;
2. the bases that can be asserted in support of the challenge;
3. who can bring the challenge; and
4. the time within which the challenge can be brought.

We will consider each of these issues in turn.

. THE ACTS THAT CAN BE CHALLENGED

In order to legally challenge an act of a Community institution, the act must be of a type that can be challenged under Article 230. The first paragraph of Article 230 addresses this issue.

The first paragraph of Article 230 specifies that certain 'acts' can be challenged, such as 'acts adopted jointly by the European Parliament and the Council', 'acts of the Council', and acts of 'the Commission and of the ECB'.

The paragraph expressly states that recommendations and opinions cannot be challenged.

The paragraph also specifies expressly that another type of 'act' can be challenged: 'acts of the European Parliament intended to produce legal effects vis-à-vis third parties'. (This language remains unchanged in the Draft Constitution.)

The language of this paragraph (apart from the reference to acts of the European Parliament), is evocative of the language of Article 249 (ex Article 189) specifying the types of legislation that can be adopted. Recall that Article 249 provides, in the relevant part:

> [T]he European Parliament acting jointly with the Council, the Council and the Commission shall make regulations and issue directives, take decisions, make recommendations or deliver opinions.

This might suggest that the 'acts' referred to in the first part of the first paragraph of Article 230, that is, the acts that can be challenged in the Court of Justice, are limited to the types of legislation specified in Article 249 (with the exception of recommendations and opinions, which are expressly excluded from challenge in Article 230).

So the first question is: are the type of 'acts' that can be challenged under Article 230 limited to the types of legislation listed in Article 249 (except for recommendations and opinions)?

The answer is no. In several cases, the Court of Justice has defined 'acts' capable of being challenged under Article 230 as being broader than the legislation listed in Article 249.

For example, in Case 22/70, *Commission v. Council (the ERTA case)* [1971] ECR 263, the Commission brought an action against the Council challenging an 'act' of the Council. The 'act' was not a regulation or a directive or a decision. Instead, the 'act' was an agreement between the Council and the member states regarding a common position to be taken in negotiations with the United Nations Economic Commission for Europe. These negotiations concerned working conditions for work crews of vehicles engaged in international road transport, which was known by its acronym, ERTA.

The Commission complained that it had not played its proper role in the discussions leading to the agreement between the member states and the Council as to the position to be taken in these negotiations with the UN.

The Council argued, firstly, that the 'act' was not the type that could be challenged under Article 230 (ex Article 173). It sought to win the case on this point. It argued that, because Article 230 excluded recommendations and opinions, this implied that only legislation of the type specified in Article 249 (ex Article 189) could be subject to a challenge under Article 230.

The court disagreed. According to the court it was illogical to conclude that the exclusion of 'recommendations and opinions' implied that only the other types of legislative instruments listed in Article 249 were open to challenge:

> Since the only matters excluded from the scope of the action for annulment open to
> the member states and the institutions are 'recommendations and opinions' – which
> by the final paragraph of Article 189 [now Article 249] are declared to have no
> binding force – Article 173 [now Article 230] treats as acts open to review by the
> court all measures adopted by the institutions which are intended to have legal force.

In other words, the court reasoned differently than the Council. The court
noted that recommendations and opinions, according to Article 249 'shall
have no binding force'. It reasoned from this observation that any action
which produced a binding legal force would therefore be capable of
challenge. The Council could take other actions, or adopt other 'acts', that
were capable of producing binding legal force. These 'acts' could be
challenged under Article 230. According to the court:

> An action for annulment must therefore be available in the case of all measures
> adopted by the institutions, whatever their nature or form, which are intended to
> have legal effects.

The court allowed the Commission to challenge the act of the Council under
Article 230.

As is often the situation with a definition of a term provided by the court,
one decision simply provokes further questions. It is clear that 'all measures ...
intended to have legal effects' are capable of being challenged under Article
230. But that leads to the question: 'What does it mean for something to have
legal effects?'

The court provided some insight into this question in Case 60/81, *IBM v.
Commission* [1981] ECR 2639 and Case C-39/93, *SFEI v. Commission* [1994]
ECR I-2681.

In *IBM v. Commission*, the multi-national corporation International
Business Machines (IBM) brought an action under Article 230 (ex Article
173). It asked the court to annul an 'act' of the Commission. The 'act' in
question was a letter from the Commission to IBM. The letter informed IBM
that the Commission had initiated an investigation against IBM and would
soon be issuing a decision concerning an alleged infringement of EC Treaty
Article 82 (ex Article 86). (This involves the competition law of the European
Union; the Commission was going to commence an investigation that could
result in a decision finding that IBM had violated this law.) The Commission
included with this letter a Statement of Objections, to which IBM was
required to respond.

IBM argued that the initiation of a procedure under Article 82 together with
the Statement of Objections was an 'act' capable of challenge under Article 230.

The court had to decide whether an 'act' capable of being challenged was
involved. It gave the following definition (emphasis added):

> In order to ascertain whether the measures in question are acts within the meaning of Article 173 it is necessary ... to look to their substance. [A]ny measure the legal effects of which are binding on, and capable of affecting the interests of, the applicant *by bringing about a distinct change in his legal position* is an act or decision which may be the subject of an action under Article 173 (now Article 230) for a declaration that it is void. [T]he form in which such acts or decisions are cast is, in principle, immaterial as regards the question whether they are open to challenge under that Article.

This definition adds to the previous definitions by specifying that the 'act' in question must bring about a distinct change in the legal position of the one challenging the act.

So how did IBM fare? Did the 'act' in question (the letter and Statement of Objections) bring about a distinct change in IBM's legal position, so as to be capable of being challenged under Article 230?

The court's answer was no. The reason was that the letter and the Statement were only the preliminary steps in proceedings that might ultimately lead to sanctions (such as fines) being imposed against IBM, and that any deficiencies in these preliminary Commission proceedings (of which, according to IBM, there were many), could be raised later to challenge the ultimate decision.

According to the court, the provisional or preliminary nature of the conduct meant it was not an 'act' capable of challenge:

> In the case of acts ... adopted by a procedure involving several stages ... an act is open for review only if it is a measure definitively laying down the position of the Commission or the Council on the conclusion of the procedure, and not a provisional measure intended to pave the way for the final decision.

The court rejected IBM's arguments that the 'acts', in particular the Statement of Objections, brought about the required 'distinct change' in legal position required under the definition provided by the court.

The court wrote that the conduct at issue did not compel IBM to change any of its behaviour:

> A Statement of Objections does not compel the undertaking concerned to alter or reconsider its marketing practices and it does not have the effect of depriving it of the protection hitherto available to it against the application of a fine ... Whilst a Statement of Objections may have the effect of showing the undertaking in question it is incurring a real risk of being fined by the Commission, that is merely a consequence of fact, and not a legal consequence which the Statement of Objections is intended to produce.

The court left open the slight possibility that in 'exceptional circumstances', a judicial review at an early stage of a Commission proceeding might be justified, 'where the measures concerned lack even the appearance of legality'. However, IBM had failed to make this case.

Thus, the commencement of an investigative procedure by the Commission that could lead to a fine does not amount to an 'act' capable of being challenged under Article 230, because it does not bring about the distinct change in legal position required to constitute a legal effect.

What about a decision by the Commission not to commence an investigation? Is that an 'act' capable of being challenged under Article 230?

The court answered this question in Case C-39/93, *SFEI v. Commission* [1994] ECR I-2681. The answer was yes.

SFEI wrote to the Commission complaining of anti-competitive behaviour by the French Government and one of SFEI's competitors. The Commission wrote to SFEI stating that it did not intend to commence an investigation of this complaint. SFEI brought an action in the Court of Justice seeking to challenge this 'act' of the Commission, that is, to annul the decision contained in the Commission's letter not to proceed with an investigation.

The Commission cited the earlier decision in the *IBM* case. It argued that its letter was merely a preliminary step and not the final step of an investigative procedure, and therefore was not an act capable of being challenged. The Court of First Instance accepted this argument, and dismissed SFEI's case. SFEI appealed to the Court of Justice.

The Court of Justice disagreed with the Court of First Instance, and ruled in favour of SFEI on this point. It concluded that the letter terminating the investigation was different to the letter in *IBM*.

According to the court the decision not to take action is fundamentally different from a decision to start an investigation:

> A decision to close the file on a complaint cannot be described as preliminary or preparatory. The decision to close the file on a complaint is the final step in the procedure. It cannot be followed by any other decision amenable to annulment proceedings.

> An institution empowered to find that there has been an infringement and to inflict a sanction in respect of it and to which private persons may make complaint, as is the case with the Commission in the field of competition, necessarily adopts a measure producing legal effects when it terminates an investigation initiated upon a complaint by such a person.

Therefore, under the circumstances pertaining in this case, a letter terminating an investigation of wrongdoing was an 'act' capable of challenge under Article 230.

What About Acts of Parliament?

Originally, the Treaties did not provide for a challenge to 'acts' of the European Parliament. This may have been because, initially, the powers of the European Parliament were so limited that there was no real need to provide for a legal challenge to acts of the European Parliament. However, in one case concerning the distribution of funds by the European Parliament to European political parties for election purposes, Case 294/83, *'Les Verts' v. European Parliament* [1986] ECR 1339, the court ruled that, because the court had jurisdiction over 'acts' if they were intended to have legal effect, it also had jurisdiction over 'acts' of Parliament (so long as they were intended to have legal effects), even though the Treaty did not expressly provide for such jurisdiction.

The court ruled that the European Parliament's decision concerning distribution of election funds was an 'act' intended to produce legal effects, and, therefore, that this act was capable of being challenged under Article 230 (ex Article 173).

Article 230 (ex Article 173) was amended by the Treaty of European Union (Maastricht Treaty), to expressly provide that: 'acts of Parliament intended to produce legal effects vis-à-vis third parties' could be challenged.

What are the Grounds for a Challenge?

The second paragraph of Article 230 sets forth the grounds that can be asserted to challenge an 'act' of a Community institution (assuming the 'act' is one that is open to challenge).

The grounds for challenging an act of a Community institution are:
1. lack of competence;
2. infringement of an essential procedural requirement;
3. infringement of the Treaty or of any rule of law relating to its application; or
4. misuse of powers.

Who Can Bring a Challenge?

The question of who has 'standing' or 'locus standi' in the Court of Justice to challenge an 'act' of a Community institution can be very complicated, especially when an individual seeks to bring a challenge.

Recall that we can divide potential challengers into three categories: privileged, quasi-privileged and non-privileged.

The Privileged

The privileged category expressly includes a member state, the European Parliament (thanks to amendments contained in the Nice Treaty), the Council and the Commission. The Court of Justice has automatic jurisdiction to hear actions brought by these parties, so long as the 'act' they are challenging is one capable of being challenged.

The Quasi-privileged

Originally, the court did not have jurisdiction to hear actions brought by the European Parliament (or by the European Central Bank or the Court of Auditors, for that matter). The court rejected suggestions by Parliament that it should have the same standing as member states and institutions of the European Union: see Case 302/87, *European Parliament v. Council* [1988] ECR 5615.

However, the Court of Justice eventually ruled that Parliament did have a limited form of standing. Specifically, in Case C-70/88, *European Parliament v. Council* [1990] ECR I-2041, the court ruled that the European Parliament had standing to challenge an act of a Community institution in order to defend its prerogatives.

The Treaty on European Union expressly amended the EC Treaty to reflect this court ruling, and also to provide the same standing for the European Central Bank and the Court of Auditors. The Nice Treaty drops this requirement for Parliament and makes the European Parliament another 'privileged' party. The Draft Constitution adds the Committee of the Regions as a party that can bring a challenge for the purpose of protecting its prerogatives (Draft Constitution, Article III–270).

The Non-privileged

The most contentious category of potential parties wishing to legally challenge an act of a Community action in the Court of Justice is also potentially the largest category. This category is that of natural or legal persons. This category includes individuals and private companies.

It is important to distinguish an action in the Court of Justice of the European Communities from other ways in which an act of a Community institution may be challenged. Due to the doctrine of 'direct effect', many acts of Community institutions can be challenged in the national courts of the member states. For example, if a state implements a directive into national law, and an individual believes the law, as implemented, violates some other principal of law (for instance, human rights), the individual can assert a claim in the national courts to test this proposition. The national court may (or must, if it is the court of last resort and other conditions are satisfied) refer the matter to the European Court of Justice. The Court of Justice would then be in a position to consider the challenge by an individual to the member state law implementing the directive and, potentially, consider the challenge by the individual to the directive itself.

In this type of challenge, the Court of Justice has been quite liberal – first, in establishing the judicially-created doctrine of direct effect, and, second, in its efforts to encourage references from the national courts of the member state to the Court of Justice.

Article 230 concerns another type of challenge altogether. Under Article 230, we are considering a direct challenge by an individual to an act of a Community institution in the Court of Justice of the European Community.

Article 230 specifies three types of challenges by an individual, over which the court has jurisdiction:

1. a decision addressed to the individual;
2. a decision addressed to another individual, which is of direct and individual concern to the person seeking to make the challenge;
3. a regulation that is, in fact, a decision that is of direct and individual concern to the person seeking to make the challenge.

We can dispose of the first and third types of challenges fairly easily. Natural justice demands that an individual should have a right to bring a challenge against a decision that is addressed to that individual. It is not surprising, therefore, that Article 230 expressly provides for such a challenge.

With respect to the third type of challenge, in practice this rarely arises; however, see Case C-50/00, *Union de Peque Agricultures v. Council* [2002] [ECR-I-6677] (involving challenge by trade association to regulation reforming the common organisation of olive oil markets). A regulation may in fact be a disguised 'decision' if it affects only a small number of people, even though drafted in the form of a wide-ranging regulation. However, it would still be necessary to show that the regulation is of direct and individual concern to the individual seeking to make the challenge.

We will focus primarily on the second type of challenge. That is, how is the court's jurisdiction determined in respect of a challenge by an individual to a decision that, although addressed to another individual, is of direct and individual concern to the individual making the challenge?

In order to determine this, we must consider when a decision addressed to another individual is of 'direct and individual concern' to the person making the challenge. We will consider these issues in reverse order, as the issue of what constitutes 'individual concern' is the most controversial. But it is important when considering this area of law not to overlook the additional requirement that the decision must be of 'direct' concern to the person seeking to make the challenge.

'Individual Concern' to the Individual Making a Challenge

In several cases, the Court of Justice has considered the requirement that, in order to invoke Article 230 to challenge a decision addressed to another, an individual must show that the decision complained of is of 'individual concern' to the individual bringing the challenge. The court has provided a definition that makes it very hard for an individual to challenge a decision addressed to another.

In Case 25/62, *Plaumann v. Commission* [1963] ECR 199, the claimants sought to annul a decision of the Commission which refused to allow Germany to suspend certain customs duties applicable to mandarins and clementines from countries outside the European Union. The parties bringing the complaint were in the business of importing clementines into Germany, and clearly were not the ones to whom the decision was addressed. The issue was, could they show that the decision, although addressed to another, was of 'individual' concern (and direct concern, for that matter), in order to have standing to invoke Article 230 (ex Article 173) and challenge the decision of the Commission?

What is a 'Decision Addressed to Another Person'?

The Commission raised several arguments. Among other things, the Commission argued that because the language of Article 230 provided that one could challenge a decision 'addressed to another person', and because the decision had been addressed to Germany, which was a country and not a person, then Article 230 could not be used at all.

The court rejected the Commission's argument. The court wrote that the Article neither defines nor limits the scope of the words 'another person'. The court then stated that:

> [P]rovisions of the Treaty regarding the right of interested parties to bring an action [e.g., Article 230] must not be interpreted restrictively.

Because the Treaty was silent on this point, 'a limitation in this respect may not be presumed'.

As we shall see, the court's comments with respect to the broad interpretation of the words 'another person' seem ironic in light of the very severe limitations that the court went on to impose on the right of an individual to use Article 230 to challenge a decision addressed to another person.

Individual Concern

The clementine importers argued that the decision, although addressed to Germany, was of individual concern to them. Clearly, they would be affected by the decision to refuse Germany permission to suspend customs duties on clementines imported from outside the European Union. The importers would have to either reduce their profit margin by paying the duty themselves, or pass on the customs duties to their customers, undoubtedly resulting in lower sales and, again, a loss of profits. Was this enough to make the decision of 'individual concern' to them?

The court said no. It laid down the following test:

Persons other than those to whom a decision is addressed may only claim to be individually concerned if that decision affects them by reason of certain attributes which are peculiar to them or by reason of circumstances in which they are differentiated from all other persons by virtue of these factors which distinguishes them individually just as in the case of the person addressed [sic].

A common-sense interpretation of the tortured language of this test might lead one to conclude that the clementine importers satisfied the test. They would seem to be differentiated from all other persons (for instance, people in other lines of work), and to be affected by the decision by reason of their attributes as clementine importers. This was not good enough for the court, which wrote:

In the present case the applicant is affected by the disputed decision as an importer of clementines, that is to say, by reason of a commercial activity which may at any time be practised by any person and is not therefore such as to distinguish the applicant in relation to the contested decision as in the case of the addressee.

This test is extremely strict. The court could have developed a less strict test. It could have said that only those individuals who were clementine importers on the date the decision was taken, or only those individuals who were clementine importers on the date the lawsuit was brought, could claim to be individually concerned with the decision. This would have prevented people from trying to take advantage of the situation by 'jumping on the bandwagon' in the event the court annulled the initial decision.

Instead, the court said that because, in theory, anyone could become a clementine importer (that is, it would not be impossible for, say, a lawyer to become a clementine importer, in theory), then clementine importers generally did not satisfy the test of 'individual concern'.

Can the Test of 'Individual Concern' ever be Met?

The test of individual concern announced in *Plaumann*, cited above, seems so strict that it is hard to imagine anyone ever satisfying it. However, the court has found at least one situation where the test has been met.

In Case 11/82, *Piaraiki-Patraiki Cotton Industry v. Commission* [1985] ECR 207, some Greek cotton exporters sought to annul a decision of the European Commission which allowed France to impose quotas for a period of time on the import of Greek cotton into France. Some of the Greek cotton exporters had contracts to export cotton to France during the time the quota would be in effect, and would not be able to export this cotton because it would have exceeded the allowable quotas.

Although the decision was addressed to 'another person', in this case the country of France, the Greek cotton exporters sought to use Article 230 to challenge the decision. They argued, among other things, that they were individually concerned because, realistically speaking:

> [T]he activity of manufacturing and exporting cotton yarn of Greek origin to France presupposes an industrial and commercial organisation which cannot be created from one day to the next and never, in any case, during the short period of application of the disputed decision.

In other words, they made the common sense observation that, as the decision allowed France to impose this quota only for a limited period of time, it was unrealistic to say that anybody, in theory, could be an exporter of Greek cotton to France. Practically speaking, if someone sought to develop the expertise and obtain the resources necessary to export Greek cotton to France, this would probably take longer than the import quota would last. In light of these observations, the Greek cotton exporters argued, it was possible to conclude that they satisfied even the strict test of 'individual concern' announced in *Plaumann*.

This argument failed. The court wrote, rather unrealistically:

> Regarding the export of the same products [Greek cotton yarn] to France, this is obviously a commercial activity which can be carried out by any enterprise at any time. It follows that the disputed decision concerns the applicants in the same way as any other firm which is, actually or potentially, in an identical situation. Consequently the mere fact that they are exporters to France is not sufficient to establish that the applicants are individually concerned by the challenged decision.

However, there was a subset of claimants who, the court decided, could satisfy the test of 'individual concern'. These were exporters of Greek cotton yarn to France who had contracts for the export of cotton during the period of the quota. This was truly a 'closed' category of claimants. That is, they were distinguished by a set of characteristics that singled them out from all others – no one, in theory or otherwise, could become an exporter of Greek cotton yarn unless they had a contract requiring them to export cotton to France during the time of the quota.

According to the court, the fact they had contracts for the period in question set them apart:

> [I]t should be observed that the fact that they had concluded, before the adoption of the disputed decision, contracts which were to be performed in the months covered by the decision constitutes a de facto situation which differentiates them from any other person concerned by the decision, in that the performance of their contracts was entirely or partially prevented by the adoption of the decision.

A similar situation arose in Case 62/70, *Bock v. Commission* [1971] ECR 897. In that case, certain German importers of mushrooms sought to annul a decision of the Commission addressed to Germany that allowed Germany to exclude from Community treatment (e.g., the free movement of goods), certain Chinese mushrooms that were in free circulation in the Benelux countries. The applicants had applied for the importation of these mushrooms at the time the German government sought the decision, and thus were individually concerned with the decision, as they could be differentiated from all others (and from the general class of mushroom importers) by the fact that they had applications pending for import of mushrooms at the time of the Commission decision.

Thus, it is possible to satisfy the test of individual concern, albeit only, it appears, in the very limited circumstances described above.

Direct Concern

Recall that an individual who seeks to use Article 230 to challenge a decision addressed to another must show that the decision is of 'direct and individual' concern. That is, in addition to showing that the matter is of individual concern according to the *Plaumann* test, the individual must show that the matter is of 'direct' concern. How has the Court of Justice interpreted this requirement?

Alcan v. Commission

The court faced this issue in Case 69/69, *Alcan v. Commission* [1970] ECR 385, in which certain Belgian companies sought to annul a Commission decision which had refused a request from the Kingdom of Belgium and the Duchy of Luxembourg to relax or open a tariff quota on aluminium imported from third countries.

The Commission sought to dismiss the application on the ground that the applicant companies could not invoke Article 230 to challenge the Commission decision, because it was not addressed to them. Specifically, the Commission argued that the decision was not of 'direct' concern to them.

The court agreed and ruled in favour of the Commission. If the Commission had granted Belgium's and Luxembourg's request, this merely would have given them permission to relax quotas on aluminium; they might not have exercised this permission. According to the court:

> [C]onsequently ... the grant ... of a tariff quota carrying a reduced rate of duty in favour of the Kingdom of Belgium or the Grand Duchy of Luxembourg would not have the effect of directly concerning undertakings which might have benefited from the award thus made.

The Belgian companies responded to this argument by arguing that they were directly concerned because the decision had denied permission to Belgium and Luxembourg. Thus, there was no possibility of them benefiting from the relaxing of tariff quotas. They argued this was different to a decision granting the request of Belgium and Luxembourg.

The court rejected this argument. Because the final decision to relax quotas would rest with Belgium and Luxembourg, the applicants could not claim to be directly concerned with the decision. According to the court:

> The annulment of the decision [refusing the request to relax quotas] cannot confer on the applicants the benefits which they seek, as such benefits can result only from the opening of tariff quotas by national authorities after an authorisation granted by the Commission to the member state concerned.

Piraiki-Patraiki

The court reached the opposite conclusion in Case 11/82, *Piraiki-Patraiki* [1985] ECR 207, although at first glance the facts appear similar to those of *Alcan*. Recall that in *Piraiki*, exporters of Greek cotton yarn to France sought to challenge a decision of the Commission to allow France to impose a quota on the import of Greek cotton. The Commission sought to have the application dismissed on the ground that, as in *Alcan*, the decision merely would have allowed France to impose a quota. In other words, even though France received permission to impose a quota, it was theoretically possible (though it seems unlikely) that they could have declined to use their permission.

The court rejected the Commission's argument. The court noted that:

1. France, even before being authorised to do so, 'maintained a very restrictive system of import licences for cotton yarn of Greek origin';
2. the request to impose a quota on Greek yarn originated from the French authorities and 'aimed to persuade the Commission to authorise an import quota scheme which was more restrictive than the scheme finally allowed'.

In light of this, the court wrote:

> Under these circumstances the possibility that the French Republic would decide not to take advantage of the power granted to it by the Commission's decision was purely theoretical, because there was no doubt whatsoever that the French authorities intended to implement the decision. Therefore it must be found that the applicants were directly concerned by the disputed decision.

Bock

The court reached a similar conclusion in *Bock*, where, you will recall, a German company sought to challenge a decision by the Commission which authorised Germany to exclude from Community treatment certain mushrooms from China that were in free circulation in the Benelux countries.

The Commission argued that the application should be dismissed because the matter was not of direct concern to the applicant. The Commission argued that the decision merely authorised (and did not compel) the German government to exempt Chinese mushrooms in free circulation in the Benelux countries from Community treatment. The German government might not have exercised this authority.

The court rejected this argument, because the appropriate German authority had already informed the applicant that they would reject its application as soon as they received authorisation from the Commission.

CONCLUSION

The court has not been very liberal in judging attempts by individuals to challenge decisions addressed to a person other than the individual making the challenge. The court has given a very restrictive interpretation to the requirement that the decision must be of direct and individual concern to the individual. The court has taken a particularly narrow view of when a decision addressed to another person is of 'individual concern' to the individual making the challenge, which makes it almost impossible for an individual to bring such a challenge.

Although most of the controversial case law under this Treaty Article concerns whether an individual bringing a challenge has 'standing', a student must not lose sight of the other issues involved, particularly the grounds for bringing the challenge, which are fairly straightforward. Students should also keep in mind the other ways that an individual can challenge a decision addressed to another, such as an action in the national court which raises the European Union law at issue.

The Draft Constitution continues the requirement that, in order for an individual to challenge an act of an institution, the individual must show that the act is of direct and individual concern to him or her. The case law is likely to remain unchanged in this regard.

Chapter 11
FREE MOVEMENT OF GOODS, PART I: DUTIES, CHARGES AND TAXES

INTRODUCTION

A primary goal of the European Union is to create an internal market or an area without internal frontiers (TEU Article 2, ex Article B). In other words, an area in which the free movement of goods, persons, services and capital is ensured in accordance with the provisions of the European Community Treaty (EC Article 14, ex Article 7a). These 'four freedoms' are a cornerstone of the European integration process agreed by the member states of the European Union.

This chapter and the following two chapters are concerned primarily with the Treaty Articles that seek to ensure the free movement of goods between member states. This chapter concerns those Articles that deal with abolition of customs duties and domestic taxes that discriminate against goods imported from another member state. The subsequent chapters deal with quantitative restrictions on goods coming from another member state.

There are primarily three sets of provisions of the European Community Treaty which deal with the free movement of goods. The first set contains a prohibition on customs duties on imports and exports between member states, as well as a prohibition on charges that have the same effect as such duties. (The latter are known as charges having equivalent effect to customs duties, sometimes referred to as CEEs.) This prohibition is principally contained at Article 25 (ex Article 12).

The second prohibition prohibits the imposition of discriminatory internal taxation on goods imported from another member state. This prohibition is contained principally in Article 90 (ex Article 95).

The third prohibition prohibits quantitative restrictions on imports and exports between member states, as well as a prohibition on restrictions that have the same effect as a quantitative restriction. (The latter are known as measures having equivalent effect to quantitative restrictions, sometimes known as MEQRs.) This prohibition is contained principally in Articles 28 and 30 EC (ex Articles 30 and 36).

THE COMPLEMENTARY ROLE OF THE THREE TREATY PROVISIONS RE FREE MOVEMENT OF GOODS

It is easy to understand the complementary role of the three sets of provisions regarding the free movement of goods by thinking about the ways in which a member state might seek to avoid implementing the free movement guarantees. The provisions of the EC Treaty with which we are concerned seek to prevent member states from thwarting the free movement of goods.

Why would a member state seek to inhibit the free movement of goods, after having agreed to a system that guarantees free movement? The theory behind the creation of a market without internal frontiers is that economic resources will move to their most efficient use. This will produce a net gain of wealth for the Union and its citizens as a whole, due to such things as economies of scale (the ability to lower the unit cost of production by increasing the scale of manufacturing operations). However, a corollary of the movement of resources is that there might be economic dislocations in particular parts of the European Union. For examples, factories in one country might shut down when the goods produced by that factory can be purchased more cheaply as imports from another country. National governments may come under pressure to prevent the import of the cheaper goods from another member state, in order to preserve local jobs.

WAYS TO PREVENT THE FREE MOVEMENT OF GOODS

A simple, straightforward way to inhibit the import of a (competing) good from another member state is to impose a customs duty or tariff on the imported good at the point that it enters the country. This would increase the price of the good to consumers (as the duty would be passed on to them) and make the domestically manufactured good more attractive.

If customs duties were abolished, it might still be possible to inhibit the importation of a good. Imposing some type of inspection of the good as it crossed the border, such as an inspection to ensure that the good meets domestic safety requirements, could do this. If a charge were imposed to pay for the cost of this 'inspection' it would have the same effect as a customs duty, raising the ultimate cost of the imported good and making the domestic good look more attractive.

If all charges imposed on a good by reason of its crossing the border were abolished (customs duties or charges that have the same effect), it might still be possible to inhibit the importation of a good from another member state. Imposing a domestic tax on the imported good at the point of sale would make it more expensive than the competing domestic good. Sales of the domestic good would benefit.

If discriminatory internal taxation were abolished, it might still be possible to discourage the import of a good from another member state. A member state could impose a quantitative restriction on the number of the good that could be imported. This does not exhaust the possible means of blocking imports of competing goods. If these quantitative restrictions were abolished, a member state could impose technical requirements for the sale of the good that could be met more easily by domestic goods. (As an example, certain labeling or packaging requirements could be imposed, knowing that domestic products already meet these requirements.) The technical requirements would have an effect equivalent to the quantitative restrictions; they would limit the numbers of the good that could come into the country.

HOW THE TREATY GUARANTEES FREE MOVEMENT OF GOODS

As we will see, Article 25 (ex Article 12) deals with the first method by which a member state may attempt to inhibit the import of a competing good from another member state. Recall, this involves imposing a duty at the point an imported good enters the country. We will consider what defences member states have raised to justify imposing a customs duty, and what charges are prohibited as equivalent to a customs duty.

Article 90 (ex Article 95) deals with discriminatory internal taxation. We will review the types of taxation that are prohibited under Article 90, and the analysis used in cases to determine whether Article 90 should apply at all.

Finally, the following chapters will deal with Articles 28 and 30 (ex Articles 30 and 36). We will consider what measures are equivalent to quantitative restrictions, and what defences are available to limit the number of a good coming into a country, or to prevent a good from entering a member state at all.

Customs Duties and Charges Having an Equivalent Effect (EC Treaty, Article 25)

Article 23 (ex Article 9) states:

1. The Community shall be based upon a customs union which shall cover all trade in goods and which shall involve the prohibition between member states of customs duties on imports and exports and all charges having equivalent effect, and the adoption of a common customs tariff in their relation with third countries.
2. The provisions of Article 25 and of Chapter 2 of this Title shall apply to products originating in member states and to products coming from third countries which are in free circulation in member states.

Article 25 (ex Article 12) states that:

> [C]ustoms duties on imports and exports and charges having equivalent effect shall be prohibited between member states. This prohibition shall also apply to customs duties of a fiscal nature.

Broadly speaking, a levy or tax or financial charge on a good that is imposed at the border is a customs duty that is prohibited by Article 25. As we will see, there are some 'exceptions' (technically, not exceptions, but charges that do not amount to customs duties or CEEs, appearances to the contrary notwithstanding), and certain limited charges imposed at the border of a member state may be allowed. But first we will deal with the basic prohibition.

Article 25 Forbids Customs Duties

If a customs duty is imposed on an imported good, the purpose of the duty is irrelevant in considering whether it is forbidden under Article 25. In other words, a member state cannot attempt to defend a customs duty by arguing that the duty has a good purpose, or that the proceeds of the duty are being applied to a good cause.

It is the effect of the duty, and not the purpose of the duty that is important. If the effect of the duty or levy or financial charge is to inhibit the free movement of goods, then the court will find the charge to be a customs duty, prohibited under Article 25.

For example, in Case 7/68, *Commission v. Italy* [1968] ECR 423, the European Commission brought an enforcement action against Italy. The Commission accused Italy of violating European Community law, and, in particular, Article 25 (ex Article 12). The facts were that Italy had imposed a tax on the export of certain historical or artistic artifacts. (Recall that Article 25 prohibits customs duties on exports as well as imports.)

Italy sought to defend the case on novel grounds. It argued that Article 25 (ex Article 12) did not apply because it was intended to promote the free movement of 'goods'. Italy argued that the term 'goods' only included goods of ordinary commercial or personal use, and not national treasures such as the type at issue in the case.

The Court of Justice rejected this argument. It gave the term 'goods' the broadest possible definition (consistent with a 'teleological' or purposeful approach to promoting the creation of single market). It ruled that goods included anything that could 'be valued in money and so be the subject of a commercial transaction'. The Italian scheme applied the tax according to the value of the artifacts that were being exported. This demonstrated that these artifacts could be valued in money and therefore they were 'goods', to which the Treaty rules applied.

Purpose of the Duty is Irrelevant

The Italian government next sought to defend the tax based on its purpose. The purpose of the tax, the Italian government argued, was not to raise money. The purpose was to prevent national artistic and historical treasures from being taken out of the country.

The court rejected this defence. It stated that:

> [T]he Treaty prohibits ... any charge which, by altering the price of the article exported, has the same restrictive *effect* on the free circulation of that article as a customs duty.

Therefore, the purpose of the charge was irrelevant; the *effect* was what mattered. Since, by Italy's own admission, the intended effect of the charge was to restrict the exportation of the 'goods' in question, it fell foul of Article 25.

Italy also sought to invoke an exception to the prohibition on customs duties that was similar to an exception to the free movement of goods that was contained in what was then Article 36 (and is now Article 30). (Article 30, ex Article 36, allows certain exceptions to the prohibition on quantitative restrictions, including an exception for the purpose of preserving national treasures of artistic value.) The court rejected this argument. It held that if Italy wished to prohibit the export of such artifacts – that is, impose a total quantitative restriction on the goods – it would have to proceed under Articles 28 and 30 (ex Articles 30 and 36).

Another case that considered whether the purpose of the customs duty could save what would otherwise violate Article 25 was Cases 2 and 3/69, *Social fonds voor de Diamantoarbeiders v. SA Ch Brachfeld & Sons* [1969] ECR 211. (This case often is referred to as the *Belgium diamond importers* case.)

In this case, importers of diamonds into Belgium were charged a levy equal to a small percentage of the value of the diamonds they were importing. The levy was used to fund a social security fund for Belgian workers in the diamond industry. An importer challenged this levy as a violation of Community law, and Belgium sought to defend the levy based on its good purpose.

The court rejected this defence. The court stated that 'customs duties are prohibited independently of any consideration of the purpose for which they are introduced and the destination of the revenue obtained therefrom'. Instead, according to the court, the justification for the prohibition in Article 25 (ex Article 12) 'is based on the fact that any pecuniary charge – however small – imposed on goods by reason of the fact that they cross a frontier constitutes an obstacle to the movement of such goods'.

Therefore, once again, it is the effect of the charge, and not its purpose, that is important in determining whether it violates Article 25 (ex Article 12).

WHAT IS A CHARGE EQUIVALENT TO A CUSTOMS DUTY?

In the previous section, we saw that a customs duty was prohibited regardless of its purpose. The court, however, did not provide a clear definition of a customs duty. Instead, it implicitly adopted a 'we know it when we see it' attitude in the cases we discussed, assuming *sub silentio* that the charge at issue amounted to a customs duty.

But what is a charge equivalent to a customs duty? Under Article 25 (ex Article 12) this type of charge is also prohibited.

Not surprisingly, the court has given a very broad definition to what constitutes a charge having an effect that is equivalent to a customs duty. For example, in Case 24/68, *Commission v. Italy* [1969] ECR 193, the Commission brought an enforcement action against Italy. The Commission alleged that Italy had violated Community law, particularly Article 25 (ex Article 12), because it imposed a charge on all exports. In form it may not have looked like a formal customs duty; such duties typically divide goods into categories and impose different charges depending on the classification of the exported good.

Italy defended the claim by arguing that the charge was not a customs duty at all. Instead, the charge was used to pay for the compiling of statistical information. Furthermore, this statistical information was of benefit to the exporters themselves.

The court rejected this argument. It stated that:

> [A]ny pecuniary charge, however small and whatever its designation and mode of application, which is imposed unilaterally on domestic or foreign goods by reason of the fact that they cross a frontier, and which is not a customs duty in the strict sense, constitutes a charge having equivalent effect within the meaning of [the Treaty], even if it is not imposed for the benefit of the state, is not discriminatory or protective in effect and if the product on which the charge is imposed is not in competition with any domestic product.

The court thus has thrown a very wide net to catch 'any pecuniary charge' that is applied to goods 'by reason of the fact they cross a frontier' without any need to look at whether the charge benefits the state, has a discriminatory effect, or benefits any goods produced within the member state that imposes the charge.

'EXCEPTIONS' TO THE BLANKET PROHIBITION ON CUSTOMS DUTIES AND CEES

The court, at least in theory, does allow certain charges that resemble customs duties. Technically, these are not 'exceptions' to the prohibition on customs duties. Instead, these charges are not customs duties at all.

Charges are allowed, in theory, in three circumstances. A member state is allowed to charge a fee that represents the cost of a benefit that actually is bestowed on the importer. The court also allows a member state to charge a fee, if the fee is to pay for a system of inspection mandated by member state law that is applied equally to domestic producers and importers. Finally, the court allows a member state to charge a fee to pay for the cost of an inspection that is mandated by Community or international law.

The court allows these charges in theory, but, in practice, it has been very hard for member states to justify the first two types of charges. The court has demanded such a degree of precision between the benefit bestowed and the charge levied, or between the cost of the inspection and the charge levied, as to make it almost impossible for member states to comply. Only in the third area, where Community law mandates the inspection, have member states been successful.

Charges for a Benefit Bestowed on the Importer (or Exporter)

The court set forth a statement of the basic rule in Case C-16/94, *Dubois & Fils SA v. Garnor Exploitation SA* [1995] ECR I-2421. It stated that Article 25 (ex Article 12) did not apply:

> to a charge that is imposed on goods by reason of the fact that they cross a frontier if that charge constitutes consideration for a specific service actually rendered to an economic agent individually and represents a proportional payment for that service.

However, as noted above, the court has demanded such precision between the value of the service and the consideration paid as to make it impossible to invoke this 'exception'. Furthermore, the court has distinguished between a benefit to the importer (or exporter) who is being charged for the service, and a benefit for society as a whole, or for a broad class of beneficiaries. If the benefit goes to more than the individual trader, then it is a customs duty caught by Article 25.

For example, in Case 24/68, *Commission v. Italy* [1969] ECR 193, Italy imposed a levy on goods exported to other member states. It used the money raised to compile statistics about trade patterns. The Commission brought an enforcement action against Italy. It claimed that the levy was a customs duty that violated Article 25 (ex Article 12).

Italy defended the claim on the ground that the levy was not a customs duty, but rather was consideration for a service rendered. The court rejected this defence. It ruled that the benefit provided by compiling the statistics was too general, and the benefit to the individual exporter could not be individually assessed in order to determine whether the charge was accurate for the benefit enjoyed by the exporter.

Specifically, the court stated:

> [T]he statistics ... constitute a benefit so general, and so difficult to assess, that the disputed charge cannot be regarded as consideration for a specific benefit actually conferred.

Similarly, in Case 132/82, *Commission v. Belgium* [1983] ECR 1649, Belgium charged importers a levy to pay for storage charges that were incurred at a special storage facility at which goods sometimes had to be kept in connection with customs inspections. This charge was levied both on importers who actually stored goods at the facility before presenting them for clearance through customs, and for goods which were presented immediately and were not actually stored at the facility. The Commission brought an enforcement action alleging a violation of Article 25 (ex Article 12). The Commission argued that the charges amounted to a CEE.

Belgium defended this argument on the ground, among others, that the charge represented consideration for the use of the storage facility, and was not a charge equivalent to a customs duty at all.

The court reiterated the rule that charges equivalent to customs duties are prohibited, but that:

> [T]he position is different only if the charge in question is the consideration for a service actually rendered to the importer and is of an amount commensurate with that service, when the charge concerned ... is payable exclusively on imported products.

However, the court rejected Belgium's defence. The problem was that some goods were not actually stored at the facility, but were merely presented there for customs clearance. However, these importers were also charged a fee. While 'the placing of imported goods in temporary storage in the special stores of public warehouses clearly represents a service rendered to traders', for which a charge might be levied, this was not true for imported goods 'presented merely for the completion of customs formalities at a special store ...'.

Therefore the court ruled that Belgium had failed to fulfil its obligations under Article 25 (ex Article 12).

Fees Charged for Complying with Member State Requirements

In theory, if a charge is imposed on an importer (or exporter) for the inspection of a good as part of a general scheme of regulation that applies equally to a domestic producer of the same good, then the charge is not equivalent to a customs duty and is not caught by Article 25 (ex Article 12). Instead, it is part of an internal scheme of taxation, which is covered by Article 90 (ex Article 95). Note that it is not sufficient that the charge is such as to offset the cost of an inspection of imported goods necessary to protect the public health. In the latter case, the charge is a CEE prohibited by Article 25.

For example, in Case 18/87, *Commission v. Germany* [1988] ECR 5427, Germany charged a fee for the inspection of imported live animals. The Commission brought an enforcement action, claiming that the fee was a CEE. The court stated in its decision that:

> [S]uch a charge escapes classification if it relates to a general system of internal dues applied systematically and in accordance with the same criteria to domestic producers and imported products alike.

However, such a defence would not be available 'if the inspection serves to guarantee, in the public interest, the health and life of animals in international transport'. If the benefit is one to society generally, then it should be borne by the member state, and not by the importer (although one could argue that by importing live animals, the importer has occasioned the need for the inspection to protect health). Also, because the benefit accrues to society generally, one cannot argue that the fee charged is consideration for a benefit bestowed specifically on the importer.

This is illustrated in Case 87/75, *Bresciani v. Amministrazione delle Finanze* [1976] ECR 129. There, Italy imposed a charge for the compulsory inspection of imported raw cowhides. On an Article 234 (ex Article 177) reference from an Italian national court, the Court of Justice was asked whether such compulsory fees, ostensibly to pay for veterinary and health inspections for the public good, amounted to a charge having equivalent effect to a customs duty.

The court ruled that the charge was a CEE and violated Article 25 (ex Article 12). It was no defence that the charge was used to pay for a system that benefited the public generally. The court stated that:

> The activity of the administration of the state intended to maintain a public health inspection system imposed in the general interest cannot be regarded as a service rendered to the importer such as to justify the imposition of a pecuniary charge.

Instead, 'the costs ... must be met by the general public which, as a whole, benefits ...'.

Fees Charged for Inspections Mandated by Community Law

Perhaps not surprisingly, the court is slightly more forgiving when it comes to assessing levies imposed by a member state on an importer (or exporter), where the fees raised are used to pay for mandatory obligations (such as inspections) under Community law.

In Case 18/87, *Commission v. Germany* [1988] ECR 5427, the German government charged a fee to pay for the cost of inspecting live animals.

However, a Community directive required the inspection. The fee was not part of a system of internal taxation, and could not be regarded as consideration for a specific benefit to the importer, because it benefited society generally.

Nevertheless, the court ruled in favour of Germany, and decided that the fee was not equivalent to a customs duty. The court stated:

> Since the contested fee was charged in connection with inspections carried out pursuant to a Community provision, it should be noted that ... such fees may not be classified as charges having an effect equivalent to a customs duty if the following conditions are satisfied:
> (a) they do not exceed the actual costs of the inspections in connection with which they are charged;
> (b) the inspections in question are obligatory and uniform for all the products concerned in the Community;
> (c) they are prescribed by Community law in the general interest of the Community;
> (d) they promote the free movement of goods, in particular by neutralising obstacles which could arise from unilateral measures of inspection adopted in accordance with Article 36 of the Treaty.

Upon an examination of the facts, the court concluded that Germany's fee satisfied these requirements.

Fees Charged for Inspections Permitted by Community Law

A distinction must be made between charges levied to pay for the cost of inspections *mandated* by Community law, and charges levied to pay for the cost of inspections that merely are *permitted* by Community law. The former charges are not CEEs if they satisfy the requirements set forth above; the latter are CEEs unless they can satisfy the conditions for a benefit bestowed on the importer (or exporter).

In Case 314/82, *Commission v. Belgium* [1984] ECR 1543, the Commission brought an action against Belgium. The Commission argued that fees charged by Belgium for the inspection of fresh, dried, salted and smoked poultry meat imported from other member states violated Community law, in particular Article 25 (ex Article 12).

Belgium defended by pointing out that a Community directive that *mandated* public health inspections of poultry meat products in the exporting country also *permitted* a member state to carry out a health inspection in the importing country, and to prohibit the marketing of the poultry meat if it were found unfit for human consumption. It therefore argued that the levy was permissible under the rule allowing such charges to be imposed where the inspections are carried out pursuant to Community law.

The court rejected this defence. The court stated that:

[I]t is sufficient to note that [the Community directive] in no way requires member states to carry out such checks on imported meat but may at most be understood as permitting them. Since they are not checks carried out in application of [the Community directive], the directive cannot be relied upon to justify the levying of an inspection charge in respect thereof.

Fees Charged for Inspections Required by International Law

In Case 89/76, *Commission v. Netherlands* [1977] ECR 1355, the Commission brought an enforcement action against the Netherlands. The Commission claimed that fees charged by the Netherlands for the inspection of plants to be exported to other member states amounted to a charge equivalent to a customs duty, in violation of Article 25 (ex Article 12).

The Netherlands defended on the ground that the fee charged was to offset the cost of an inspection that was required under the terms of an international treaty to which the Netherlands was a party, and which concerned the export of such plants.

The court ruled in favour of the Netherlands. It reasoned that such charges were not unilateral measures adopted by the Netherlands that hindered trade, but rather were part of an operation under an international treaty designed to overcome obstacles to the free movement of such goods.

The court stated that:

[T]he fees charged for such inspections cannot be regarded as charges having an effect equivalent to customs duties, provided that their amount does not exceed the actual cost of the operations in respect of which they are charged.

Hence, the court was considerably more accommodating of obligations imposed under international agreements, than of obligations unilaterally adopted for the general welfare of the member state.

DISCRIMINATORY INTERNAL TAXATION

Introduction

At the beginning of the chapter, we pointed out that Article 25 (ex Article 12) was part of a broader scheme of Treaty Articles designed to ensure the free movement of goods. In other words, the elimination of customs duties (and charges having equivalent effect) is a necessary, but not a sufficient condition for ensuring the free movement of goods within the European Union.

If customs duties and charges having equivalent effect were eliminated, member states might still be able to protect local goods and prevent the importation of competing goods from other member states. One way that they might do this would be to impose a higher internal tax on the imported good than on a similar, domestically produced good. They might do this directly, or they might attempt to be clever and adopt a tax that appeared to be neutral with respect to the origin of the good (that is, foreign or domestically produced) but that, in application, only applied to the imported good.

Of course, there might be goods that, while not technically similar to the domestic good, were in competition with that good. An example of this would be beer and wine. If a country, like France, produced a great deal of wine, they might want to protect domestic manufacturers of wine from having to compete with beers, the vast majority of which is imported. They might increase the tax on beer in order to give wine manufacturers a competitive advantage.

Article 90 (ex Article 95) is designed to deal with each of the situations described above. Its two paragraphs provide:

> No member state shall impose, directly or indirectly, on the products of other member states any internal taxation of any kind in excess of that imposed directly or indirectly on similar domestic products.

> Furthermore, no member state shall impose on the products of other member states any internal taxation of such a nature as to afford indirect protection to other products.

Member States Free to Devise System of Internal Taxation

At the outset, it is important to note that, in the absence of harmonisation by the European Union, each member state is free to devise its own system of internal taxation. (The harmonisation of internal taxation was one of the issues discussed at the Nice Summit. The Commission sought, unsuccessfully, to extend qualified majority voting to certain aspects of internal taxation that concerned single market issues. Ireland opposed the introduction of QMV to these areas of internal taxation. Ireland believes it is very important to set its own internal taxes. It can set low corporate tax and attract foreign investment.)

The freedom of member states to devise their own system of internal taxation is subject to certain restrictions. There is no requirement that taxes must be equal between member states. Different member states are free to impose taxes at different levels for the same good. However, taxes must be non-discriminatory. That is, as a general proposition (as noted above), member states cannot charge different taxes on similar goods depending upon whether these goods are domestic or imported from another member state (so as to charge higher taxes on the imported goods). (Note that it is not prohibited to charge a lower rate of tax on imported goods; that form of discrimination – in favour of imports – is allowed under Article 90.) Furthermore, member states cannot impose higher taxes on imported goods to provide protection to domestic goods against which it competes.

As the court stated in Case C-68/96, *Grundig Italiana v. Ministero delle Finanze* [1998] ECR I-3775:

> [T]he aim of Article 90 (ex Article 95) of the Treaty is to ensure free movement of goods between member states in normal conditions of competition by the elimination of all forms of protection which result from the application of internal taxation which discriminates against products from other member states.

Articles 90 and 25 are Mutually Exclusive

It is also important to note that Articles 90 and 25 (and Article 28, for that matter) are mutually exclusive. In other words, a charge levied by a member state on a good imported from another member state is either a customs duty (or charge having an equivalent effect) or a charge levied pursuant to an internal system of taxation. The charge cannot be both a customs duty (or equivalent charge) and a tax under a general system of internal taxation.

Thus, the analysis of a charge imposed by a member state must proceed either under Article 90 or Article 25. Sometimes, it can be difficult to tell the difference between a charge levied as part of an internal tax, and a customs duty (or equivalent charge).

Article 90(1) and Direct Discrimination

The first paragraph of Article 90 forbids both direct and indirect discrimination on similar goods. At first glance, we might think it is easy to detect direct discrimination against an imported good under an internal system of taxation. Some forms of direct discrimination are likely to be blatant and easy to detect – a higher rate of tax may be charged for an imported good, for instance. Some other forms of direct discrimination, however, may be more difficult to detect.

As an overview, we should note that the prohibition on direct discrimination does not mean only that the rate of taxation must be the same. In addition, there cannot be discrimination in the manner in which the tax is calculated, nor in the way in which it is collected.

A case from Ireland illustrates how a member state can violate Article 90(1) by discriminating directly between domestic and imported goods, even if the rate of tax is the same.

In Case 55/79, *Commission v. Ireland* [1980] ECR 481, Irish law provided that domestic producers and importers of spirits, beer and wine both paid the same rate of excise duty. However, the law provided for deferment of payment by Irish domestic producers for a period of four to six weeks, while importers had to pay the excise duty on the date of importation or delivery to customs warehouse. The Commission brought an enforcement action against Ireland. It claimed that the Irish law constituted direct discrimination under a system of internal tax.

The Irish government expressed a willingness to abolish the different method of tax collection 'within the context of the harmonisation of tax legislation', that is, only if the Community adopted directives or regulations harmonising national tax legislation. However, Ireland refused to concede that, in the absence of harmonisation, its scheme violated Article 90.

The government of Ireland, represented by Nial Fennelly, who later became an Advocate General and, after that, an Irish Supreme Court Justice, argued that Article 90 (ex Article 95) only prohibited a member state from imposing on the products of other member states a rate of tax 'in excess of' that imposed on a domestic product. Ireland argued that the prohibition did not reach differences in the method of collecting the tax.

The court rejected this argument. It concluded that discrimination against importers in the way the tax was collected also violated Article 90 (ex Article 95).

It does not have to be shown that all imported goods of a certain type pay a higher rate of tax than the domestic good to establish a case of direct discrimination. Article 90(1) is violated if some imported goods have to pay a higher tax.

Another case of direct discrimination under Article 90(1) is Case 127/75, *Bobie Getränkevertrieb v. Hauptzollamt Aachen-Nord* [1966] ECR 205. Germany adopted an internal system of taxation on beer. The German system imposed different rates of tax on beer, depending on whether it was produced domestically or imported. For domestic beer, there was a 'sliding scale', i.e. the rate of tax increased depending upon the amount of beer produced by the domestic manufacturer; the more beer produced, the higher the rate (percentage) of tax. This system of taxation had been adopted, Germany maintained, in order to benefit small, domestic manufacturers of beer.

For imported beer, a flat rate of tax applied. A foreign brewer of beer paid the same rate of tax, regardless of how much beer it produced.

Not all importers of beer were charged higher tax than domestic producers. For example, a very large foreign brewer of beer probably was charged less than its German counterpart. This is because the large foreign brewer paid a flat rate of tax that was less than the rate that applied to that level of production under the sliding scale applicable to domestic brewers. However, the opposite was true of small foreign brewers. The flat rate of tax they had to pay was less than the tax paid by a domestic German brewer of the same size.

There were probably far more large brewers importing beer into Germany than small brewers. Therefore, if one took an overall view of the 'discriminatory' tax rates, it would probably be true that, overall, importers of beer to Germany benefited from the differing rates of tax. Germany argued that this meant the tax scheme did not violate Article 90(1).

The Court of Justice rejected this argument. It concluded that the tax scheme violated Article 90(1).

Of course, Germany could have remedied the problem if it had made the same tax rates available to both domestic and foreign brewers of beer. That is, if Germany had applied the flat rate of tax to both domestic and foreign brewers, there were have been no violation of Article 90(1). Similarly, if Germany applied the sliding scale to foreign brewers, this also would have remedied the problem under Article 90(1). (Of course, it might have created another problem, namely, how to verify the amount of beer being produced by the foreign brewer.)

A similar case of direct discrimination under Article 90(1) resulting from differing tax rates is Case C-213/96, *Outokumpu Oy* [1998] ECR I-1777. In *Oy*, the Finnish government charged a different rate of excise duty on domestically produced electricity depending on the method of its production. Foreign-produced electricity was charged a flat rate. The Finnish government sought to justify its tax scheme by arguing that it was meant to protect the environment.

The court rejected the Finnish government's argument. The court accepted that, in the absence of tax harmonisation, the Finnish government was free to charge a different rate of excise duty on electricity depending upon the way in which the electricity was produced. However, the Finnish government had to apply this same rate of tax to both domestic and imported electricity. To do otherwise would violate the prohibition of direct discrimination contained in Article 90(1), even though, as in the *Bobie* case, cited above, it could be shown that not all imported electricity was charged at a higher rate than domestic electricity.

A recent case involving various forms of directly discriminatory internal taxation in violation of Article 90(1) is Case C-68/96, *Grundig Italiana v. Ministero delle Finanze* [1998] ECR I-3775.

There were essentially three differences in the way that an internal tax was calculated for domestic goods and similar goods imported from another member state. First, the same rate of tax was applied to domestic and imported goods, but the value of the goods on which the tax was levied was calculated in a different fashion. For domestic goods, no transport or distribution costs were included in the taxable amount, whereas for goods imported from other member states, the taxable amount included the cost of delivery to the Italian border, less transport or distribution costs incurred in Italy. This difference in calculation resulted in a higher value being ascribed to the similar goods imported from another member state, and thus a higher tax being paid.

Second, domestic producers were allowed to deduct a flat rate of thirty-five per cent from the value of the good to be assessed as tax, representing the (assumed) cost of transport within Italy. Producers of goods imported from another member state were not allowed to take the thirty-five per cent deduction, but had to 'itemise' the actual costs of transport within Italy.

Third, producers of goods imported from another member state paid the tax at the point of import, while producers of domestic goods made quarterly returns at which time they paid the tax.

The court found that the differing methods of taxation violated Article 90(1), because they amounted to direct discrimination against goods imported from another member state.

Direct Discrimination in Favour of Imported Goods Allowed

We should note that Article 90(1) does not prohibit all discriminatory internal taxation between similar domestic and imported goods. Specifically, a member state is allowed to discriminate against domestic goods and in favour of similar goods imported from another member state: see Case 86/78, *Peureux v. Directeur des Services Fiscaux* [1979] ECR 897.

Finally, recall that Article 90 does not apply to goods imported from outside the European Union. It applies only to goods imported from other member states (including goods that are in 'free circulation' within the EU, although originally from outside of the EU). As the court stated in Case C-68/96, *Grundig Italiana v. Ministero delle Finanze* [1998] ECR I-3775:

> [Article 90] is intended to cover all products from member states, including products originating in non-member countries which are in free circulation in the member states.

ARTICLE 90(1) AND INDIRECT DISCRIMINATION

Article 90(1) prohibits both direct and indirect discrimination. To understand the prohibition against indirect discrimination, we must first define it.

Before defining indirect discrimination, it will help to review what constitutes direct discrimination, and what is prohibited by Article 90(1) with regard to direct discrimination.

In cases of direct discrimination, there is express reference to the origin of the goods in the internal tax system under consideration.

The discrimination may be blatant, such as an outright higher rate of internal tax for the goods imported from another member state. Or the discrimination may be more subtle, such as differing methods of calculating the value of the similar domestic goods and goods imported from other member states, or differing methods of payment for producers of domestic goods and goods imported from other member states.

It is important to remember that having a different method of taxing domestic goods and similar goods imported from another member state does not, in itself, violate the prohibition against direct discrimination contained in Article 90(1). Instead, the differing system violates Article 90(1) only if it results in a higher tax being paid by the producer of goods imported from another member state.

Advocate General Lenz made the latter point clear in Case C-68/96, *Grundig Italiana v. Ministero delle Finanze* [1998] ECR I-3775, when he stated, in considering whether differing methods of calculating tax due on domestic goods and similar goods imported from another member state violated Community law:

> [T]he provisions of Article 90 (ex Article 95) give a member state the option of applying to the imported product a system of taxation different from that to which the similar domestic product is subject, but only if the charge [or] tax on the imported product remains the same or lower than the charge applicable to the similar domestic product.

However, Article 90(1) does not only prohibit direct discrimination against goods imported from another member state. Indirect discrimination is also prohibited.

Generally speaking, indirect discrimination means that the system of taxation makes no express reference to the origin of the goods, but, in practice, a higher rate of taxation applies to the imported goods. In other words, the system is facially neutral with respect to the origin of the goods, but has a disproportionate impact on goods imported from other member states.

Article 90(1) prohibits indirect discrimination, *unless there is an objective justification for the discrimination.* We will see that it can be difficult to determine when the court will accept a justification for a facially neutral scheme that has a disproportionate impact.

Examples of Indirect Discrimination

A classic example of indirect discrimination is provided by Case 112/84, *Humblot v. Directeur des Services Fiscaux* [1985] ECR 1367. Mr Humblot sought a refund of a French road tax he had paid on a Mercedes purchased in France. Under the French road tax system, the amount of road tax paid for a car increased with the increasing horse-power of the car. The amount of tax increased gradually up to a maximum of 1100 French francs for a car with an engine rating of 16-CV. At 16-CV, the amount of tax suddenly increased to a flat rate of 5,000 French francs, that is, there was a sudden increase of more than 400 per cent on the amount of road tax due on a car purchase.

Notice that the road tax makes no reference to the origin of the car. However, Mr Humblot showed that France did not make any cars with an engine rating above 16-CV. Therefore, the higher rate of tax fell exclusively on imported cars, including cars imported from other member states.

This is an example of indirect discrimination. On the surface, the French road tax seems neutral with respect to the origin of the car, but the tax falls disproportionately heavily on imported cars.

The Commission argued that the amount of road tax could never be determined by a sliding scale that referred to the engine capacity of the car. The court rejected this argument.

However, the court did find that the French road tax was capable of violating Community law, in particular Article 90(1) and the prohibition against indirect discrimination.

The court concluded:

> Article 90 (ex Article 95) ... prohibits the charging on cars exceeding a given power rating for tax purposes of a special fixed tax the amount of which is several times the highest amount of the progressive tax payable on cars of less than the said power rating for tax purposes, where the only cars subject to the special tax are imported, in particular from other member states.

(Note that the court did not specify how great a difference in tax rates could be tolerated in the progressive tax scheme.)

Thus, wherever a system of internal taxation results, in practice, in higher tax being paid on goods imported from other member states than on similar goods produced domestically, the tax may amount to indirect discrimination, in violation of Article 90(1), even if the tax does not expressly differentiate between domestic and imported goods.

ARTICLE 90(1), INDIRECT DISCRIMINATION AND OBJECTIVE JUSTIFICATION

Note that while a system of internal tax that indirectly discriminates against goods imported from another member state may violate Article 90(1), it does not necessarily violate Article 90(1) in all circumstances. An internal tax, which indirectly discriminates against goods imported from another member state, does not violate Article 90(1) if it has an objective justification.

(Note that an internal tax that directly discriminates against a good imported from another member state always violates Article 90(1); a member state cannot attempt to justify the directly discriminatory tax by offering an objective justification.)

Objective Justification

In Case 196/85, *Commission v. France* [1987] ECR 1597, the Commission brought an enforcement action against France. The Commission claimed that by establishing a system of differential taxation for 'natural sweet wines' and liqueur wines, France had violated the prohibition against (indirectly) discriminatory internal taxation contained in Article 90(1).

The French tax scheme provided that liqueur wines and similar wines were generally subject to a certain amount of tax. However, certain such wines were taxed at a lower rate. The wines taxed at a lower rate were those whose production was 'traditional and customary'.

The Commission argued that the preferential scheme was discriminatory because although it did not differentiate expressly between domestic wines and those imported from other member states, the condition could only be fulfilled by domestically produced wines, and because the criteria 'traditional and customary' production was so subjective as to make its application inherently unfair. That is, the French authorities could claim that imported wine had not been produced by methods that were 'traditional and customary' and there would be no objective criteria to refer to in order to disprove the authorities and obtain the tax advantage.

The French defended the tax scheme on the grounds that it was intended to benefit producers of natural sweet wines in France, who typically manufacture such wines in areas characterised by low rainfall and poor soil. The difficulty of growing crops in these areas made them heavily dependent on production of natural sweet wines. Furthermore, the French argued that the criteria 'traditional and customary' production could be applied to imported goods and was not applied in a discriminatory manner.

The court ruled in favour of France. The court stated that:

> Community law does not restrict the freedom of each member state to lay down tax arrangements which differentiate between certain products, even products which are similar within the meaning of the first paragraph of Article 90 [ex Article 95], on the basis of objective criteria, such as the nature of the raw materials used or the production processes employed.

However, the court approved granting a tax advantage based on the production process only if 'such preferential systems are extended without discrimination to imported products conforming to the same conditions as the preferred domestic products'.

And what about the Commission's argument that the criteria employed – 'traditional and customary' production methods – carried with it the potential for discrimination because it was so subjective?

The court rejected the Commission's argument. It was not enough that the system had the potential for discriminatory abuse. Such abuse had to be shown in fact. The court stated that:

> [N]ational [tax] provisions which cover both domestic and imported products without distinction cannot be regarded as contrary to Community law merely because they might lend themselves to discriminatory application, unless it is proved that they are actually employed in that way.

Thus, a potentially indirectly discriminatory system of internal taxation can be justified if there is an objective justification for the differentiation in taxes imposed on similar products, so long as there is no evidence that the scheme actually has been applied in a discriminatory manner.

The issue of objective justification also arose in Case C-132/88, *Commission v. Greece* [1990] ECR I-1567. This case was very similar to *Humblot v. France*, but a different result was reached. In fact, it is difficult to reconcile the two cases. It may indicate that the court has become more willing to accept a member state's claim of objective justification at face value.

In *Commission v. Greece*, the Commission brought an enforcement action against Greece. The Commission claimed that the internal tax system for cars violated Article 90(1) and its prohibition against indirect discrimination.

In Greece, the amount of tax that had to be paid on a new car progressed according to the cylinder capacity of the car. However, the progression of the tax was not constant. The tax increased at a certain rate up to 1200 cc. The tax then increased more steeply for cars with a cylinder capacity of from 1200 to 1800 cc. Above 1800 cc the tax rose dramatically. Between 1800 and 1801 cc the tax rose by more than 50 per cent.

Greece only manufactured cars with a cylinder capacity of less than 1600 cc. The Commission claimed that the internal tax indirectly discriminated against cars imported from other member states in violation of Article 90(1).

Greece argued that there was an objective justification for the different tax rates charged for similar products (cars). It said that cars above 1800 cc were viewed as luxury items in Greece, exclusively for people with very high incomes, and thus it was legitimate to subject them to high taxation. Also, Greece had very poor roads, and it was legitimate to charge higher tax for larger cars, which did more damage to the roads.

The court ruled in favour of Greece. The court stated:

> Member states are at liberty to subject products such as cars to a system of tax which increases progressively in amount according to an objective criterion, such as cylinder capacity, provided that the system of taxation is free of any discriminatory or protective effect.

And what about the Commission's argument that the system did in fact have a discriminatory or protective effect? In appearance, the Greece tax system looked much like the French tax system that had been condemned in *Humblot*. (Advocate General Mischo had recommended in his opinion that the court find that the tax violated Article 90(1).)

The court concluded that there was no unlawful discrimination. The court suggested that:

> [A] system of taxation cannot be regarded as discriminatory solely because only imported products ... come within the most heavily taxed category.

The court found that even if the tax discouraged Italian consumers from purchasing cars with a cylinder capacity in excess of 1800 cc:

> those consumers will choose either a model in the range of cars having cylinder capacities between 1600 and 1800 cc or a model in the range of cars having cylinder capacities below 1600 cc. All the models in the first-mentioned category are of foreign manufacture. The second range includes cars of both foreign and Greek manufacture.

In other words, people discouraged from buying (imported) cars with a cylinder capacity of more than 1800 cc might still buy an imported car with a cylinder capacity of between 1600 and 1800 cc (which Greece did not manufacture) or a foreign car with a cylinder capacity of less than 1600 cc (in which range Greece did manufacture cars).

However, if we think back to the *Humblot* case, it was true there also that if people were discouraged from buying an (imported) car of more than 1800 CV, they might still choose to buy an imported car with less horsepower.

Thus, it is difficult to reconcile these cases, except to say that the *Humblot* case was a more extreme case of discrimination, and that the court may be becoming more willing to accept a member state's objective justification.

The court continues to wrestle with these issues. In Case C-421/97 *Tarantik v. Direction des Services Fiscaux de Seine-et-Marne* [1999] ECR 2313, the court once again confronted progressive tax rates for automobiles in France.

ARTICLE 90(1) AND (2) AND 'SIMILAR' GOODS

Recall that Article 90(1) prohibits discriminatory taxation between domestic goods and goods imported from other member states, if those goods are 'similar'. Article 90(2) prohibits discrimination between domestic goods and goods that are imported from other member states, even if the goods are not similar, if the effect of the tax on the imported good is such as to afford indirect protection to the domestic product.

If the court strikes down an internal tax as violating Article 90, it sometimes does not conclusively rule whether the first or second paragraph of Article 90 applies. Instead, the court rules that the system violates Article 90, either because the goods are similar and the tax amounts to direct or indirect discrimination in violation of Article 90(1), or, in the alternative, although the goods are not similar, the tax is such as to afford indirect protection to the domestic product in violation of Article 90(2).

However, the court sometimes determines whether or not two goods or products are similar, so as to decide expressly whether Article 90(1) or Article 90(2) applies. That poses the issue, how do we determine whether two products – one an imported good from another member state and the other a good produced domestically – are similar?

The court suggested in Case 27/67, *Fink-Frucht GmbH v. Haupzollamt* [1968] 223 that two goods were similar if they fell within the same tax category. However, although being in the same tax category in the member state is strong evidence that the goods are similar, the goods might be similar even if they did not fall into the same tax category. In subsequent cases, the court considered a number of factors to determine whether the goods were similar. These factors included the ways in which the goods were manufactured, the substances used in their manufacture and whether consumers would regard the goods as substitutes for each other.

ARTICLE 90(2) AND DISCRIMINATION THAT PROTECTS A DOMESTIC PRODUCT

If two products are not similar, it is still possible that a system of differential internal taxation – that is, one that imposes a higher tax on goods imported from another member state than that imposed on a good produced domestically – may violate Article 90(2). Community law will be violated if the tax is such as to afford indirect protection to the good that is produced domestically.

It can be very difficult to determine whether a discriminatory internal tax affords indirect protection to domestic products. This may explain why the court sometimes 'fudges' on the issue of whether Article 90(1) or Article 90(2) applies. Instead of conclusively ruling whether the goods are similar and proceeding only under Article 90(1) or Article 90(2), the court concludes overall that the tax scheme is discriminatory, and condemns it on the basis that it violates whichever of the two sections applies.

We can appreciate the difficulty in determining whether Article 90(2) has been violated by considering Case 170/78, *Commission v. United Kingdom* [1983] ECR 2265, known as the *United Kingdom (Beer and Wine)* case. In that case, the Commission brought an action against the UK. It claimed that the UK had set taxes on wine so high as to afford indirect protection to beer. Of course, the UK manufactured a great amount of beer and little wine.

The court concluded that beer and wine were not similar. That meant that Article 90(1) did not apply to the case. The court then had to consider whether the internal tax scheme violated Article 90(2), by affording indirect protection to beer.

A number of issues immediately posed themselves. The first concerned the simple issue of measurement. That is, how to measure whether the tax was discriminatory at all.

Do we compare the tax rate applied to the volume of the different beverages? Or do we compare the tax rate as applied to the alcoholic content of the different beverages? The measure that we choose will affect our conclusion as to the difference between the rates of tax applied to the different beverages.

Another issue concerned measuring the impact of the (discriminatory) tax. Do we compare the amount of beer consumed in the UK with the amount of all wine consumed? Do we measure this by the amount of money spent or by the volume of liquid consumed? Should we compare beer consumption with all wine consumption, or conclude that beer only competes with a certain segment of the wine market, for example, cheap wines?

After wrestling with these issues for a number of years, and requiring the parties to make additional submissions, the court concluded that the British system of taxation violated Article 90(2).

However, thereafter the court showed a marked preference for taking a 'global' or overall approach to considering whether a system of internal taxation violated Article 90.

CONCLUSION

The application of Article 25 (ex Article 12) and the prohibition against custom duties and charges having an effect equivalent to customs duties, have been relatively straight-forward. The Court of Justice has applied an 'effects' test, and has rejected defences for charges applied solely by reason of a good crossing a border. The court has regarded any charges applied at the border with suspicion, but has been more lenient when these are used to pay for an inspection mandated by EU law.

The Court of Justice has had to provide active guidance on the proper application of Article 90(1) and Article 90(2) (ex Article 95(1) and (2)), and it has not always been easy to interpret and apply the court's rulings.

The *Humblot* case and the factually-similar *Greece* case are almost impossible to distinguish, and one would be wise to follow the latter *Greece* case. Efforts to apply Article 90(2) in the *United Kingdom (Beer and Wine)* case proved so difficult that the court is likely to confine its analysis to Article 90(1), or else not precisely specify which part of Article 90 is being applied.

However, as we shall see, the court's rulings in the remaining area relevant to the free movement of goods, Articles 28 and 30 (ex Articles 30 and 36), have been as complex as anything we have encountered thus far.

Chapter 12

FREE MOVEMENT OF GOODS, PART II: QUANTITATIVE RESTRICTIONS, 'DISTINCTLY APPLICABLE' MEQRS, AND JUSTIFICATIONS

INTRODUCTION

This chapter takes a look at two Treaty Articles, Article 28 (ex Article 30) and Article 30 (ex Article 36). These Articles complement the provisions of Article 25 (ex Article 12) and Article 90 (ex Article 95), that is, the other Treaty provisions that seek to promote the free movement of goods by eliminating customs duties (or charges having equivalent effect) (Article 25) and by prohibiting discriminatory internal taxation (Article 90).

It would be easy for a member state to protect producers of domestic goods from competition with producers of goods in other member states, even if Community law prohibited customs duties and discriminatory taxation. A member state could simply impose a quota on imports from another member state, or simply ban importation of a good from another member state altogether (that is, impose a quota of 'zero').

Article 28 (ex Article 30) is designed to plug the remaining gap in Community law regarding the free movement of goods by prohibiting quantitative restrictions on goods imported from other member states, or measures that are equivalent to quantitative restrictions (sometimes referred to as MEQRs.) However, Article 30 (ex Article 36) is designed to allow member states to invoke certain exceptions. These exceptions allow them, in certain circumstances, to ban the importation of goods from other member states, at least in the absence of Community-wide harmonisation of the law pertaining to the good in question.

We should note that, while Article 25 (ex Article 12), pertaining to customs duties, and Article 90 (ex Article 95), pertaining to discriminatory internal taxation, are mutually exclusive, the same is not true with respect to Article 25 (ex Article 12) and Article 28 (ex Article 30). That is, we saw in a previous chapter that a charge imposed on a good imported from another member state was either:

1. a customs duty (or charge having equivalent effect) – and thus subject to scrutiny under Article 25 (ex Article 12); or
2. part of a system of internal taxation – and thus subject to Article 90.

It could not be both. We had to decide which it was, before we could decide which Treaty Article applied.

However, we will see that a certain measure may be subject to scrutiny both as a measure equivalent to a quantitative restriction under Article 28 (ex Article 30) and as a charge equivalent to a customs duty under Article 25 (ex Article 12). We will return to this later in our discussion.

BALANCING COMPETING INTERESTS AND JUDICIAL ACTIVISM

Several comments should be made at the outset. First, it is easy to get confused by the unfortunate coincidence of the new numbering system that has resulted in 'Article 30' being part of both the old and new numbering scheme regarding Community law pertaining to quantitative restrictions. When reading the cases of the Court of Justice (and there are a great many in this area of law) it is easy to become confused.

Second, even more so than in the other areas pertaining to the free movement of goods, Article 28 (ex Article 30) and Article 30 (ex Article 36) represent an express attempt to balance two interests. One interest is the Community goal of creating 'an area without internal frontiers' or an internal market in which, among other things, the free movement of all legal goods is guaranteed. A competing interest is the legitimate interest of a member state to prevent the importation of goods that might be freely available in another member state. A classic example of this is the importation of pornographic films that might be legally available in the Netherlands (or elsewhere) into Ireland, which still maintains a system of film censorship.

Third, this is an area where the Court of Justice has been particularly active, and has not hesitated to take an aggressive, 'purposive', approach when it felt that the free movement of goods was at stake. For example, the court gave such a broad definition to what constituted a measure equivalent to a quantitative restriction (MEQR) that the definition applied to commercial rules and regulations that seemingly had nothing to do with imports or exports of goods – including opening hours for shops, and labour law concerning working hours. The court was forced in Cases 267-268/91, *Keck and Mithouard* (1993) ECR I-6097, to 'backpedal' and 'reverse' its decisions (although it did not specify which ones) in order to prevent a flood of lawsuits by businesses that wished to challenge restraints on their freedom to do business by arguing that every rule was really an MEQR.

Finally, we should appreciate that the court's activism is due, at least in part, to the absence of Community legislation that would more widely harmonise rules pertaining to the free movement of goods. In the absence of such legislative harmonisation, the court has been forced to address the issues of quantitative restrictions arising under Article 28 (ex Article 30) and Article 30 (ex Article 36) on a case-by-case basis, which can lead to seeming inconsistencies and difficulties in interpretation. These difficulties can be reflected in academic works, such as this one, that seek to categorise and explain the court's thinking in this area. In other words, it can be hard to figure out and explain all of the court's decisions in this area and to place them within an easily accessible framework.

With the foregoing comments in mind, we can begin our review of Articles 28 (ex Article 30) and Article 30 (ex Article 36). First, we will consider the express prohibition contained in Article 28 (ex Article 30). This prohibition includes quantitative restrictions and measures equivalent to quantitative restrictions. We will cover quantitative restrictions briefly, and then consider the two types of MEQRs: distinctly applicable; and indistinctly applicable. We will focus, initially, on distinctly applicable MEQRs, leaving aside, for the moment, detailed consideration of indistinctly applicable MEQRs. (However, we will briefly mention the court's 'u-turn' on the issue of how far the definition of MEQR reaches.)

We next will review Article 30 (ex Article 36), and the various grounds for defending distinctly applicable MEQRs, that is, the express grounds for justifying burdens placed distinctly on imported (or exported) goods. Finally, we will consider, at considerable length, the development of the court's jurisprudence regarding 'indistinctly applicable' MEQRs, the limitations on the reach of MEQRs, and the judicially-created 'rule of reason' for justifying certain indistinctly-applicable measures that may hinder trade between member states.

ARTICLE 28 (EX ARTICLE 30), QUANTITATIVE RESTRICTIONS AND MEQRS

Article 28 simply provides that:

> Quantitative restrictions on imports and all measures having equivalent effect shall be prohibited between member states.

(Article 29 contains the same prohibition with respect to exports between member states.) It is hard to believe that such a brief Treaty Article could spawn the complicated case law associated with Article 28.

In Case 2/73, *Geddo v. Ente* [1973] ECR 865, the Court of Justice defined a quantitative restriction as 'measures which amount to a total or a partial restraint of, according to the circumstances, imports, exports, or goods in transit'. Recall that a quantitative restriction can consist of a total ban of goods, that is, a quota of zero. This has confused some courts.

While the definition of a 'quantitative restriction' is relatively straightforward, it has been more difficult to come up with a definition of a measure equivalent to a quantitative restriction or MEQR.

MEQRs and Commission Directive 70/50

An early Commission directive addressed the issue of what constituted a measure equivalent to a quantitative restriction. This directive, Directive 70/50 on the abolition of measures that have an effect equivalent to quantitative restrictions on imports, is no longer in force, and is of only historical significance. However, it is useful to note similarities to, and differences from, later attempts by the Court of Justice to define MEQRs.

The Commission directive distinguished between two types of MEQRs: those that applied distinctly to goods imported from other member states; and those that applied equally to goods imported from other member states and those goods that were manufactured domestically.

The directive provided that the first type of MEQR was prohibited. That is, a member state could not adopt a measure that hindered imports from other member states and which did not apply equally to domestically produced goods. Specifically, the directive prohibited measures that made an imported good subject to a condition that did not apply to a domestically produced good, or subject to a different condition than one that applied to a domestic good. It also forbad measures that favoured domestic goods over goods imported from another member state by imposing favourable conditions for the domestic good and not making these conditions available to the imported good.

The directive provided examples of this first type of MEQR, that is, a 'distinctly applicable' MEQR. Examples included measures that set minimum or maximum prices for imported goods, or that fixed profit margins for imported goods, or that made access to markets for imported goods conditional on having an agent present in the member state, or that required a giving of a guarantee that was not required for domestic goods, or that imposed conditions concerning shape, size, weight, composition or presentation that were different than those for domestic products, or that limited publicity in respect of imported products only.

The directive was not limited to 'distinctly applicable' measures; it also extended to 'indistinctly applicable' measures, that is, to 'measures governing the marketing of products which deal, in particular, with shape, size, weight, composition, presentation', and which applied equally to domestic and imported goods. These measures were not prohibited outright. Instead, these measures were prohibited only if 'the restrictive effects on the free movement of goods are out of proportion to their purpose', or 'the same objective can be obtained by other means which are less of a hindrance'.

We will hear echoes of these definitions in the cases decided by the Court of Justice.

Court of Justice and Definition of an MEQR

The Court of Justice attempted to define an MEQR in Case 8/74, *Procureur du Roi v. Dassonville* [1974] ECR 837. As we will see, the court defined an MEQR so broadly that it was forced in a later case, Cases 267-268/91, *Keck and Mithouard* [1993] ECR I-6097, to revise its definition to limit the scope of its application, at least with respect to indistinctly applicable trading rules that hindered intra-Community trade. We will discuss the development of the law with respect to indistinctly-applicable trading rules in a subsequent chapter.

In *Dassonville,* Belgian law provided, essentially, that the sale of Scotch whiskey had to be accompanied by a certificate from the UK government authenticating that the Scotch whiskey came from Scotland. Belgian traders purchased Scotch whiskey in France, imported it into Belgium, and sold it without a certificate of authenticity from the UK. (France did not require such a certificate, and it would have been extremely difficult to obtain one.) The traders were charged with violating Belgian (criminal) law. They defended themselves by arguing that the Belgian law violated Community law regarding the free movement of goods, in particular Article 28 (ex Article 30) and its prohibition on measures that were equivalent to a quantitative restriction. (The Belgian law did not impose a numerical quota on imports from other member states, and, thus, would have, if anything, amounted to a measure equivalent to a quantitative restriction.)

The Belgian court made an Article 234 (ex Article 177) reference to the European Court of Justice. The court faced the issue: did the Belgian law amount to a measure equivalent to a quantitative description?

In order to answer this question, the Court of Justice had to provide a definition of a measure equivalent to a quantitative restriction, in order to have something against which to test the Belgian law. In defining a measure equivalent to a quantitative restriction, the court gave a very broad definition.

The court stated, in paragraph 5:

> All trading rules enacted by member states which are capable of hindering, directly or indirectly, actually or potentially, intra-Community trade are to be considered as measures having an effect equivalent to quantitative restriction.

The court went on to conclude that the trading rule that Belgium had adopted was a measure equivalent to a quantitative restriction.

The court suggested that, in the absence of Community harmonisation, a member state might be free to adopt 'reasonable' measures to protect such things as consumer welfare. We will see, in a subsequent chapter, that the court's jurisprudence allows for such a defence to indistinctly applicable measures. (Note that the definition of an MEQR in *Dassonville* includes both indistinctly and distinctly applicable trading rules, even though the rule in *Dassonville* was only distinctly applicable, that is it applied to an imported good.) The court's basic approach was to throw a very wide net, catching any trading rule that directly or indirectly, actually or potentially, hindered trade, and then allow a member state to seek to defend the rule on the ground of reasonableness. Ultimately, as we will see, the court narrowed the definition of MEQR to exclude a certain type of indistinctly applicable trading rule, specifically, a trading rule concerned with 'commercial selling arrangements'. See Cases 267-268/91, *Keck and Mithouard* [1993] ECR I-6097. We will discuss this in detail in a subsequent chapter.

For the moment, we will concern ourselves with the application of the *Dassonville* definition of an MEQR to distinctly applicable trading rules, that is, those trading rules that apply only to goods imported from another member state. We will see that such trading rules can only be justified, if at all, under Article 30 (ex Article 36). Before giving examples of distinctly applicable trading rules and defences under Article 30, we must consider certain threshold issues, such as whether Article 28 (ex Article 30) applies to private or only public behaviour.

What Constitutes a 'Measure' for Article 28?

Article 28 does not apply to (or 'reach') purely private behaviour. Recall that the court in *Dassonville* described a 'measure' as a trading rule 'enacted by' a member state. There must be some involvement by a member state before Article 28 can be invoked.

However, it can be difficult to draw a line between 'public' behaviour, to which Article 28 applies, and purely private behaviour, which would not be subject to Article 28. The court considered the issue in the following cases, which illuminate some of the issues.

In Case 249/81, *Commission v. Ireland ('Buy Irish')* [1982] ECR 4005, the court considered the issue of whether there was sufficient public action to invoke Article 28. In this case, known as the *'Buy Irish'* case, the Commission brought an action against Ireland, in which the Commission alleged a violation of Article 28 (ex Article 30). They claimed the violation arose from a campaign designed to persuade Irish consumers to purchase goods manufactured in Ireland. The issue that arose was whether this was purely private behaviour, or was it public behaviour to which Article 28 applied.

The 'Buy Irish' campaign had commenced with an announcement from the Irish Minister for Industry, Commerce and Energy. The Minister announced that the goal of the campaign was to switch consumption from imports to Irish goods. The goal was a three per cent switch. The Irish government had taken a number of steps to promote the campaign. It had organised a free information service, provided exhibition facilities, encouraged the use of a 'guaranteed Irish' symbol, and had organised an Irish Goods Council.

The Irish Goods Council was organised under Irish company law. The management of the Council consisted of ten persons, each appointed in their individual capacity by the Irish Minister. The Irish government paid most of the expenses of the Council, although private businesses also contributed a portion of the expenses.

By the time the action reached the court, only two aspects of the 'Buy Irish' campaign continued to operate: the advertising campaign; and the use of the 'Guaranteed Irish' symbol.

The Commission argued that the 'Buy Irish' campaign as a whole amounted to a measure equivalent to a quantitative restriction. The Irish government argued that the term 'measures' only applied to 'binding provisions emanating from a public body', such as laws or statutory instruments. The Irish government argued that since there were no such provisions at issue, the 'Buy Irish' campaign was not subject to Article 28 (ex Article 30).

The court rejected Ireland's argument and agreed with the Commission that Article 28 (ex Article 30) applied. The court concluded that the advertising campaign and the use of the 'Guaranteed Irish' symbol 'form part of a government programme' and that 'the two activities in question amount to establishment of a national practice, introduced by the Irish government and prosecuted with its assistance'. Therefore, the court concluded that:

> [S]uch a practice cannot escape the prohibition laid down in Article 28 (ex Article 30) of the Treaty solely because it is not based on decisions which are binding upon undertakings.

The court stated, in what we can regard as a general rule:

> Even measures adopted by the government of a member state which do not have binding effect may be capable of influencing the conduct of traders and consumers in that state and thus of frustrating the aims of the Community as set out in Article 2 and enlarged upon in Article 3 of the Treaty.

Thus, in concluding that the activities in the *'Buy Irish'* case could be reached by Article 28, the court looked at the effects of the actions by the member states, in light of the purpose of the Treaty in creating a common market without internal frontiers.

In Case C-325/00, *Commission v. Germany* [2002] ECR I-9977, the Court of Justice faced a case very similar to the *'Buy Irish'* case. Germany had enacted a law establishing a central fund. The fund was for the purpose of promoting German agricultural products, both within and outside Germany. The money for the fund was raised by compulsory donations from the agricultural sector. Among other things, the fund promoted indication of origin and quality labels. Some members of the central board responsible for administering the fund were appointed by a German government minister. It should not be surprising that the Court of Justice agreed with the European Commission that the acts could be ascribed to the government of Germany, for the purposes of considering whether these activities violated Article 28. In other words, public rather than private behaviour was involved.

In the following case, the court considered whether Article 28 (ex Article 30) applied to the activities of a 'private' organisation.

ARTICLE 28 AND 'PRIVATE' ORGANISATIONS

In Case 266-267/87, *Pharmaceutical Society of Great Britain* [1989] ECR 1295, the court had to consider whether Article 28 (ex Article 30) applied to a 'private' organisation. It concluded that, under the circumstances of the case, Article 28 did apply.

The Pharmaceutical Society of Great Britain, the pharmacists' professional body, had adopted a Code of Ethics that prohibited a pharmacist from substituting a generic equivalent for a brand name drug prescribed by a physician, even if the generic substitute (which, typically, cost less and provided the pharmacist with a greater profit margin) had an equivalent therapeutic effect. That is, even if the generic equivalent was in virtually all respects identical to the brand name drug that had been prescribed (except for its cost, of course) a pharmacist could not substitute it for the brand name drug without violating the Code of Ethics. A violation in the Code of Ethics could result in the pharmacist being 'struck off' the rolls. (Another rule, adopted by the National Health Service, also prohibited substitution of generic equivalents for prescribed brand name drugs, although it encouraged doctors to prescribe the lower cost generic equivalent.)

The Association of Pharmaceutical Importers challenged these rules in court proceedings in the UK, relying on the direct effect of Article 28 (ex Article 30). The British court made an Article 234 (ex Article 177) reference to the Court of Justice.

Before the court could consider whether the rules at issue violated Community law, it had to decide 'whether a measure adopted by a professional body such as the Pharmaceutical Association of Great Britain', could be reached by Article 28 (ex Article 30). The court concluded that the Pharmaceutical Society's activities could be reached by Article 28 (ex Article 30).

The following factors persuaded the court:
1. the Society was established by a Royal Charter;
2. its existence was recognised by British legislation;

3. it was the sole professional body for pharmacy;
4. it maintained the register on which pharmacists must appear in order to carry on their business;
5. it adopted rules of ethics;
6. British legislation established a disciplinary committee within the Society, which could order that pharmacists be struck off the register; and
7. an appeal from the disciplinary committee could be taken to the High Court.

The court stated, in what we can regard as a general rule, that:

> [M]easures adopted by a professional body on which national legislation has conferred powers of that nature [such as those described in the preceding paragraph of this text] may, if they are capable of affecting trade between member states, constitute 'measures' within the meaning of [Article 28 (ex Article 30)].

Finally, the court has considered whether government 'inaction' may constitute a 'measure' capable of being caught by Article 28 (ex Article 30).

GOVERNMENT INACTION AND ARTICLE 28

In Case C-265/95, *Commission v. France* [1997] ECR I-6959, the court considered whether Article 28 applied when private parties carried out the acts that interfered with the free movement of goods. The court concluded that Article 28 did apply, and that France could be liable for a violation of Community law, where France failed to take adequate steps to stop the private behaviour that interfered with the free movement of goods. However, the facts were particularly egregious, and it is probably a rare case in which a member state will be liable for acts of private individuals.

In *Commission v. France*, French farmers had engaged in civil disobedience, including violent acts of destruction of private property, in order to disrupt the free movement of goods, particularly Spanish strawberries. These incidents had been occurring for up to ten years. The French authorities seemed unable to stop these incidents, and it appeared that many times they did not intervene to stop them. Very few French farmers had been arrested and charged with a crime.

The Commission brought an enforcement action against France. The Commission argued that France's inaction in the face of the disruption of the free movement of goods amounted to a violation of Article 28 (ex Article 30). France defended this claim on the ground that it had not ignored these activities, and it also argued that if it took a stronger line against the farmers, this would cause further disruption of civil society.

The court ruled in favour of the Commission. The court stated that:

> [H]aving regard to the frequency and seriousness of the incidents cited by the Commission, the measures adopted by the French government were manifestly inadequate to ensure freedom of intra-Community trade.

Furthermore, with regard to the argument of the French government that violent protests would occur if the government cracked down on the farmers, the court wrote that: 'apprehension of internal difficulties cannot justify a failure by a member state to apply Community law correctly'. The court stated that France must use 'all appropriate measures to guarantee the full scope and effect of Community law'.

The only possible exception would occur if France could prove that 'action on its part would have consequences for public order with which it could not cope by using the means at its disposal'. In other words, the court did not rule out, in theory, a possible defence that enforcing EC law might provoke public disorder with which the member state could not cope. However, the court stated that:

> In the present case, the French government has adduced no concrete evidence proving the existence of a danger to public order with which it could not cope.

Furthermore, it would not be enough to point to a generalised fear of public disorder: 'that argument can ... be put forward only with respect to a specific incident'.

ARTICLE 28 AND EXAMPLES OF DISTINCTLY APPLICABLE MEASURES EQUIVALENT TO A QUANTITATIVE RESTRICTION

Distinctly applicable measures are those that apply only to imported goods. The Commission has targeted a number of different types of acts by a member state as amounting to a distinctly applicable measure to which Article 28 applies. The court has taken a fairly liberal approach as to what types of activities are caught by Article 28 (ex Article 30), consistent with its purposive or teleological approach.

THE 'IRISH SOUVENIRS' CASE

In Case 113/80, *Commission v. Ireland* [1981] ECR 1625 (known as the '*Irish Souvenirs*' case), the Commission brought an action against Ireland under Article 29 (ex Article 30). Ireland had passed laws that required that certain imported goods must bear the word 'foreign'. The law applied to 'tourist items' that were souvenirs of Ireland, and that represented certain 'classic' Irish things or scenes, such as round towers, shamrocks, and wolfhounds.

The Commission claimed that the Irish laws constituted measures equivalent to a quantitative restriction, and that they were subject to Article 28 (ex Article 30). Note that the 'measures' are distinctly applicable, inasmuch as they only apply to imported goods.

Ireland protested that the laws did not constitute measures equivalent to a quantitative restriction. Recall that, at the time of this case, a measure equivalent to a quantitative restriction was a trading rule that potentially hindered imports of goods from another member state. Ireland argued that it was not discriminating between similar goods. It argued that items manufactured in Ireland and those manufactured abroad were essentially two different types of goods. The court rejected this argument. It stated that:

> [T]he essential characteristic of the souvenirs in question is that they constitute a pictorial reminder of the place visited, which does not by itself mean that a souvenir … must necessarily be manufactured in the country of origin.

Ireland also argued that the measure could be justified on the grounds of consumer protection. Note, however, that the measure is distinctly applicable, that is, it applies only to imported goods. Distinctly applicable measures can only be justified by reference to the exceptions set forth in Article 30 (ex Article 36). Consumer protection is not included in the exceptions contained in this Article. According to the court:

> [I]n view of the fact that neither the protection of consumers nor the fairness of commercial transactions is included amongst the exceptions set out in Article 30 [ex Article 36], those grounds cannot be relied upon as such, [in defence of a distinctly applicable measure].

In Case 207/83, *Commission v. United Kingdom* [1985] ECR 1202, the court faced an issue similar to the '*Irish Souvenirs*' case. The UK had adopted a law requiring that all goods be marked with their place of origin. The UK argued that this measure applied equally to domestic and imported goods. However, the court remarked that:

> [T]he indication of origin of goods are applicable without distinction to domestic and imported products only in form because, by their very nature, they are intended to enable the consumer to distinguish between these two categories of products, which may thus prompt him to give his preference to national products.

The court concluded that the UK had failed to fulfil its obligations under Article 28 (ex Article 30).

JUSTIFICATION FOR DISTINCTLY APPLICABLE MEQRS UNDER ARTICLE 30 (EX ARTICLE 36)

A outright quantitative restriction or a distinctly applicable measure equivalent to a quantitative restriction (that is, a trading rule that hinders intra-Community trade but that applies only to imported products, rather than to imported and domestic products equally) can only be justified by reference to the exceptions contained in Article 30 (ex Article 36).

Article 30 allows member states to restrict imports from (or exports to) other member states for any of the following reasons:
1. public morality;
2. public policy or public security;
3. protection of health and life of humans, animals or plants;
4. the protection of national treasures possessing artistic, historic or archaeological value; or
5. the protection of industrial or commercial property.

Because Article 30 (ex Article 36) provides an exception to the free movement of goods, it is interpreted narrowly. This has several implications. The first implication of the narrow construction is that the list of categories contained at Article 30 (ex Article 36) is exhaustive or exclusive. One cannot argue that the list is merely illustrative, and that other, similar, concerns (such as consumer protection) are implicitly contained in Article 30 (ex Article 36) and can be used to justify a quantitative restriction or a distinctly applicable measure equivalent to a quantitative restriction. The court made this point clear in Case 113/80, Commission v. Ireland ('Irish Souvenirs' case):

> ... neither the protection of consumers nor the fairness of commercial transactions is included amongst the exceptions set out in Article 30 (ex Article 36), [and] those grounds cannot be relied upon as such in connection with that Article.

A second implication is that each of the specific grounds will be interpreted strictly, and that member states cannot rely on generalisations in support of their arguments.

Article 30 (ex Article 36) also anticipates that a member state might pretend to rely on one of the grounds outlined in that Article, but actually would be using the Article to protect local producers. It states that:

> Such prohibitions or restrictions [on imports or exports] shall not, however, constitute a means of arbitrary discrimination or a disguised restriction on trade between member states.

The following sections consider some of the exceptions contained in Article 30 (ex Article 36) and how these grounds have been applied by the Court of Justice.

Public Morality

In Case 34/79, *R. v. Henn and Darby* [1979] ECR 3795, the defendants were charged with a crime for importing obscene material into Great Britain in violation of UK customs laws. They sought to overturn their conviction by arguing that the ban on importation of obscene materials violated Community law.

There was an Article 234 (ex Article 177) reference to the European Court of Justice. In the court there was no question that the ban on such materials amounted to a quantitative restriction, and that Article 28 (ex Article 30) applied. (In the British Court of Appeal, Lord Chief Justice Widgery upheld the convictions: see *Henn and Darby v. Director of Public Prosecutions* [1978] All ER 1190, CA. He wrongly concluded, among other things, that a total ban on imports was not a quantitative restriction, and ruled that European Community law did not apply. Of course, as we know, a total ban on imports is a quantitative restriction, but the quantity equals zero. The House of Lords caught his error and made a preliminary reference to the Court of Justice.)

The UK sought to rely on Article 30 (ex Article 36) to defend the ban on import of obscene goods. Specifically, the UK invoked the public morality exception to Article 28 (ex Article 30).

The court concluded that, in the abstract, there was no problem with the UK, or any other member state, establishing its own 'moral code'. The court stated:

> [I]t is for each member state to determine in accordance with its own scale of values and in the form selected by it the requirements of public morality in its territory ... [T]he statutory provisions applied by the UK in regard to the importation of articles having an indecent or obscene character come within the powers reserved to the member states by the first sentence of [Article 30, ex Article 36].

The only issue was whether the UK could prove that it had established a 'moral code' that sought to prohibit the manufacture and sale of obscene or indecent materials. If such materials could be freely manufactured or sold domestically, then the quantitative restriction contained in the customs law would be seen not as a means of protecting morality, but rather as 'a means of arbitrary discrimination or a disguised restriction on trade between member states'. In that case, the UK would be guilty of a violation of Community law.

One difficulty with the UK position was that, as any visitor to the Soho neighborhood of London realises, obscene or indecent materials can be purchased in licensed sex shops in certain parts of the UK. This is because the regulation of such matters is left largely to the local authorities, which have taken various approaches to the issue. Many local authorities ban such materials outright, while other local authorities, primarily in larger UK cities, have allowed the sale of such materials under certain conditions.

Thus, in *Henn and Darby*, one issue facing the European Court of Justice was whether the UK had to be able to point to a uniform national law prohibiting the sale of obscene or indecent materials in order to justify the quantitative restriction on the import of such goods. In other words, was the quantitative restriction really justified on the grounds of public morality, or was it merely a disguised restriction on trade?

As it was an Article 234 (ex Article 177) reference, it would be for the national court ultimately to decide the factual issues in the case. However, the Court of Justice virtually assured the outcome of the case (as it often does) when it ruled that:

> Whatever may be the differences between the laws on this subject in force in the different constituent parts of the UK, and notwithstanding the fact that they contain certain exceptions of limited scope, these laws, taken as a whole, have as their purpose the prohibition, or at least, the restraining, of the manufacture and marketing of publications or articles of an indecent or obscene character.

The court concluded that 'there is no lawful trade in such goods in the United Kingdom'. Therefore, the national court almost certainly would conclude that the quantitative restriction on such imports was justified under the public morality clause of Article 30 (ex Article 36) and did not amount to a disguised restriction on trade.

The Court of Justice reached a contrary conclusion in Case 121/85, *Conegate v. Customs and Excise Commissioners* [1986] ECR 1007. In that case, customs officials had confiscated inflatable 'love love' dolls that were being imported into the UK. Again, the law that imposed a ban on such material was regarded as a quantitative restriction, subject to Article 28 (ex Article 30). Once again, the UK sought to invoke the public morality exception contained in Article 30 (ex Article 36). However, this time the UK was not successful.

In *Conegate*, the UK failed to make a convincing case that its law prohibited or restricted the domestic trade in such goods. The court stated that:

> [A]lthough Community law leaves the member states free to make their own assessments of the indecent or obscene character of certain articles … the fact that goods cause offence cannot be regarded as sufficiently serious to justify restrictions on the free movement of goods where the member state concerned does not adopt, with respect to the same goods manufactured or marketed within its territory, penal measures or other serious and effective measures intended to prevent the distribution of such goods in its territory.

The only restrictions on the manufacture or marketing of such goods in the UK were that they could not be sold by mail, and could not be displayed in certain areas or sold without a special license.

The court concluded that Article 30 (ex Article 36) could not be relied upon on grounds of public morality to prevent import of goods:

where the same goods may be manufactured freely on its territory and marketed on its territory subject only to an absolute prohibition on their transmission by post, a restriction on their public display and, in certain regions, a system of licensing of premises for the sale of those goods ... .

Public Policy and Public Security

In Case 72/83, *Campus Oil v. Minister for Industry and Energy* [1984] ECR 2727, a challenge was brought to an Irish law that mandated that importers of oil into Ireland had to purchase a certain proportion of their oil requirements from a refinery located in Ireland. On an Article 234 (ex Article 177) reference, the Court of Justice clarified some of the issues arising under the Public Policy and Public Security exceptions contained in Article 30 (ex Article 36).

In *Campus Oil,* Ireland sought to justify the mandatory purchasing requirement on a number of grounds. The court, while ultimately ruling in favour of Ireland, ruled out a justification based on economic considerations alone. The court stated that:

> Goods cannot ... be exempt from the application of that fundamental principle [of free movement] merely because they are of particular importance to the life or the economy of a member state.

The court's ruling in this respect makes sense. The creation of a single market anticipates that some economic dislocation may occur. That is, with free movement of goods guaranteed, certain producers may prosper and others – deprived of protection previously afforded by customs duties, discriminatory taxation or quantitative restrictions – may fail. If economic considerations alone were sufficient to justify an exception to the principles embodied in Article 28, it would undercut the guarantees and anticipated outcomes of free movement. It would make little sense to guarantee free movement in the first place if the failure of a producer could be used to justify an exception from the free movement guarantees.

However, Ireland pleaded something in addition to the economics of a failing company in support of a public security exception. Ireland argued that national security required that the country have at least one oil refinery, and that unless the exception were granted, Ireland's sole oil refinery would fail. The court accepted this argument.

Protection of Life and Health of Humans, Animals and Plants

There has been considerable litigation over the Article 30 (ex Article 36) exception that allows a derogation from the free movement guarantees of Article 28 (ex Article 30) on the grounds of protection of the life and health of humans, animals and plants. The court's judgments in this area tend to focus on whether the principle is being abused as a disguised restriction on trade. The court also has an antipathy to 'dual inspection', that is, to requiring imported goods to be inspected in the importing country if they already have been inspected in the exporting country.

In Case 40/82, *Commission v. United Kingdom* [1982] ECR 2793, the Commission challenged the UK's effective import ban on poultry meat and eggs from other member states. The UK defended the policies as being required to prevent the spread of Newcastle disease, which was a disease affecting poultry.

The court found in favour of the Commission and found that the UK had violated Community law. The factors that influenced the court's decision were the timing of the ban (it occurred in the run-up to Christmas, when UK poultry manufacturers typically face stiff competition from other producers in other member states) and that the UK had demanded, as a condition of import, that other countries prove stronger protective measures against Newcastle disease than the UK government had imposed on UK farmers.

When viewed in the light of the foregoing facts, the UK import ban did not appear to be a legitimate measure to protect the life and health of humans and animals. Instead, the UK policies more closely resembled a disguised restriction on intra-Community trade, designed to protect domestic poultry manufacturers.

However, in Case 53/80, *Officer van Justitie v. Koniklijke* [1981] ECR 409, the court took a more lenient view of a member state's efforts to protect the health and life of human and animals. The Dutch government restricted the amount of vitamins that could be contained in snacks sold over the counter. The scientific evidence on the effects of eating a large amount of vitamins was mixed – some evidence pointed to harmful effects, other evidence suggested eating a large amount of vitamins was harmful. However, the court upheld the Dutch trading rule as a permissible exception to Article 28 (ex Article 30) justified on the ground of protection of the health of humans under Article 30 (ex Article 36). Generally speaking, in the absence of Community harmonisation (such as a directive specifying permissible levels of vitamin content in snack bars), a member state will be allowed to set its own health and safety standards, in the absence of evidence that it is a disguised restriction on trade.

However, the court has expressed disapproval of dual inspection requirements, that is, of requiring imported goods to be inspected if they already have been inspected in the exporting country. See Case 124/81, *Commission v. United Kingdom (UHT Milk)* [1983] ECR 203. The court's attitude has been that dual inspection requirements are disproportionate. Less restrictive measures could be taken to meet public health concerns. One less restrictive measure would be to announce standards that the imported product must meet, but accept certification from the exporting member state that these standards have been met.

CONCLUSION

This chapter primarily has addressed the issue of outright quantitative restrictions on imported goods, and 'distinctly applicable' measures equivalent to a quantitative restriction. After determining that a trading rule is either a quantitative restriction or a distinctly applicable MEQR under Article 28 (ex Article 30), it can only be justified, if at all, by reference to the categories set forth in Article 30 (ex Article 36).

Member states have sometimes been accused of trying to avoid the requirements of Article 28 through various means. These means include portraying certain activities as being strictly of a 'private' nature (and thus beyond the reach of Article 28, which only applies to 'measures enacted by' a member state) or by virtually ignoring (illegal) behaviour which undermines the free movement of goods. However, the Commission and the court have focused primarily on the effects of certain activities, and have been willing to ascribe those effects to the member states, if these effects threaten a fundamental principle such as the free movement of goods.

Although the Treaty allows an express exception to quantitative restriction and distinctly applicable quantitative restrictions, the court has policed the asserted reasons of member states very carefully to detect 'disguised restrictions' on trade between member states.

The next chapter focuses on indistinctly applicable MEQRs, that is, trading rules that apply equally to imported and domestic products, but that can, at least potentially, hinder intra-Community trade. We will see that this category of trading rule has caused the court some difficulty, and resulted in a major revision of the case law in this area.

Chapter 13

FREE MOVEMENT OF GOODS, PART III: 'INDISTINCTLY APPLICABLE' MEQRS AND 'MANDATORY REQUIREMENTS'

INTRODUCTION

So far, we have examined ways in which the law of the European Union prevents member states from protecting domestic industries by erecting barriers to the import (or export) of goods from (or to) other member states. We have seen that the EC Treaty prohibits the imposition of duties or tariffs on the import of goods from other member states. The Treaty also prohibits charges on imports that would be equivalent to import duties. The elimination of tariffs and charges equivalent to tariffs was one of the core goals in the establishment of the original European Economic Community.

Of course, even if tariffs, duties or other charges on the import of goods from other member states were completely eliminated, it might still be possible for one member state to erect barriers to the import of goods from other member states. (The pressure to erect such barriers might come from domestic industries that are having trouble competing with goods imported from other countries, where competitors are based.) One way of blocking goods from other member states would be to impose numerical quotas or quantitative restrictions on the import of such goods.

Thus, it would not be adequate simply to prohibit tariffs or duties on imports. It also is necessary for European Union law to prohibit quantitative restrictions on the imports of goods. The law of the European Union prohibits quantitative restrictions on goods from other member states. These have been covered in a previous chapter.

However, the prohibitions on tariffs and on quantitative restrictions on the import of goods from other member states are not enough. It would still be possible for a member state to prevent the import of (competing) goods from other member states by enacting what are known as measures equivalent to quantitative restrictions. Measures such as these might not impose a numerical limit on the amount of goods that could be imported from another member state. However, the practical consequence of the measure might be to limit the number of goods imported from another member state, or to prevent any goods from being imported.

Some of these measures might be directed only at goods imported from another member state. These are known as distinctly applicable measures equivalent to a quantitative restriction (MEQRs). We have covered these in detail in a previous chapter. An example of this might be a measure that sets certain conditions only on imported products with respect to price, or packaging, or other conditions. For example, a rule that Italian sausages can only be sold in clear plastic wrapping for no more than a certain price and only from a butcher's shop, when Irish sausages are not subject to the same requirements, would be an example of a 'distinctly applicable' MEQR.

Some measures, however, might apply equally to domestic goods and goods imported from another member state. These are known as 'indistinctly applicable' MEQRs. These measures might make it more difficult to import goods into Ireland, even though they apply equally to domestic and imported goods. For example, a rule that certain electrical equipment must meet safety standards laid down by an Irish safety board, even if applied equally to domestic and imported goods, might make it difficult to import electrical equipment from other member states. Even seemingly innocent rules pertaining to packaging, presentation or selling arrangements that applied equally to domestic and imported goods might be shown to have a negative impact on the importation of goods from other member states.

The question is whether these 'indistinctly applicable' measures should be 'caught' by Article 28 (ex Article 30) EC Treaty, which prohibits quantitative restrictions and MEQRs. If these 'indistinctly applicable' measures are 'caught' by Article 28, how, if at all, can they be justified and not struck down as violating Community law?

One of the primary goals of the European Union is to create a single market, that is, an area where goods, among other things, can move freely. Therefore, at first blush, we might think that any national measure that hindered the free movement of goods between member states, whether the measure is distinctly or indistinctly applicable, should not be allowed. But there is a tension here. A member state may have a legitimate interest in such things as consumer protection, and a measure may represent a sincere desire to protect the consumer even though it has an impact on trade between member states. On the other hand, even a measure that applies equally to imported and domestic goods, and thus appears on the surface to have nothing to do with trade, may in reality be a devious method of hindering imports of goods in order to illegitimately protect some domestic industry.

It is important to note that, in many areas, these issues could be resolved by the adoption at Community level of measures relating to safety standards, consumer protection, and similar rules, either in the form of directives or regulations. If the Community 'harmonised' these standards throughout the member states of the European Union, then there would be no need (nor ability) on the part of the member states to adopt standards that might vary one from the other and thus pose potential hindrances to the free movement of goods.

How can we identify which measures should be tested against the Community's laws regarding the free movement of goods? What test should we apply to determine whether the measure is legitimate and should be allowed, or is an illegitimate attempt at protectionism?

This chapter explores these issues through examining Community law regarding what are known as indistinctly applicable measures equivalent to quantitative restrictions (MEQRs). We shall see that the European Union, and particularly the Court of Justice, has struggled to provide a working formula for resolving these issues. There is some unavoidable overlap with the previous chapter when we deal with these so-called indistinctly applicable MEQRs.

COMMISSION DIRECTIVE 70/50

Commission Directive 70/50 [now only of historical interest] sought to deal with 'measures' that had 'an effect equivalent to quantitative restrictions on imports'. It dealt both with those types of measures which applied only to imports (i.e., 'distinctly applicable' MEQRs), and with 'measures' that applied equally to domestic and to imported products, but which had the effect of hindering the importation of goods made in other member states (i.e., 'indistinctly applicable' MEQRs).

Directive 70/50 and 'Distinctly Applicable' MEQRs

Directive 70/50 sought to abolish 'distinctly applicable' measures equivalent to a quantitative restriction, that is, in the words of the directive:

> [M]easures which make imports or the disposal, at any marketing stage, of imported products subject to a condition … which is required in respect of imported products only, or a condition differing from that required for domestic products and more difficulty to satisfy. Equally, it covers … measures which favour domestic products or grant them a preference … to which conditions may or may not be attached.

The directive provided examples of such 'measures':
1. measures which lay down minimum or maximum prices for imported products only;
2. measures which lay down conditions for payment for imported products only;
3. measures which subject imported products only to conditions regarding shape, size, weight, composition, presentation, identification;

4. measures which limit publicity in respect of imported products only.

This is only a partial list. This directive and the notion of the prohibition on distinctly applicable measures (which can be justified, if at all, only by reference to the grounds set out in Article 30, ex Article 36), is, of course, familiar to us from a previous chapter.

Directive 70/50 and 'Indistinctly Applicable' MEQRs

Directive 70/50 also dealt with 'indistinctly applicable' measures, as we know from a previous chapter. That is, in the words of the directive:

> This directive also covers measures governing the marketing of products which deal, in particular, with shape, size, weight, composition, presentation, identification or putting up and which are equally applicable to domestic and imported products ... .

However, the directive did not seek to 'abolish' such indistinctly applicable measures outright. Rather, such measures were prohibited:

> [W]here the restrictive effect of such measures on the free movement of goods exceeds the effects intrinsic to trade rules.
>
> This is the case, in particular, where:
> 1. the restrictive effects on the free movement of goods are out of proportion to their purpose;
> 2. the same objective can be attained by other means which are less of a hindrance to trade.

As we shall see, in dealing with the same issue, the Court of Justice has come full circle, finally articulating a position that is not far from the position taken by the European Commission back in 1970 in Directive 70/50.

European Court of Justice and MEQRs

In Case 8/74, *Procureur du Roi v. Dassonville* [1974] ECR 837, a father and son were prosecuted by Belgian authorities. They were accused of violating a Belgian law which prohibited the import or sale of certain spirits unless the sale was accompanied by a certificate of origin from the country of origin. The Dassonvilles were prosecuted for importing into Belgium and selling 'Scotch Whiskey' without the required certificates of origin. The whiskey had been bought legally in France, where a certificate of origin was not required. Although such a certificate could have been obtained from the country of origin (the UK), it would have been impractical to do so.

On a reference from the national court, the European Court of Justice first had to address the issue whether the Belgian measure, that is, the criminal law prohibiting import or sale of certain goods without a certificate of origin, was a 'measure equivalent to a quantitative restriction'. The court announced the following test for making this determination:

> All trading rules enacted by member states which are capable of hindering, directly or indirectly, actually or potentially, intra-Community trade are to be considered as measures having an effect equivalent to quantitative restrictions.

Note that this definition is very wide. Although the facts of the case concern imported goods (thus making the Belgian law 'distinctly applicable'), the definition does not limit itself to distinctly applicable rules. It would appear to apply to 'all trading rules', whether these rules are distinctly or indistinctly applicable.

Ordinarily, a quantitative restriction and a (distinctly applicable) MEQR can only be justified by reference to the (exclusive) category of justifications contained in Article 30 (ex Article 36), e.g., public morality. However, in a prescient comment, the court hinted that, in some cases, there might be other ways of justifying an MEQR:

> In the absence of a Community system guaranteeing for consumers the authenticity of a product's designation of origin, if a member state takes measures to prevent unfair practices in this connection it is subject to the condition that these measures should be reasonable and that the means of proof required should not act as a hindrance to trade between member states and should, in consequence, be accessible to all Community nationals.

Thus, the court in *Dassonville* hinted at a 'rule of reasonableness' for testing whether or not a member state rule could be justified (in the absence of Community harmonisation in the area). However, the court seemed to indicate that the means of complying with the measure must not hinder trade. This reasoning seems circular. If the measure did not hinder trade – directly or indirectly, actually or potentially – than it would not constitute a MEQR and would not be caught by Article 28 in the first place.

The court soon had an opportunity to clarify some of the issues raised by the *Dassonville* case.

European Court of Justice and Indistinctly Applicable MEQRs

In Case 120/78, *Rewe-Zentrale AF ('Cassis de Dijon')* [1979] ECR 649, the Court of Justice considered a German law pertaining to the sale of certain types of fruit liqueur.

The plaintiff applied to the German authorities to import a fruit liqueur known as Cassis de Dijon into Germany from France. However, German law prohibited selling this type of fruit liqueur unless it contained a certain minimum amount of alcohol content, and this brand contained less than the minimum amount specified. France did not have such a law and this type of fruit liqueur could be freely purchased there.

The court refined the ruling it had given in *Dassonville*. The court stated:

In the absence of common rules relating to the production and marketing of alcohol ... it is for the member states to regulate all matters relating to the production and marketing of alcohol and alcoholic beverages on their own territory.

Obstacles to movement within the Community resulting from disparities between the national laws relating to the marketing of the products in question must be accepted insofar as those provisions may be recognised as being necessary in order to satisfy mandatory requirements relating in particular to the effectiveness of fiscal supervision, the protection of public health, the fairness of commercial transactions and the defence of the consumer.

If one reads the quoted portion of the judgment quickly, one might conclude that Germany won the case. This would be wrong. In fact, Germany lost the case. (Technically, the judgment was entered by the national court after the decision of the European Court was sent back, but the judgment of the European court left no doubt as to the outcome of the case.)

In order to understand the outcome, and the rule for future cases as derived from *Dassonville* and *Cassis*, we must take the issues one by one.

First, was the German law prohibiting the sale of certain liqueurs below a minimum alcoholic content a 'measure equivalent to a quantitative restriction' (MEQR) under Article 28?

Recall that the German law did not discriminate in its application. It applied to both domestic and imported goods. In other words, it was 'indistinctly applicable'. In *Dassonville*, the application of the Belgian law was 'distinctly applicable'.

The court implicitly decided the German law was an MEQR, even though it was indistinctly applicable. If we apply the *Dassonville* formula, we can see that the German law satisfies the test. The German law *actually and directly* hindered intra-Community trade: specifically, liqueurs freely available in France could not be sold in Germany. Thus, the *Cassis* judgment indicated that the *Dassonville* formula was not limited to measures that were distinctly applicable.

Because the German law was an MEQR, did this mean that it had to satisfy one of the justifications listed under Article 30 (ex Article 36)?

The German law did not have to satisfy one of the criteria outlined under Article 30 (ex Article 36). Instead, to survive challenge, the German government had to show that the German law was:

... necessary in order to satisfy the mandatory requirements relating in particular to the effectiveness of fiscal supervision, the protection of public health, the fairness of commercial transactions and the defence of the consumer [italics added].

This has become known as the 'mandatory requirements' test. This is sometimes called the 'rule of reasonableness test' from the language of the earlier *Dassonville* case. It is important to note that, by using the words, 'in particular', the court was indicating that, unlike the criteria listed under Article 30 (ex Article 36), the criteria listed in describing the mandatory requirements test were not exclusive. Fiscal supervision, public health, and fairness of commercial transactions were merely examples of the type of justifications that could be offered by a member state to justify an indistinctly applicable measure that had the effect of hindering trade between member states. If the member state satisfied the 'mandatory requirements' test, than the law or regulation would not violate Community law (in particular Article 28) even though it was an MEQR.

Germany sought to defend the MEQR by arguing that it was necessary in order to satisfy the mandatory requirements of public health, specifically, in order to fight alcoholism. The government argued that if the alcoholic content of liqueurs was too low, people would be tempted to drink too much of it and become alcoholic.

The court rejected this argument, and stated:

> [T]he requirements relating to the minimum alcohol content of alcoholic beverages do not serve a purpose which is in the general interest and such as to take precedence over the requirements of the free movement of goods.

SUMMARY

To summarise, then, the state of the law after the court's judgments in *Dassonville* and *Cassis* is as follows:

1. The court in *Dassonville* gave a very broad definition of what constitutes an MEQR under Article 28 (ex Article 30); that is: '*All* trading rules enacted by member states which are capable of hindering, directly or indirectly, actually or potentially, intra-Community trade are to be considered as measures having an effect equivalent to quantitative restrictions'.

2. The definition of what constitutes an MEQR under Article 28 (ex Article 30) applies both to distinctly and indistinctly applicable 'measures'; that is, even if the law or regulation applies equally to domestic and imported goods, it is an MEQR if it satisfies the very low threshold set by the *Dassonville* formula.

3. If the measure does not actually or potentially, directly or indirectly hinder intra-Community trade, then it is not 'caught' by the definition of an MEQR under Article 28 and no justification is required against a claim that it violates Community law.

4. However, if the measure is 'caught' by Article 28, it has to be justified or it violates Community law.

5. If the measure is 'distinctly applicable', that is, applies only to imported

goods, then it has to satisfy one of the exclusive justifications contained in Article 30 (ex Article 36).

6. However, if the 'measure' that hinders intra-Community trade is indistinctly applicable, then it could be justified by reference to a wider range of justifications than those listed in Article 30.

7. Specifically, an indistinctly applicable MEQR does not violate Community law if it is necessary in order to satisfy the *mandatory requirements* relating in particular to the effectiveness of fiscal supervision, the protection of public health, the fairness of commercial transactions or the defence of the consumer.

As a result of the *Dassonville* and *Cassis* judgments, several things became clear. First, there was a general presumption that if a good was lawfully marketed in one member state, it could be lawfully marketed in another member state. This indicated a level of trust in the member states to protect their own citizens, such that it was not necessary to second-guess the exporting member state by imposing additional requirements in the importing member state. (Of course, a member state could still do so if it was able to satisfy the requirements of Article 30 (ex Article 36) or the 'mandatory requirements' test.)

Second, it was clear that the court was going to throw a very broad net in the first instance in deciding which 'measures', that is, national laws and regulations, amounted to an MEQR. The court's rationale may have been to be overly cautious against the possibility that a member state would creatively employ seemingly neutral regulations in order to protect domestic industries from competing imported goods.

However, almost any business regulation, even one that has nothing to do with trade, has at least the potential to indirectly hinder intra-Community trade. If one were so inclined, one could challenge any number of business regulations on the ground that they were 'measures equivalent to quantitative restrictions'. Member states could be required to justify the application of the regulation under the 'mandatory requirements' test and/or Article 30.

Lawyers for many businesses were inclined to make such arguments. The court was forced to reconsider the *Dassonville* and *Cassis* rules concerning the test for what constituted an MEQR. We will consider this in the following sections.

TESTING THE LIMITS OF ARTICLE 28

Cases 60 and 61/84, *Cinetheque v. Fédération Nationale des Cinemas* [1985] ECR 2605, represents a (partially) successful attempt to stretch the limits of Article 28 to 'catch' national trading rules that seem to have nothing to do with trade between member states.

In *Cinetheque*, a French law prohibited the sale of movies on videocassette until a year after the date of the movie's release in the cinema. This was done to encourage movie production generally and support cinema owners by encouraging people to go to the movies. Certain film producers entered into agreement with distributors in France that resulted in certain movies being offered for sale on videocassette before the expiration of the deadline for the selling of such videocassettes. The Fédération Nationale des Cinemas, a sort of trade association of movie house owners, obtained court orders based on the French law that prohibited the sale of videocassettes.

The parties who wished to sell the videocassettes brought an action in a French court, claiming, among other things, that the French law amounted to a measure equivalent to a quantitative restriction, and, as such, was prohibited under Article 28 of the Treaty. The French national court made a preliminary reference to the European Court of Justice, seeking a ruling on this issue of Community law.

The Court of Justice faced the threshold issue of whether or not the French regulation amounted to a measure equivalent to a quantitative restriction. If the French regulation was not an MEQR, then the French regulations would be upheld, and it would not be necessary to prove anything else. Article 28 would not apply at all.

However, if the French regulation constituted an MEQR, then the regulation would have to be justified by showing, for example, that the regulation satisfied the 'mandatory requirements' test, that is, that the regulation promoted an important national interest, and did so in the least restrictive way possible.

Obviously, the French government in defending the regulation would have preferred if the court had ruled that, as a matter of law, the law was not an MEQR. The parties challenging the regulation would have preferred the opposite ruling – that is, that the regulation was an MEQR. If the measure was an MEQR, then the parties challenging the ruling would 'live to fight another day' – that is, they would be able to challenge the law by arguing that the French law could not satisfy the 'mandatory requirements' test.

The defendants defended the regulation by arguing, among other things, that it was not an MEQR, and that, therefore, Article 28 did not apply at all. According to the court's description of their argument:

> The Fédération Nationale des Cinemas Français, the defendant in the main proceedings, contends that the legislation in question applies to imported and national products alike, that it was adopted in the absence of Community legislation in the field falling within the exclusive competence of the member states, and that it was justified by the mandatory requirements of the general interest.

They took a multi-pronged approach, but led with an argument that the French law *did not* fall within Article 28. The French government backed them in their argument, and explained the justification for the rule as well.

The Commission made a submission to the court, in which it argued that Article 28 *did* apply. According to the court, the Commission would have applied Article 28, although it gave a strong indication that the law could be justified:

> The Commission states that the national legislation in question, by prohibiting the marketing of video-cassettes of cinematographic works shown in cinemas, undeniably has the effect of hindering imports of video-recordings lawfully produced and marketed in another member state and in free circulation there ... The Commission maintains, however, that cultural aims may justify certain restrictions on the free movement of goods provided that those restrictions apply to national and imported products without distinction, that they are appropriate to the cultural aim which is being pursued and that they constitute the means of achieving them which affects intra-Community trade the least.

In other words, the Commission argued that Article 28 should apply, and that the French law would have to satisfy the 'mandatory requirements' test. If the French law did not pass the mandatory requirements test, then it would violate Community law (although the Commission gave a strong hint that the French regulations would satisfy the mandatory requirements test).

The court ruled that Article 28 did apply. On the one hand, the court accepted the French government's argument that:

> [S]uch a system [i.e., the French regulations prohibiting sale of video-cassettes for a period of time], if it applies without distinction to both the video-cassettes manufactured in the national territory and to imported video-cassettes, does not have the purpose of regulating trade patterns; its effect is not to favour national production as against the production of other member states, but to encourage cinematographic production as such.

However, the court went on to conclude that, even though the law did not have the purpose of regulating trade between member states and its effect was not discriminatory or designed to protect local producers, it nevertheless was 'caught' by Article 28 and had to satisfy the 'mandatory requirements' test. According to the court, it was the effects of the law that influenced its decision:

> [T]he application of such a system may create barriers to intra-Community trade in video-cassettes because of the disparities between the systems operated in the different member states and between the conditions for the release of cinematographic works in the cinemas of those states. In those circumstances a prohibition of exploitation laid down by such a system is not compatible with the principle of the free movement of goods provided for in the Treaty unless any obstacle to intra-Community trade thereby created does not exceed that which is

necessary in order to ensure the attainment of the objective in view and unless the objective is justified with regard to Community law.

Cinetheque represents the outer limits of the reach of Article 28. *Cinetheque* stands for the proposition that it does not matter that the trading regulation at issue does not concern trade between member states, nor that is applies equally to domestic and imported goods (that is, that it is indistinctly applicable). If it satisfies the *Dassonville* formula, then it is subject to 'mandatory requirements' test. (The court in *Cinetheque* did rule that the French regulation satisfied the 'mandatory requirements' test.)

A number of other cases also followed the reasoning of *Cinetheque*. In Case 382/87, *Buet v. Ministére Public* [1989] ECR 1235, the court ruled that a French trading rule that prohibited door-to-door selling was caught by Article 28 and was subject to the mandatory requirements test. In Case C-362/88, *GB Inno,* the court ruled that restrictions on the content of advertising flyers, although indistinctly applicable, were caught by Article 28.

Although the foregoing cases might give a different impression, the court did find that certain trading rules did not affect trade between member states, and were not caught by Article 28. Challenges to these rules were dismissed without the member state having to satisfy the mandatory requirements test. For example, in Case 148/85, *Direction Générale des Impôts v. Forest* [1986] ECR 3449, the court ruled that French regulations imposing quotas on the use of flour in certain types of bread were not capable of hindering trade and did not have to satisfy the mandatory requirements test.

One might inquire whether it makes any difference if the court sets the threshold for being caught by Article 28 low or high, so long as the mandatory requirements defence is available. That is, even if the court finds that an indistinctly applicable regulation is 'caught' by Article 28, the member state (hopefully) can show that the regulation satisfies the mandatory requirements test.

However, several cases, known as the *'Sunday Trading'* cases, demonstrate that there is a significant difference between finding that a trading regulation is not caught by Article 28 at all, and finding that, even though it is caught, it satisfies the mandatory requirements test. This difference results from the fact that, pursuant to the preliminary reference procedure described in another chapter, it is usually the member state court that must apply and decide the 'mandatory requirements' test. This is not an easy test to apply. In fact, different member state courts applying the same test to similar fact situations might reach different conclusions. This would threaten one of the most important goals of the law of the European Union – the harmonisation of EU law. The following sections illustrate how this occurred, and how the court reacted by revising the law in this area.

The 'Sunday Trading' *Cases*

In Case C-145/88, *Torfaen Borough Council v. B & Q plc* [1989] ECR 3851, a retail DIY shop was prosecuted by the local authorities because it had sold certain items on a Sunday, in violation of British regulations that prohibited certain items from being sold on a Sunday. These regulations, the Sunday trading laws, prohibited certain items from being sold on a Sunday, while allowing other items – including liquor, tobacco and newspapers – to be sold.

The retail outlet defended by arguing that the regulations prohibiting Sunday trading were 'a measure equivalent to a quantitative restriction (MEQR) and that these regulations could not be justified by reference to the mandatory requirements test.

The national court had found that the ban on Sunday trading of certain items had the effect of reducing the total amount of goods sold by the retail outlet, and that a certain proportion of these goods were imported from other member states.

The local authorities, according to the court, denied that the ban on Sunday trading constituted a measure having an effect equivalent to a quantitative restriction on the ground that it applied to domestic and imported products alike and did not put imported products at any disadvantage.

The British court referred the case to the European Court of Justice for guidance on the issue.

The European Court of Justice, citing the *Cinetheque* case (and applying its very broad interpretation of the *Dassonville* formula), indicated that, generally:

> [S]uch a prohibition [is] not compatible with the principle of the free movement of goods provided for in the Treaty unless any obstacle to Community trade thereby created [does] not exceed what [is] necessary in order to ensure the attainment of the objective in view and unless that objective [is] justified with regard to Community law.

The European Court accepted that: 'national rules governing the opening hours of retail premises' pursued a legitimate objective. The court concluded that such rules were, essentially, similar to rules pertaining to 'hours of work, delivery and sale', which themselves constituted 'a legitimate part of [national] economic and social policy, consistent with the objectives of public interest pursued by the Treaty'.

However, the fact that the national regulations pursued a legitimate objective was not sufficient to justify the regulations under the mandatory requirements test. According to the court:

> [I]t is necessary to ascertain whether the effects of such national rules exceed what is necessary to achieve the aim in view.

Furthermore, and crucially:

> The question whether the effects of specific national rules do in fact remain within
> that limit is a question of fact to be determined by the national court.

Inconsistent rulings resulted from the application of the 'mandatory requirements' test to similar fact patterns in the different UK national courts. That is, some national courts, applying the mandatory requirements test, decided that Sunday trading laws did not violate EU law, specifically the guarantee of the free movement of goods contained in Article 28. Other national courts, applying the same mandatory requirements test, decided that Sunday trading laws did violate EU law, and struck down those laws. Thus, a situation developed where in some areas, EU law did not permit national laws prohibiting Sunday trading, while in other areas, EU law did permit national laws prohibiting Sunday trading. One of the important goals of EU law, the harmonisation of laws, was being undermined. It is not surprising that the Court of Justice changed its mind.

Stoke on Trent *and a U-turn by the European Court*

In Case C-169/91, *Stoke on Trent v. B & Q plc* [1992] ECR I-6635, the issue of Sunday trading returned to the European Court. Two local authorities had prosecuted a retail outlet for violating Sunday trading regulations. The retail outlet had defended on the basis that regulations were an MEQR and violated Article 28 because they did not satisfy the mandatory requirements test. The national court was confused over how to apply the mandatory requirements test. The national court asked, among other things:

> [O]n what criteria and by reference to what, if any, factual or other evidence must
> the national court determine the question whether or not the restrictive effects on
> intra-Community trade which may result from national rules such as [Sunday
> trading regulations] exceed 'the effects intrinsic to rules of that kind' within the
> meaning of that phrase used in the ruling of the Court of Justice in [*Torfaen
> Borough Council v. B & Q plc*, cited above]?

The European Court of Justice did not answer this question directly. Instead, it decided to issue a blanket rule that Sunday trading regulations did not violate Article 28. The court stated that Article 28 of the Treaty: 'is to be interpreted as meaning that the prohibition which it lays down does not apply to national legislation prohibiting retailers from opening their premises on Sunday'.

This solved the problem of retail merchants repeatedly seeking to challenge such things as Sunday trading regulations by invoking Article 28 and claiming that the national regulations were an MEQR that failed to satisfy the mandatory requirements test. However, businesses remained free to challenge every other sort of national business regulation under the same sort of argument. The court was besieged by cases brought by businesses challenging all sorts of national business regulations. In order to deal with this, the Court of Justice sought to lay down a bright line test, in order to simplify the law in this area. Some people have questioned whether the court succeeded. The next sections deal with these issues.

A Bright Line Test for Article 28

In Case C-267 and 268/91, *Keck and Mithouard* [1993] ECR I-6097, the European Court of Justice sought to establish a bright line test to indicate which national trading regulations were caught by Article 28 (and thus subject to the mandatory requirements test) and which regulations were not caught by Article 28 (and thus could not be challenged as being an MEQR and a violation of Community law regarding the free movement of goods).

Messrs Keck and Mithouard were criminally prosecuted for violating a French law that prohibited selling goods at a loss. They defended on the basis that the French criminal law prohibiting certain below-cost sales was a measure equivalent to a quantitative restriction that did not satisfy the mandatory requirements test.

The French court made a preliminary reference to the European Court of Justice, seeking guidance on this issue.

The judgment of the European Court of Justice was decided by the entire court, and was simultaneously released in all the official languages of the European Community. Clearly, the court regarded the case as important.

The court, unusually, took note of something quite outside the issue directly facing them in the case. The court referred to the many challenges brought under Article 28 (ex Article 30):

> In view of the increasing tendency of traders to invoke Article [28] of the Treaty as a means of challenging any rules whose effect is to limit their commercial freedom even where such rules are not aimed at products from other member states, the court considers it necessary to re-examine and clarify its case law on this matter.

The court reviewed the state of law as laid down in *Cassis de Dijon*. It summarised this law as follows:

> [O]bstacles to free movement of good which are the consequence of applying, to goods coming from other member states where they are lawfully manufactured and marketed, rules that lay down requirements to be met by such goods (such as those relating to designation, form, size, weight, composition, presentation, labelling, packaging) constitute measures or equivalent effect prohibited by Article [28]. This is so even if those rules apply without distinction to all products unless their application can be justified by a public-interest objective taking precedence over the free movement of goods.

However, the European Court then did something it rarely does. It expressly overruled its prior case law. (Unfortunately, the court did not indicate which cases, exactly, it was overruling.) The court stated:

> By contrast [to the above statement of law], *contrary to what has previously been decided*, the application to products from other member states of national provisions restricting or prohibiting certain selling arrangements is not such as to hinder directly or indirectly, actually or potentially, trade between member states within the meaning of [the *Dassonville* formula] so long as those provisions apply to all relevant traders operating in the national territory and so long as they affect in the same manner, in law and in fact, the marketing of domestic products and of those from other member states [italics added].

In other words, the court was attempting to draw a bright line. On one side of the line were national trading regulations that concern the characteristics of a good, such as its weight, size, labelling, etc. These regulations were still caught by Article 28, and had to meet the mandatory requirements test, even if the regulations were indistinctly applicable (that is, applied equally to imported and domestic goods). On the other side of the line were national trading regulations pertaining to 'selling arrangements', such as hours of operation (like the Sunday trading regulations). These latter regulations were not caught by Article 28, since, as a matter of law, they did not affect trade between member states, so long as:

1. they applied to all producers equally; and
2. they did not affect imported products differently than domestic products.

Bright Line or Further Ambiguity?

The *Keck* case was meant, among other things, to clarify the law regarding indistinctly applicable MEQRs, by providing bright lines as to which trading regulations were subject to Article 28 and which were not. The European Court did this by dividing trading regulations into two sorts: those concerned with the characteristics of a good (size, shape, packaging), and those concerned with 'selling arrangements' (hours during which goods can be sold).

As to the former, the usual rules applied: indistinctly applicable trading rules concerning the characteristics of a good that met the *Dassonville* formula were MEQRs and were subject to Article 28. They could be justified only by reference to the 'mandatory requirements' test and/or the criteria under Article 30. On the other hand, indistinctly applicable trading rules that concerned 'selling arrangements' were not capable of hindering trade, as a matter of law, and did not amount to MEQRs, provided two conditions were met:

1. the trading regulations applied to all producers (foreign and domestic) equally; and
2. the trading regulations did not affect the imported product more severely than the domestic product.

It may not always be possible to distinguish between the two types of trading rules. One can imagine a situation where a trading regulation might seem to straddle the border of the dividing line. For example, what if the Minister for Health sought to combat alcohol abuse among young people by prohibiting the sale of so-called 'Alco-Pop' drinks after 10 p.m. on weekends? Would this be a trading rule that concerned 'selling arrangements' (since it only concerned the hours at which a good could be sold), or would it be a trading rule that concerned 'characteristics of a good' (since it applied only to 'Alco-Pop' drinks)?

Also, what about advertising? What if trading rules prohibit advertising of certain products? Would this be a 'selling arrangement' (and not subject to Article 28) or would it concern the 'characteristics of a good' (and be subject to Article 28)?

The European Court addressed this issue in Case C-412/93, *Leclerc-Siplec v. TFI Publicité* [1995] ECR I-179. Leclerc-Siplec brought a lawsuit in the French courts after TFI Publicité refused to accept television advertisements from Leclerc. French trading regulations provided that certain goods could not be advertised on television. In addition to prohibiting television advertising of such things as certain alcoholic drinks, it prohibited advertising of distribution methods. Leclerc wanted to advertise the distribution of fuel at its convenience stores, and TFI Publicité refused to accept these ads because it was prohibited from doing so by French law.

Leclerc sued TFI Publicité in the French courts and the national court made a preliminary reference to the European Court of Justice, seeking guidance on whether Article 28 applied to the French regulations concerning advertising.

The European Court of Justice ruled that Article 28 did not apply. The court stated:

> The application to products from other member states of national provisions restricting or prohibiting certain selling arrangements is not such as to hinder directly or indirectly, actually or potentially, trade between member states within the meaning of the *Dassonville* judgment, cited above, so long as those provisions apply to all relevant traders operating within the national territory and so long as they affect in the same manner, in law and in fact, the marketing of domestic products and of those from other member states. Provided that those conditions are fulfilled, the application of such rules to the sale of products from another member state meeting the requirements laid down by that state is not by nature such as to prevent their access to the market or to impede access any more than it impedes the access of domestic products. Such rules therefore fall outside the scope of Article [28] of the Treaty.

The European Court turned its attention to the types of French regulation at issue in the case. The court stated:

A provision such as that at issue in the main proceedings concerns selling arrangements since it prohibits a particular form of promotion (televised advertising) of a particular method of marketing products (distribution). Furthermore, those provisions, which apply regardless of the type of product to all traders in the distribution sector, even if they are both producers and distributors, affect the marketing of products from other member states and that of domestic products in the same manner.

It is still an open question whether it would be open to the foreign producer to argue that a ban on advertising would have a heavier impact on imported goods than on domestic goods, particularly if the domestic goods are well established in the market, and the imported goods are trying to break into the market through, e.g., advertising.

CONCLUSION

The European Court of Justice has sought to strike a balance between the legitimate concern of the member states in protecting its citizens, and the unfortunate tendency of member states to adopt trading regulations which are disguised restrictions on trade designed to protect local manufacturers.

The European Court's initial attempts to throw a very wide net and subject even indistinctly applicable trading rules to the 'mandatory requirements' test proved unworkable. Businesses tried to challenge every restriction on their practices by arguing that trading regulations that had nothing to do with intra-Community trade were 'caught' by Article 28 and had to satisfy, on a case by case basis, the mandatory requirements test laid down by the European Court (but applied, more often than not, by the national court).

The European Court responded to the difficulties caused by the original *Dassonville* formula by refining its rules to eliminate a broad swathe of trading regulations from scrutiny under Article 28. Specifically, in *Keck*, the court ruled that indistinctly applicable trading rules concerned with 'selling arrangements' were not caught by Article 28, so long as two criteria were met:
1. the rules applied to domestic and foreign producers equally; and
2. they did not affect imported goods more heavily than domestic goods.
The bright line of *Keck* may dim in the future and may prove difficult to apply in particular situations. Also, it may be open to importers to argue that restrictions on advertising will always have a heavier impact on imported goods, when faced with an entrenched domestic product.

Chapter 14

FREE MOVEMENT OF WORKERS AND FREE MOVEMENT OF CITIZENS

INTRODUCTION

The EC Treaty always envisaged the creation of a common market among the member states. In a 'customs union', tariffs and quotas between participating states are removed and a common external tariff is imposed on trade with non-members. In a 'common market', the free movement of goods characterising a customs union is supplemented by the free movement of the factors of production, i.e. labour, capital and enterprise. Article 14 of the EC Treaty states that 'the internal market shall comprise an area without internal frontiers in which the free movement of goods, persons, services and capital is ensured'. The free movement of persons is therefore one of the four fundamental freedoms of Community law.

Economic theory postulates that when goods can move freely, consumer choice is enhanced and wealth-creation is maximised. The provisions of the EC Treaty concerning the free movement of persons, services and capital reflect the same idea. Labour is one of the economic factors of production, i.e. the elements involved in the making of a product. The Treaty seeks to ensure the optimal allocation of resources within the Community by enabling the factors of production to move to the area where they are most valued. Thus, the free movement provisions ensure that workers can move from areas of the Community with high unemployment and low wages, to areas of labour shortages and high wages, thereby creating a more efficient allocation of resources.

Various Treaty provisions deal with the free movement of persons. Firstly, Articles 39-42 (ex Articles 46-51) cover the free movement of employed persons, i.e., 'workers'. Secondly, Articles 43-48 (ex Articles 52-58) concern the free movement of self-employed persons and companies (i.e. the freedom of establishment). Thirdly, Articles 49-55 (ex Articles 59-66) deal with the freedom to provide services, a freedom which also has implications for the free movement of persons within the Community. It is also worth noting that Article 12 (ex Article 6) contains a general, overarching prohibition on discrimination on grounds of nationality.

Free movement rights are accorded primarily to those involved in an economic activity. With its overriding goal of market integration, Community law has traditionally attached importance to the categorisation of persons as past or future economic actors. However, in more recent years, and particularly since the entry into force of the Treaty on European Union (TEU), the EU has begun to expand its areas of competence beyond the purely economic sphere. The TEU introduced the concept of Union citizenship – the rights accorded to citizens of the EU are now set out in Articles 17-22 (ex Articles 8(1)-8(e)). Increasingly, it would appear from the case law of the court that the enjoyment of rights of free movement is not dependent on the exercise of an economic activity.

In this chapter, we will focus primarily on the orthodox principles relating to the free movement of workers, as set out in Articles 39-42. However, we will also consider the rights accorded to workers' families, students and, more generally, to Union citizens. In particular, we will consider the impact of the citizenship provisions on the existing law relating to the free movement of persons within the Community.

It should be noted that secondary legislation has been introduced to supplement the provisions of Article 39, the principal measures being:
1. Regulation 1612/68 which fleshes out the principal of equal treatment in relation to access to and conditions of employment;
2. Directive 64/221 governing member states' right to derogate from the free movement of workers on grounds of public policy, public security and public health; and
3. Directive 68/360 concerning rights of entry and residence.

These measures will be considered in greater detail below.

Free Movement of Workers: EC Treaty, Articles 39-42 (ex Articles 48-51)

Article 39(1) provides that 'freedom of movement of workers shall be secured within the Community'. Obviously, the definition of the term 'worker' is crucial in determining the scope of the provision. However, the term is defined neither in Article 39 itself, nor in the relevant secondary legislation. As a result, the definition of a 'worker' for the purposes of Article 39 has been left to the Court of Justice of the European Communities. It should be noted, however, that Regulation 1612/68 restricts the definition of the term to workers who are nationals of the member states. As a result, the rights accorded to 'workers' under Community law do not extend to 'third country nationals', i.e. persons who are not citizens of an EU member state. The rights afforded to third country nationals under Community law are very limited. For example, such persons may enjoy certain rights in their capacity as family members of Community workers. However, these rights are purely derivative, e.g. the rights afforded to the spouse of a Community worker are entirely contingent on the continuing existence of a marital relationship. This issue will be considered in greater detail below.

Unsurprisingly, the Court of Justice of the European Communities has held that the term 'worker' is a Community concept, to be defined by the Community courts and not by individual member states. The court's approach is designed to avoid discrepancies between different member states in the application of Article 39. Furthermore, it should be observed that the European Court of Justice has interpreted the term 'worker' very broadly, while construing the derogations provided for in Article 39(3) and the public service exception in Article 39(4) very narrowly. In so doing, the court seeks to give the broadest possible effect to the free movement of workers, as one of the fundamental freedoms on which the Community is based.

Part-time Employment and Definition of 'Worker'

It is worth examining some of the cases in which the court has been called upon to clarify the ambit of Article 39. Of particular importance are the 'borderline' cases in which the court has considered the application of Article 39 to part-time workers. In Case 53/81, *Levin v. Staatssecretaris van Justitie* [1982] ECR 1035, a British citizen living in the Netherlands had her application for a residence permit refused by the Dutch authorities on the basis that her employment as a part-time chambermaid did not provide sufficient means for her support. The question arose as to whether Ms Levin fell within the scope of Article 39 in circumstances where her earnings were below the minimum subsistence level under Dutch law.

In a preliminary ruling, the European Court of Justice stated that the enjoyment of free movement rights could not be made dependent on a worker's earnings being equal to or above the national minimum wage. It went on to state that part-time employment was not excluded from the scope of Article 39, but declared that the rules relating to the free movement of workers covered only the pursuit of 'effective and genuine activities, to the exclusion of activities on such a small scale as to be regarded as purely marginal and ancillary'. The crucial factor was, therefore, whether a person was pursuing a genuine economic activity. It did not matter that Ms Levin did not earn a living wage and received financial support from her family. It also did not matter that Ms Levin's motive for going to work was to avoid deportation. The fact that a worker chose to supplement his or her earnings with income from other private sources was deemed to be irrelevant, as was the motive for taking the job.

In Case 139/85, *Kempf v. Staatssecretaris van Justitie* [1986] ECR 1741, a German national living and working in the Netherlands as a music teacher, giving approximately twelve one-hour lessons per week, was refused a residence permit. The Dutch government claimed that work providing an income below the minimum subsistence level in a member state could not be regarded as 'genuine and effective' work where the person doing the work was in receipt of social assistance payments from public funds. The European Court of Justice rejected this argument, declaring that it was irrelevant whether supplementary means of subsistence were derived from private or public funds when considering the application of Article 39.

General Definition of 'Worker'

While the European Court of Justice had elaborated a general definition of the term 'worker' in the *Levin* case, it was not long before national courts sought further and more detailed assistance. In Case 66/85, *Lawrie-Blum v. Land Baden-Württemburg* [1986] ECR 2121, the court sought to give greater guidance on the requirements that work be 'genuine and effective' and not 'marginal and ancillary'. In the case, the European Court of Justice was asked to consider whether a trainee teacher undertaking a period of teacher training would qualify as a 'worker'.

The European Court of Justice noted that the essential feature of an employment relationship was that 'for a certain period of time a person performs services for and under the direction of another person in return for which he receives remuneration'. On the facts, the court suggested that a trainee teacher who, under the direction and supervision of the school authorities, was undergoing a period of service in preparation for entry into the teaching profession during which she provided services by giving lessons and received remuneration must be regarded as a 'worker' within the meaning of Article 39(1).

In subsequent cases, the European Court of Justice was asked to consider the issue of remuneration in greater detail. Case 196/87, *Steymann v. Staatssecretaris van Justitie* [1988] ECR 6159 concerned a German national living in the Netherlands, where he was a member of a religious community. The plaintiff carried out plumbing and general domestic work for the community, but his application for a Dutch residence permit had been refused on the ground that he was not an employed person receiving a wage and was thus not a 'worker' for the purposes of Article 39. On a preliminary reference, the court ruled that the work in question could in principle be regarded as a genuine economic activity. The European Court of Justice noted that, in return for providing services of economic value, the plaintiff's material needs had been looked after by the community. In other words, while the plaintiff had not received wages in the formal sense, there had nonetheless been a *quid pro quo* for the services performed. This qualified as 'renumeration', and, since he performed his duties under the direction of another, he satisfied the definition of a 'worker'.

In Case 344/87, *Bettray v. Staatssecretaris van Justitie* [1989] ECR 1621, decided in the following year, the European Court of Justice took a more restrictive approach to the application of Article 39. The case concerned a German national who had been refused a residence permit by the Dutch authorities. He was involved in therapeutic work as part of a drug rehabilitation programme under Dutch law. The court started by reiterating the definitions of a 'worker' laid down in *Levin* and in *Lawrie-Blum*. However, the European Court of Justice qualified its previous case law by stating that work under a social integration scheme was not an effective and genuine economic activity if it constituted merely a means of rehabilitation or reintegration for the person concerned. This case would seem to be an anomaly because the court usually does not look into a worker's motives.

Substantive Rights of Workers: EC Treaty, Article 39(3)

Article 39(3) sets out the rights enjoyed by Community workers, and these include:
1   the right to accept offers of employment actually made (Article 39(3)(a));
2.   the right to move freely within the territory of the member states for the purpose of accepting offers of employment (Article 39(3)(b));
3.   the right to remain for employment (Article 39(3)(c)); and
4.   the right to remain after employment (Article 39(3)(d)).
This latter right has been elaborated on by Regulation 1251/70.

Article 39(3) makes no reference to any right to move to and reside in the territory of another member state for the purpose of seeking employment. However, that issue was dealt with by the European Court of Justice in Case C-292/89, *R v. Immigration Appeal Tribunal, ex parte Antonissen* [1991] ECR I-745.

The case concerned a Belgian national who had entered the UK in 1984. Mr Antonissen had not yet found employment when, in 1987, he was imprisoned in the UK for a drug-related offence. Following his release, the Secretary of State decided to deport him. When Antonissen sought to challenge his deportation, the national court made a reference to the European Court of Justice. Under UK law, a non-national could be deported if he had not found employment within six months of being admitted to the country. The UK government argued that, according to the wording of Article 39, Community nationals were given the right to move freely within the territory of the member states for the purpose only of accepting offers of employment actually made. However, the European Court of Justice rejected such a strict interpretation of Article 39(3). It pointed out that such a construction would render the provision ineffective: if nationals could move to another member state only when they already had an offer of employment, few people would exercise their rights of free movement under the Treaty. The court concluded that Article 39(3) was to be interpreted in a *non-exhaustive* manner as including:

> the right for nationals of member states to move freely within the territory of other member states and to stay there for the purposes of seeking employment.

It should be noted that a member state retains the power to expel a national of another member state who has not found work after a certain period of time. The European Court of Justice noted in *Antonissen* that the period of six months laid down in UK law did 'not appear in principle to be insufficient' to enable persons to apprise themselves of job offers and to take the necessary steps to obtain employment. The court added, however, that if, after the expiry of that period, a person provided evidence that he was continuing to seek employment and that he had genuine chances of being employed, the member state was not entitled to deport.

Documentation: Directive 68/360

Directive 68/360, which was adopted under what is now Article 40, seeks to clarify certain formal requirements relating to the right of entry and residence of Community workers. Article 3 of the directive states that a European Community national should be entitled to enter another member state simply on producing a valid identity card or passport. No visa requirement may be imposed. Community workers are also entitled to five-year, automatically renewable, residence permits as proof of their right of residence. To obtain such a permit, the worker must produce the document with which he or she entered the territory and proof of engagement from an employer.

Article 5 of Directive 68/360 indicates that the rights to reside and work are not conditional upon satisfaction of the administrative formalities set out in the directive, a point clearly illustrated by Case 48/75, *Royer* [1976] ECR 497. In the *Royer* case, a French national living in Belgium was ordered to leave the country, since he had not complied with the necessary administrative formalities of entry on the population register when he first arrived in Belgium. The European Court of Justice pointed out that the directive simply clarified the scope of rights *already directly conferred by the Treaty*. It noted that the grant of a residence permit was therefore not a measure giving rise to rights. Accordingly, mere failure to comply with national legal formalities concerning the movement and residence of aliens could not justify a decision ordering expulsion. However, the court has recognised the possibility of imposing alternative sanctions, such as fines and detention, provided such penalties are proportionate and comparable to sanctions imposed on nationals for similar offences.

PROHIBITION ON DIRECT AND INDIRECT DISCRIMINATION ON GROUNDS OF NATIONALITY

Article 39(2) (ex Article 48(2)) states that:

> [F]reedom of movement for workers shall entail the abolition of any discrimination based on nationality between workers of the member states as regards employment, remuneration and other conditions of work and employment.

The terms of Article 39 are supplemented by the much more detailed provisions of Regulation 1612/68, which seeks to facilitate the exercise of the rights conferred by the Treaty. It should be noted that Article 39 prohibits not only direct discrimination against EC workers on grounds of nationality, but also all forms of indirect discrimination.

Language Requirements

Article 3(1) of Regulation 1612/68 states that a member state shall not be prohibited from imposing 'conditions relating to linguistic knowledge required by reason of the nature of the post to be filled'. Case 379/87, *Groener v. Minister for Education* [1989] ECR 3967 concerned a Dutch national who had been refused a permanent post at the Dublin College of Marketing and Design (now part of the Dublin Institute of Technology) because she did not hold the requisite certificate of proficiency in the Irish language. Ms Groener argued that the conditions laid down by the Minister were contrary to Article 39 and to Article 3 of Regulation 1612/68 because knowledge of the Irish language was not actually necessary to carry out her relevant duties. However, the European Court of Justice recognised the importance of Irish government policy in promoting the use of Irish 'as a means of expressing national identity and culture'. It emphasised the importance of the role of teachers in implementing the state policy in question and concluded that a language requirement of this kind fell within the scope of the exception in Article 3(1) of Regulation 1612/68, provided it was not disproportionate. Among other things, this meant Ms Groener had to be given another opportunity to take the Irish language test (which, happily, she passed).

The issue of linguistic knowledge arose in a different context in Case C-281/98, *Angonese v. Cassa di Riparmio di Bolzano* [2000] ECR I-4139. The case concerned an Italian national who had applied for a job in a bank in the German-speaking Bolzano region of Italy. Candidates for the post were required to produce an official certificate of bilingualism given by the Bolzano authorities. Mr Angonese did not possess the necessary certificate and sought to rely instead on degrees he had obtained in language studies at Vienna University as evidence of his bilingualism. The European Court of Justice ruled that, while it was legitimate to require applicants to have minimum linguistic knowledge, refusal to consider qualifications acquired in other member states was disproportionate to that aim.

The court noted that the requirement imposed by the bank was likely to put nationals of other member states at a disadvantage by comparison with residents of the province and was thus contrary to Article 39. Of interest also in the *Angonese* decision is the court's emphatic assertion that the prohibition of discrimination on grounds of nationality set out in Article 39 of the Treaty is applicable to the actions of private persons, as well as to those of public authorities. It is clear, therefore, that Article 39 produces horizontal, as well as vertical, direct effect.

Conditions of Employment and Work

Article 7(1) of Regulation 1612/68 stipulates that a Community worker may not be treated differently from national workers by reason of his nationality in respect of 'any conditions of employment and work'. The case law of the European Court of Justice confirms that this provision covers both direct and indirect discrimination. Indirect discrimination can occur when a rule that appears on the surface to be neutral has a disproportionate impact in practice on one group over another. In Case 152/73, *Sotgiu v. Deutsche Bundespost* [1974] ECR 153, the decision of the German Post Office to increase the separation allowance paid to workers employed away from their place of residence within Germany was found to be potentially incompatible with Article 7(1) of the regulation.

The increase in payment was not paid to workers, whatever their nationality, whose residence at the time of their initial employment was situated outside Germany. The European Court of Justice pointed out that Article 39 of the EC Treaty and Article 7 of Regulation 1612/68 prohibit not only overt discrimination on grounds of nationality, but also 'all covert forms of discrimination which, by the application of other criteria of differentiation, lead in fact to the same result'.

The court ruled that the criterion based on the residence of a worker was capable of breaching the principle of non-discrimination, since it was tantamount, as regards its practical effect, to discrimination on grounds of nationality. In other words, the vast majority of non-residents would also be non-nationals; thus, the national law tended to place workers from other member states employed in Germany at a disadvantage in comparison with their German counterparts.

Social and Tax Advantages

Article 7(2) of Regulation 1612/68 provides that a Community worker shall enjoy the same 'social and tax advantages' as national workers. This provision has given rise to considerable litigation and has been interpreted very broadly by the European Court of Justice to ensure equal treatment for Community workers and their families, going beyond purely economic rights linked to a worker's contract of employment. In Case 137/84, *Ministère Public v. Mutsch* [1985] ECR 2681, a Luxembourg national resident in a German-speaking part of Belgium was charged with certain criminal offences following an extended pub-crawl. Mr Mutsch wished to have the proceedings conducted in German rather than French, but the Belgian authorities argued that the option of having proceedings conducted in German was only available to Belgian nationals.

The European Court of Justice adopted an extremely wide definition of Article 7(2), declaring that it covered advantages generally granted to national workers primarily because of their status as workers *or* by virtue of the mere fact of residence in the national territory. The court concluded that the Belgian rule violated Article 39 of the EC Treaty and Article 7(2) of the regulation, holding that EC workers were entitled to choose a language for proceedings before a member state court on the same conditions as nationals of that state.

A novel interpretation of the concept of a 'social advantage' contained in Article 7(2) can be seen in Case 59/85, *Netherlands v. Reed* [1986] ECR 1283. The case concerned an unmarried cohabiting British couple living in the Netherlands. The male partner (Mr W) enjoyed a right of residence in the Netherlands as a Community worker. Mr W's long-term partner, Ms Reed, was not employed in the Netherlands but sought to claim a right of residence on the basis of her relationship with Mr W. Article 10 of Regulation 1612/68 guarantees a right of residence for the spouse of a Community worker.

The European Court of Justice ruled that, in the absence of consensus among all member states concerning the status of unmarried companions, the term 'spouse' applied only to a person in a marital relationship and did not extend to cohabitation. While Ms Reed was therefore denied a right of residence as the spouse of a Community worker under Article 10 of Regulation 1612/68, the court instead focused on Article 7(2) concerning social advantages. The court noted that under Dutch law, a person who had a stable relationship with a Dutch worker was treated as that worker's spouse. It concluded that the possibility for a migrant worker to have his unmarried companion reside with him in another member state constituted a social advantage for the purposes of Article 7(2), which would assist integration, and to which he was entitled on the same basis as a national of that state. Of course, reliance on Article 7(2) of the regulation in a case such as *Reed* is entirely dependent on the status afforded to cohabiting couples under national law.

The decision in Case 316/85, *Centre public d'aide sociale de Courcelles v. Lebon* [1987] ECR 2811 illustrates the potential limitations of Article 7(2). The case concerned a French national who was the adult married daughter of a French national working in Belgium. Ms Lebon had never worked in

Belgium, but claimed to be seeking employment there, and had been refused the Belgium 'minimex', a minimum income payment. The court ruled that since Ms Lebon was not in employment in Belgium as a 'worker', she could not rely directly on Article 39 of the EC Treaty or on the provisions of Article 7(2) of Regulation 1612/68 relating to social advantages. The court further ruled that Ms Lebon could only claim entitlement to the minimex *if she was dependent on her father*. If that were the case, the payment would constitute a social advantage to her father, a Community worker. Whether or not Ms Lebon was dependent on her father was deemed by the European Court of Justice to be a matter of fact for the national court.

NON-DISCRIMINATORY BARRIERS TO THE FREE MOVEMENT OF WORKERS

We have seen that Article 39 of the Treaty, as supplemented by Regulation 1612/68, prohibits both direct and indirect discrimination on grounds of nationality in the context of Community workers. Until recently, however, it was unclear whether Article 39 applied to measures which restricted the free movement of workers, but which were neither directly nor indirectly discriminatory. The issue first emerged in the context of the free movement of workers in the famous *Bosman* case (Case C-415/93, *Union Royale Belge des Sociétés de Football Association and Others v. Bosman* [1995] ECR I-4921).

Under the rules regulating football in Europe, when a player was transferred at the expiry of his contract, his former club was entitled to a compensation fee for development or training. At the expiry of his contract with Liège FC, Bosman was put on the transfer list, but no other club showed any interest. Bosman was suspended by Liège and effectively prevented, by the UEFA transfer rules, from playing for any other club. He instituted proceedings in the Belgian courts seeking a declaration that the transfer rules were contrary to Community law and, in particular, that they were contrary to Article 39.

Note that the UEFA transfer rules applied even if a player moved to a new club in the same member state, and applied irrespective of a player's nationality. The European Court of Justice ruled, however, in *Bosman* that the fact that the transfer system applied equally to players moving from one club to another within a state, and that a player's nationality was irrelevant *did not* prevent the system from being caught by Article 39. The court noted that the transfer rules directly affected players' *access to the employment market* in other member states and were capable of impeding freedom of movement for workers. Thus, it is clear that even non-discriminatory rules may fall foul of Article 39, provided they potentially affect access to the employment market in another member state.

Case C-176/96, *Lehtonen* [2000] ECR I-2681 concerned a Finnish national who had signed a contract of employment with a Belgian basketball team. The rules of the International Basketball Federation on international transfers within the European zone stipulated that a player could not transfer to a club in a country of which he was not a national after 28 February each year.

Lehtonen transferred from his club in Finland and started to play with a Belgian team at the end of March 1996. He played in two games which the team won, but the points were subsequently deducted as a penalty for the breach of the International Federation's rules. Proceedings were instituted before the Belgian courts alleging that the Federation's rules constituted a breach of Article 39.

Applying *Bosman*, the European Court of Justice held that the contested rules constituted an obstacle to the free movement of workers, since they were liable to restrict the movement of workers who wished to pursue their activity in another member state, by preventing clubs from fielding players from other member states where such players had been engaged after a specified date. The court recognised that the setting of deadlines for transfers could be justified on grounds of ensuring the proper functioning of competitions, since late transfers might be liable to change substantially the sporting strength of a particular team in the course of the championship. However, the court noted that players from outside the European zone were subject to a transfer deadline of 31 March, rather than 28 February. It was left to the national court to determine whether the rule applicable to transfers within the European zone was proportionate to the objective pursued.

DEROGATIONS FROM THE FREE MOVEMENT OF WORKERS: EC TREATY, ARTICLE 39(3)

Under Article 39(3), a member state may impose limitations on the free movement of Community workers on grounds of 'public policy, public security or public health'. As with the derogations from the free movement of goods provided for in Article 30, the European Court of Justice has interpreted the justifications set out in Article 39(3) in an extremely restrictive manner.

Directive 64/221 provides guidance as to the measures a member state may adopt on grounds of public policy, security and health. It should be noted that the directive applies not only to workers, but also to the self-employed and to service providers. It is also worth noting that Article 2(2) of the directive stipulates that none of the derogations may be invoked 'to service economic ends'.

While the public health and public security justifications are rarely invoked, the public policy exception has given rise to considerable litigation.

Of particular interest in this regard is Article 3(1) of Directive 64/221, which states that 'measures taken on grounds of public policy or public security shall be based exclusively on the personal conduct of the individual concerned'. One of the earliest cases in which the European Court of Justice was required to consider the public policy justification was Case 41/74, *Van Duyn v. Home Office* [1974] ECR 1337, a decision which also established that the provisions of a directive may produce direct effect.

In *Van Duyn,* the UK sought to justify the refusal to allow a Dutch Scientologist to enter the state. The Church of Scientology was considered by the UK authorities to be anti-social and harmful, but was not prohibited under UK law.

Firstly, the European Court of Justice recognised that member states retained discretion as regards the public policy exemption. Thus, the practice of Scientology could legitimately be considered contrary to public policy in one member state, but tolerated in all other states. The court went on to declare that current active participation in a particular organisation could constitute 'personal conduct' within the meaning of Article 3(1). Finally, the European Court of Justice held that the UK was entitled to prevent a national from another member state from taking up employment with a particular organisation, even though no similar restriction was placed on its own nationals.

Subsequent case law illustrates that, in certain respects, the ruling in *Van Duyn* no longer represents the law. In Cases 115 and 116/81, *Adoui and Cornuaille v. Belgian State* [1982] ECR 1665, two French nationals working in Belgium had been refused residence permits on grounds of public policy. The authorities believed that both women were working as prostitutes. Of particular significance in this case was the fact that prostitution itself was not illegal in Belgium. The European Court of Justice recognised that the derogations provided for in the Treaty permitted member states to adopt measures which discriminated against non-nationals, since a state had no authority to expel its own nationals from its territory. However, the court stressed that a member state was not entitled to adopt measures which had the effect of applying an 'arbitrary distinction' to the detriment of nationals of other member states. It concluded that conduct could not be regarded as sufficiently serious to justify deportation, where a member state did not adopt 'repressive measures or other genuine and effective measures' to combat the same conduct on the part of its own nationals. A comparison can be drawn with the decision in Case 121/85, *Conegate Ltd. v. Commissioners of Customs and Excise* [1986] ECR 1007 relating to the application of the public morality justification under Article 30. A justification invoked by a member state under Article 39(3) must be *bona fide* and not a means of effecting arbitrary discrimination.

CRIMINAL CONVICTIONS AND DEROGATION FROM FREE MOVEMENT GUARANTEES

Article 3(2) of Directive 64/221 provides that previous criminal convictions shall not in themselves constitute grounds for the taking of measures on grounds of public policy or public security. In Case 30/77, *R v. Bouchereau* [1977] ECR 1999, the European Court of Justice considered the circumstances in which previous criminal convictions might be relevant.

The *Bouchereau* case concerned a French national working in the UK who had been convicted twice for unlawful possession of drugs. A preliminary reference was made to the European Court of Justice asking whether past conduct resulting in a criminal conviction could be taken into account in considering whether to deport a Community national.

The court held that a previous criminal conviction could only be taken into account insofar as the circumstances giving rise to that conviction were 'evidence of personal conduct constituting a present threat to the requirements of public policy'. It went on to clarify the grounds on which a member state was entitled to derogate from the free movement of persons, declaring that the concept of public policy required the existence of a 'genuine and sufficiently serious threat to the requirements of public policy affecting one of the fundamental interests of society'. The ruling emphasises the fact that a member state may not have recourse to the public policy exception unless very substantial grounds for restricting the free movement rights of a Community national can be established.

In Case C-348/96, *Criminal Proceedings against Calfa* [1999] ECR I-11, the court reiterated its earlier ruling in *Bouchereau*. It should be noted that the *Calfa* case concerned the free movement of services, rather than the free movement of workers. However, as we will see in the following chapter, the grounds of derogation from the free movement of workers, the freedom of establishment and the free movement of services are identical.

Ms Calfa was an Italian tourist charged with possession of drugs for personal use while on holiday in Crete. Under Greek law, the relevant offence was punishable by a term of imprisonment. However, foreign nationals convicted of the offence could be expelled from the country for life. On conviction, Ms Calfa was sentenced to three months' imprisonment and expelled from Greece for life.

The European Court of Justice pointed out that the public policy exception was to be interpreted restrictively. Applying *Bouchereau*, the European Court of Justice declared that a previous conviction could only be taken into account insofar as it provided evidence of a present threat to public policy. It also pointed out that public policy required the existence of a 'genuine and sufficiently serious threat to the requirements of public policy affecting one of the fundamental interests of society'. The contested national legislation was found to violate both the Treaty and the directive by virtue of the automatic nature of the sanction of expulsion. Expulsion for life automatically followed a criminal conviction: no account was taken of the personal conduct of the offender or of the danger that person posed to society.

PUBLIC SERVICE EXEMPTION: EC TREATY, ARTICLE 39(4)

Article 39(4) states that the provisions of Article 39 'shall not apply to employment in the public service'. Unsurprisingly, the concept of 'employment in the public service' has been construed very restrictively by the European Court of Justice, since Article 39(4) constitutes a derogation from one of the fundamental principles on which the Community is based. It should be noted that the public service exemption set out in Article 39(4) is similar to the derogation from the freedom of establishment and the free movement of services applicable in respect of activities connected with the 'exercise of official authority' (considered in the following chapter).

In Case 149/79, *Commission v. Belgium* [1980] ECR 3881, the Commission took infringement proceedings against Belgium for breach of Article 39. Under Belgian law, possession of Belgian nationality was required as a condition of entry for an array of posts within local authorities, regardless of the nature of the activities to be performed, including the posts of unskilled railway workers, hospital nurses and night watchmen. The European Court of Justice held that posts covered by the public service exception presumed on the part of those occupying them the 'existence of a special relationship of allegiance to the state and reciprocity of rights and duties which form the foundation of the bond of nationality'. Posts falling within the scope of Article 39(4) must involve 'direct or indirect participation in the exercise of powers conferred by public law' *and* must entail 'duties designed to safeguard the general interests of the state or of other public authorities'. On the facts of the case, the court ruled that it did not have enough information to determine which posts fell within the public service exception.

Two years later in Case 149/79, *Commission v. Belgium II* [1982] ECR 1837, the court ruled that with the exception of a certain limited number of posts – including those of night watchman and architect with the municipality of Brussels – none of the contested posts fell within the ambit of the public service exception. In Case 307/84, *Commission v. France* [1986] ECR 1725, the European Court of Justice declared that the post of nurse in a public hospital was not employment in the 'public service' for the purposes of Article 39(4). Accordingly, a law making possession of French nationality a precondition for appointment to the post of nurse in French public hospitals was deemed to constitute discrimination on grounds of nationality, as prohibited by Article 39(2).

RIGHTS OF WORKERS' FAMILIES: REGULATION 1612/68

From the outset, it was recognised that labour mobility within the Community would be severely undermined unless the rights of free movement and residence accorded to Community workers were extended also to the families of such workers. This sentiment is reflected in the preamble to Regulation 1612/68. The rights of workers' families are dealt with in Articles 10 to 12 of the regulation.

Article 10 lists the family members who have the right to install themselves with a Community worker employed in another member state. These include: a worker's spouse; their descendants who are under the age of 21 or who are dependants; and dependent relatives in the ascending line of the worker and his spouse. As noted previously, the rights accorded to spouses under the regulation do not extend to cohabitees. In *Netherlands v. Reed*, cited above, the European Court of Justice held that the term 'spouse' in Article 10 of the regulation applied only to a person in a marital relationship and did not extend to cohabitation.

The derivative nature of the rights accorded to workers' families is illustrated in a number of cases. Case 267/83, *Diatta v. Land Berlin* [1985] ECR 567 concerned a Senegalese national who had married a French national, both of whom were resident in Germany. The couple separated with the intention of divorcing and moved into separate accommodation. The applicant was refused a residence permit on the ground that she was no longer a family member of an EC national.

On a preliminary reference, the European Court of Justice held that Article 10 of Regulation 1612/68 did not require that a member of a worker's family live permanently under the same roof as the worker in order to qualify for a right of residence. However, the European Court of Justice emphasised that the members of a worker's family had *no independent right of residence*, but rather that the rights conferred on the worker's family were entirely conditional upon the right of residence of the worker. The court noted that the marital relationship in the instant case had not yet been dissolved and that the likelihood of divorce did not affect the spouse's rights under EC law. It is clear that the rights conferred on the third country national spouse of a Community worker under Regulation 1612/68 are entirely contingent on the continued existence of a marital relationship.

Reverse Discrimination?

It should be noted that certain anomalies can arise in this area in the context of so-called 'wholly internal situations'. In Cases 35 and 36/82, *Morson and Jhanjan v. Netherlands* [1982] ECR 3723, two Dutch nationals living and working in the Netherlands sought to bring their parents, of Surinamese nationality, into the country to reside with them. The applications of the two Surinamese women for residence permits were refused by the Dutch authorities. On a preliminary reference, the European Court of Justice held that the provisions of EC law relating to the free movement of workers could not be invoked by workers living and working in their own member state who had never exercised the right to free movement within the Community. Had the workers been nationals of any other member state working in the Netherlands, they would have been entitled to rely on Article 10 of Regulation 1612/68 to have their dependent parents reside with them.

The issue of reverse discrimination also arose in Case C-370/90, *R v. IAT and Surinder Singh, ex parte Secretary of State for the Home Department* [1992] ECR I-4265, but in that case a period spent by the applicant and spouse working in another member state was of crucial significance. The case concerned an Indian national who had married a British national and travelled with her to Germany, where they had both worked for some years before returning to the UK. The couple separated and commenced divorce proceedings. Before the divorce became final, the UK authorities sought to deport Mr Singh. The question arose as to whether Mr Singh enjoyed a right of residence in the UK as the spouse of a Community worker.

The UK sought to argue that the case was governed entirely by national law, since it concerned the right of the spouse of a UK national to reside in the UK. However, the European Court of Justice held that the period of time spent working in another member state triggered the application of EC law. The court pointed out that a worker might be deterred from leaving his country of origin to work in another member state, if, on his return, the conditions of entry and residence were not at least equivalent to those enjoyed in the territory of another member state.

Education Rights of Workers and Their Families

The preamble to Regulation 1612/68 recognises that close links exist between freedom of movement for workers and vocational training. Indeed, education and training are seen as being intrinsic to greater labour mobility within the Community and to the creation of a more competitive European market. It should be noted that Community law recognises different categories of persons for the purposes of education rights, with certain categories being more privileged than others.

Education Rights of Community Workers

Article 7(3) of Regulation 1612/68 provides that a Community worker shall have access to training in vocational schools and retraining centres under the same conditions as national workers. In Case 39/86, *Lair* [1988] ECR 3161, the European Court of Justice interpreted Article 7(3) quite restrictively, declaring that the concept of a vocational school was a limited one and referred 'exclusively to institutions which provide only instruction either alternating with or closely linked to an occupational activity, particularly during apprenticeship'. As a result, it held that a university course did not fall within the scope of Article 7(3). However, the court pointed out that a Community worker might nevertheless be entitled to invoke Article 7(2) of Regulation 1612/68 in respect of studies in an institution that did not fall within the definition of a 'vocational school'. The court noted that a grant awarded for maintenance and training with a view to the pursuit of university studies leading to a professional qualification constituted a 'social advantage' within the meaning of Article 7(2) of Regulation 1612/68. However, the court stressed that where a Community worker sought to rely on Article 7(2) to claim entitlement to a university maintenance grant, there had to be some 'continuity between the previous work activity and the course of study'. In effect, the court sought to prevent Community nationals from abusing the provisions relating to the free movement of workers so as to take advantages of more attractive educational benefits in other member states.

In Case 197/86, *Brown v. Secretary of State for Scotland* [1988] ECR 3205, the applicant, who held dual French-British nationality, had undertaken an eight-month period of pre-university industrial training in Edinburgh prior to commencing engineering studies at Cambridge University. He claimed that the refusal of the Scottish authorities to award him a maintenance grant constituted a breach of his rights as a Community worker under Article 7 of Regulation 1612/68. The European Court of Justice declared that where a person acquired the status of worker exclusively as a result of his being admitted to university to pursue studies in a related field, the employment relationship was *merely ancillary to the studies*. Such a person was not entitled to rely on Article 7(2) of Regulation 1612/68 to claim entitlement to a maintenance grant. It should be noted that the practical implications of the ruling in *Brown* have been significantly diminished by more recent decisions of the European Court of Justice in the area of citizenship (see below).

Education Rights of Children of Community Workers

The children of Community workers enjoy the most generous educational rights. Article 12 of Regulation 1612/68 states that 'the children of a national of a member state who is or has been employed in the territory of another member state shall be admitted to that state's general educational, apprenticeship and vocational training courses under the same conditions as the nationals of that state, if such children are residing in its territory'. In other words, Article 12 places the children of Community workers residing in a particular member state in the same position as the children of nationals of that state insofar as education is concerned.

The scope of the educational rights of children of migrant workers has been clarified in the case law of the European Court of Justice. In Case 76/72, *Michel S* [1973] ECR 457, the European Court of Justice ruled that the list of courses outlined in Article 12 was not exhaustive. In Case 9/74, *Casagrande v. Landeshauptstadt München* [1974] ECR 773, the court focused on the second paragraph of Article 12, which states that member states must encourage all efforts to enable the children of Community workers to attend educational courses 'under the best possible conditions'. The European Court of Justice declared that the principle of equal treatment in Article 12 applied not only to admission to courses, but extended to any general measures intended to facilitate educational attendance. As a result, the court suggested that the child of an Italian national working in Germany was entitled to avail of an educational grant payable to German secondary school students.

In Cases 389 and 390/87, *Echternach and Moritz* [1989] ECR 723, the European Court of Justice held that the rights enjoyed by the children of migrant workers in the host member state under Article 12 continue to apply, even where the child's parents (i.e. the Community workers) had returned to their home state. The case concerned two students of German nationality who had been refused educational grants by the Dutch authorities on the basis that their parents, who had worked in the Netherlands, had returned to Germany.

RIGHTS OF STUDENTS AND NON-ECONOMICALLY ACTIVE PERSONS

With moves towards greater political integration, Community law is no longer purely driven by economic considerations. In recent years, increasing measures have been taken to facilitate the free movement of those who are not economically active. In 1990, the Community adopted three new directives conferring rights of residence on retired persons (Directive 90/365), students (Directive 90/366, replaced by Directive 93/96) and all nationals of member states with sufficient resources to avoid becoming a burden on the social assistance system of the host member state (Directive 90/364).

Aside from rights of residence, the case law of the European Court of Justice has also conferred other significant rights on students. As a result of a number of important cases decided by the European Court of Justice, students who have no family link to the host member state are now recognised as enjoying substantial rights under Community law. Case 293/83, *Gravier v. City of Liège* [1985] ECR 593 concerned a French national who challenged the requirement under Belgian law for non-Belgians to pay an enrolment fee for admission to a third level art school. In a judgment with far-reaching consequences, the European Court of Justice held that the imposition on non-nationals of the enrolment fee, in circumstances where the same fee was not imposed on students who were nationals of the host member state, constituted discrimination on grounds of nationality contrary to Article 12 of the EC Treaty.

As we have mentioned previously, Article 12 stipulates that: 'within the scope of application of [the] Treaty ... any discrimination on grounds of nationality shall be prohibited'. The European Court of Justice succeeded in bringing the *Gravier* case 'within the scope of application of the Treaty' by relying on what was then Article 128 of the EC Treaty, a provision which envisaged the creation of a common vocational training policy. In Case 24/86, *Blaizot v. University of Liège* [1988] ECR 379, the European Court of Justice stated that university education could constitute vocational training, unless the course was one intended to improve general knowledge rather than prepare a person for an occupation.

As we will see in the following section, the provisions on Union citizenship introduced by the TEU have served to further expand the rights enjoyed by students within the Community (see, in particular, the decision in Case C-184/99, *Rudy Grzelczyk* [2001] ECR I-6193, considered below).

IMPACT OF UNION CITIZENSHIP ON FREE MOVEMENT LAW

While the concept of 'European citizenship' had been discussed in political and academic circles for many years, it only found formal expression in Community law with the adoption of the Treaty on European Union, which amended the EC Treaty to add a new Part Two (now Articles 17-22) entitled 'Citizenship of the Union'.

Article 2 of the TEU also states that one of the objectives of the EU is:

[T]o strengthen the protection of the rights and interests of the nationals of its member states through the introduction of a citizenship of the Union.

Articles 17-22 contain the core citizenship provisions. These provisions contain a definition of those who are to be considered 'citizens' and an enumeration of the specific rights accorded to Union citizens. Article 17(1) states that 'every person holding the nationality of a member state shall be a citizen of the Union'. Article 18 confers on every citizen the right to move and reside freely within the territory of the member states. The rights to vote in and to stand for municipal elections in one's member state of residence, and in elections to the European Parliament, are accorded by Article 19. Meanwhile, Article 20 provides the right to the diplomatic and consular assistance of any member state in the territory of a third country in which a Union citizen's member state of nationality is not represented. Finally, the rights to petition the European Parliament and to apply to the Ombudsman are enshrined in Article 21.

With the entry into force of the TEU, the question soon arose as to whether the new citizenship provisions would add anything to the existing principles of Community law. In particular, it remained to be seen whether the 'right to move and reside freely within the territory of the member states' conferred on the Union citizen by Article 18 would have any impact on the existing Community rules governing the free movement of workers. Initially, the European Court of Justice showed little willingness to entertain arguments based on citizenship, preferring instead to continue to categorise persons as economic actors and to apply the more specific Community provisions governing the free movement of workers, the freedom of establishment and the free movement of services. In more recent cases, however, the court has begun to afford greater consideration to the concept of Union citizenship – with some far-reaching results.

Case C-85/96, *Martinez Sala* [1998] ECR I-2691 related to a refusal by the German state of Bavaria to grant a child-raising allowance to Ms Sala, a Spanish national who had lived in Germany almost continuously since 1968. German law made the grant of child-raising allowance to non-nationals dependent on the possession of a formal residence permit. Save for a brief period of employment in 1989, Ms Sala had not worked since 1986 and was in receipt of social assistance. She was not in possession of a residence permit at the time when she made the application for the child-raising allowance. The national court asked the European Court of Justice to rule on the compatibility with Community law of a requirement that Community nationals seeking to avail of child-raising allowance be in possession of a formal residence permit.

In its decision, the European Court of Justice declared that that the requirement that non-German EC nationals produce a residence permit in order to receive child-raising allowance was indeed tantamount to 'unequal treatment'. Of course, such treatment could only constitute discrimination under Article 12 if Ms Sala's situation fell *within the scope of application of the Treaty*.

The child-rearing allowance was found to fall within the 'material scope' of Community law, since it constituted a 'social advantage' within the meaning of Regulation 1612/68. However, bringing Ms Sala within the 'personal scope' of Community law was more difficult, since she did not appear to fall within one of the categories of economically active persons granted rights by the

Treaty. In its judgment, the court made its first important statement on the significance of the new citizenship provisions, declaring that:

> ... [A] citizen of the European Union, such as the appellant in the main proceedings, lawfully resident in the territory of the host member state, can rely on Article 6 [now Article 12] of the Treaty in all situations which fall within the [material scope] of Community law.

Applying this reasoning, the court suggested that as a national of a member state lawfully residing in the territory of another member state, Ms Sala came within the personal scope of the Treaty provisions on European citizenship. Since Article 17(2) attaches to the status of citizen of the Union the rights and duties laid down by the Treaty, she was entitled to invoke the non-discrimination principle embodied in Article 12 in any situation falling within the material scope of the Treaty. Thus, Ms Sala's status as a Union citizen was invoked to bring her within the personal scope of Community law; it was not necessary that she establish her involvement in an economic activity.

The concept of European citizenship was again invoked by the European Court of Justice in Case C-184/99, *Rudy Grzelczyk* [2001] ECR I-6193. The case concerned a French national studying in Belgium who had been refused payment of a minimum subsistence allowance (the 'minimex') under Belgian law on the ground that he was not a Belgian national. Under Belgian law, entitlement to the minimex had been extended to persons to whom Regulation 1612/68 applied. However, Mr Grzelczyk was not a 'worker' and, as such, did not fall within the ambit of the regulation. In preliminary reference proceedings, the European Court of Justice reiterated its previous assertion in *Martinez Sala* that a Union citizen, lawfully resident in the territory of a host member state, could rely on the Article 12 prohibition of discrimination on grounds of nationality in all situations which fell within the material scope of Community law. Most significantly, however, the court went on to find that a citizen exercising the right to move and reside freely in another member state, as enshrined in Article 18 of the Treaty, came within the material scope of Community law. Thus, the concept of Union citizenship and the free movement rights conferred on citizens by Article 18 were used to bring the applicant within both the personal and material scope of Article 12. The court concluded that Articles 12 and 18 of the Treaty precluded entitlement to a non-contributory social benefit, such as the Belgian 'minimex', from being made conditional, in the case of nationals of member states other than the host state where they were legally resident, on their falling within the scope of Regulation 1612/68 when no such condition applied to nationals of the host member state.

Other important decisions on citizenship include Case C-224/98, *D'Hoop v. Office national de l'emploi* [2002] ECR I-6191 and Case C-413/99

Baumbast v. Secretary of State for the Home Department [2002] ECR I-7091. In the *D'Hoop* case, the question arose as to whether Community law precluded a member state from refusing to grant a particular unemployment allowance to one of its nationals (a student seeking her first employment), on the sole ground that the student in question had completed her secondary education in another member state. Ms D'Hoop could not be regarded as a Community worker and, accordingly was not in a position to rely on either Article 39 of the Treaty or the provisions of Regulation 1612/68. Having reiterated the essence of its decision in *Grzelczyk*, the court declared that:

> [A] citizen of the Union must be granted in all member states the same treatment in law as that accorded to the nationals of those member states who find themselves in the same situation.

The court found that it would be incompatible with the right of freedom of movement conferred by Article 18 if a Union citizen, in the member state of which she is a national, were to receive treatment less favourable than she would enjoy if she had not exercised her rights of free movement under the Treaty. Community law was held to preclude a member state from refusing to grant an allowance to one of its nationals, a student seeking her first employment, on the sole ground that she had completed her secondary education in another member state.

In the *Baumbast* case, cited above, the European Court of Justice declared that a citizen of the European Union who no longer enjoyed a right of residence as a migrant worker in the host member state could, as a citizen of the Union, enjoy a right of residence by direct application of Article 18 of the Treaty. The court recognised that the exercise of that right was subject to the 'limitations and conditions' referred to in Article 18, but stated that the competent authorities and the national courts in the state in question were required to ensure that those limitations and conditions were applied in compliance with the general principles of Community law and, in particular, with the principle of proportionality.

CONCLUSION

The free movement of workers is one of the four fundamental freedoms recognised by Community law. Articles 39-42 of the EC Treaty set out the basic principles applicable in this area, with further detail on the rights enjoyed by Community workers contained in secondary legislation, most notably in Regulation 1612/68. The European Court of Justice has interpreted the term 'worker' very broadly, while construing the derogations provided for in Article 39(3) and the public service exemption contained in Article 39(4) very narrowly – an approach designed to maximise the scope of application of the Community free movement rules. Central to the law governing the free movement of workers is the principle of equal treatment. As we have seen in this chapter, Article 39 of the Treaty, as supplemented by Regulation 1612/68, prohibits both direct and indirect discrimination against workers on grounds of nationality. Regulation 1612/68 also contains important provisions relating to the rights of workers' families. With the introduction of the concept of Union citizenship, however, the classification of a person as an economic actor is becoming less important. Recent decisions such as *Martinez Sala* and *Grzelczyk* illustrate the far-reaching influence that the citizenship provisions have begun to exert on the development of Community law.

Chapter 15

FREEDOM OF ESTABLISHMENT AND FREE MOVEMENT OF SERVICES

INTRODUCTION

The free movement of persons is one of the four fundamental freedoms recognised by Community law. A Community national may exercise his or her free movement rights as a 'worker', in which case Articles 39-42 (ex Articles 48-51) and the relevant secondary legislation adopted under those provisions will be applicable. However, a national of one member state may wish to move on a permanent or semi-permanent basis to another member state with the intention of working there in a self-employed capacity. In this case, the Treaty provisions concerning the freedom of establishment apply (Articles 43-48, ex Articles 52-58).

Free movement rights may also be exercised by persons established in one member state who wish to provide or receive services in another member state on a temporary or periodical basis. The Community rules governing the free movement of services are set out in Articles 49-55 (ex Articles 59-66). It should be noted that the free movement of services provisions can also come into play in situations involving no cross-border movement of persons. For example, cross-border transmission of television programmes constitutes the provision of services within the meaning of the Treaty, despite the fact that neither the provider nor the recipient of the services moves from one state to another.

In this chapter, we will consider the principles applicable to the freedom of establishment and to the free movement of services. As we will see, the rules governing both areas are similar in many respects. Indeed, certain parallels can be drawn between the Treaty provisions concerning each of the four fundamental freedoms. In particular, the grounds of derogation from the free movement of workers, the freedom of establishment and the free movement of services are identical. These justifications – public policy, public security and public health – were considered in the previous chapter in the context of the free movement of workers, but will be considered in further detail below insofar as they apply to the freedom of establishment and the free movement of services. As we will see later, the rules on establishment and services do not apply 'so far as any given member state is concerned, to activities which in that state are connected, even occasionally, with the exercise of official authority'. This is known as the 'official authority' exception, and echoes the 'public service' exception set out in Article 39(4) in the context of the free movement of workers.

SECONDARY LEGISLATION GOVERNING ESTABLISHMENT AND SERVICES

It is important to note that the Treaty provisions concerning establishment and services, and the case law interpreting those provisions, cannot be considered in isolation. Secondary legislation, particularly in relation to the recognition of professional qualifications, also plays an extremely important role. While a whole array of 'sectoral' directives have been adopted providing for the mutual recognition of qualifications in specific fields, we will focus primarily on the more general principles enshrined in the Treaty and developed by the European Court of Justice.

Other important legislative provisions in the field of establishment and services include Directive 73/148 and Directive 75/34. Directive 73/148 provides for the abolition of restrictions on movement and residence within the Community for nationals of member states with regard to establishment and the provision of services. The directive is analogous to Directive 68/360, considered in the previous chapter, concerning rights of entry and residence for Community workers. Directive 75/34 concerns the right of nationals of one member state to remain in the territory of another member state after having pursued an activity there in a self-employed capacity.

DISTINCTION BETWEEN ESTABLISHMENT AND SERVICES

In Case C-55/94, *Gebhard v. Consiglio dell-Ordine degli Avvocati e Procuratori di Milano* [1995] ECR I-4165, the European Court of Justice declared that the Treaty provisions governing the free movement of workers, the right to establishment and the free movement of services were 'mutually exclusive'. Thus, the situation of a Community national who has moved to another member state in order to pursue an economic activity will fall to be examined under only one of those three categories. While it is relatively easy to ascertain whether a person constitutes a 'worker' for the purposes of Article 39, the dividing line between establishment and provision of services is often difficult to draw. In the *Gebhard* case, the European Court of Justice sought to provide guidance on this issue. It noted that the concept of 'establishment' was a very broad one, allowing a Community national 'to participate, on a stable and continuous basis, in the economic life of a member state other than his state of origin […]'.

In contrast, where the provider of services moves to another member state on a temporary basis, the Treaty provisions relating to services apply. The temporary nature of the activities in question was, according to the court, to be determined in light not only of the 'duration of the provision of the service', but also by reference to its 'regularity, periodicity or continuity'. Despite the temporary nature of the provision of services, the European Court of Justice in *Gebhard* recognised that a service provider was entitled to equip himself with some form of infrastructure in the host state (including an office, chambers or consulting rooms) insofar as such infrastructure was necessary for performing the services in question.

FREEDOM OF ESTABLISHMENT: EC TREATY, ARTICLES 43-48

Article 43 of the EC Treaty prohibits restrictions on the freedom of establishment of nationals of a member state in the territory of another member state. The prohibition also applies to:

> restrictions on the setting up of agencies, branches, or subsidiaries by nationals of any member state established in the territory of any member state.

The second paragraph of Article 43 states that freedom of establishment shall include:

> the right to take up and pursue activities as self-employed persons and to set up and manage undertakings ... under the same conditions laid down for its own nationals by the law of the country where such establishment is effected [...].

Direct Effect of EC Treaty, Article 43

Under the original Treaty, Article 52 (now Article 43) provided that restrictions on the freedom of establishment were to be abolished by progressive stages during a transitional period. The Treaty envisaged the adoption of legislative measures (including a general programme and harmonising directives) by the Community to attain this objective. On the expiry of the transitional period in 1970, a number of directives had been adopted eliminating restrictions in certain specific fields. However, significant obstacles remained and the question soon arose as to whether Article 43 (ex Article 52) was capable of producing direct effect.

In Case 2/74, *Reyners v. Belgium* [1974] ECR 631, a Dutch national had obtained a legal diploma in Belgium giving the right to take up the profession of *avocat* (lawyer), but was refused admission to the Belgian Bar solely by reason of his nationality. Rejecting the arguments of the Belgian government, the European Court of Justice held that Article 43 produced direct effect and could therefore be relied upon by Mr Reyners before the Belgian courts to challenge the discriminatory national law. The court was determined to ensure that in the absence of harmonising directives, individuals could directly invoke the prohibition of restrictions on the right of establishment contained in Article 43.

Scope of Application of EC Treaty, Article 43: Definition of 'Establishment'

The freedom of establishment enshrined in Article 43 entails the right to engage in an economic activity in another member state on a permanent or semi-permanent basis. The case law of the European Court of Justice provides guidance on the meaning of the term 'establishment'. In Case C-55/94, *Gebhard v. Consiglio dell-Ordine degli Avvocati e Procuratori di Milano* [1995] ECR I-4165, a German national who had qualified as a lawyer in Germany opened an office in Italy, but was prohibited by the Milan Bar Council from using the Italian title *avvocato* (lawyer) and suspended from practice for six months. On a preliminary reference, the European Court of Justice was called upon to clarify the concepts of 'establishment' and 'provision of services'.

In relation to establishment, the court noted that the term was a very broad one, which allowed a Community national to participate, on a 'stable and continuous basis', in the economic life of a member state other than his state of origin. The court suggested that Mr Gebhard, as a national of a member state who pursued a professional activity on a stable and continuous basis in another member state from an established professional base, came within the scope of the Treaty provisions relating to the right of establishment and not those relating to services.

In Case C-221/89, *R v. Secretary of State for Transport, ex parte Factortame (No. 2)* [1991] ECR I-3905, the European Court of Justice declared that the concept of establishment within the meaning of Article 43 involved the 'actual pursuit of an economic activity through a fixed establishment in another member state for an indefinite period'.

It should be noted that a Community national may exercise the right of establishment in more than one member state at the same time. In Case 107/83, *Ordre des Avocats au Barreau de Paris v. Klopp* [1984] ECR 2971, a German lawyer already practising in Düsseldorf was refused permission by the Paris Bar Council to practise simultaneously as a member of the Paris Bar. Under the rules of the Paris Bar, a lawyer could only have chambers in one place, which was required to be in the region of the court with which he was registered (the 'single chambers' rule). The European Court of Justice ruled that the freedom of establishment implied the right to establish oneself in another member state without surrendering one's existing establishment elsewhere.

The court accepted that a host state had the right, in the interest of the proper administration of justice, to require lawyers practising in its territory to conduct their practice in such a way as to maintain sufficient contact with their clients and with the judicial authorities. However, modern means of transport and telecommunications made it possible for a lawyer to maintain appropriate contact with judicial authorities and clients, even where he had a second set of chambers in another member state. The decision in *Gebhard*, cited above, confirmed that a person may be established in more than one member state – for example, through the setting up of agencies, branches or subsidiaries, or by establishing a second professional base.

Professional Qualifications: Case Law of the European Court of Justice

The decision in *Reyners*, cited above, clearly illustrates that laws restricting the exercise of a particular trade or profession to nationals of the member state in question will be regarded as incompatible with Article 43. However, such explicitly discriminatory rules are relatively rare. In practice, the most significant barriers to the freedom of establishment arise in the area of qualifications. If access to certain trades and professions is made dependent on the possession of qualifications that can only be obtained in the host state, nationals from other member states possessing qualifications obtained in their home state will effectively be precluded from exercising their rights of free movement.

In order to make it easier for persons to take up and pursue activities as self-employed persons, Article 47 (ex Article 57) provides for the adoption of directives for the harmonisation or mutual recognition of qualifications in a particular trade or profession. Before examining some of the secondary legislation adopted under Article 47, it is worth considering the general principles on recognition of qualifications developed by the European Court of Justice. In Case 71/76, *Thieffry v. Conseil de l'Ordre des Avocats à la Cour de Paris* [1977] ECR 765, a Belgian lawyer's application for admission to the Paris Bar had been rejected on the ground that he did not hold a degree in law from a French university. Mr Thieffry held a Belgian diploma of Doctor of Laws which had been recognised by a French university as being equivalent to a French law degree. The Paris Bar Council argued that, in the absence of any directives under Article 47 governing the legal profession, Article 43 had no application to the question of recognition of foreign diplomas.

Rejecting this argument, the European Court of Justice held that a Community national could not be denied the benefit of the Treaty provisions on freedom of establishment solely by virtue of the fact that, for a particular profession, the directives envisaged by Article 47 had not yet been adopted. On the facts of the case, the French authorities were not justified in refusing the applicant admission to the Paris Bar solely on the ground that he did not possess a French qualification. Mr Thieffry had obtained a Belgian diploma which had been recognised by the French university as being an equivalent qualification to a French law degree. In addition, he had passed the necessary professional examination for admission to the profession of *avocat* in France.

The issue of equivalence of qualifications was further examined by the European Court of Justice in Case C-340/89, *Vlassopoulou* [1991] ECR 2357. The case concerned a Greek lawyer who had practised with a firm of lawyers in Germany for a number of years. She had obtained her professional qualification in Greece and held a doctorate in law from a German university. In 1988, her application for admission to the German Bar was refused on the ground that she had not passed any of the necessary examinations for admission to the profession of lawyer in Germany. The European Court of Justice noted that, even in the absence of any actual discrimination on grounds of nationality, national laws on qualifications could nonetheless have the effect of hindering the freedom of establishment guaranteed under Article 43. That would be the case, for example, if the national rules in question took no account of knowledge and qualifications already acquired in another member state. The court held that if a member state received a request to admit a person to a profession to which access, under national law, depended on the possession of a diploma or a professional qualification then the member state was required to take into consideration the diplomas, certificates and other evidence of qualifications acquired by that person in another member state. Thus, national authorities were found to be obliged, even in the absence of any directive governing the particular trade or profession, to undertake an *assessment of equivalence*, by making a 'comparison between the specialised knowledge and abilities certified by those diplomas and the knowledge and qualifications required by the national rules'. It should be noted that the *Vlassopoulou* case arose prior to the expiry of the deadline for the implementation of Directive 89/48 (considered below).

Principle of Mutual Recognition: Legislative Developments

Article 47 (ex Article 57) provides for the adoption of directives for the 'mutual recognition of diplomas, certificates and other evidence of formal qualifications' and directives 'for the co-ordination of the provisions laid down by law, regulation or administrative action in member states concerning the taking-up and pursuit or activities as self-employed persons'. Initially, the Community pursued a policy of harmonisation, targeting specific trades and professions and establishing uniform, minimum standards of education and training necessary to obtain qualifications in those fields. Known as 'sectoral harmonisation', this process was extremely complex and time-consuming. Directives adopted using this method covered professionals such as architects, pharmacists, dental practitioners, veterinary surgeons and doctors. These can be called 'vertical' directives.

An example of a sectoral directive is Directive 75/362 (the 'Doctors' Directive'), now repealed and replaced by Directive 93/16, which provided for the mutual recognition of diplomas, certificates and other evidence of formal qualifications in medicine. In Case 246/80, *Broekmeulen v. Huisarts Registratie Commissie* [1981] ECR 2311, a doctor who had qualified in a member state other than that of his nationality by means of a qualification listed in Article 3 of the directive was held to be entitled to practise as a general practitioner in his country of nationality without undergoing any additional periods of training required under national law. Thus, where a directive has been adopted governing a particular profession, a member state may no longer require compliance with training requirements beyond those imposed under the terms of the directive. Under the Doctors' Directive, additional training requirements could only be imposed by a member state in respect of specialists; a general practitioner was not regarded as a specialist under the directive.

By the 1980s, the task of harmonising qualification requirements for individual professions had become so arduous that the Council finally resolved to pursue a different strategy. Instead of seeking to fix uniform standards for *every individual trade and profession*, the Community moved to a *general system* of 'mutual recognition'. These can be called 'horizontal' directives. Directive 89/48 was the first directive to embody this new approach, providing for 'a general system for the recognition of higher-education diplomas awarded on completion of professional education and training of at least three years' duration'. The directive applies to all regulated professions for which university-level training of at least three years is required and which are not covered by a specific directive. In essence, where a person has completed the necessary training to take up a profession falling within the scope of the directive in one member state, he or she cannot be precluded from practising that profession in another member state solely on grounds of inadequate qualifications.

A second 'general system' directive was adopted in 1992 – Directive 92/51 extends the principles of mutual recognition to certain qualifications not covered by Directive 89/48. A third 'general system' directive, Directive 99/42, was adopted in 1999. The legislative regime currently governing the mutual recognition of education and training comprises seventeen main directives i.e. the three general system directives just mentioned, and other sectoral directives dealing with individual professions, particularly in the health sector. Both Directives 89/48 and 92/51, and a number of the sectoral directives were recently amended by Directive 2001/19. This new directive aims to simplify existing rules on recognition of professional qualifications.

While more detailed consideration of the Community directives on the recognition of professional qualifications is beyond the scope of this work, particular attention should be drawn to recent legislation covering the legal profession. Directive 98/5 on the establishment of lawyers enables a lawyer qualified in one member state to practise permanently and without restriction, under his or her original professional title, in another member state on the same basis as the host country's own lawyers. Lawyers who are fully qualified in one member state are simply required to register with the Bar or other competent authority in the host member state on the basis of their registration in the home member state, without the need to pass an aptitude test or to undergo any adaptation period. Most significantly, after practising for three years in the host member state, a lawyer is entitled to gain admission to the profession in the host member state and to acquire the relevant professional title of that member state. The deadline for the implementation of Directive 98/5 was 14 March 2000. In Case C-362/01, *Commission v. Ireland* [2002] ECR I-11433, the European Court of Justice found that Ireland had failed to adopt the necessary measures to transpose the directive into its domestic legal system before the expiry of the deadline for implementation.

Reverse Discrimination: EC Treaty, Article 43 and 'Purely Internal Situations'

Article 43 prohibits restrictions on the freedom of establishment of nationals of a member state *in the territory of another member state*. In contrast, the prohibition of restrictions on the setting up of agencies, branches or subsidiaries is expressly stated to apply in respect of nationals of *any* member state established in the territory *of any member state*. The wording of Article 43 appears to suggest that the provision cannot be invoked by a national against his own member state. However, the case law of the European Court of Justice suggests that, in certain circumstances, a national may succeed in relying on Article 43 in a seemingly 'wholly internal situation'. As is the case in relation to the free movement of workers, certain factors must be present in order to trigger the application of Community law.

A period of time spent in another member state acquiring a qualification may be sufficient to bring a case within the ambit of Article 43. In Case 115/78, *Knoors v. Secretary for State for Economic Affairs* [1979] ECR 399, the European Court of Justice recognised the right of a Dutch plumbing contractor to rely on Article 43 *against his member state of origin* when seeking to exercise his freedom of establishment on the national territory using a trade qualification acquired during a period of lawful residence in another member state. The court held that the application of Article 43 extended to a person such as Mr Knoors who had lawfully resided in another member state and acquired a trade qualification there which was recognised by the provisions of Community law. On the facts, Mr Knoors was entitled to rely on the provisions of Directive 64/427 on the recognition of certain trade qualifications.

In Case C-61/89, *Bouchoucha* [1990] ECR I-3551, the European Court of Justice ruled that in the absence of Community rules on the professional practice of osteopathy, each member state was free to regulate the exercise of that activity within its territory, provided it did not discriminate as between its own nationals and those of other member states. As a result, Mr Bouchoucha, a French national who had qualified as an osteopath in the UK, was not entitled to rely on Article 43 to challenge a French law restricting the practice of osteopathy to qualified medical doctors. The fact that the UK diploma was not covered by any of the then existing directives on the recognition of professional qualifications distinguished the situation from that in *Knoors* and would appear to have been fatal to the applicant's case.

It is worth noting, however, that the subsequent decision in Case C-19/92, *Kraus v. Land Baden-Württemberg* [1993] ECR I-1663 suggests that a person may be entitled to rely on Article 43 against his or her own member state, even in the absence of Community legislation providing for recognition of the professional qualification at issue. In any event, the adoption of the three 'general system' directives, mentioned above, has radically extended the scope of application of the principle of mutual recognition and rendered a situation such as that which arose in *Bouchoucha* less likely to occur today.

The question of 'wholly internal situations' arose again recently in the context of the free movement of services in Case C-60/00, *Carpenter v. Secretary of State for the Home Department* [2002] ECR I-6279. The issue for consideration was whether Ms Carpenter, a national of the Philippines married to a British citizen, enjoyed a right of residence in the UK under Community law. Ms Carpenter argued that her husband's business potentially required him to travel to other member states, providing and receiving services, and that he could do so more easily when she was looking after his children from his first marriage. He had been providing services to companies located in other member states by placing advertisements for them in UK publications. As a result, she argued that her threatened deportation from the UK would restrict her husband's right under Community law to provide and receive services, and that as a result, she had a right of residence under Article 49.

The European Court of Justice rejected her argument. However, the court ruled in her favour. It held that her husband's activities in providing services and potentially traveling to another member state supplied the necessary 'Community element' for the application of fundamental EU law principles of human rights. Furthermore, fundamental principles of human rights pertaining to the family precluded deporting Ms Cooper. However, this did not provide Ms Cooper with a right of residence directly under Article 49.

Discriminatory and Non-discriminatory Obstacles to the Freedom of Establishment

As we have noted above, Article 43 provides for a right of establishment 'under the conditions laid down for its own nationals' by the law of the host member state. Thus, Article 43 could be construed as prohibiting only discriminatory restrictions on the freedom of establishment. In other words, the provision would be breached only if a person exercising the right of establishment were treated less favourably than nationals of the host state. However, the European Court of Justice has adopted a more expansive interpretation of Article 43, holding that it prohibits not only discriminatory, but also non-discriminatory obstacles to the freedom of establishment.

The *Reyners* case, cited above, provides an example of a case in which discrimination on grounds of nationality was found to breach Article 43. In that case, a law restricting the right to practise as a lawyer in Belgium to Belgian nationals was deemed to be incompatible with the freedom of establishment. Similarly, in Case 197/84, *Steinhauser v. City of Biarritz* [1985] ECR 1819, a law providing that only French nationals were entitled to rent lock-ups as business premises from the local municipality was held to infringe Article 43.

However, cases such as *Klopp* and *Gebhard* (both cited previously) indicate that non-discriminatory obstacles to the exercise of the right of establishment may also be caught by Article 43. In *Klopp*, the European Court of Justice found that the French 'single chambers' rule violated Article 43, despite the fact that it applied equally to both nationals and non-nationals. The subsequent ruling in *Gebhard* echoed the decisions in *Dassonville* and *Cassis,* considered earlier, on the free movement of goods, with the European Court of Justice in *Gebhard* indicating that Article 43 could apply to any national measure 'liable to hinder or make less attractive the exercise of fundamental freedoms guaranteed by the Treaty'. The application of Article 43 to national laws *liable to hinder* the freedom of establishment mirrors the prohibition of indistinctly applicable trade rules under Article 28.

The decision in *Gebhard* also indicates that non-discriminatory restrictions on the freedom of establishment may be justified on grounds beyond those set out in Article 46 (i.e. public policy, public security and public health). In *Gebhard*, the European Court of Justice stated that national measures liable to hinder or make less attractive the exercise of fundamental freedoms guaranteed by the Treaty must fulfil four conditions:

1. they must be applied in a non-discriminatory manner;
2. they must be justified by imperative requirements in the public interest;
3. they must be suitable for securing the attainment of the objective which they pursue; and
4. they must not go beyond what is necessary in order to attain it.

The reference to 'imperative requirements in the public interest' echoes the 'mandatory requirements' jurisprudence developed by the court under Article 28 in relation to the free movement of goods.

Application of Freedom of Establishment Rules to Companies and Other Legal Persons

As noted previously, freedom of establishment is defined by Article 43 as including the right to 'set up and manage undertakings' under the same conditions as laid down for its own nationals by the host member state. Thus, it is clear that the Community rules governing freedom of establishment apply not only to those who wish to set up in business in a self-employed capacity in another member state, but also to those who wish to set up and manage companies in other member states (primary establishment). Article 43 also prohibits the imposition of restrictions on the setting up of agencies, branches or subsidiaries by nationals of any member state established in the territory of any member state (secondary establishment).

Article 48 (ex Article 58) provides that companies and firms formed in accordance with the law of a member state and having their registered office, central administration or principal place of business within the Community are to be treated in the same manner as natural persons who are nationals of member states. In other words, the rights enjoyed by self-employed persons under Articles 43-48 are expressly stated to apply equally to companies and firms. The phrase 'companies or firms' is defined as meaning 'companies or firms constituted under civil or commercial law, including co-operative societies, and other legal persons governed by public or private law, save for those which are non-profit-making'.

A company formed under the law of a member state and having its central administration or principal place of business *anywhere* within the Community is entitled to rely on the principle of equal treatment set out in Article 48. This will be the case even if the company carries on all of its business through some form of secondary establishment (i.e., through a subsidiary, branch or agency) and conducts no business in the state in which it is registered. In Case C-212/97, *Centros* [1999] ECR I-1459, the Danish authorities refused to allow a private limited company incorporated in the UK to register a branch of the company in Denmark. The company, which did not actually carry on any business in the UK, argued that the refusal constituted a breach of the freedom of establishment enshrined in Articles 43 and 48 of the Treaty. The Danish authorities contended that the company was, in reality, seeking to establish its principal establishment in Denmark, but had been incorporated in the UK with a view to circumventing the stricter Danish rules on the paying-up of minimum share capital. In its judgment, the European Court of Justice held that the refusal of a member state to register a branch of a company which had its registered office in another member state constituted an obstacle to the exercise of the right of establishment. While a member state was entitled to take measures to prevent its nationals from attempting improperly to circumvent national legislation, the fact that a national of a member state chose to form a company in the member state whose rules on company law seemed to him the least restrictive and to set up a branch in another member state could not in itself constitute an abuse of the right of establishment. The court also ruled that the fact that a company did not conduct any business in the member state in which it had its registered office and pursued its activities only in the member state where its branch was established was not sufficient to prove the existence of abuse or fraudulent conduct which would entitle the latter member state to deny the company the benefit of the Community provisions on freedom of establishment.

In the absence of complete harmonisation of national laws on the regulation of companies, the European Court of Justice has been somewhat more circumspect in applying the rules on freedom of establishment to legal persons than it has been in dealing with natural persons. In Case 81/87, *R v. HM Treasury, ex parte Daily Mail* [1988] ECR 5483, a company which had been registered in the UK sought to transfer its corporate residence (i.e., its central management and control), but not its place of registration, to the Netherlands. The proposed transfer of corporate residence was designed to lessen the company's tax liability. Under UK law, a company seeking to transfer its residence was required to obtain the prior consent of the UK authorities. In this case, the company claimed that the Treaty rules on freedom of establishment gave it the right to transfer its central management and control to another member state without having to obtain prior consent. Rejecting this argument, the European Court of Justice declared that, in the present state of Community law, Articles 43 and 48 of the Treaty could not be interpreted as conferring on a company incorporated under the law of one member state a right to transfer its central management and control and its central administration to another member state while retaining its status as a company incorporated under the legislation of the first member state.

FREE MOVEMENT OF SERVICES: EC TREATY, ARTICLES 49-55

Article 49 (ex Article 59) states that:

> [R]estrictions on freedom to provide services within the Community shall be prohibited in respect of nationals of member states who are established in a state of the Community other than that of the person for whom the services are intended.

Article 50 (ex Article 60) provides that:

> [S]ervices shall be considered to be 'services' within the meaning of [the] Treaty where they are normally provided for remuneration, insofar as they are not governed by the provisions relating to freedom of movement for goods, capital and persons.

The distinction between 'establishment' and 'provision of services' has already been considered above. Article 50 states that a service provider may 'temporarily pursue his activity in the state where the service is provided, under the same conditions as are imposed by that state on its own nationals'. In Case C-55/94, *Gebhard v. Consiglio dell-Ordine degli Avvocati e Procuratori di Milano* [1995] ECR I-4165, the European Court of Justice noted that where a service provider moves to another member state, the Treaty provisions on services envisage that he is to pursue his activity there on a *temporary basis*. The temporary nature of the activities in question was, according to the court, to be determined in light not only of the 'duration of the provision of the service', but also by reference to its 'regularity, periodicity or continuity'.

Despite the temporary nature of the provision of services, the European Court of Justice in *Gebhard* recognised that a service provider was entitled to equip himself with some form of infrastructure in the host state (including an office, chambers or consulting rooms) insofar as such infrastructure was necessary for performing the services in question. In contrast, in Case 205/84, *Commission v. Germany (Re Insurance Services)* [1986] ECR 3755, the court held that an insurance company that maintained a *permanent presence* in a member state came within the scope of the Treaty provisions on the freedom of establishment and not those on the free movement of services.

It is also worth distinguishing the scope of application of the Treaty rules on the free movement of services from those relating to the free movement of workers. In Case C-43/93, *Vander Elst v. Office des Migrations Internationales* [1994] ECR I-3803, the European Court of Justice held that workers employed by an undertaking established in one member state who were temporarily sent to another member state to provide services did not in any way seek access to the labour market of that second state if they returned to their country of origin or residence after the completion of their work. Persons exercising rights of free movement in such circumstances would fall to be dealt with under Articles 49 and 50 on the free movement of services, rather than under Article 39 on the free movement of workers.

Direct Effect of EC Treaty, Article 49

Under the original Treaty, restrictions on the free movement of services were to be abolished during a transitional period. Article 63 (now Article 52) provided for the drawing up by the Commission of a 'general programme' for the abolition of such restrictions, which was to be implemented by a series of directives. In Case 33/74, *Van Binsbergen* [1974] ECR 1299, the question arose as to whether Article 49 was capable of producing direct effect, i.e. whether it created rights that could be relied on by individuals before national courts. Echoing its earlier decision in *Reyners*, cited above, the European Court of Justice held that the provisions of Article 49 had become unconditional on the expiry of the transitional period. The court concluded that, insofar as they prohibited discrimination on grounds of nationality or on the basis of residence, Articles 49 and 50 of the Treaty were directly effective.

Application of Treaty Rules to Recipients of Services

As noted previously, Article 49 prohibits restrictions on freedom to *provide* services within the Community. Similarly, Article 50 guarantees a right of equal treatment to persons 'providing a service'. The Treaty makes no reference to any right to *receive* services, although Directive 64/221 governing member state derogations from the Community rules on the free movement of persons is expressly stated to apply to recipients of services.

The status of recipients of services under Community law was considered in Cases 286/82 and 26/83, *Luisi and Carbone v. Ministero del Tesoro* [1984] ECR 377. The case concerned criminal proceedings against two Italian nationals for breach of Italian currency laws limiting the amount of foreign currency which could be taken out of Italy. On a preliminary reference, the European Court of Justice ruled that the freedom to move temporarily to another member state to receive services was a 'necessary corollary' of the freedom to provide services. The court declared that:

> [T]he freedom to provide services includes the freedom, for the recipients of services, to go to another member state in order to receive a service there, without being obstructed by restrictions [...].

It went on to note that 'tourists, persons receiving medical treatment and persons travelling for the purposes of education or business are to be regarded as recipients of services'.

In Case 186/87, *Cowan v. Trésor Public* [1989] ECR 195, a British national who was visiting France as a tourist had been mugged outside a Paris metro station and was refused compensation from the French Criminal Injuries Compensation Board on the ground that he was not a French national or resident. The European Court of Justice reiterated that the freedom to provide services included the freedom for the recipients of services to go to another member state in order to receive services there, without being obstructed by restrictions. The court noted that tourists were to be regarded as recipients of services and, as such, were entitled to rely on the general prohibition of discrimination on grounds of nationality now laid down in Article 12.

Application of EC Treaty, Articles 49 and 50 to 'Illegal' or 'Immoral' Services

Problems may arise in certain cases regarding the types of services which are covered by Articles 49. Since member states remain free to regulate a wide variety of economic activities at national level, the question has inevitably arisen as to whether a person established in one member state and engaged in an activity which is lawful in that state may rely on the Treaty rules regarding the free movement of services to pursue that activity in another member state in which it is not lawful.

Case C-159/90, *SPUC v. Grogan* [1991] ECR I-4685 concerned the then existing ban under Irish law on the dissemination of information on abortion services lawfully available in other member states. Among the questions referred to the European Court of Justice for a preliminary ruling, the Irish High Court asked whether medical termination of pregnancy constituted a service within the meaning of Article 50. SPUC contended that the provision of abortion could not be regarded as a 'service' on the grounds that it was grossly immoral and involved the destruction of human life. Rejecting this argument, the European Court of Justice declared that it was not for it to 'substitute its assessment for that of the legislature in those member states where the activities are practised legally'. Accordingly, abortion was found to constitute a 'service' within the meaning of Article 50 of the Treaty.

In Case C-275/92, *Customs and Excise v. Schindler* [1994] ECR I-1039, two German nationals had been charged with an offence under UK lotteries legislation following the interception of lottery advertisements and application forms which had been sent from Germany to households in the UK. Despite arguments to the contrary submitted by a number of member states, the European Court of Justice ruled that lotteries were to be regarded as 'services' within the meaning of the Treaty. While lotteries were subject to strict regulation and control by the public authorities in various member states, the court noted that lotteries were not actually prohibited in any state. While the morality of lotteries was considered by some to be questionable, the court reiterated that it was not for it to substitute its assessment for that of the legislatures of the member states where the activity in question was practised legally.

Discriminatory and Non-discriminatory Obstacles to the Free Movement of Services

Article 50 states that a service provider is entitled to pursue his activity on a temporary basis in the state where the service is provided, under the same conditions as are imposed by that state on its own nationals. In other words, the principle of equal treatment applies to service providers and (according to the case law of the European Court of Justice considered above) to recipients of services. While Article 50 clearly prohibits discrimination against service providers on grounds of nationality, the question remains as to whether non-discriminatory rules applied equally both to those established in the regulating state and those established in another member state may be caught by the Community rules on the free movement of services. For example, can the application of rules governing a particular profession to both persons established on the national territory and persons providing services there on a temporary basis constitute a breach of the principle of the free movement of services?

In Case C-76/90, *Säger v. Dennemeyer* [1991] ECR I-4221, the European Court of Justice declared that Article 49 required not only the abolition of all discrimination against service providers on grounds of nationality, but also the abolition of any restriction, even if it applied without distinction to national service providers and to those in other member states, which was:

> liable to prohibit or otherwise impede the activities of a provider of services established in another member state where he lawfully provides similar services.

Dennemeyer was an English company which provided patent renewal services. Under German law, a person providing such services was required to hold a special licence.

The European Court of Justice found that a member state was not entitled to make the provision of services in its territory subject to compliance with all the conditions required for establishment, since this would deprive the Treaty provisions on free movement of services of all practical effectiveness. It noted, however, that restrictions could in certain circumstances be imposed on the provision of services by persons or companies established in other member states. Specifically, the court held that the freedom to provide services could be restricted only by provisions which were objectively justified by imperative reasons relating to the public interest and which were imposed on all persons or undertakings operating in the state in question, insofar as that interest was not already safeguarded by the provisions to which the service provider was subject in the member state of his establishment. The court also stated that restrictions on the free movement of services must not exceed what is necessary to achieve the desired objective, i.e., the national law must not be disproportionate.

In many respects, the decision in *Säger* merely echoed the court's previous rulings in cases such as Case 33/74, *Van Binsbergen* [1974] ECR 1299 and Case 205/84, *Commission v. Germany (Re Insurance Services)* [1986] ECR 3755. Those earlier cases also dealt with the issue of 'objective justification' of non-discriminatory restrictions on the free movement of services. In *Van Binsbergen*, for example, the European Court of Justice stated that a national law imposing a residence requirement on service providers was capable of breaching Article 49. On the facts of the case, a Dutch lawyer who had transferred his residence from the Netherlands to Belgium sought to challenge a Dutch law under which only persons established in the Netherlands could act as legal representatives before courts in that country. The European Court of Justice found that a permanent residence requirement could be permissible where it was objectively justified in order to ensure observance of professional rules of conduct. However, a residence requirement was not compatible with Article 49 where the objective in question could have been achieved by less restrictive means.

The recent decision in Cases C-369/96 and C-376/96, *Arblade* [1999] ECR I-8453 confirmed that Article 49 applies not only in the context of discriminatory restrictions on the free movement of services, but also to non-discriminatory obstacles and impediments. In its judgment, the European Court of Justice declared that Article 49 requires not merely the elimination of all discrimination on grounds of nationality against service providers established in another member state, but also the abolition of any restriction:

> liable to prohibit, impede or render less advantageous the activities of a provider of services established in another member state where he lawfully provides similar services.

Similar views were expressed by the court in its earlier decision in Case C-384/93, *Alpine Investments* [1995] ECR I-1141.

DEROGATIONS FROM THE TREATY PROVISIONS ON ESTABLISHMENT AND SERVICES

Article 46 provides that member states may derogate from the Treaty rules on the freedom of establishment on grounds of 'public policy, public security or public health'. By Article 55, these derogations are also deemed to apply to the Treaty provisions on the free movement of services. As a result, the grounds of derogation from the free movement of workers, the freedom of establishment and the free movement of services are identical. These justifications – public policy, public security and public health – were considered in detail in the previous chapter. As we noted in that chapter, the justifications have been interpreted by the European Court of Justice in an extremely restrictive manner. Directive 64/221, mentioned previously, provides guidance as to the measures a member state may adopt on grounds of public policy, security and health. The directive applies not only to workers, but also to the self-employed and to service providers.

As we have seen in this chapter, the narrow list of derogations provided for in the Treaty has been supplemented by a more expansive category of justifications developed by the European Court of Justice. The existence of these 'objective justifications' or 'imperative requirements' has been recognised in cases such as *Gebhard* (in the context of establishment) and *Van Binsbergen* (in the context of services). In essence, the court has held that non-discriminatory restrictions on the freedom of establishment and the free movement of services may be justified on grounds beyond those set out in the Treaty.

OFFICIAL AUTHORITY EXCEPTION

Article 45 states that the Treaty provisions on the freedom of establishment shall not apply in any member state to activities 'connected, even occasionally, with the exercise of official authority'. Under Article 56, the 'official authority' exception is also made applicable in the context of services. As with the 'public service' exemption set out in Article 39(4) and considered in the previous chapter, the official authority exception has been interpreted very restrictively by the European Court of Justice. It is clear from the case law of the court that the exception applies to specific activities which involve the exercise of official authority, rather than to entire professions.

In Case 2/74, *Reyners v. Belgium* [1974] ECR 631, a Dutch national was refused admission to the Belgian Bar solely by reason of his nationality. The Belgian Bar Council argued that the whole profession of *avocat* was exempt under Article 45 from the Treaty rules on establishment by reason of the fact that it was connected organically with the public service of the administration of justice. In contrast, a number of member states contended that only certain activities within the legal profession were actually connected with official authority. In its judgment, the court ruled that the Article 45 exemption was limited to those activities which, taken on their own, constituted a direct and specific connection with the exercise of official authority. In the context of the legal profession, it noted that activities such as consultation and representation of parties in court could not be said to involve a direct and specific connection with the exercise of official authority.

CONCLUSION

The Treaty rules on establishment and services contribute to the wider goal of creating a common Community market in which the free movement of goods, persons, services and capital is ensured. The freedom of establishment entails the right to pursue an economic activity on a stable and continuous basis in another member state, while the Treaty provisions on services envisage the pursuit of an economic activity in the host state on a temporary basis. Despite the fact that the right to establishment and the right to provide services appeared under the Treaty to be conditional on the adoption of directives, the European Court of Justice has held that both Article 43 (freedom of establishment) and Articles 49 and 50 (free movement of services) are directly effective. It should be noted, however, that secondary legislation plays an extremely important role in the field of establishment and services. As we have seen above, the legislative regime currently governing the mutual recognition of education and training comprises seventeen main directives, i.e., the three general system directives and other sectoral directives dealing with individual professions, particularly in the health sector. While the Treaty explicitly prohibits discrimination against persons or companies exercising the right of establishment, or the right to provide or receive services, the European Court of Justice has declared that the rules on establishment and services apply also to non-discriminatory obstacles and impediments to free movement. In that respect, interesting parallels can be drawn between the Community principles governing goods, persons and services. Of course, the right of establishment and the freedom to provide and receive services are not absolute and unconditional. Member states may derogate from these freedoms on grounds of public policy, public security or public health. The court has also recognised the existence of a broader category of objective justifications capable of being invoked in the context of non-discriminatory restrictions. In addition, the 'official authority' exception provides an exemption from the Treaty rules on establishment and services for activities 'connected, even occasionally, with the exercise of official authority'. As is the case with all limitations on the 'fundamental freedoms', these grounds of derogation have been interpreted very narrowly so as to maximise the scope of application of the Community free movement rules.

Chapter 16
COMPETITION LAW: CARTELS AND OTHER COLLUSIVE BEHAVIOUR

EC COMPETITION LAW: INTRODUCTION

A market economy is one in which the allocation of resources is primarily determined by supply and demand. In a free market, firms are encouraged to produce efficiently what people want to buy, thereby achieving an optimal allocation of resources. Competition between firms or undertakings allows for the allocation of scarce resources in accordance with consumer choice, so as to avoid waste and stimulate efficiency. Traditional economic theory indicates that goods and services will be produced in the most efficient manner where there is competition between undertakings in the market. Even if one firm is particularly successful and expands its operations, other firms will notice its success and seek to enter the market. Thus, a successful firm will not go on enjoying market power for long unless it remains more than usually efficient or unless other firms cannot enter the market freely by virtue of the existence of barriers to entry.

AIMS AND OBJECTIVES OF EC COMPETITION LAW

It should be noted that the aims of EC competition policy are not limited to enhancing allocative efficiency, that is, ensuring that goods are produced in the most efficient manner possible, so as to maximise consumer welfare. A further objective of EC competition law is to promote the creation of a single European market. As outlined in previous chapters, the EC Treaty provides for the free movement of goods, persons, services and capital within the common market.

It is clear that the Treaty rules relating to free movement would be entirely frustrated if undertakings, in the absence of protectionist state rules, were free to enter into private agreements to keep out of each other's markets and thus partition the Community market along national lines. For example, state tariffs protecting the domestic cement industry might be replaced by a collusive agreement between cement producers within the EU to stay out of each other's territories.

Other suggested objectives of EC competition law include consumer protection and the protection of small and medium-sized firms from large aggregations of economic power. Integration brings with it the risk that small and medium-sized firms, formerly protected by customs duties and quotas, may find it difficult to compete successfully with larger firms operating from other member states. However, the objective of protecting smaller firms is controversial and difficult to reconcile with the overriding aim of enhancing allocative efficiency within the Community. For example, is it desirable that small shops be helped to compete against large supermarkets, even if they are less efficient in producing what consumers want to buy and charge more? Although largely based on the liberal philosophy of the free market, it should be noted that EC competition policy has not always been oblivious to social and human demands.

OVERVIEW OF RELEVANT TREATY PROVISIONS

The EC Treaty contains various provisions relating to competition. Article 3(g) states that the activities of the Community include the putting in place of a system ensuring that competition in the internal market is not distorted. Article 86 provides for the application of competition rules to public undertakings and undertakings to which member states have granted special or exclusive rights. Article 87 prohibits the granting of state aids which distort competition.

However, the most important Treaty rules relating to competition are those contained in Articles 81 and 82. In this chapter, we will focus on Article 81 (formerly Article 85), while in the next chapter we will examine Article 82 (formerly Article 86). At the outset, it should be noted that competition law cannot be studied or understood in isolation. Increasingly, lawyers and policy-makers recognise the fundamental importance of economics in the development and application of competition law.

EC TREATY, ARTICLE 81: CARTELS AND OTHER COLLUSIVE BEHAVIOUR

Article 81 prohibits anti-competitive agreements, decisions or concerted practices entered into by two or more undertakings which affect trade between member states and which have as their object or effect the prevention, restriction or distortion of competition within the common market. Article 81(1) sets out a useful, but non-exhaustive, list of the types of practices that are capable of falling within the scope of the prohibition. In essence, Article 81 seeks to prohibit cartels and other forms of collusive behaviour between undertakings.

Why is it necessary to have laws of the European Union that prohibit cartels and other forms of agreements in restraint of trade? As the famous economist Adam Smith wrote in his famous work, *The Wealth of Nations* (1776):

> People of the same trade seldom meet together, even for merriment and diversion, but the conversation ends in a conspiracy against the public, or in some contrivance to raise prices.

Article 81 is an acknowledgement of this fact of life, and seeks to protect the public against such conspiracies.

Article 81(2) provides that any agreement or decision which infringes the Article shall be automatically void. However, Article 81(3) provides for an exemption from the prohibition contained in Article 81(1) in certain circumstances. We will consider the various provisions of Article 81 in turn.

Elements of EC Treaty, Article 81(1)

A number of the key elements of the Article 81(1) prohibition require closer scrutiny. It should be noted that the various elements of Article 81(1) are not defined in the Treaty and have, therefore, been interpreted by the Commission, the Court of Justice and the Court of First Instance.

What Constitutes an 'Undertaking' Under EC Treaty, Article 81(1)?

Article 81(1) prohibits certain types of behaviour on the part of undertakings, but the term 'undertaking' itself is not defined in the Treaty. Unsurprisingly, the Commission and the Community courts have opted for a broad interpretation. In Decision 86/398, *Polypropylene* [1988] 4 CMLR 347, the Commission asserted that the term 'undertaking' was not confined to those entities which possessed legal personality, but covered any entity engaged in commercial activity. In Case C-41/90, *Höfner and Elser v. Macrotron GmbH* [1991] ECR I-1979, the term was held to cover any entity engaged in an economic activity, regardless of its legal status and the way in which it is financed. In that case, a public employment agency engaged in the business of employment recruitment was held to constitute an 'undertaking' for competition law purposes. In subsequent cases, the term has been held to encompass corporations, partnerships, sole traders, trade associations, co-operatives and state and semi-state companies.

It is worth noting, however, that an agreement between two or more entities within the same corporate group will not fall foul of Article 81(1). In Case C-73/95P, *Viho Europe BV v. Commission* [1996] ECR I-5457, the European Court of Justice held that a distribution policy which had been pursued by a parent company of dividing national markets between subsidiaries could not fall within the scope of Article 81(1), where the parent company and its subsidiaries formed a 'single economic unit' within which the subsidiaries did not enjoy any real autonomy in determining their course of action on the market.

Agreements and Decisions for the Purposes of EC Treaty, Article 81(1)

The operation of Article 81(1) is dependent on the existence of an agreement, decision or concerted practice between two or more undertakings. It should be noted that the technical classification of particular behaviour as 'agreement', 'decision' or 'concerted practice' is unimportant. The purpose of dividing activities into three distinct categories is simply to make Article 81(1) as all-encompassing as possible.

Both the court and the Commission have construed the term 'agreement' very broadly. In Cases 41, 44-45/69, *Quinine Cartel* [1970] ECR 661, a number of firms had agreed to fix prices and divide the market in quinine. While they had made an explicit agreement to this effect covering trade with non-member states, they had reached a less formal 'gentlemen's agreement' governing sales within the Community. The European Court of Justice held that this form of informal collusion was caught by Article 81.

In the *Polypropylene Cartel* case (Decision 86/398, *Community v. ICI and Others* [1988] 4 CMLR 347), the Commission found that an 'agreement' had been reached by a number of petrochemical companies involved in the production of polypropylene, even though the agreement in question was oral and despite the absence of any formal sanctions for its breach. The Commission further held that it was not necessary for the agreement to be intended to be legally binding on the parties. Instead, an agreement is deemed to exist:

> [I]f the parties reach a consensus on a plan which limits or is likely to limit their commercial freedom by determining the lines of their mutual action or abstention from action in the market.

Definition of 'Concerted Practice' Under EC Treaty, Article 81(1)

If the prohibition contained in Article 81(1) only operated when an explicit agreement (whether written or oral) had been made, it would be of very limited use. Business people who enter into anti-competitive agreements, particularly those involved in cartels, are likely to know that such conduct is anti-competitive and will seek to destroy all evidence of collusion. Accordingly, Article 81(1) applies not only to overt agreements, but extends to all forms of collusive behaviour between firms which have an anti-competitive object or effect. However, the notion of a 'concerted practice' poses certain interpretative problems, most particularly in the context of *oligopolistic* markets. An oligopoly exists where there are relatively few sellers in the market, each anticipating the others' reactions. Each seller has approximately the same share of the market. For example, there might be five sellers with approximately twenty per cent of the market each. Barriers to entry are high and product-differentiation is low. In an oligopolistic market, firms may naturally end up pricing at the same level, not as a result of any actual collusion, but rather because of the structure of the market itself and the mutual interdependence of firms in that market.

If the term 'concerted practice' is interpreted too expansively it may condemn certain behaviour as collusion, even though the parallel conduct of undertakings in a particular market – for example in pricing policy – may not in fact be the result of collusion at all, but may instead be simply a rational response of firms in that market. The Commission and the Community courts have had to consider whether such parallel behaviour falls within the ambit of the Article 81(1) prohibition.

The concept of a 'concerted practice' was considered by the European Court of Justice in the leading *Dyestuffs* case (Case 48/69, *ICI v. Commission* [1972] ECR 619). In that case, the Commission had instituted proceedings against a number of undertakings which it believed had participated in a concerted practice of price-fixing in relation to dyestuffs. As a result of investigations, the Commission had noted the occurrence of three separate, uniform price increases announced by Community dyestuffs producers between 1964 and 1967. On appeal against fines imposed by the Commission, the producers sought to argue that the price increases in question resulted not from any collusion, but rather from the oligopolistic structure of the market. In its decision, the European Court of Justice defined a concerted practice as:

> ... a form of co-ordination between undertakings which, without having reached the stage where an agreement properly so-called has been concluded, knowingly substitutes practical co-operation between them for the risks of competition.

The court noted that parallel behaviour did not of itself prove the existence of a concerted practice, but asserted that it amounted to strong evidence of such a practice if it led to conditions of competition which did not correspond to the normal conditions of the market. On the facts of the case, the European Court of Justice rejected the 'market structure' argument, finding that the similar price increases which occurred within the industry in 1964, 1965 and 1967 were not spontaneous, but resulted from collusion.

In the *Sugar Cartel* case (Cases 40-48, 50, 54-56, 111, 113 and 114/73, *Suiker Unie v. Commission* [1975] ECR 1663), the court noted that the criteria of co-ordination and co-operation used in determining the existence of a concerted practice did not require the 'working out of an actual plan' between undertakings. The court further observed that while the requirement of independence did not deprive economic operators of the right to adapt themselves intelligently to the existing and anticipated conduct of their competitors, it did strictly preclude any direct or indirect contact between such operators the object or effect whereof is either to influence the conduct on the market of an actual or potential competitor or to disclose to such competitors the course of conduct which they themselves have decided to adopt or contemplate adopting on the market. The crucial factor is that an undertaking must operate independently on the market. On the facts of the *Sugar Cartel* case, the court found that the competing undertakings had contacted each other and had pursued the aim of removing in advance any uncertainty as to their future conduct. Such conduct amounted to a concerted practice.

In Cases 89, 104, 114, 116-7, 125-9/85, *Ahlström v. Commission (Wood Pulp Cartel)* [1993] ECR I-1307, the Commission concluded that a large number of producers of wood pulp had been engaged in concerted practices as regards price announcements. It found that the wood pulp market was not oligopolistic in nature, since there were a large number of firms operating on the market. However, the European Court of Justice subsequently annulled a significant part of the Commission's decision, holding that the parallelism of price trends could be 'satisfactorily explained by the oligopolistic tendencies of the market'. The court asserted that parallel conduct could not be regarded as proof of concertation unless concertation constituted the only plausible explanation for such conduct. On the facts, the parallel conduct on the wood pulp market found to exist by the Commission was held not to amount to evidence of collusion.

When is There an 'Effect on Trade Between Member States'?

It is not enough to prove an agreement in restraint of trade, in order to establish a violation of Article 81(1). In order for Article 81(1) to apply, the impugned conduct must have an 'effect on trade between member states'. This requirement is of particular significance, since if it is not satisfied the matter will remain within the jurisdiction of the relevant national competition authority. That is, the conduct may violate Irish competition law, and be prosecuted by the Irish Competition Authority.

In practice, the European Court of Justice has adopted a broad interpretation of the concept of an effect on trade between member states. Thus, the mere fact that all the parties to an agreement are based in one member state will not preclude the application of Article 81(1). In Case 56/65, *Société Technique Minière v. Maschinenbau Ulm* [1966] ECR 235, the European Court of Justice held that the relevant test was whether it was possible to:

> foresee with a sufficient degree of probability on the basis of a set of objective factors of law or of fact that the agreement in question may have an influence, direct or indirect, actual or potential, on the pattern of trade between member states.

For example, a particular anti-competitive agreement between undertakings in Ireland may have a detrimental effect on market entry for competitors from other member states, thereby producing a potential effect on trade between member states.

Meanwhile, in Cases 56 and 58/64, *Consten and Grundig v. Commission* [1966] ECR 299, the European Court of Justice held that the effect on trade between member states necessary to trigger the application of Article 81(1) was not required to be negative. The fact that an agreement purportedly enhanced the volume of trade between member states was therefore irrelevant for this purpose; the agreement was still held to produce an 'effect on trade between member states' for the purposes of Article 81(1). In other words, the requirement of an effect on trade is a purely neutral jurisdictional requirement, a mere prerequisite to the application of Article 81(1).

The 'De Minimis' Doctrine

It is clear from the case law of the European Court of Justice that an agreement will not be caught by Article 81(1) if it does not have an appreciable impact on competition or does not affect trade between member states. These are separate issues. In Case 5/69, *Völk v. Vervaecke* [1969] ECR 295, Völk manufactured less than one per cent of the washing machines produced in Germany. The European Court of Justice ruled that even absolute territorial protection granted to the producer's exclusive distributor for Belgium and Luxembourg would not infringe Article 81(1) if it did not appreciably restrict competition. This principle has become known as the *de minimis* doctrine.

In order to reduce uncertainty surrounding the application of the *de minimis* rule and the concept of 'appreciable effect', the Commission has published Notices governing Agreements of Minor Importance. In its Notice (*Commission Notice on Agreements of Minor Importance* [1997] OJ C372/13), the Commission stated its view that Article 81(1) does not apply to agreements between undertakings where the aggregate market shares held by all of the participating undertakings do not exceed, on any of the relevant markets, a five per cent threshold where the agreement is made between undertakings operating at the same level of production ('horizontal agreements') or a ten per cent threshold where the agreement is made between undertakings operating at different economic levels ('vertical agreements'). While the Commission Notice does not alter the text of the Treaty or supplant the rulings of the Community courts, it nonetheless constitutes a useful interpretative guide.

The Commission replaced its 1997 Notice in 2001, when it published the *Commission Notice on Agreements of Minor Importance which do not Appreciably Restrict Competition under Article 81(1)* [2001] OJ C368/13.

The Commission emphasised that its Notice only addressed appreciable restrictions on competition; it did not address the separate issue concerning the required affect on trade between member states, although the Commission indicated that agreements between small and medium-sized enterprises would not ordinarily have the required affect on trade member states.

In this later Notice, thresholds and nomenclature are changed. For agreements between competitors, if the aggregate market share held by the competitors in the relevant market does not exceed ten per cent, there is no appreciable effect on competition. For agreements between non-competitors, if the market share held by each of the parties to the agreement does not exceed fifteen per cent on any of the relevant markets affected by the agreement, then those not appreciable restriction or competition.

Object or Effect of Preventing, Restricting or Distorting Competition

Article 81(1) prohibits agreements, decisions or concerted practices that have as their 'object or effect the prevention, restriction or distortion of competition'. It is clear from the decision in Cases 56 and 58/64, *Consten and Grundig v. Commission* [1966] ECR 299 that the requirement of an 'object or effect' is an alternative, and not a cumulative, test. In its ruling, the European Court of Justice noted that there was no need to take account of the concrete *effects* of an agreement once it appeared that it had as its *object* the prevention, restriction or distortion of competition. In Case 56/65, *Société Technique Minière v. Maschinenbau Ulm* [1966] ECR 235, the court again asserted that the phrase 'object or effect' indicated the existence of alternative, not cumulative, requirements. Thus, a cartel established with the objective of fixing prices might be caught by the prohibition in Article 81(1) even where it had not succeeded in its objectives. In *Société Technique Minière*, the European Court of Justice further noted that the object of an agreement was to be considered in light of the economic context in which it was to be applied. In other words, the object of an agreement may be assessed in an objective manner, rather than by reference to the parties' actual, subjective intentions.

Where an anti-competitive 'object' cannot be discerned, the Commission or the court may still have regard to the 'effect' of the agreement. In assessing the effect of a particular agreement, the Commission or the court will normally engage in some form of market analysis. In Case C-234/89, *Delimitis v. Henniger Bräu* [1991] ECR I-935, the European Court of Justice emphasised the importance of assessing the effects of an agreement in the context of the market, rather than in isolation. However, the extent of the economic analysis carried out by the Commission and the court has varied from case to case, with many commentators accusing the Commission in particular of engaging in inadequate market analysis. This issue will be examined in more detail in the following paragraphs.

EC Treaty, Article 81(1) and the Rule of Reason

As noted previously, Article 81(1) prohibits all agreements that have as their object or effect the 'prevention, restriction or distortion of competition'. The phrase has generated a substantial body of case law and academic literature, with various problems surrounding its interpretation. All commercial contracts entail some restriction on competition by constraining undertakings to some extent in their dealings with third parties. That is, if a company enters into a contract with another company, it foregoes the freedom to enter into an identical contract with a third party. However, to assert that every contract ought thus to be caught by the rules on competition would be illogical. It has been recognised that a particular agreement may have features which both enhance and restrict competition. For example, the contract may create a market where one previously did not exist. Certain specific restrictions, or ancillary restraints, might have been essential to the conclusion of the deal: a distributor may not be willing to accept the risks inherent in entering into a distribution agreement with a manufacturer in respect of a new market without some form of exclusivity. The question arises as to whether an agreement containing such restrictions should fall within the ambit of Article 81(1), with the possibility of exemption under Article 81(3), or whether it should fall outside the scope of Article 81(1) entirely.

Under the rule of reason applied in US antitrust law, courts may balance the pro- and anti-competitive effects of an agreement and exempt from the prohibition contained in section 1 of the Sherman Act (broadly analogous to Article 81(1)) those restraints deemed to be reasonable and ancillary to the main purpose of the agreement. The extent to which this 'rule of reason' analysis is employed in Community competition law is far from clear. In contrast to US antitrust law, EU law already possesses a formal mechanism whereby an agreement which distorts competition can be exempt from the prohibition set out in Article 81(1): the existence of the Article 81(3) exemption provision could be said to render any separate 'rule of reason' approach superfluous. This argument is strengthened by the recent adoption of Regulation 1/2003 (discussed below), which renders Article 81(3) directly effective in national courts and by national competition authorities.

It should also be noted that the objectives underpinning EU competition law – in particular, the goal of promoting market integration – differ in some important respects from those pursued by the US antitrust enforcement authorities. Thus, a vertical distribution agreement between a manufacturer and a distributor, whereby the manufacturer agreed to afford its distributor in a particular member state absolute territorial protection would fall foul of Article 81(1) on the ground that it served to partition the common market along national lines. Neither the Commission nor the court would be swayed by a rule-of-reason argument which sought to assert the pro-competitive effects of such an agreement. While the agreement might promote interbrand competition (that is, competition between different manufacturers of the same product) in the member state in question by facilitating the penetration of the market by a new manufacturer, its market-partitioning effect would be regarded as incompatible with the creation of a single European market.

Status of the Rule of Reason: Decisions Under EC Treaty, Article 81(1)

As noted previously, an agreement may contain provisions that both restrict and enhance competition. In order to ascertain whether such an agreement distorts competition within the meaning of Article 81(1), detailed economic analysis is desirable. While the European Court of Justice has shown a willingness to engage in detailed market investigation, the Commission has on occasion adopted a more formalistic approach. *Consten and Grundig v. Commission*, cited above, provides a good example of a case in which both the Commission and the court avoided any in-depth market analysis.

In 1957, Grundig had appointed Consten as sole distributor of its electronic products in France. Consten had to provide advertising and after-sale services and undertook not to sell the products of competing manufacturers. Furthermore, the agreement between Consten and Grundig provided for absolute territorial protection: Consten agreed not to sell the goods outside the contract territory and Grundig distributors in other countries were also subject to a similar prohibition. Grundig permitted Consten to register the 'Gint' trademark (which appeared on all Grundig products at the time) under French law, so as to confer protection on Consten against unauthorised sales of Grundig products in France.

In 1961, a parallel importer, UNEF, bought Grundig products from sellers in Germany and started to sell them in France at prices more favourable than those charged by Consten. When Consten brought an action in the French courts for infringement of its trademark, UNEF sought a declaration from the Commission that the entire agreement between Consten and Grundig was void on the ground that it violated Article 81(1). In those proceedings, the Commission concluded that the agreement in question did indeed infringe Article 81. The European Court of Justice upheld the Commission's finding, concluding that since the contested agreement aimed at isolating the French market for Grundig products and artificially maintaining separate national markets with the Community, it distorted competition within the common market contrary to Article 81(1). The court declared that no possible favourable effects of the agreement could lead to a different conclusion.

The decision in *Consten and Grundig* has been severely criticised on the ground that both the Commission and the court failed to engage in any proper market analysis. Certain commentators have pointed out that Consten incurred significant costs and risks when it undertook to promote the Grundig brand in France. Without territorial protection, Consten would have faced competition from parallel importers taking a free ride on its investment in promotion and after-sales service and might have decided not to enter the market at all. It could be argued that while the agreement had the effect of reducing intra-brand competition, it served to stimulate inter-brand competition by creating the conditions whereby Grundig could enter the French market. However, other commentators have suggested that the court's apparent hostility to economic analysis in *Consten and Grundig* should be considered in the light of the facts of the case: the absolute territorial protection conferred on Consten had the effect of partitioning the Community market along national lines and as such could never be justified.

A Different Approach to the Rule of Reason?

In the *Société Technique Minière* case (cited above), a French undertaking, STM, had been granted the exclusive right to sell in France certain machines produced by a German company, Maschinenbau Ulm. Unlike the position in *Consten and Grundig*, the contract did not have the effect of insulating the French territory. STM was free to sell the goods outside France and parallel imports could be obtained from other countries and sold on the French market. When a contractual dispute arose between the parties in 1962, STM sought to argue before the French courts that the agreement violated Article 81(1).

In the preliminary reference proceedings which ensued, the European Court of Justice held that, in deciding whether the exclusive distribution clause in the agreement at issue had the object or effect of preventing, restricting or distorting competition, it was necessary to examine the actual context of the agreement and to consider whether the agreement was necessary for the penetration of a new market by an undertaking. The court specified various factors to be taken into account in determining whether the agreement was anti-competitive, including:

1. the nature and quantity of the products covered by the agreement;
2. the position and importance of the parties on the market;
3. the isolated nature of the agreement or its position in a series of agreements;
4. the severity of the clause protecting the exclusive distributorship; and
5. the opportunities allowed for parallel imports and exports.

The court also appeared to endorse a 'rule of reason'-type approach, noting that it was doubtful whether there could be any distortion of competition if an agreement seemed 'really necessary for the penetration of a new area by an undertaking'. It could be argued, for example, that the German company could not have attempted to enter the French market without co-operation from a local exclusive dealer (in this case STM) who would require a certain level of protection to induce investment.

Further examples of this more flexible approach include the decisions in Case 258/78, *Nungesser v. Commission* [1982] ECR 2015, Case 161/84, *Pronuptia de Paris* [1986] ECR 353, Case C-234/89, *Delimitis v. Henniger Bräu* [1991] ECR I-935 and, most recently, in Case C-309/99, *Wouters v. Dutch Bar Council* [2002] ECR I-1577. In these cases, the European Court of Justice showed a clear willingness to engage in economic analysis and accepted that certain ancillary restraints did not constitute restrictions on competition within the meaning of Article 81(1). In *Pronuptia*, the court ruled that certain restrictions imposed by a franchisor on a franchisee (such as the obligation on the franchisee only to sell the merchandise covered by the agreement in premises set up and decorated according to the franchisor's specification) were indispensable to the proper functioning of the franchising system and did not infringe Article 81(1). It is worth noting, however, that the recent decision in Case T-112/99, *Métropole Télévision and Others v. Commission* [2001] ECR II-2459 appears to exhibit a more restrictive approach, with the Court of First Instance emphatically asserting that that it was not necessary to balance the pro- and anti-competitive effects of an agreement when determining whether Article 81(1) was applicable.

ROLE OF THE COMMISSION IN THE ENFORCEMENT OF EC COMPETITION LAW

The Commission has played a crucial role in the enforcement of EC competition law. Under Article 85 (ex Article 89), the Commission is given the task of ensuring the application of the principles laid down in Article 81 and in Article 82. The Commission is empowered to investigate cases of suspected infringement of these principles and to propose measures to bring such breaches to an end. Its powers of investigation and inspection were originally contained in Regulation 17/62, which was replaced by Regulation 1/2003 with effect from 1 May 2004. Investigations can be conducted on the Commission's own initiative or on the basis of complaints received from aggrieved parties. In recent years, the Commission has intensified its efforts to combat large-scale cartels and other serious anti-competitive practices, and has increased the levels of fines imposed on undertakings engaged in such conduct. Among the practices targeted by the Commission are secret cartels between two or more competitors aimed at fixing prices, sharing markets, fixing production or sales quotas or restricting imports or exports.

The method for calculating fines is set out in Commission Guidelines adopted in 1998, which stipulate that the final amount calculated may not in any case exceed ten per cent of the world-wide turnover of the undertakings concerned. Among the factors which may be taken into account in determining the amount of the fine are the gravity and duration of the infringement. Article 23(2) of Regulation 1/2003 reiterates that the fine imposed on an undertaking found to have infringed Article 81 or Article 82 of the Treaty may not exceed ten per cent of its total turnover in the preceding business year. In the 2001 *Vitamins Cartel* case, the Commission imposed record fines amounting in total to over €855 million on eight undertakings found to have been involved in secret market-sharing and price-fixing cartels affecting vitamin products (Commission Decision 2003/2, (2003) OJ L6/1). Under the Commission's Leniency Notice (*Commission notice on immunity from fines and reduction of fines in cartel cases* [2002] OJ C45/3) adopted in February 2002, an undertaking which co-operates with the Commission's investigation into an alleged cartel may be granted total or partial immunity from fines.

EXEMPTION UNDER EC TREATY, ARTICLE 81(3)

An agreement that falls within the scope of Article 81(1) is rendered automatically void by Article 81(2), unless it benefits from exemption under the terms of Article 81(3). As noted previously, an agreement between two or more undertakings, while imposing certain restrictions on the conduct of those undertakings, may also confer significant pro-competitive advantages. In other words, if the economic and consumer benefits conferred by the agreement outweigh its anti-competitive effects, Article 81(1) may be declared inapplicable. Article 81(3) sets out the conditions which must be satisfied for the grant of an exemption:

The provisions of [Article 81(1)] may, however, be declared inapplicable in the case of:
– any agreement or category of agreements between undertakings;
– any decision or category of decisions by associations of undertakings;
– any concerted practice or category of concerted practices;
which contributes to improving the production or distribution of goods or to promoting technical or economic progress, while allowing consumers a fair share of the resulting benefit, and which does not:
(a) impose on the undertakings concerned restrictions which are not indispensable to the attainment of these objectives;
(b) afford such undertakings the possibility of eliminating competition in respect of a substantial part of the products in question.

Individual Exemptions: the Impact of Regulation 1/2003

Regulation 17/62, adopted in 1962, conferred upon the Commission the *sole power* to grant exemptions under Article 81(3), thereby establishing a centralised authorisation system based on prior notification. While Article 81(1) always produced direct effect and could therefore be applied by national courts, the Commission until recently had the sole power to grant exemptions under Article 81(3). Any undertakings wishing to avail of an individual exemption under Article 81(3) were obliged to notify their agreements to the Commission. With the passage of time and the enlargement of the Community, this notification system became increasingly unworkable. The Commission, with its limited administrative resources, was unable to respond by way of formal decision to the thousands of individual notifications it received. Among the strategies employed by the Commission to deal with this problem were the adoption of block exemption regulations declaring Article 81(1) inapplicable to certain categories of agreements, and the issuing of 'comfort letters' – informal, non-legally binding letters which simply informed an undertaking that, according to the information in the Commission's possession, the notified agreement either did not meet the conditions for the application of Article 81(1) or qualified for exemption.

The *White Paper on Modernisation of the Rules Implementing Articles 81 and 82 EC* (Commission Programme No. 99/027) published in April 1999 identified the main problems with the application of Article 81, namely, the overbroad interpretation of Article 81(1) adopted by the Commission and the fact that only the Commission could grant exemptions under Article 81(3). The White Paper summarised the situation as follows:

> It is essential to adapt the system so as to relieve companies from unnecessary bureaucracy, to allow the Commission to become more active in pursuit of serious competition infringements, and to increase and stimulate enforcement at national level.

In the White Paper, the Commission favoured a radical shift to a directly applicable exemption system whereby agreements would no longer need to be validated in advance by the Commission in order to be lawful.

The debate engendered by the White Paper led to the adoption on 16 December 2002 of Regulation 1/2003 on the implementation of the rules of competition laid down in Articles 81 and 82 of the Treaty, which entered into force on 1 May 2004. The regulation, which replaces Regulation 17/62, marks a radical shift from the prior authorisation system, under which agreements had to be notified to the Commission in order to obtain approval under Article 81(3), to a directly applicable exemption system. Under the new decentralised enforcement regime, the provisions of Article 81(3) can for the first time be applied by national courts. Article 1 of Regulation 1/2003 provides that an agreement, decision or concerted practice caught by Article 81(1) of the Treaty which satisfies the conditions of Article 81(3): '... shall not be prohibited, no prior decision to that effect being required'. As a result of the radical reforms effected by the new regulation, businesses will henceforth have to decide for themselves whether their agreements meet the criteria for exemption without the option of seeking an individual exemption or comfort letter from the Commission.

The new regulation also aims to strengthen the enforcement of competition rules within the Community by enhancing co-operation between the Commission, national competition authorities and national courts. Part IV of the regulation contains detailed provisions concerning co-operation between the Commission and the competition authorities of the member states, and between the Commission and national courts. Part V of the regulation prescribes the Commission's powers of investigation and inspection, while Part VI sets out the rules governing the payment of fines by undertakings found to have infringed Article 81 or Article 82 of the Treaty. With the entry into force of Regulation 1/2003 and the ending of the notification system, it is envisaged that the Commission will be in a position to concentrate its efforts and resources on combating more serious infringements of Community competition law.

Block Exemptions Under EC Treaty, Article 81(3)

As noted previously, the Commission has the power to declare Article 81(1) inapplicable to categories of agreements. Using this power, the Commission has adopted a series of block exemption regulations which render Article 81(1) inapplicable to certain types of agreement, thereby obviating the need for undertakings to make individual notifications to the Commission. Of course, on the entry into force of Regulation 1/2003, the requirement of prior notification will be abolished, with national courts and competition authorities having jurisdiction to consider the compatibility of restrictive practices with Article 81 as a whole. Despite the move to a directly applicable exemption system, block exemption regulations will continue to play an important role. With the move to decentralised enforcement of Article 81, block exemption regulations will assist in ensuring consistency and uniformity in the application of Community competition rules by national courts and national competition authorities.

If a firm can devise an agreement or contract so as to fall within the scope of one of the block exemption regulations, such an agreement will not fall foul of the Article 81(1) prohibition. Examples of block exemption regulations currently in force include:

1. Regulation 2790/1999 (vertical distribution, purchasing and franchising agreements);

2. Regulation 240/96 (technology transfer agreements);
3. Regulation 1400/2002 (vertical agreements and concerted practices in the motor vehicle sector);
4. Regulation 2658/2000 (specialisation agreements); and
5. Regulation 2659/2000 (research and development agreements).

CONCLUSION

In conclusion, Article 81 of the Treaty provides a vital legal weapon in the fight against cartels and other forms of anti-competitive collusion between undertakings within the Community. The prohibition enshrined in Article 81(1) extends not only to agreements and decisions, but also to other more tacit forms of collusion characterised as 'concerted practices'. As noted above, the definition of this latter term has posed certain interpretative difficulties for the Commission and the Community courts, specifically in the context of oligopolistic markets. Considerable controversy also surrounds the extent to which the pro- and anti-competitive effects of an agreement should be balanced under Article 81(1). An agreement found to infringe Article 81(1) is automatically void, unless it satisfies the criteria for exemption set out in Article 81(3). While the Commission traditionally enjoyed the sole power to grant exemptions, the recent radical overhaul of Community competition law, initiated by the 1999 White Paper, has resulted in the decentralisation of the application of Article 81(3). Regulation 1/2003 abolishes the prior notification system and renders Article 81(3) directly applicable by national competition authorities and national courts. The various block exemption regulations currently in force will form an important part of the new regime, ensuring consistency and uniformity in the application of Article 81 by national courts and national competition authorities. Most significantly, it is hoped that the entry into force of Regulation 1/2003 will ease the administrative burden on the Commission and enable it to focus its efforts on combating those restrictive practices that most seriously distort competition and impede market integration.

Chapter 17
COMPETITION LAW: ABUSE OF
A DOMINANT POSITION

INTRODUCTION: EC TREATY, ARTICLE 82

The second principal Treaty provision dealing with competition policy is Article 82 (formerly Article 86), which stipulates that:

> [A]ny abuse by one or more undertakings of a dominant position within the common market or in a substantial part of it shall be prohibited as incompatible with the common market insofar as it may affect trade between member states.

Certain examples of abusive conduct are set out in Article 82 itself – such as the imposition of unfair purchase or selling prices, and the limiting of production, markets or technical development to the prejudice of consumers – but these examples are not exhaustive.

In the sphere of competition law, the Commission enjoys quasi-judicial powers under Regulation 17/62 (which was replaced by Regulation 1/2003 with effect from 1 May 2004). Where the Commission, acting on its own initiative or on the basis of a complaint, finds that an undertaking has infringed Article 82, it may issue a decision requiring the undertaking to bring the abusive conduct to an end and imposing an appropriate penalty. As noted in the previous chapter, Article 23(2) of Regulation 1/2003 provides that the fine imposed on an undertaking found to have infringed Article 82 of the Treaty may not exceed ten per cent of its total turnover in the preceding business year. It should also be noted that Article 82 produces direct effect and is therefore capable of being invoked by private parties in, and applied by, national courts.

If an undertaking wishes to challenge a Commission decision under Article 82, it may use the annulment procedure provided for in Article 230 of the Treaty. That mechanism allows the Commission's decision to be reviewed by the Court of First Instance, and by the European Court of Justice, on appeal. Many such actions are fought on the issue of market definition, with the undertaking concerned arguing that the Commission has adopted an overly narrow definition of the relevant market (which, in turn, increases the undertaking's share of the market). Of course, it is important to emphasise at the outset that Article 82 does not prohibit dominance *per se*. An undertaking will not be found to have infringed the provision unless it has engaged in some form of abusive conduct. In this chapter, we will consider the constituent elements of Article 82. Firstly, we will examine the issue of market definition – the conduct of an undertaking cannot be caught by the Article 82 prohibition unless the undertaking occupies a dominant position within a defined product and geographical market. Secondly, we will discuss the criteria to be used in assessing dominance. Consideration will also be given to the jurisdictional requirement of an 'effect on trade between member states' necessary to trigger the application of Article 82, and to the concept of joint or collective dominance. Finally, we will look at some of the specific types of abusive conduct that have been condemned by the Community courts.

DEFINITION OF THE RELEVANT MARKET

Central to the application of Article 82 is the concept of a 'dominant position'. Dominance cannot be assessed in the abstract, rather it must be considered by reference to a defined market. In order to determine whether an undertaking occupies a dominant position, it is necessary to consider two main factors:
1. the product market; and
2. the geographical market.
Obviously, the narrower the definition of the market, the more likely it is that the undertaking in question will be found to occupy a dominant position for the purposes of Article 82. In many of the decided cases, the Commission has advocated a narrow market definition, while the undertakings involved have sought to have the market defined in much broader terms.

Product Market

In determining the scope of the relevant product market, both the Commission and the court generally consider the issue of interchangeability, i.e., the extent to which consumers regard other products as being substitutable with the accused undertaking's products. The Commission tends to focus primarily on demand-side substitutability in order to determine whether two products are competing on the same product market. However, supply-side substitutability can also be relevant. (This means the ease with which new suppliers can enter the product market.) Interchangeability can be measured by cross-price elasticity. Cross-price elasticity on the demand side is high where an increase in the price of one product will lead buyers to switch to another product. (Supply-side price elasticity is high when an increase in the price of a product attracts new suppliers of that product.) Where cross-price elasticity is high, two products are regarded as forming part of the same product market. In the past, the Commission and the court have been accused of ignoring more sound economic analysis in favour of an approach based on the physical characteristics of products.

Demand-side Substitutability

In Case 27/76, *United Brands v. Commission* [1978] ECR 207, a banana manufacturer was accused of having engaged in various abusive practices contrary to Article 82. Before examining the alleged abusive conduct, the European Court of Justice had to consider, as a preliminary issue, the definition of the relevant product market. United Brands argued that bananas formed part of a larger market in fresh fruit, since consumers regarded bananas as being interchangeable with other kinds of fresh fruit.

However, the Commission maintained that bananas formed a distinct product market, since the banana formed an important part of the diet of certain sections of the community. It argued that the specific qualities of the banana influenced consumer preference and rendered other fruits unacceptable as substitutes. In its judgment, the European Court of Justice noted that in order for the banana to form a market distinct from other fresh fruits, it had to be singled out by:

> ... such special features distinguishing it from other fruits that it [was] only to a limited extent interchangeable with them and [was] only exposed to their competition in a way that [was] hardly perceptible.

The court focused on the physical characteristics of the banana, asserting that it had specific features, namely appearance, taste, softness and seedlessness, which enabled it to satisfy the requirements of an important section of the population consisting of the very young, the old and the sick. Since such consumers were not enticed away from consumption of bananas by the arrival of other fresh fruits on the market, the court concluded that the banana market constituted a discrete product market, sufficiently distinct from the market for other fresh fruit.

Supply-side Substitutability

While the Commission and the court have traditionally placed most emphasis on demand-side factors, supply-side substitutability is also taken in account in certain cases. In Case 322/81, *Michelin v. Commission* [1983] ECR 3461, the Commission brought an action against a tyre manufacturer alleging abusive conduct in the awarding of discounts. The Commission considered Michelin to have a dominant position in the market for new replacement tyres for lorries, buses and similar heavy vehicles. Michelin argued that this definition was too narrow and that regard should also be had to tyres for lighter vehicles, such as cars and vans. It was clear that these different types of tyre were not regarded by customers as interchangeable from a demand perspective. However, Michelin argued for a broader market definition based on a supply-side analysis. It argued that a car tyre manufacturer could easily adapt its existing plant to become a manufacturer of lorry tyres and thus a competitor of Michelin.

The European Court of Justice rejected this argument, asserting that there was no elasticity of supply between tyres for heavy vehicles and tyres for cars, owing to significant differences in production techniques. The considerable time and investment required to modify production processes for the manufacture of heavy-vehicle instead of light-vehicle tyres meant that, on a supply-side analysis, car tyres and lorry tyres did not form part of the same product market. As a result, the Commission had been correct to assess Michelin's market share with reference to replacement tyres for lorries, buses and other heavy vehicles and to exclude consideration of car and van tyres.

Commission Notice on Market Definition

The *Commission Notice on the definition of the relevant market for the purposes of Community competition law* [1997] OJ C372/5 provides guidance for firms on the issue of market definition. In previous decades, as we have seen, the Commission tended to examine the question of substitutability by reference to product characteristics and intended use. In more recent years, however, the Commission has begun to heed the criticisms of competition lawyers and economists and has started to use more detailed economic analysis.

In the 1997 Notice, the Commission reiterates the orthodox principles relating to demand and supply-side substitutability, but goes on to outline the more sophisticated manner in which those principles will be applied. In particular, the Commission endorses the application of the so-called SSNIPs test, a mechanism for measuring demand substitutability drawn from US antitrust practice.

SSNIP is an acronym for 'small but significant non-transitory increase in price'. The test involves a speculative experiment, postulating a hypothetical small, lasting change in relative prices and evaluating the likely reactions of consumers to that increase. The essential question is whether such a hypothetical small, but permanent relative price increase (in the range of five to ten per cent) would cause customers to switch to readily available substitutes or to suppliers located elsewhere. If customers were to switch, making the price increase unprofitable due to loss of sales, these additional substitute products and geographical areas are to be included in the relevant market. This iterative process is repeated until the set of products and geographical areas is such that small, permanent increases in relative prices would be profitable.

In paragraph 18 of the Notice, the Commission seeks to illustrate the application of the SSNIPs test in a practical context. Its example envisages the merger of two soft-drink bottlers and the test to be applied in determining whether such a merger would have the effect of creating a dominant position on the relevant market. In this example, it is necessary to determine whether different flavours of soft drink belong to the same market. If the price of flavour A were to increase by five to ten per cent, would consumers switch to another flavour? If a sufficient number of consumers switched to flavour B, making the flavour A price increase unprofitable due to loss of sales, the relevant product market will be deemed to comprise at least flavours A and B. The process would have to be extended to other flavours until a set of flavours was identified for which a price rise would not induce a sufficient substitution in demand.

Geographical Market

In order to determine whether an undertaking occupies a dominant position for the purposes of Article 82, it is also necessary to consider the geographical market in which it operates. Obviously, it will be impossible to calculate the market share of the firm in question unless one has ascertained the relevant geographical market. An undertaking might enjoy a huge market share in Ireland in a particular product market, but only a tiny fraction of the Community market. Obviously, a firm involved in proceedings under Article 82 will be anxious to have the geographical market defined as broadly as possible in order to minimise the likelihood of a finding of a large market share and the likely finding of dominance. In many cases, the relevant geographical market has been held to be the entire Community. In other instances, the existence of special factors results in a more narrow definition of the market. For example, in the case of bulky goods, high transport costs mean that distribution within an extremely wide geographical area is unfeasible. Similarly, if goods are highly perishable, a producer may only be able to supply a relatively narrow geographical market.

Commission and Court of Justice and Dominant Market

In *United Brands* (cited above), the European Court of Justice stated that the relevant geographical market was 'an area where a dominant undertaking may be able to engage in abuses which hinder effective competition' and 'an area where the objective conditions of competition applying to the product in question must be the same for all traders'. The European Court of Justice also referred to the relevant geographical market as being an area where conditions of competition are 'sufficiently homogeneous' for all traders. The court concluded that the Commission had been correct in defining the relevant geographical market as comprising Germany, Denmark, Ireland and the three Benelux countries (the Community comprised nine member states at the time). The remaining three member states – France, Italy and the UK – were excluded even though United Brands operated in those jurisdictions. The European Court of Justice endorsed the Commission's finding that the objective conditions of competition were not the same for all traders in those three states due to the existence of preferential tariff regimes for banana imports originating in their respective overseas territories and former colonies. United Brands' bananas did not compete on equal terms in France, Italy and the UK with the bananas which benefited from a preferential tariff system in those three states.

In Case IV/D-2/34.780, *Re Virgin/British Airways* [2000] 4 CMLR 999, the Commission found that British Airways had infringed Article 82 in the operation of certain commission and incentive schemes involving UK travel agents. In its decision, the Commission cited its own 1997 Notice on market definition, declaring that:

> [T]he relevant geographic market comprises the area in which the undertakings concerned are involved in the supply and demand of products or services, in which the conditions of competition are sufficiently homogeneous and which can be distinguished from neighbouring areas because the conditions of competition are appreciably different in those areas.

On the facts of the case, the Commission found that the relevant geographical market was the UK.

Substantial Part of the Common Market

In order for Article 82 to apply, the relevant geographical market must also constitute either the entire common market or at least a substantial part thereof. If an undertaking's behaviour affects no more than a purely local market, with no intra-Community effects, it should not fall within the scope of Article 82. Abuses of a dominant position that affect a non-substantial part of the common market are best regulated by national competition authorities through the application of national competition laws.

Both the Commission and the Community courts have been reluctant to formulate a test for defining what constitutes a substantial part of the common market, most likely fearing that the elaboration of a rigid test might serve to exclude from the scope of Article 82 the activities of an undertaking which, although ostensibly affecting a relatively small geographical area, might nonetheless have serious implications for intra-Community trade. The territory of a single member state, or an even smaller geographical region, may be deemed to represent a substantial part of the common market. For example, the Netherlands was deemed to constitute a substantial part of the common market in *Michelin* (cited above). Both the port of Genoa (Case C-179/90, *Merci Convenzionali* [1991] ECR 5889) and the port of Holyhead

(Case IV/34.174, *B & I Line/Sealink* [1992] 5 CMLR 255) have also been held to constitute substantial parts of the common market for the purposes of Article 82.

ASSESSING DOMINANCE UNDER EC TREATY, ARTICLE 82

Once the Commission or the court has defined the relevant product and geographical market, it must decide whether the undertaking in question is dominant on that particular market. In the *United Brands* case (cited above), the European Court of Justice defined a dominant position as:

> [A] position of economic strength enjoyed by an undertaking which enables it to prevent effective competition being maintained on the relevant market by giving it the power to behave to an appreciable extent independently of its competitors, customers and ultimately of its consumers.

A dominant undertaking is one which enjoys market power, in that it has the ability to act in a manner whereby its freedom of action is largely unrestrained by the activities of its competitors. As the European Court of Justice noted in *United Brands*, however, an undertaking need not have eliminated all opportunity for competition in order to be found dominant. In Case 85/76, *Hoffmann La Roche v. Commission* [1979] ECR 461, the European Court of Justice observed that a dominant position allows an undertaking to determine, or at least have an appreciable influence on, the conditions under which competition will develop. The court declared that the existence of a dominant position may derive from several factors which, taken separately, are not necessarily determinative. Among such factors, according to the court, a highly important one is the existence of a very large market share.

Market Share and Dominance

It is clear that the market share possessed by an undertaking is perhaps the most crucial factor in determining whether that firm occupies a dominant position. There are no definitive rules as to what percentage of market share will bring an undertaking within the scope of Article 82. The case law of the European Court of Justice indicates that it is not necessary to hold a statutory monopoly (i.e. occupying a one hundred per cent market share) in order to be caught by Article 82.

In *United Brands* (cited above), a market share of forty to forty-five per cent of the banana market in the relevant states was held to be sufficient, although the court also considered other factors which were indicative of dominance, such as the strength of rival undertakings and the existence of barriers to entry on the relevant market. In *Hoffmann La Roche* (cited above), the European Court of Justice ruled that the firm was not dominant in the market for B3 vitamins in which it held a forty-three per cent share, primarily because it was not satisfied that there were other factors supporting a finding of dominance.

In more general terms, the court noted that the existence of very large market shares was in itself, and save in exceptional circumstances, evidence of the existence of a dominant position. It asserted that an undertaking with a very large market share, which had been held for some time, occupied a position of strength which made it an unavoidable trading partner and which secured the freedom of action that was the hallmark of a dominant position.

Other important cases on the criterion of market share include Case C-62/86, *Akzo Chemie BV v. Commission* [1991] ECR I-3359, where the European Court of Justice suggested that a market share of fifty per cent was, in itself, indicative of dominance. Similarly, in Case T-30/89, *Hilti AG v. Commission* [1991] ECR II-1439, the Court of First Instance held that a market share of between seventy per cent and eighty per cent was, in itself, a clear indication of the existence of a dominant position in the relevant market.

Other factors are frequently taken into account in determining whether a firm occupies a dominant position, including the relationship between the market share of the undertaking concerned and its competitors, and the existence of barriers to entry such as superior technology, access to capital and legal provisions. In *Hoffmann La Roche* (cited above), for example, the European Court of Justice declared the following factors to be relevant in assessing dominance:
1. the relationship between the market shares of the undertaking concerned and of its nearest competitors;
2. the technological lead of an undertaking over its competitors;
3. the existence of a highly developed sales network; and
4. the absence of potential competition.

Controversy surrounds the concept of barriers to entry, with many commentators arguing that many such barriers result merely from the superior efficiency of the incumbent undertaking and should not be taken into account when assessing dominance. It has been argued that factors such as economies of scale, capital strength and access to technology enjoyed by existing firms in the market should not be categorised as entry barriers. These are not artificially created barriers which shield existing players from new entrants to the market, but rather represent the costs that are incurred by all firms wishing to enter the market. If an undertaking has obtained economies of scale or developed its own costly and sophisticated technology, should those factors count against it in an enquiry into its possible dominance? It would be somewhat anomalous if an over-broad view of barriers to entry had the effect of stifling efficiency and discouraging firms from competing to their full potential.

Joint or Collective Dominance Under EC Treaty, Article 82

In contrast to the position under Article 81 considered in the previous chapter, the unilateral behaviour of a single undertaking is sufficient to trigger the application of Article 82. The vast majority of cases dealt with under Article 82 have concerned the abusive conduct of a single undertaking. However, the phrase 'any abuse *by one or more undertakings* of a dominant position ...' which appears in Article 82 has been construed by the Commission and the Community courts as importing the notion of joint or collective dominance. The question has arisen as to whether the parallel conduct of firms in an oligopolistic market may come within the ambit of Article 82.

In Cases T-68, 77-78/89, *Re Italian Flat Glass: Società Italiana Vetro v. Commission* [1992] ECR I-1403, the Court of First Instance held that:

> [There is] nothing, in principle, to prevent two or more independent economic entities from being, on a specific market, united by such economic links that, by virtue of that fact, together they hold a dominant position vis-à-vis the other operators on the same market.

This could be the case where two or more undertakings jointly had, through agreements or licences, a technological lead affording them the power to behave to an appreciable extent independently of their competitors, their customers and ultimately of their consumers. However, the court emphasised that it was not sufficient for the Commission to recycle the facts relevant to its decision under Article 81 as the basis for a finding of collective dominance under Article 82. On the facts, the court annulled the Commission's findings in relation to Article 82 on the ground that the Commission had not adduced the necessary proof of collective dominance.

In Cases C-395-396/96P, *Compagnie Maritime Belge Transports v. Commission* [2000] ECR I-1365, the European Court of Justice gave further consideration to the 'economic links' between undertakings necessary to support a finding of collective dominance. In order to establish the existence of a collective entity, it is necessary to determine whether the links between two or more undertakings are such as to enable them to act together independently of their competitors, their customers and consumers.

The court noted that the mere fact that two or more undertakings were linked by an agreement, decision or concerted practice within the meaning of Article 81(1) did not, of itself, constitute a sufficient basis for establishing the existence of a collective entity. It went on to declare that a finding of collective dominance could flow from:

> the nature and terms of an agreement, from the way in which it is implemented and, consequently, from the links or factors which give rise to a connection between undertakings which result from it.

Significantly, the European Court of Justice stated that the existence of an actual agreement or of other links in law was not indispensable to a finding of collective dominance. Such a finding could be based on other connecting factors and depended on an assessment of the structure of the market in question. On the facts of the *Compagnie Maritime Belge* case, cited above, the European Court of Justice found that two shipping companies, who were both members of a shipping conference operating between Zaire and certain Northern European ports, had abused their position of collective dominance by their efforts to eliminate an independent competitor from the market.

Effect on Trade Between Member States

Under Article 82 of the Treaty, abusive conduct by a dominant undertaking is prohibited 'insofar as it may affect trade between member states'. In practice, the Commission and the Community courts have adopted a broad interpretation of this jurisdictional requirement. If the requisite effect on trade between member states is not found to exist, the matter will fall to be dealt with under national competition law, such as the Irish Competition Authority.

In Cases C-241 and 242/91P, *RTE and ITP v. Commission* [1995] ECR I-743, the European Court of Justice held that, in order to satisfy the condition under Article 82 that trade between member states must be affected, it was not necessary that the conduct in question should in fact have substantially affected that trade. It was sufficient to establish that the conduct was *capable* of having such an effect. The practical application of this approach can be seen clearly in Case 322/81, *Michelin v. Commission* [1983] ECR 3461. In this case, the relevant geographical market had been found to be the Netherlands. The applicant, a tyre manufacturer accused of having engaged in abusive behaviour, argued that conduct confined to the territory of a single member state could not affect trade between member states within the meaning of Article 82. Rejecting this argument, the European Court of Justice pointed out that conduct obstructing the access to the market by competitors was capable of affecting patterns of trade and competition within the wider common market. Michelin's conduct in offering target discounts to dealers had the effect of impeding the entry onto the Dutch market of tyre manufacturers based in other member states.

EXAMPLES OF ABUSIVE CONDUCT UNDER EC TREATY, ARTICLE 82

Article 82 does not prohibit the existence or acquisition of a dominant position, but rather the abusive exploitation of that position. Competition law of its essence encourages firms in the market to compete, ensuring that the most efficient firms will be the most successful. Clearly, it would be somewhat invidious to penalise an undertaking for simply having acquired market power by virtue of being more competitive that its rivals. While dominance *per se* is not prohibited under Article 82, an undertaking occupying a dominant position has been recognised by the Community courts as having a special responsibility not to allow its conduct to impair genuine undistorted competition within the common market (see Case 322/81, *Michelin v. Commission* [1983] ECR 3461). The instances of abusive behaviour set out in Article 82 are not exhaustive. Further examples of abusive conduct can be identified in the case law of the Court of First Instance and the European Court of Justice. In the remainder of this chapter, we will focus on some of the specific types of conduct that have been found to infringe Article 82.

Discriminatory and Selective Pricing

Article 82(c) explicitly prohibits the 'application of dissimilar conditions to equivalent transactions with other trading parties, thereby placing them at a competitive disadvantage'. The notion of price discrimination for the purposes of Article 82 does not refer simply to differences in the price at which goods are sold, but rather to price differences which are not related to objective differences in costs. For example, it is permissible for a wine producer operating in Italy to charge higher prices to distributors in Finland than to those in France, since it will have incurred different transport costs in the two instances (assuming that transport costs were, in fact, incurred by the producer). However, a dominant undertaking may not charge different prices to different customers in the absence of any objective justification.

In Case 27/76, *United Brands v. Commission* [1978] ECR 207, discussed previously, the applicant undertaking (United Brands) had been found to occupy a dominant position on the relevant market. United Brands, one of the largest importers of bananas operating in the Community, shipped bananas from Central America to ports in northern Europe, from where it sold them to ripener/distributors.

Acting on foot of a number of complaints received from other importers, the Commission initiated proceedings against United Brands in 1975, alleging that it sold the bananas at different prices to distributors from different member states, without objective justification. Although buyers came to two ports, either Rotterdam or Bremerhaven, in order to purchase from United Brands and were responsible for transporting the bananas back to their respective member states, the firm sold the product to different buyers at different prices.

The firm asserted that the price set for each national buyer was calculated by reference to the anticipated price at which the bananas would be sold in retail outlets in each national market in the following week. The European Court of Justice held that the discriminatory prices charged by the firm were not objectively justified, led to a rigid partitioning of national markets, created price levels which were artificially different and placed certain ripeners at a competitive disadvantage. United Brands' conduct had the effect of applying dissimilar conditions to equivalent transactions with other trading parties contrary to Article 82.

The decision in *United Brands* clearly illustrates the court's hostility to market behaviour which entails the division of markets along national lines. The market-partitioning effect of the discriminatory prices charged by United Brands to different buyers was exacerbated by the contractual prohibition it placed on the resale of unripened, green bananas by ripeners. The contractual restriction had the effect of rendering trade between ripeners in different member states impossible. As a result, a retailer could only obtain supplies from a ripener situated in his own member state, a practice which had the inevitable effect of maintaining artificial price differences between national markets.

A further example of discriminatory pricing can be seen in Case C-62/86, *Akzo Chemie v. Commission* [1991] ECR I-3359. Both Akzo and its competitor, ECS, were involved in the manufacture of organic peroxides. One particular organic peroxide, benzoyl peroxide, was used both in the manufacture of plastics and as a bleaching agent for flour. ECS initially supplied its product to flour millers only, but decided in 1979 to start supplying the plastics market also. In response, Akzo launched a targeted price offensive on the flour additives market designed to 'discipline' ECS and, ultimately, to force its withdrawal from the plastics market. One of its strategies involved the practice of selective pricing on the market for flour additives. The European Court of Justice found that Akzo had charged different prices to buyers of comparable size without objective justification – the differences did not relate to the quality of the products sold or to special production costs. The prices charged by Akzo to its own customers were higher than those offered to customers of ECS, leading the court to conclude that the firm's intention was to damage ECS and to force it to withdraw from the plastics market.

Predatory Pricing

Article 82(a) states that abuse may consist in: 'directly or indirectly imposing unfair purchase or selling prices ...'. The charging of unfairly low prices by a dominant undertaking may, in certain circumstances, amount to predatory pricing. Predatory pricing can be defined as pricing low in the short term with the aim of driving competitors out of the market or preventing new firms from entering. The predatory undertaking trades at a loss for a short period of time in order to eliminate a competitor or competitors. Once its rivals have been driven out of the market, it will be free to raise prices and to recoup the losses made during the period of predation.

The leading European case on predatory pricing is *Akzo Chemie v. Commission* (cited above), in which the European Court of Justice found that Akzo had abused its dominant position by engaging in predatory pricing on the flour additives market designed to eliminate a rival producer from that market. In its judgment, the European Court of Justice drew an important distinction between sales below 'average total costs' (fixed costs plus variable costs) and sales below 'average variable costs' (those costs which vary depending on the quantities produced). It would appear that sales below average variable costs will automatically be regarded as abusive. The court in the *Akzo* case stated:

> Prices below average variable costs (that is to say, those which vary depending on the quantities produced) by means of which a dominant undertaking seeks to eliminate a competitor must be regarded as abusive. A dominant undertaking has no interest in applying such prices except that of eliminating competitors so as to enable it subsequently to raise its prices by taking advantage of its monopolistic position ... .

On the other hand, sales below average total costs, but above average variable costs, enable the dominant undertaking to recover a significant portion of its costs and, as such, will only be regarded as abusive if they form part of a determined plan for eliminating a competitor.

Discounts and Rebates

The awarding of discounts or rebates by a dominant undertaking will not automatically infringe Article 82. In certain circumstances, however, the granting of discounts or rebates by a dominant firm may amount to the application of 'dissimilar conditions to equivalent transactions with other trading parties' and thereby violate Community competition rules. For example, the effect of fidelity rebates is that two purchasers pay a different price for the same quantity of the same product depending on whether they obtain their supplies exclusively from the dominant undertaking or have several sources of supply.

In Case 85/76, *Hoffmann La Roche v. Commission* [1979] ECR 461, the Commission had imposed a fine on a Swiss pharmaceutical firm for abuse of a dominant position on the vitamins market in the manner in which it operated a system of fidelity rebates. The European Court of Justice noted that an undertaking which is in a dominant position abuses that dominant position where it ties purchasers – even if it does so at their own request – by an obligation or promise on their part to obtain all or most of their requirements exclusively from that undertaking. It did not matter whether the obligation was stipulated without further qualification or whether it was undertaken in consideration of the grant of a rebate. The same applied if an undertaking, without tying purchasers by a formal obligation, applied a system of fidelity rebates, i.e., discounts conditional on the customer's obtaining all or most of its requirements from the dominant undertaking. The court noted that loyalty or fidelity rebates had a tying effect on customers, preventing them from obtaining their supplies from competing producers. It drew an important distinction between *quantity discounts*, which are considered to be objectively justifiable and compatible with Article 82, and *fidelity rebates* which are not. A quantity discount is based on the volume of products bought from the same firm, while a loyalty discount is based on the proportion of requirements bought from it.

Refusal to Supply Existing Customers

As noted previously, an undertaking occupying a dominant position has been recognised as having a 'special responsibility' not to impede genuine and effective competition on the market. Thus, specific conduct on the part of a non-dominant firm might not amount to an infringement of Community competition law, while the same behaviour practised by a dominant undertaking might be classified as abusive under Article 82. The 'special responsibility' placed on dominant undertakings is well illustrated in the case law on refusal to supply.

One of the allegations of abusive conduct made in Case 27/76, *United Brands v. Commission* [1978] ECR 207 (discussed previously) was that United Brands had refused to continue to supply Olesen, a Danish distributor, when the latter became involved in an advertising campaign for a rival brand of bananas. In its judgment, the European Court of Justice declared that an undertaking in a dominant position cannot stop supplying a longstanding customer who abides by regular commercial practice, if the orders placed by that customer are in no way out of the ordinary. While the dominant firm was entitled to take reasonable steps to protect its own commercial interests, such behaviour was not permitted if its actual purpose was to strengthen and abuse a dominant position.

The action taken by United Brands in relation to Olesen was deemed to be disproportionate and liable to discourage other ripener/distributors from supporting the advertising of other brands. The impugned conduct was held to amount to a serious interference with the independence of small and medium-sized firms in their commercial relations with United Brands, an independence which implied the right to give preference to a competitor's goods.

In Cases C-6 and C-7/73, *ICI and Commercial Solvents Corporation v. Commission* [1974] ECR 223, CSC produced the raw materials used in the manufacturing of ethambutol, an anti-tuberculosis drug. One of CSC's main customers was Zoja, an Italian firm which manufactured ethambutol products. When CSC started to manufacture the finished product itself in 1970, it informed Zoja that it had changed its commercial policy and that it would no longer be supplying it with the raw material necessary to produce ethambutol. In its decision, the European Court of Justice held that by refusing to supply Zoja, CSC had abused its dominant position within the meaning of Article 82. The court declared that an undertaking which occupies a dominant position in respect of the production of raw material and which is therefore able to control the supply to manufacturers of derivatives cannot, just because it decides to start manufacturing these derivatives itself (in competition with its former customers), act in such a way as to eliminate their competition.

Refusal to Deal and the Essential Facilities Doctrine

In a number of more recent cases, the courts of the European Union have considered the issue of refusal to supply in the absence of a pre-existing commercial relationship. A debate has arisen, in particular, as to whether a dominant undertaking that owns an 'essential facility' can be compelled to share that facility with its competitors. Cases C-241 and 242/91P, *RTE and ITP v. Commission* [1995] ECR I-743 related to the publication of TV guides in Ireland and Northern Ireland. Each of the three broadcasting organisations transmitting programmes that could be received in Ireland and Northern Ireland published its own weekly guide to programmes on its channels. When *Magill* magazine started to publish a comprehensive guide to programmes on RTE, ITV and the BBC, an injunction was obtained by the three broadcasters restraining *Magill* from infringing their copyrights in the programme listings. In 1988, the Commission, acting on foot of a complaint from *Magill*, held that by refusing to grant licences for the reproduction of their advance weekly programme listings, the three companies had abused their dominant positions contrary to Article 82.

The Court of First Instance, and on appeal the European Court of Justice, upheld the Commission decision, declaring that the companies were obliged to grant compulsory licences for the listings to third parties on request on reasonable terms. By refusing to grant licences, the broadcasters had prevented the emergence of a new product for which there was potential consumer demand and had effectively reserved the market for weekly television guides to themselves.

Cases T-374, 375, 384 and 388/94, *European Night Services v. Commission* [1998] ECR II-3141 concerned four European railway undertakings which had come together to create ENS, a company established to provide and operate overnight rail services between points in the UK and points on the Continent. ENS had notified certain agreements concerning the carriage of passengers by rail through the Channel Tunnel to the Commission for exemption under Article 81(3). The Commission declared Article 81(1) inapplicable and exempted the agreements subject to the condition that the parties to ENS supply the same necessary rail services they had supplied to ENS to any other transport operator wishing to operate night passenger trains through the Channel Tunnel. The condition required that train paths, locomotives and crews be supplied to third parties on the same basis as to ENS since they constituted essential facilities. The Court of First Instance subsequently annulled the Commission decision primarily on grounds of insufficient reasoning. Of particular significance, the court held that a product or service cannot be considered as essential unless there are 'no real or potential substitutes'. On the facts, the court noted that locomotives and crew did not constitute essential facilities. A facility could not be regarded as essential unless, by reason of special characteristics (e.g., the prohibitive costs involved or the time required to reproduce it), there were no viable alternatives available to potential competitors who wished to enter the market.

In Case C-7/97, *Oscar Bronner v. Mediaprint* [1998] ECR I-7791 the publisher (Bronner) of a daily newspaper in Austria with 3.6 per cent of national circulation made an application to an Austrian court seeking an order requiring Mediaprint, the publisher of two rival newspapers, to grant Bronner access to its nationwide home-delivery service in return for fair remuneration.

Bronner contended that the owner of an 'essential facility' – in this case the only economically viable home-delivery scheme existing in Austria on a national scale – was obliged to allow access to the scheme by competing products. Mediaprint argued that it had built up its delivery system at great financial and administrative cost and that it should not be obliged to afford assistance to its competitors.

The national court made a reference to the European Court of Justice seeking to determine whether Mediaprint's refusal to allow Bronner access to its home-delivery system constituted an abuse of a dominant position. In its ruling, the court stated that the refusal by a dominant undertaking to allow the publisher of a rival newspaper to have access to its nationwide home-delivery scheme in return for appropriate remuneration did not constitute an abuse of a dominant position within the meaning of Article 82. The court noted the existence of other forms of distribution such as post, shops and kiosks, and observed that there were no technical, legal or economic obstacles making it impossible for other publishers to establish home-delivery systems. It also pointed out that the conduct in question would only amount to abuse if the refusal to allow access was:

1. likely to eliminate all competition in the daily newspaper market on part of Bronner;
2. incapable of being objectively justified; and
3. if the delivery service operated by Mediaprint was indispensable to carrying on of Bronner's business in that there were no actual or potential substitutes.

Tying

Article 82(d) sets out a further example of abusive conduct, namely, 'making the conclusion of contracts subject to acceptance by the other parties of supplementary obligations which, by their nature or according to commercial usage, have no connection with the subject of such contracts'. This phenomenon, known as 'tying', was discussed in Case C-333/94P, *Tetra Pak v. Commission (Tetra Pak II)* [1996] ECR I-5951.

The case concerned an undertaking which had developed the process and machinery required for the packaging of liquid and semi-liquid food products. Tetra Pak required customers to whom it supplied machines to use only Tetra Pak cartons. The Commission, the Court of First Instance and the European Court of Justice found that the practice of tied sales of cartons and filling machines amounted to an abuse of a dominant position in the relevant markets. The European Court of Justice noted that the practice of tying was intended to strengthen Tetra Pak's dominant position by reinforcing its customers' economic dependence on it. The system of tied sales could not be justified on grounds of protecting public health and went beyond the recognised right of an undertaking in a dominant position to protect its commercial interests.

CONCLUSION

Article 82 of the Treaty seeks to control the behaviour of firms with market power by prohibiting dominant undertakings from behaving in a manner that is liable to distort competition within the common market. In applying Article 82, several factors fall to be considered. As a preliminary matter, it is necessary to determine whether the firm in question occupies a 'dominant position'. Dominance cannot be measured in abstract terms; rather it must be assessed by reference to a defined market. In any case which involves the application of Article 82, the detailed evidence of expert economists is usually called upon in ascertaining the relevant geographical and product markets. The Commission's 1997 *Notice on market definition* provides guidance for businesses on the economic tests to be used in determining the scope of the relevant market. Many of the cases considered in this chapter were vigorously contested on the issue of market definition, with the undertakings concerned seeking to have the market defined in as broad a manner as possible, so as to reduce the likelihood of a finding of dominance. Once the relevant market has been identified, certain criteria are employed in assessing whether a firm is actually dominant on that market. Of these factors, market share plays the most important role, although the existence of barriers to entry may also be relevant. Finally, and most importantly, it is necessary to determine whether an undertaking found to occupy a dominant position has, in fact, abused that position. It should always be borne in mind that Article 82 targets not the existence of dominance itself, but rather the abusive conduct of a firm occupying a dominant position.

INDEX